GERARD MANLEY HOPKINS

THE CRITICAL HERITAGE

Edited by
GERALD ROBERTS
Stonyhurst College

ROUTLEDGE & KEGAN PAUL
LONDON AND NEW YORK

First published in 1987 by
Routledge & Kegan Paul Ltd
11 New Fetter Lane, London EC4P 4EE

Published in the USA by
Routledge & Kegan Paul Inc.
in association with Methuen Inc.
29 West 35th Street, New York, NY 10001

Set on 10/12pt Bembo
by Thomson Press (India) Limited,
New Delhi
and printed in Great Britain
by T J Press (Padstow) Ltd
Padstow, Cornwall

Library of Congress Cataloging in Publication Data

Gerard Manley Hopkins, the critical heritage.
(The Critical heritage series)
Bibliography: p.
Includes index.
1. Hopkins, Gerard Manley, 1844–1889—Criticism and interpretation.
I. Roberts, Gerald. II. Series.
PR4803.H44Z6445 1987 821'.8 86-13884

British Library CIP Data also available

ISBN 0-7102-0414-0

General Editor's Preface

The reception given to a writer by his contemporaries and near-contemporaries is evidence of considerable value to the student of literature. On one side we learn a great deal about the state of criticism at large and in particular about the development of critical attitudes towards a single writer; at the same time, through private comments in letters, journals or marginalia, we gain an insight upon the tastes and literary thought of individual readers of the period. Evidence of this kind helps us to understand the writer's historical situation, the nature of his immediate reading-public, and his response to these pressures.

The separate volumes in the *Critical Heritage Series* present a record of this early criticism. Clearly, for many of the highly productive and lengthily reviewed nineteenth- and twentieth-century writers, there exists an enormous body of material; and in these cases the volume editors have made a selection of the most important views, significant for their intrinsic critical worth or for their representative quality—perhaps even registering incomprehension!

For earlier writers, notably pre-eighteenth century, the materials are much scarcer and the historical period has been extended, sometimes far beyond the writer's lifetime, in order to show the inception and growth of critical views which were initially slow to appear.

In each volume the documents are headed by an Introduction, discussing the material assembled and relating the early stages of the author's reception to what we have come to identify as the critical tradition. The volumes will make available much material which would otherwise be difficult of access and it is hoped that the modern reader will be thereby helped towards an informed understanding of the ways in which literature has been read and judged.

B.C.S.

Contents

Comments 1877–1918

Poems of Hopkins (1918)

CONTENTS

CONTENTS

CONTENTS

CONTENTS

Preface

I have tried to make this collection of Hopkins criticism from his own time up to 1940 representative, rather than comprehensive. Criticism which is purely descriptive, pseudo-biographical, or simply repetitive cannot be entirely excluded, but it has not been emphasised; whatever is 'interesting' (for a variety of reasons) I have tried to include.

I have 'cut' and extracted fairly freely in dealing with some material, but I hope the end result is to provide a sharper outline of attitudes to Hopkins's poetry over some fifty years than might otherwise have been the case.

No attempt has been made to cover reactions to the prose, although these naturally enter into judgments of Hopkins from 1935 onwards.

There is nothing inevitable about 1940 as a terminus date. Tom Dunne's *Hopkins: A Comprehensive Bibliography*, which has been an invaluable starting-point for this book, reveals the acceleration of writing about Hopkins throughout the thirties and forties. I have also found the following volumes in the *Critical Heritage Series* helpful in plotting the course of Hopkins's reputation in the modern period: *T.S. Eliot*, ed. Michael Grant, vol. I, London, 1982: *W.H. Auden*, ed. John Haffenden, London, 1983. However, all Hopkins's major work was published (or re-published) in the thirties (the *Sermons*, 1959, has a more limited interest), and the criticism in this volume is still therefore close to the time of the poetry's publication. The peculiar circumstances of the belated appearance of Hopkins's work means that some of the principles laid down in the Preface by the General Editor of this series cannot be applied, but this is amply compensated for by the insight we gain into the 'tastes and literary thoughts of individual readers' at a time of remarkable aesthetic upheaval.

Acknowledgments

It is a pleasure to thank the staff of the British Library in Bloomsbury and the Newspaper Library at Colindale for their helpfulness while I have been preparing this book. I am also grateful for the assistance of the staff at the University Library, Lancaster, and at the National Library of Scotland in Edinburgh. Fr F. Turner, SJ, Librarian and Archivist at Stonyhurst College, has again been generous with his time and knowledge, and I am grateful to Heythrop College of the University of London for their hospitality when my researches took me to London.

The editor and publishers would like to acknowledge with thanks the following permissions from holders of copyright: Burns & Oates for No. 35; Cambridge University Press for Nos 67 and 77; Chatto & Windus and New Directions Publishing Corporation for No. 43, from William Empson, *Seven Types of Ambiguity* (All Rights Reserved. Reprinted by permission); Chatto & Windus and University of Michigan Press for No. 63; Malcolm Cowley for No. 56; Gerald Duckworth and Co. for No. 74; the English Association for No. 88; Faber & Faber for Nos 76 and 92; Mrs W.H. Gardner for Nos 90 and 97; Grafton Books, a Division of the Collins Publishing Group, for No. 71; the late Geoffrey Grigson for Nos 53 and 82; the *Glasgow Herald* for Nos 12 and 49; David Higham Associates for Nos 7, 64, 69, 93 and 102; the *Methodist Recorder* for No. 22; the *Month* for Nos 16, 28, 81, 89 and 100; *New Blackfriars* for No. 86; *New Catholic World* (Ramsey, N.J.) for Nos 4 and 27; *New Republic* for Nos 52 and 83; the *New Statesman* for Nos 18 and 62; the *Observer* for Nos 54 and 80; Orthological Institute (London) for No. 94; Oxford University Press for Nos 1, 21, 32, 40, 44, 68, 78, 79, 91 and 103; A.D. Peters and Co. Ltd. for Nos 75 and 96; Prentice-Hall, Inc, for No. 99, from Cornelius Weygandt, *The Time of Yeats* (© 1937, renewed 1965); Mrs Dorothea Richards for Nos 36 and 39; *Saturday Review* (Washington, D.C.) for No. 72 (© 1934 *Saturday Review* magazine); Society of Authors for No. 26; *Spectator* for Nos 20 and 34; *Studies*

(Dublin) for No. 55; *The Tablet* for Nos 19 and 46; the *Times Literary Supplement* for Nos 47, 66 and 71.

Much time has been spent in trying to establish copyrights, but in some cases without success. The editor apologises for any omissions in this respect.

Introduction

There is no doubt that, for all the belated circumstances of
Hopkins's arrival on the literary scene, he became available to
English readers at a most auspicious moment. T.S. Eliot, with
much encouragement from Ezra Pound, had published his first
'modernist' poems in 1915: the 'Love Song of J. Alfred Prufrock'
and 'Portrait of a Lady' duly shocked the general public and pleased
the progressive critics. May Sinclair in the *Little Review* warned
that Eliot's genius 'is in itself disturbing. It is elusive; it is difficult;
it demands a distinct effort of attention. ... [Francis Thompson]
was in the poetic tradition all right. People knew where they were
with him.... But Mr. Eliot is not in any tradition at all.'[1] It was
these very qualities of obscurity, aesthetic challenge, and revolt
against tradition that identified Eliot as unofficial leader of the new
movement. The time of the new poetry, at least in some critics'
minds, had arrived. The *New Statesman*, reviewing *Prufrock and
Other Observations* in 1917, might say 'much of what [Eliot] writes
is unrecognisable as poetry at present',[2] but a reviewer of Hardy's
Moments of Vision, in the following year, argued more positively:

Mr. Hardy's poems have been written in an age which is in at least one
sense fortunate. It may be an exaggeration to talk as though there had been
a revival of poetry in the last few years, but there has certainly been a
revival of the habit of reading poetry—especially of reading new poetry.[3]

A combination of luck and editorial foresight meant that the
publication of the *Poems of Gerard Manley Hopkins* in 1918 plunged
the poet into the revolutionary atmosphere of modern literature.
Although his reputation as a 'modern' grew only slowly though the
twenties, the intellectual rigour and thematic seriousness that such
outspoken critics as I.A. Richards and Robert Graves identified in
his verse, strengthened his critical position.

By 1930, and the second edition of the *Poems*, another distinguished living poet, W.H. Auden, joined Hopkins before the
reviewers. Auden's own *Poems* (published in September, two
months before Hopkin's) were as controversial as Eliot's: the

1

response ranged from enthusiastic admiration to outright bewilderment and rejection. Obscurity was again the quality noted. Naomi Mitchison advised readers 'not to get angry at once with the unintelligibility, but re-read and accept [Auden's poems] as beautiful and new and a sign of the times'.[4] The challenge to treat obscurity as rewarding and not the frustrating barrier that, for example, Bridges had found it, was meeting increasing acceptance. It can be plotted from Eliot's essay on the Metaphysical Poets (1921), 'We can only say that it appears likely that poets in our civilisation, as it exists at present, must be *difficult*',[5] through I.A. Richards, 'It is a good thing to make the light-footed reader work for what he gets'[6] (*Dial*, 1926), to Leavis in 1932, 'We expect some measure of difficulty in modern verse; indeed we are suspicious when we find none.'[7] Even Edmund Gosse, a critic of the older school, ruefully admitted in 1913 that the modern poet 'will achieve effect and attach interest … [by] …wrapping the truth in darkness'.[8]

The changing taste of changing times brought Hopkins in the twenties and thirties those readers whom a variety of circumstances had earlier deprived him of. It is one of the well known facts of literary history—and nearer to the truth than most—that virtually no one knew Hopkins was a poet when he died. Some of his poems had, in fact, been published in obscure circumstances, and some of his relatives and friends knew that he wrote poetry, but he neither sought nor had a public in the accepted sense of the word. His Jesuit obituary did not suggest that he was a poet, though it conceded that he had 'all the elements of an eminent artist or literary man'.[9] A few years later, when his admirer Canon Dixon was shown round the college at St Stephen's Green by a friendly priest, the situation was hardly changed: indeed, Hopkins was, Fr Cormac regretted, 'fond of pursuing niceties to an extent that rather stood in the way of his general usefulness'.[10] Nor were fellow-Jesuits who knew his work necessarily sympathetic: Fr Barraud, who had been with him at St Beuno's, later remarked that his poetry 'was full of tremendous power, yet rough and often rudely grotesque'.[11]

In August 1884 Hopkins made for Bridges's benefit a list of all whom he had allowed to see his verses, amounting to a dozen relatives, friends, and Jesuits: with one exception, none of these suggested he should make his work more widely known. It is true that in 1879 he wrote, 'A poet is a public in himself',[12] and the previous year, also addressing Bridges: 'I do not write for the public. You are my public',[13] but is it not helpful for even such a limited audience as Bridges represented to be a sympathetic one? Almost all Bridge's side of the correspondence has been destroyed, but Hopkins's replies (of which a selection appears in the following pages) show that he struggled unsuccessfully to modify his friend's fundamentally conservative attitude. The Preface to the Notes in the 1918 edition of the *Poems* is Bridges's formulation of his suspicions of Hopkins's innovative practices.

It has been argued that Hopkins's lack of a public had its advantages. As Morton Dauwen Zabel suggested in *Poetry*, December 1930,

Hopkins's labours were wholly divorced from the commercial and personal influences of the literary market, and from the politics of esthetic schools. He wrote under no stimulus of clerical or public approbation.[14]

Humphry House attributed his independence specifically to his being a Jesuit, since 'very few of them knew or cared whether he was a poet at all'.[15] We shall never be able to do more than speculate whether Hopkins would have benefited from being better known to his contemporaries, but there is evidence for doubting if they would have liked his poetry had it been easily available. The poet Laurence Binyon, who would have been twenty when Hopkins died and who was, through Bridges, a great admirer of sprung rhythm, later deplored the utterly traditional taste of the period: 'Hopkins's poems, if not wholly ignored, would have been thought a deliberate outrage, and simply execrated'.[16] The very mixed reaction of Hopkins's correspondents reflects the probable truth of Binyon's conclusion, and Bridges's criticisms may be taken as representative, not exceptional.

EARLY REACTION: BEFORE 1918

In his letter of 21 August 1877 from St Beuno's (No. 1), Hopkins referred to Bridges as parodying 'The Wreck of the Deutschland' and calling its style 'presumptious jugglery'. He defended his use of sprung rhythm as the 'native and natural rhythm of speech', and emphasised the need to read the poem *aloud* (later critics recognised the importance of both these points). Elsewhere he differed with

Bridges over the question of obscurity on the grounds that it was a common feature of great poetry, and pointed out that true appreciation comes slowly, while 'first criticisms ... come easiest'. If his poetry was 'odd', it was odd because it expressed his own individual view of experience, and in this sense he rejoiced in being 'queer'.

What is striking about this defence is that critics of the twenties and thirties would have accepted most of Hopkins's assumptions without question. In time, his poetry would succeed in having itself judged according to the principles on which it had been written: any reader of the documents that follow must be impressed by the way in which successive critics of Hopkins's poetry did become 'more weathered to the style and its features'. The modern movement that began with Eliot had to fight the same prejudices, but unlike Hopkins its success was almost instantaneous: time and numbers were on its side.

Coventry Patmore (No. 1), with whom Hopkins was not acquainted until 1883, was not so much unsympathetic as completely puzzled by his friend's work. He had begged to see his poetry with, as it turned out, the unfortunate remark that although slow in making up his mind he based his judgment on a 'contempt for what is meretricious'. Much to his chagrin, after reading the poems, he had to write back complaining of the 'novelties' and the obscurity, and saying he could never become reconciled to the 'strangenesses' of 'The Wreck of the Deutschland'. Later, to Bridges, he again wrote, regretfully, of the 'poetical novelties', and summed up his impression of Hopkins's verse as 'veins of pure gold imbedded in masses of unpracticable quartz'; it was a rhetorically attractive phrase which caught the fancy of later critics trying to explain the bewildering clashes and contrasts of Hopkins's writing. Patmore concluded by saying that he felt 'absolutely sure that he would never conciliate' the critics.

The most appreciative of Hopkins's friends was Richard Dixon (No. 1), an Anglican cleric and minor poet, who tried, unsuccessfully, to persuade him to go before that wider public that Hopkins was paradoxically fond of recommending to other poets, but of refusing for himself. Dixon found him 'amazingly original', praised his sincerity, and, more enigmatically, admired his power in carrying 'one out of one's self with healing'. The therapeutic value he found in Hopkins's poetry is also suggested in the remark

that 'no one could read ['The Loss of the Eurydice'] without the
deepest and most ennobling emotions' and in his reference to the
'health-breathing and ... powerful ... faculty' which Hopkins
possessed. Some understanding of what he meant by Hopkins's
originality may be deduced from that intriguing phrase, 'terrible
pathos' ('inadequate word') which he used for the first time in
October 1881, and further defined as a 'right temper which goes to
the point of the terrible'. Coined long before the Dublin poems, the
phrase, though often quoted, is puzzling: does it mean a tragic
sense of existence, which, it might be argued, is expressed in 'The
Wreck of the Deutschland'? Herbert Read referred to the latter
poem in suggesting the meaning of 'beauty of terror',[17] and pointed
to the poem's emphasis on fear, rather than love, of God. As for
Hopkins's views on metre, Dixon was no more convinced than
Bridges had been, and regarded them as an attempt to systematise
what was by its very nature unsystematic and determined by the
need of the individual poem; in this scepticism, Dixon has been
followed by later critics.

W.H. Gardner has suggested[18] that Bridges, Patmore, and
Dixon each represented a distinctive response to Hopkins, ranging
from the critical, through the puzzled, to the appreciative. The
generalisation is not entirely fair to Bridges, whose Introductions
to Hopkins in the Miles anthology and the 1918 *Poems* certainly
show fitful moments of appreciation, more than might be guessed
from a reading of the Correspondence. Perhaps, too, any genuinely
new poet would evoke just those divided reactions coincidentally
summed up in Hopkins's three friends. They are, however, our
only source of contemporary criticism, and their concerns—
obscurity, metrical and linguistic oddity, originality, conflicting
demands of poet and priest—continued to be those of the first
generation of critics. Similarly, what they do not discuss, Hopkins's thought, only slowly became a subject for criticism: not until
the mid-thirties did Scotism and the Ignatian *Exercises* receive
authoritative treatment.

It was said by many, and it has been said by a modern critic and
poet, Anthony Thwaite,[19] that Hopkins is not a suitable model for
poets because 'what shows through is the mannerism, not the
mind', as if, one feels like adding, he was another Swinburne. The
parallel is salutary, for, once considered, the fullness and interest of
Hopkins's thought is surely realised: the mind *does* show through,

but it is a Catholic and Jesuit one, and not to be appreciated without some effort and conscious rejection of bias by the reader (one is asking for no more preparation than other serious poets demand). Perhaps, after all, Auden's enigmatic remark that Hopkins 'ought to be kept on a special shelf like a dirty book, and only allowed to readers who won't be ruined by him',[20] was a back-handed compliment to the message, rather than the technique.

When, following Hopkins's death, the verse became Bridges's responsibility, he decided after some hesitation on the policy of releasing a few poems at a time, in order to prepare and encourage a taste for an eventual full edition. Convinced as he was that Hopkins would be caviare to the general, he still felt a special responsibility towards him as a friend whose gifts as a poet, however specialised, did not deserve to be neglected. His decision to work through anthologies brought some important readers: Leavis and Auden—who remarked that the 'anthology ... is the best form of advertising'[21]—both first became interested in Hopkins through Bridges's selection in the *Spirit of Man*, and those who continue to criticise Bridges for not preparing an earlier edition should bear in mind the immense success of that anthology (compared with, for example, the first edition of the *Poems* which took ten years to sell out less than a thousand copies).

Until 1918, then, public knowledge of Hopkins was based on some twenty-five poems published in mainly obscure anthologies or periodicals. Two anthologies, however, were important. In 1893, as part of Alfred Miles's epic ten-volume series, *The Poets and the Poetry of the Century*, Bridges made his first selection of a dozen complete or partial poems. The impact, however, was lessened by the unfortunately diffident terms in which he introduced them (No. 2). He spoke of Hopkins's 'natural eccentricity', 'love for subtlety and uncommonness', 'unusual and difficult rhythms', of poems 'removed from the ordinary simplicity of grammar and metre', and a 'neglect of those canons of taste which seem common to all poetry'. He also suggested that a full volume of Hopkins's work would constitute a 'unique effort in English literature' with 'verses of the rarest beauty', praise that was unlikely to outweigh the overriding impression of a poet for whom the reader would have to make many allowances: such poems 'could never be popular'. Finally, remarks about his unhappy priestly life were a tempting starting point for later developments of the theme of the priest and poet in conflict.

It is possible that Bridges deliberately went out of his way to draw attention to the difficulties in order to anticipate and so soften the hostile reaction which he obviously expected. He wrote to Fr Joseph Keating, one of Hopkins's most enthusiastic admirers in the Society of Jesus, that he proposed to put Hopkins's verse 'out of reach of criticism' by means of an introduction that he would place before it.[22] Both what he wrote for Miles and the Preface of 1918 are attempts to create a sympathetic attitude by acknowledging the untraditional elements the reader would have to face. If this was an error, it was as much tactical as critical, and certainly not malicious as the tone of some attacks on Bridges by later writers seems to imply.

For whatever reason, the response to the Miles selection was muted. One of the few comments seemed to bear out all Bridges's misgivings, when the *Manchester Guardian*,[23] criticising what it claimed to be the excessive length of the volume, added: 'Curiosities like the verses of the late Gerard Hopkins should be excluded, while introductions like those contributed to his work by Mr Bridges should, if possible, be multiplied, but employed on worthier objects.'

It might have been this selection, or the author's personal acquaintance with Bridges, that led George Saintsbury, a few years later, to make a brief reference to Hopkins in a history of nineteenth-century literature, where he assigned him to the Pre-Raphaelites and regretted that his 'remarkable talents' were wasted by his life with the Jesuits.[24] In 1910, in his *History of English Prosody*,[25] Saintsbury talked of him as belonging to the 'anti-foot and pro-stress division' and dismissed his poems summarily by saying: 'It is quite clear that all were experiments.' All these verdicts contributed to the impression that Hopkins was not likely to appeal to the general reader, and this reputation for unconventionality grew quietly around the turn of the century. A review of Basil Champneys's biography of Patmore praised some letters from Hopkins, 'an Oxford man of remarkable intellect and some very remarkable, but too eccentric poetic performances'.[26] Another book about Patmore, by Edmund Gosse, described him as a 'remarkable man of imperfect genius'.[27]

7

In 1906, his own Society (with only brief acknowledgment of his work as a poet) began printing extracts from his journals in its own private publication, *Letters and Notices* (No. 3). In some introductory remarks, eccentricity was again a theme; Fr John MacLeod, the editor, declared that Hopkins was 'A man of a very original cast of mind, of very marked character, and of quaint and somewhat extravagant poetic fancy. It was often by no means easy to understand the line of his thought or the play of his imagination.'

A more balanced as well as enthusiastic view was taken by the American Katherine Brégy, in the first essay on Hopkins to appear in a public journal, the *Catholic World* of January 1909 (No. 4). The tone is sometimes cloying—'And on the 8th of June—the month he had loved so well!—Gerard Hopkins's soul marched quietly over the borderland to victory'—but, for a pioneer essay, it is not without sensitivity and insight. She wrote of 'Spring' that, 'In one of the most hackneyed of poetic subjects, we are come upon an original vein of poetry; a spiritual motivation, a vigor of word-painting, and a metrical proficiency of very real distinction'. Her phrase 'passionate sincerity' happily describes one aspect of Hopkins's poetry, but the view that he was 'essentially a minor poet' whose verses 'were not written for the public' reflects the same limited estimate of his achievement that was also held by Bridges.

The article gained some notice and probably had some influence. It prompted an insert in *Letters and Notices* for April 1909,[28] asking for any Hopkins material to be made available for a project of 'collecting and publishing Father Hopkins' Poems with a suitable memoir'. The reviewer of Brégy's essay in the *Month* lamented the difficulty of getting hold of Hopkins's verse and hoped that the poems in the care of Bridges, 'ultimately, we trust, are destined to see the light' (No. 5). The *Academy*[29] too protested at the fact that Hopkins had 'hitherto received so small a meed of recognition' and that there was still no collected edition.

Bridges, however, was not to be hurried. In October 1909, after Fr Keating had printed a selection of letters to Hopkins, with a plea for a collection of his verse 'as a distinct and valuable addition to the literary heritage of the Catholic Church',[30] Bridges wrote as follows:

I do not think that the peculiar qualities which rendered [the poems] unintelligible and distasteful (and, therefore, practically unknown) to his contemporaries would find much favour now. .... The attention which his memory has lately received—which must be traced to Mr Miles's book—is easily accounted for, since in literary circles it is common to demand anything that is withheld.[31]

Nor was Bridges impressed by the argument of conferring a benefit on the Catholic Church: he regarded Hopkins's religious supporters as unreliable judges of good poetry and thought his directly religious poems among the weakest he wrote.

A final and perhaps overlooked reason for Bridges's reluctance relates to his own experience in publishing the poems of another friend, Canon Dixon. In a memoir that prefaced his selection from Dixon in 1909, he explained his disappointment at the public response to some of Dixon's poetry which he had published earlier; hence his reluctance with the present edition:

I had always hitherto refused, or had rather deferred doing this office for my friend, because I could not see in the public taste the sign of any feeling that would welcome the book, or even regard it with the respect necessary to its acceptance.[32]

This memory must have contributed to his caution about Hopkins.

In tracing the slow development of Hopkins's reputation before 1918, published comment is so slight that each piece of the jigsaw has its value. Another review of Brégy's essay in *Studies*, a periodical edited by the Irish Jesuits, showed that Bridges's suspicion of Catholic objectivity was not always justified. Although the author, George O'Neill, SJ, was Professor of English at University College, Dublin, and had been personally acquainted with Hopkins, he was decidedly of the opinion that he had been over-praised by Brégy: 'Father Hopkins is a tiny harp indeed' (No. 6).

Very different was the enthusiasm of the American Catholic convert Joyce Kilmer, later to die on the Western Front, who hailed Hopkins as the 'most scrupulous word-artist of the nineteenth century'. Writing in *Poetry* for September 1914,[33] he described all the poems as 'successions of lovely images, each a poem in itself', called 'The Habit of Perfection' in particular 'true poetry', and criticised Bridges for his narrow views. Kilmer, of course, could not have known more than a dozen or so of Hopkins's poems, but his article was further evidence of American interest in Hopkins, encouraged by Katherine Brégy, Louise Guiney, and members of the Society of Jesus in that country.

In the same year in England, the two Brett Young brothers, sharing a mutual enthusiasm for both Hopkins and Bridges, published a study of the latter's work (No. 7). Like Bridges, they were most interested in Hopkins's prosody, and although they thought he possessed a 'very real poetic gift', his work was 'so obscure in metre and diction that there is little chance of its ever becoming popular'. The younger of the two brothers later wrote an appreciative account of the poetry for the magazine *Today* (No. 10), possibly to raise interest in Hopkins for the publication of the *Poems* later the same year, 1918. He noted the change in Hopkins's poetry before and after his conversion, but thought that in his deliberate 'pursuit of a new technique' his successes were often won 'at the expense of baffling disregard of grammar'. Such an observation again suggests Bridges's influence.

Among books inspired by the Great War, Bridges's anthology *The Spirit of Man* must rank, at least in its time, as one of the best-known. It was not a religious anthology, but its contents were intended to suggest that 'spirituality is the basis and foundation of human life',[34] as well as to encourage the Allied war effort. Hopkins would have been pleased at the patriotic setting of his six pieces: 'We can therefore be happy in our sorrows,' wrote the editor in the Preface, 'happy even in the death of our beloved who fall in the fight; for they die nobly, as heroes and saints die, with hearts and hands unstained by hatred or wrong.'[35] The book's popularity certainly won more attention for Hopkins. Fr Martindale of his own Society, writing in the *Dublin Review*,[36] may well have been surprised at his 'pessimism', but the *New Statesman*,[37] in the first of several appreciative reviews it printed of Hopkins over the next twenty years, discovered 'A curious sincerity and elaborateness of diction which, if it delights at all, delights the reader deeply'. The reviewer continued pregnantly: 'He is little known; but he was one of the most original of modern poets.' Hopkins was soon to be celebrated as 'modern' in a more specific sense than was here intended.

The *New York Times* (No. 8) was full of praise on rather more traditional grounds, only regretting that two stanzas of 'The Habit of Perfection', and not the whole poem, had been printed, as it was the author's 'best claim to literary immortality'. In the

Catholic World,[38] from the same city, the editor was given at least as much credit as some of his contributors:

The gain is ours when a man of true taste and discernment brings forth and puts in circulation the best things from second or third rate poets, especially of our own time. And so we are thankful that Mr. Bridges has a fondness for Darley and Dixon and Dolben and Hopkins and Yeats.

George Saintsbury returned to Hopkins when he gave him a small place in the *Cambridge History of English Literature* (No. 9), describing him as having 'partially acute, but not generally sound, notions on metre', but a more important contribution to his reputation was the essay by the Irish writer J.M. Hone in the *New Statesman* of 9 June 1917.[39] This was a general introduction to Hopkins, clearly intended to interest the ordinary reader, but also making the important claim that he was 'in reaction against most of the literary influences of the nineteenth century'. This recognition that Hopkins was not merely unusual, but a revolutionary in conflict with the conventions and traditions of Victorian literature, may be considered the starting point to what was eventually to become a cliché about his place in literary history, until challenged in its turn in the 1930s.

The moment at which the first edition of Hopkins was due to be published is a convenient point at which to look back and distinguish some general trends in the development of his reputation from the time of his death to 1918. That something had been done—perhaps more than has been realised—to bring his name before the public cannot be denied. From being a poet whose least interesting verses had appeared in one or two obscure publications during his lifetime, his poetry had come to be written about in British and American books and periodicals, some of influential circulation. Bridges's promotion had clearly been a key factor. Nevertheless, the exceptional nature of his poetry had not yet been grasped—could hardly be, with so little of it in print—and his critics, headed by the same man who had introduced him to the general public, had stated his failings: eccentric and perverse in diction and syntax, rhythmically awkward, obscure as a result of these faults, and particularly and even narrowly Catholic. Against these vices were to be set—as even the same critics claimed—his virtues: originality in language and metre which had its own appeal, sincerity and power of feeling, an unusually direct spirituality. None of this early criticism was particularly perceptive: readers' responses had been fashioned by literature which, generally speaking, acknowledged different priorities from Hopkins: his poetry had to create the taste to judge it. The difficulty that untraditional poetry has in finding a fit audience was well put by a reviewer of the 1st edition of Hopkins's *Poems* who wrote: 'It requires nearly as much inspiration to appreciate a great poem as to create one.'[40]

THE FIRST EDITION OF 1918

'This edition', wrote Bridges of the *Poems of Gerard Manley Hopkins*, published late in 1918, 'was undertaken in response to a demand that, both in England and America, has gradually grown up from the genuinely poetic interest felt in the poems which I have gradually introduced to the public' (No. 11). The 'genuineness', in the editor's eyes, was their appeal to the cultured reader, and not to the Catholic enthusiast. By charging an expensive 12*s*. 6*d*. for the book, the Oxford University Press appeared to be reflecting Bridges's ingrained prejudice that Hopkins would only appeal to the few, that he was a poet who would primarily 'interest poets'. Even these few found difficulty at the best London bookshops in obtaining copies of the 750 printed.[41]

Its appearance on the contemporary scene was on the whole welcomed, although the poetry's unusualness was quickly noted. Hopkins's reputation had preceded him: one of his reviewers entitled his article 'The Prophet Unveiled',[42] others spoke of his following as a 'cult', implying, one presumes, a small but fanatic band of devotees. (On the unresolved aesthetic battlefield of 1918, some parallel might be drawn with Eliot, who, until the substantial *Poems* of 1920, had assumed myth-like qualities, his name pronounced as a 'shibboleth or a red flag'.)[43]

In his Preface to the Notes, Bridges struggled to avoid any impression of endorsing those aspects of Hopkins's poetry which made it seem 'peculiar', and as a result, the *Times Literary Supplement* (No. 13), along with several reviewers, commented that 'Mr. Bridges, in his notes, enumerates the defects of Hopkins's poetry'. Bridges stressed Hopkins's unconventionality: his 'extravagances', 'freaks' and 'idiosyncrasy'. There were references, too, to 'faults of taste', to oddity and obscurity, while 'The Wreck of the Deutschland', in an unhappily memorable image, was described as a 'great dragon folded in the gate to forbid all entrance'. Insensitive remarks about 'exaggerated Marianism' raised doubts about the editor's religious objectivity, and even though the Preface ended with a tribute to the 'rare masterly beauties' of the verse, the general tone was that of qualification and regret.

Shortly before the volume was published, Bridges wrote to Fr Keating with ingenuous frankness:

I cannot tell how far you will like my book, but whatever feelings or animus it may discover (lurking in it) against the medievalism which I cannot sympathise with, that no doubt will appear in anything that I write, and I do not go out of my way to express it or disguise it.[44]

There is no doubting his sincerity—he told Shane Leslie that in his selection he was 'guided entirely by what I knew [Hopkins's] prayers and wishes had been'[45]—but it is difficult not to feel that his prejudice against Hopkins's religion narrowed his critical sympathies.

Nevertheless, the Poet Laureate's name on the title-page ensured that the volume was widely reviewed and given a fair reading. The *Glasgow Herald* (No. 12) was tolerant of the 'crudities' in a book where there was not a 'shred of the commonplace'. In the *Times Literary Supplement*, Arthur Clutton-Brock, a regular contributor, devoted one and a half columns of thoughtful discussion to it. He admitted Hopkins was difficult, and concentrated on style, not matter. Still, he was impressed, though not quite clear why: 'You fight your way through the verses, yet they draw you on.'

This ambivalent attitude found its way into several reviews. In the *New Witness* (edited by G.K. Chesterton), Hopkins emerged as a martyr to the demands of the muse, 'the flagellant of song', and the reviewer was impressed by his technical achievement: Hopkins 'was more modern than the most freakish modern would dare to be. Ezra Pound is stale set beside this poet' (No. 14). But his undeniable obscurity was never an 'affectation'. This article seems to have been the first to claim a parallel between Hopkins and contemporary poets, although it had no obvious influence at the time.

Bridges received his meed of praise from, for example, the reviewer in *Everyman* (No. 15) who found him the perfect commentator of an 'ecstatic and difficult poet', and Imogen Guiney rushed to his defence in the columns of the *Universe*, the Catholic paper,[46] when he was attacked by the *Saturday Westminster Gazette* (No. 17) for omitting some of Hopkins's religious verse. Shortly before, she had written an appreciative account of the *Poems* in the *Month*, drawing particular attention to the sprung rhythm—as well as pointing to its tradition in English verse—and calling Hopkins 'the most choral of English poets' (No. 16). The importance of the aural element of his poetry had been recognised from the first, though like his diction and syntax, its very obviousness as a feature drew a disproportionate amount of attention in these early years.

The generally sympathetic approach to the *Poems* in the first few months of 1919 received its first major check with the review by the poet Edward Shanks in the normally appreciative *New Statesman* (No. 18). Shanks mocked the long build-up to the 'unveiling' of Hopkins, a poet of mystery, known until then only through anthologies, and conceded that he was indeed 'the writer of the strangest [poetry] that has been published in England'. Shanks found it impossible (as many before and after) to follow his metrical explanations, but, in any case, considered that sprung rhythm was only one aspect of his 'general and prevailing eccentricity'. He observed that Hopkins's metrical aim was to 'approach as nearly as possible to the effect of music', a shrewd perception of the intentions of a writer who laid so much store by the 'performance' of his poetry. Hopkins was 'too rare and too difficult' for the ordinary reader.

Did Shanks count himself one? Or was his remark a discreet way of expressing his lack of sympathy for Hopkins's poetry? Whatever his meaning, Bridges must have felt himself at home with much of the essay. Whereas E.M. Harting's 'Gerard Hopkins and Digby Dolben' in the *Month*,[47] written in the romantic-religious vein, justified some of Bridges's worst fears, with such specimens as 'In [Hopkins's and Dolben's] outpouring of worship, there is something akin to the ecstasies of the saints.'

But it was in a Catholic weekly, the *Tablet* (No. 19) that one of the best reviews appeared. Written by Fr Geoffrey Bliss, SJ, who also contributed to the *Month*, it emphasised Hopkins's concern for both sound and sense in his choice of diction, and the importance of his use of alliteration. The author admitted that Hopkins made 'large demands upon his readers', but 'a pioneer can do no otherwise'. Unlike Bridges, he was able to see how the last sonnets, despite appearances, show the poet triumphing over despair. Apart from this review, the *Tablet* continued the subject of Hopkins over the next two weeks and made the first of many pleas that appeared over the next fifteen years for the publication of his letters.

Praise for Bridges was usually accompanied by at least a measure of disapproval for his protégé (this principle also tended to operate in reverse when Bridges was criticised). Both the *Spectator* and the *Oxford Magazine* (Nos. 20 and 21) thought well of Bridges, but the first took Hopkins to task on the grounds that 'lyrics which do not sing themselves would, in our opinion at least, be better in prose'. The *Oxford Magazine* wondered if the time was ripe for the new poet, and castigated the forced rhythms, the rhymes, 'the violent breaches of grammar and syntax', and, of course, the 'obscurities'; consequently, 'these poems are almost all immediately incomprehensible'.

As the first six months of reviewing neared its end, opinion showed no sign of arriving at a simple conclusion about Hopkins. Although the *Methodist Recorder* (No. 22) predicted unpopularity, it also forecast a 'place on the shelf of the discerning' for this poet of 'Browning obscurity...verbal violence...and mystic glooms'. In America, the *Dial* (No. 23), still reorganising itself for the challenge of contemporary literature, had little doubt of the poems' unpopularity, and complained of their 'antique tone oddly incongruous with the time of publication'. This verdict on the style—which has its justification—must be compared with later views that saw instead the contemporaneity of Hopkins's writing. Like most critical judgments these are not incompatible, but reflect a difference in emphasis from one critic and his period to another.

One of the better-known of these early reviews is Middleton Murry's in the *Athenaeum* (No. 26), yet it is hardly one of his most distinguished pieces. He claimed Hopkins had little to say, that his 'whole achievement' was a 'failure' (the poet's religious outlook obviously made little sense to him), and that 'music' was the most outstanding feature of his verse: 'he must remain a poet's poet'. Much to the later disgust of F.R. Leavis, Murry attempted to find parallels with Shelley, and it is not a comparison which has found favour with critics in general, in their search for Hopkins's poetic ancestors. A more interesting if curious observation about his literary context, came from a reviewer in the *Irish Monthly* (a periodical edited by the Jesuits in Dublin), who praised the originality of Hopkins's poetry which, 'for all its strangeness and tangled passages, stands out in refreshing contrast to the derivative, groove-confined verses which make up a large part of the output of modern English poets' (No. 29). One must presume that the reference is not to Eliot and Pound, but, perhaps, to the Georgians.

For most readers, knowledge of the life of Hopkins was limited to the incidental contributions of Bridges. The brief, whimsical reminiscences of Fr Barraud in the *Month* for August 1919 did not add much, but because they came from a contemporary of the poet were of special interest. Their appearance at all suggested that the subject was achieving an increasingly wide appeal. Barraud, however, duly confirmed the traditional Jesuit picture of Hopkins's eccentricity: 'He wilfully set all tradition at defiance' (No. 28). One must take account of the fact that in a veteran Jesuit's mind, originality was not likely to be seen as a virtue.

The year 1919 may be taken as a convenient terminus date for the second phase of Hopkins criticism, directly arising from the first edition of the *Poems*. After this date, and until the second edition in 1930, comment becomes increasingly sporadic, although not without some writing of exceptional distinction. Except to state the obvious—that readers were not yet ready for Hopkins—it is difficult to explain the apparent lack of interest over the next ten years. As has been described, much critical reaction to the first edition (admittedly, with a strong Catholic element) had been positive, although Bridges's Preface dictated the terms, if not in some cases the opinions, of many reviewers. Even if they took a more sympathetic view of 'originality', their remarks usually reflected Bridges's concern with metre, rhyme, and syntax, with the eccentricity of diction, and his doubts about the likely extent of the poetry's appeal. But it was not only Bridges who gave technique most attention: there was a general reluctance to venture into a serious discussion of Hopkins's 'doctrine', and one of the causes for the paucity of Hopkins criticism in the twenties was the ignorance of his life and his religious viewpoint.

BETWEEN TWO EDITIONS: 1919–30

George O'Neill's *Essays on Poetry* (1919) is interesting in its development of the idea of Hopkins as a 'modern'. The author saw

parallels in contemporary writers, and made the farsighted statement that he was 'quite ahead of his own generation and anticipated
doings still far off in the twentieth century' (No. 30). These insights
into his contemporaneity were no longer isolated. Alan Porter in
the *Spectator* (No. 34) declared that Hopkins was being read by the
'youngest generation of poets' and that his obscurity was 'necessary
...the impress of himself'. In a similarly enlightened, if belated
review of the *Poems*, Edward Sapir in *Poetry* (No. 31) recognised
the same quality as a 'symbolic reflection of the tumult that raged in
his soul'. Although he did not describe him as modern he had
no hesitation in calling Hopkins one of the 'half dozen most
individual voices in the whole course of English nineteenth-
century poetry'.

Some note was also taken of Hopkins's debt to classical
languages and literature, but it was made a cause of reproof, rather
than the starting-point for much-needed research. The perceptive
comment[48] that, 'His love of compound words and his involved
syntax may, perhaps, be due to his classical learning, particularly
Greek', was followed by the chastening criticism that 'He casts his
words about, forgetting that when using an uninflected language
this cannot be done unduly without involving the sense in
obscurity'. And Sapir similarly complained that Hopkins's 'scholarship in Latin made him forget that an uninflected language has
need of' articles and pronouns.

In the early 1920s Hopkins was still a puzzle, a poet of
contradictions. The American Catholic writer George Shuster
found his poetry full of 'oddities', but 'gifted with power'; 'he was
a master of the phrase but a mere tinker at composition' (No. 33).
Another critic summed him up as 'A fascinating failure'.[49] Shane
Leslie's Introduction to the *Anthology of Catholic Poets* (No. 35) also
gave a mixed impression, particularly difficult to interpret in
Leslie's overpowering purple prose: 'Hopkins's poems remained
hidden like violets, whilst his whole life became a passion-flower in
the Jesuit Conservatory'.

But in September 1926, the *Dial* printed I.A. Richards's essay on
Hopkins (No. 36), the most influential piece of writing since
Bridges's Preface. The opening paragraphs, with their enunciation
of the virtues of difficulty, were a constructive defence of
Hopkins's poetic and a rejection of a basic assumption of Bridges
and of 'traditional' criticism:

Poets who can compel slow reading have...an initial advantage. The effort, the heightened attention, may brace the reader....These are arguments for some slight obscurity in its own right....We should be clear (both as readers and writers) whether a given poem is to be judged at its first reading or at its *n*th.

Hopkins's oddities, said Richards, were deliberate, and modern poets were attempting 'independently' 'some of his most daring innovations'. Sound was very important in his verse, but the general question of his prosody had been given too much importance: 'Many people just ripe to read Hopkins have been and will be too busy asking "does he scan?" to notice that he has anything to say to them.'

The remarks are enlightening, but even Richards is sometimes guilty of misapplied principles: to say that 'The poet in him was often oppressed and stifled by the priest' is to transform an observation about poems into a generalisation about Hopkins's life. He also asserts that the conflict found in most of Hopkins's poetry was only resolved by a 'stoic acceptance of sacrifice': 'All Hopkins's poems are in this sense poems of defeat.' But, of course, sacrifice is not defeat, and the last poems of Hopkins salvage Christian hope out of despair.

However, Richards's commitment to the ideals of accurate and sensitive reading were further demonstrated by his use of 'Spring and Fall' as one of the test-pieces of *Practical Criticism* (1929), a work that was the product of his teaching at Cambridge (No. 39). Christopher Isherwood has recalled Richards's lectures on modern poetry in the mid-twenties: 'He revealed to us in a succession of astounding lightning flashes the entire expanse of the Modern World.'[50] *Practical Criticism* itself revealed that being a student at Cambridge was no guarantee of close reading: misunderstandings of the poems placed before the students were rife; Richards justifiably observed after some particularly misguided interpretations that 'We may remind ourselves here that these are the opinions of serious and professed students of English.' 'Spring and Fall' suffered as much as any poem in the collection, and was, as the figures in the Appendix showed, one of the less popular poems. This chapter certainly discourages any suggestion that Hopkins's poetry was universally known and liked in the twenties.

Richards's work, and particularly the *Dial* essay, was both an important part of and important influence on a new style of

Hopkins criticism which above all emphasised close reading of the text. The new critics showed that his choice of language was not determined on superficial grounds, but controlled by the overall intention of the poem. His sensitive handling of words put him in revolt, so it seemed, against a standardised poetic diction which had grown up over the past fifty years. Nor did his style seem limited by any social or cultural boundaries: current speech, dialect, archaisms all jostled together (in a time of both social and artistic egalitarianism this was no mean recommendation).

There were other, more subjective reasons why the new criticism took over from Bridges the patronage of Hopkins. Religious differences were no longer esteemed grounds for critical judgment, whereas what was felt to be personal sincerity was: religious experience could be read in terms of emotional and psychological responses, common to all thinking people. (The point was made by a number of thirties writers who discussed Hopkins as a religious poet whose experiences were conceivable in purely human terms.) Lastly, Bridges's somewhat grudging managing of Hopkins provided an all-too-obvious opportunity for deprecating establishment attitudes in literature: reading attack after attack on the Poet Laureate's editorship, one is irresistibly led to the conclusion that he was the critics' scapegoat for a despised and rejected cultural tradition.

Laura Riding and Robert Graves's *Survey of Modernist Poetry* (1927) (No. 37) fitted naturally into the Richards-inspired movement of close reading (Graves later claimed that it was he who had stimulated the new interest in Hopkins) and made great play with Bridges's shortcomings. They challenged traditionalists with condemning Hopkins simply because he had broken with convention, and ironically praised Bridges for helping to turn Hopkins into a modernist by delaying his publication for thirty years. More obviously influenced by Richards was Alec Brown's 'Gerard Hopkins and Associative Form' for the *Dublin Magazine* (April–June 1928) (No. 38). The writer suggested that grammatical logic was not necessary in poetry and that Hopkins was most successful, as in 'Tom's Garland', when least inhibited by it:

... It is not surprising ... that one of the chief elements even of the most reasoned pseudo-classical 'poetry' is the introduction of characteristics entirely unnecessary to the argument—words associated by sound, rhyme, assonance, alliteration—or even by mere metrical position.

The passage says a good deal about Hopkins's method, but it underestimates the meaningfulness of such devices; to confess otherwise is to admit the charge that he was characteristically—and not occasionally—guilty of merely aural effects.

It was Hopkins's style—and nothing else—that encouraged comparisons with the Victorian writer and traveller Charles Doughty (whose consciously archaic manner Hopkins, in fact, thoroughly detested). Edward Shanks made the first comparison in the *New Statesman* in March 1919, and a more substantial parallel was drawn by D.M. Mirsky in a review of Barker Fairley's *Charles M. Doughty* in the *London Mercury*[51] eight years later. He commented on the 'curious likeness of Doughty's rhythmical practice to that of Gerard Hopkins ... both were effective workers in destroying the "Spenserian" fluency of English verse'. In the same periodical, in June 1935, Barker Fairley also pointed to certain parallels in the use of language. Later in the same year, however, a *Times Literary Supplement* reviewer responded that there was no comparison in depth of experience between the two writers, and Michael Roberts remarked in the *Faber Book of Modern Verse* (No. 92) that Doughty's poetry lacked 'that intensity which, in the poetry of Hopkins, was the expression of an important moral conflict'. F.R. Leavis's article in *Scrutiny*, December 1935 (No. 87) emphatically disowned any parallels in style: to compare Doughty's use of language with that of Hopkins was to 'betray a complete inappreciation of Hopkins's poetry'. Doughty's writing carried 'to an extreme the spirit of Victorian romanticism', whereas Hopkins was 'working in the spirit of the living English language'.

The superficial attractiveness of this parallel, and the firmness with which it was rejected, are an interesting commentary on the place of Hopkins in contemporary criticism. His usefulness as a name to publicise another writer suggests the rise of his own reputation; the repudiation of the comparison by his admirers reflects their regard for his uniqueness: Hopkins was not to be associated with what was, in their eyes, outworn tradition. The dogma now, as stated by Harold Monroe in *Twentieth Century Poetry*, one of the better anthologies of the period, was that he belonged 'temperamentally and technically to the 20th century'.[52]

Early in 1930, Fr Lahey's biography was published, the first major attempt to supply a want only sparsely filled so far by

Bridges's introductions, and occasional information in esoteric Jesuit publications. It was sympathetically handled by most reviewers, particularly for its extracts from the Diaries, but there was some disappointment at the paucity of biographical information, and the occasional critic was very severe. Morris Schappes in the *Symposium* for January 1931 (No. 48) clinically pointed out its shortcomings, and summed it up as 'blunt, badly written, and actually misleading'. It has only historical interest for the modern reader, who now has access to all Hopkin's letters and journals, some modern biographical studies, and the expectation of a definitive one from Dr. Norman White.

Lahey's work, and the knowledge of an impending second edition of the *Poems*, revived interest in Hopkins. Reviewing Lahey in the *Nation*, April 1930 (No. 41), Isidor Schneider particularly remarked on the contemporary willingness to accept experiment, in contrast with 1918. He thought that Hopkins's example had encouraged individuality in general, and metrical experiment in particular, but he repeated the old warning that his style was 'very dangerous to copy'. As if to show that it could be equally perilous to adapt it, the poet and critic Sturge Moore, in the *Criterion* in July,[53] proceeded to rewrite 'The Leaden Echo' in order to demonstrate the virtues of an economic style: the final result deprived the poem of all the qualities that had made it worth reading in the first place.

A very old-fashioned attack on Hopkins was provided by an anonymous critic in the *New York Times Book Review* (No. 42), who dismissed interest in the poet as part of the modern fad for being different. Hopkins's poems should have been allowed to 'remain in that oblivion to which [his] contemporaries seemed content to consign' them. As the poet Stanley Kunitz pointed out in the *Wilson Bulletin*,[54] Hopkins's contemporaries did not have the opportunity to read his poetry in the first place: this critic was a 'dullard'. He ended: 'I know of no young poet of talent in this country today whose face is not turned to him, though it will be many generations before a popular audience will even know his name.' Kunitz was happily proved wrong in the latter forecast; while Hart Crane, who died in 1932, was at least one American poet who admitted to being influenced by Hopkins.

William Empson's references to Hopkins in *Seven Types of Ambiguity* (1930) (No. 43) helped to underline the ease with which the new criticism assimilated his poetry. This book, with its clear and stated debt to Richards, regarded ambiguity of meaning as a measure of poetic excellence, and in 'Spring and Fall' and 'The Windhover' Empson found ample evidence of the 'use of poetry to convey an indecision, and its reverberation in the mind'. Empson's use of Hopkins was not extensive, but it completed a chain of approval—Richards, Riding and Graves, and now Empson—which securely established the poet among the ideal writers of the new critical anti-establishment. Leavis's later praise of Empson's treatment seemed a logical continuation.

Surveying criticism between 1919 and 1930, one is impressed by the picture of a period of transition, from traditional to modern, from Bridges to Richards. The pendulum had swung from general value judgments, whether of approval or disapproval, to stringent analysis of text determined, in the first place, by the aim of understanding what Hopkins meant. In making this analysis, of course, the new critics found in Hopkins a man and a poet of considerable interest, with whose mind they could empathise and whose art they could admire. Their critical procedures were a more sensitive means for exploring Hopkins than the watered-down conventions of Romantic criticism. If Hopkins was not widely read during this period, his readers nevertheless seem to have been among the poets and critics most likely to influence taste in the succeeding generation. This, at any rate, provides a possible explanation for the astonishing outburst of writing that started to appear towards the end of 1930 as a result of the appearance of the second edition of the *Poems*.

FAME I: THE 2ND EDITION, 1930–5

For this development, the new editor must take some credit. Charles Williams was a very different personality from his predecessor: more open-minded towards what was original in both character and art, he remained a committed Anglican while holding wide theological interests. Hopkins's Catholicism was no barrier, and Williams's Introduction is free of the suspicions manifest in Bridges's comments. But although the first editor had died in April 1930, his hand was still very much in evidence in the new volume. Indeed, basically the edition was still Bridges's: his Preface and

Notes were retained, and the only important changes were the addition of Williams's Introduction and an Appendix of previously omitted poems and their notes. These poems are of minor importance, and on critical grounds at least their earlier omission seems justified.

Reviewers were therefore dealing with a volume which was substantially the same as before (though the cheaper price of 7s. 6d. suggested hopes of a wider market), so that, apart from Williams's Introduction, there could be no question of explaining the surge of interest that was to come on any other grounds than a general revival of interest in Hopkins. The appreciativeness of Charles Williams's Introduction was an encouragement to sympathetic reading. His analysis of the functional quality of such techniques as alliteration and interior rhyme is full of insight, and he specified two vital qualities in Hopkins's work, 'passionate emotion' and 'passionate intellect'; Milton was the poet who offered the best parallel.

Williams's criticisms, although more gently expressed than Bridges's, were essentially the same: he regretted his 'poetic tricks, his mannerisms, his explorations in the technique of verse', and believed they would have vanished if he had lived longer (comparison with one of Bridges's final sentences is obvious).

The first reviews were decidedly positive. Hester Pickman in *Hound and Horn* (October–December 1930)[55] observed that 'Hopkins was trying to do something with the language that others have tried since, but was unknown to his English contemporaries'. His so-called obscurity was in fact evidence of his modernism. Morton Dauwen Zabel took up these two popular themes of modernism and obscurity in his review in *Poetry* in December (No. 45) when he praised the verse for its 'astonishing originality and subtlety' which 'anticipated by a quarter century the most searching experiments of contemporary writers'. He made the distinction that unlike the private language of Joyce, Hopkins's obscurity was accessible to patience and intelligence. In her book *Discovering Poetry*, Elizabeth Drew also noted the difference between understanding Hopkins and a poet like Blake. It was the 'suggestion and overtones'[56] that made him difficult, not mysterious symbolism or esoteric ideas.

The latter seemed not, however, the opinion of 'E.O.' writing the first English review in the *Tablet* (No. 46). He thought Hopkins was 'nearly always difficult, and often obscure. His worst faults are so bad that they will forever disable him from popularity'. In 'risking' the quotation of 'Pied Beauty', which he described as 'like all truly Hopkinsy Hopkins...for ear-reading, not for eye-reading', 'E.O.' showed that he considered that the concern with sound was an important reason for Hopkins's obscurity. Similarly, Ernest de Selincourt, Oxford Professor of Poetry, accused him of forcing language 'to fit his rhythmical purpose', so that his meaning became 'impenetrably obscure'.[57] Against this one may place the *Nation's* view that no one else had 'brought sense and sound into so perfect or beautiful a unity' (No. 50). Judgments continued to reflect the element of puzzle and contradiction that critics found in his work. The *Venerabile*, the journal of the English College in Rome,[58] must have confounded its readers by on one hand telling them to read Hopkins, but warning that 'obscurity and oddity' would always tell against him. Alan Pryce-Jones explained in the *London Mercury* (No. 59) that 'In an attempt to show concisely the splendour of an obscure poet, I have shown nothing but his faults.' Oliver Elton, in *The English Muse* (1933)[59] implied this element of paradox when he declared that although Hopkins was 'deliberately and invincibly queer', these difficulties were still 'worth facing'.

One of the most notable essays of the thirties on Hopkins appeared in F.R. Leavis's *New Bearings* (1932) (No. 63). It was a confident assertion of his greatness, with a strong criticism of Bridges for insensitivity, that was arguably responsible for the renewed baiting of Hopkins's earliest editor that characterised some thirties writing. But the main section of the essay was a constructive examination of certain aspects of his work, with particular attention to 'The Wreck of the Deutschland' (reclaiming it from Bridges's strictures) and the later poems. Leavis declared that Hopkins's genius comprised 'technical originality....insepar-able from the rare adequacy of mind, sensibility and spirit that it vouches for'. The various devices of Hopkins's style were not mannerisms but functional in intensifying the poem's meaning. Leavis was therefore emphatically denying charges of lack of thematic seriousness and of verbal appropriateness; at the same time he wanted to reject parallels between Hopkins and the Victorian poets and Shelley (by Murry) and endorse a link with the

Metaphysical poets. This, of course, represented the state of Leavis's own preferences in literature.

Great though Leavis admitted 'The Wreck of the Deutschland' to be, he felt that Hopkins's powers were more fully extended in such pieces as 'The Windhover' and 'Spelt from Sibyl's Leaves', a poem that 'magnificently justifies most of the peculiarities of his technique'. 'The 'terrible' sonnets were perhaps too personal and less technically accomplished, yet the use of language in them reflected the 'living idiom', the 'speaking voice'; no one could come from studying Hopkins's work 'without an extended notion of the resources of English'. Leavis concluded with the comprehensive tribute, 'He is likely to prove, for our time and the future, the only influential poet of the Victorian age, and he seems to me the greatest.'

This is an essay that continues to be read and reprinted, even if the definitive and aggressive tone seems more grating today than in the atmosphere of the controversial thirties. Just as it has been claimed that 'The influence of Leavis in making Eliot [also the subject of an essay in *New Bearings*] into perhaps the most powerful literary figure of the 1930's cannot be overestimated',[60] his admirataion for Hopkins must be regarded as at least as important to the latter's reputation as the work of I.A. Richards. Indeed, Leavis, as the more active literary critic, in the front-line of controversy, may have lost Hopkins some of the sympathy the more traditional critics were prepared to give. Yet Leavis was not an undiscriminating supporter, and the history of his references to Hopkins, culminating with his lecture in 1971 to the Hopkins Society, will show that personal taste and critical principle were never stultified.

Bridges's name had not lost its influence, nor necessarily was it only quoted by Hopkins sceptics. So enthusiastic an admirer of Hopkins as Geoffrey Grigson (No. 53) recommended Bridges's notes to the enquiring reader. Edward Thompson in the *Observer* (No. 54) praised the editing and criticised Hopkins for anticipating the 'left-wing' movement in literature. B. Ifor Evans, an active critic in the thirties, thought Bridges was right and that Hopkins remained an 'original if erratic poet'.[61]

But by far the most interesting example of the Bridges factor was the review of his verse by Yvor Winters in *Hound and Horn* in January–March 1932 (No. 61). Winters professed an admiration of Hopkins's poetry, but a preference for that of Bridges, whom he found less vague in thought and more sensitive in technique. Originality was a dubious virtue: 'Extreme originality of method almost always involves extreme departure from the norm of experience, involving specialization and limitation of feeling.'

No direct answer seems to have been given to this critique, and Winters continued to express his doubts about Hopkins into the next decade. It might have influenced a similar, but less respectful, devaluation of Hopkins that appeared early in 1933 in the *Times Literary Supplement*.[62] Suggesting that Hopkins's rejection of tradition went too far, the reviewer went on: 'Hopkins chooses to forget that he is using a language which has expressed itself in literature for four centuries. Bridges does not.' He concluded: 'His poetry, with all its power and suggestiveness, is in fact just such a failure as Bridges said it was.' The same year also produced Herbert Read's almost Leavisian denunciation of Bridges in *English Critical Essays* (No. 69) and the complaint that the standard he applied in judging Hopkins 'was not that of the indicted... [Hopkins's] values were so fundamentally opposed to common practices, that only by an effort of the imagination could they be comprehended.' Bridges could not make that effort. This attack was certainly more typical of the 'spirit of the age' than those defences just quoted.

The whole decade from 1930 to 1940 is the story of Hopkins's growth in reputation to 'classic' status, and the perception of him as a modern is the major theme running through these years. His influence on contemporaries was commented on by several critics. W.J. Turner, the Georgian poet, remarked that modern poets looked to him for his 'strange powers' (No. 47). Technically, he was a 'great liberating influence in English verse'. Malcolm Cowley (No. 56) thought that one reason for reading him was because he was a 'source for other poets', and Auden was regularly pointed to as one who stemmed 'directly from Gerard Manley Hopkins'.[63]

One of Hopkins's most enthusiastic advocates as a modern was the already quoted Herbert Read, the art critic whose interests in literature were particularly welcoming to new developments. He saw Hopkins as a characteristic modern writer, grappling with problems of faith and belief and attempting to use language in new and personal ways. He again thought new poets were much influenced by him, though in the area of style, rather than content. Read's essay in the *Criterion* in April 1931 (No. 57) was the first of several pieces in which he took a positive view of Hopkins's achievement.

Extreme claims in literature rarely go unchallenged for long. The fact that Hopkins had lived and written in mid-Victorian England made it difficult to maintain his complete uniqueness in the period. G.W. Stonier, writing in the *New Statesman and Nation* (No. 62) defiantly declared that he was a 'Victorian in style, outlook and feeling, and... was a Catholic priest who wrote poetry to the glory of God'. Without going quite as far, Humphry House also argued that Hopkins had been 'wrenched out of his context' (No. 71). F.W. Bateson suggested that both Victorian and personal influences had moulded Hopkins: he praised him as one of the few nineteenth-century poets who had contributed to the 'catholicity of diction' of post-war poetry, but claimed that so powerful was the effect of Victorian poetic diction that in striving to counteract it his own vocabulary had been forced into awkwardness (No. 78).

C. Day Lewis classified him as a 'naif' poet, one of those 'whose voice seems to come out of the blue, reminding us of nothing we have heard before'; an 'unconscious revolutionary' who, unlike Wordsworth, didn't realise what conventions he was rebelling against (No. 75). In the same work, suggestively called *A Hope for Poetry*, Lewis noted his influence on the style of modern poetry, which like Hopkins's own writing often combined unusual language in a prosody based 'on the rhythm of common speech'. Lewis also thought that modern verse had attempted to imitate Hopkins's alliteration, assonance, and repetition.

The degree to which Hopkins had become the favourite of the trendsetters was more informally apparent in William Rose Benét's column in the American *Saturday Review of Literature* (No. 72). He complained of the modern 'cult' of Hopkins whose name was 'at present the Open Sesame to poetic converse with the intelligentzia, if you wish to meet the "right people"' (which was hardly Hopkins's fault).

One suspects that Benét's irritation was partly religious in source, but most writers in the period 1930–5 were at least objective, if not positively sympathetic in this debatable area. The best answer to any who might still fear that Catholics were too favourable to Hopkins came from Babette Deutsch,[64] who turned the objection on its head by remarking that 'In dealing with Hopkins's work the question of belief is so fundamental that one could wish that his critics would state frankly their position.' Joan Bennett in *Four Metaphysical Poets* (No. 77) did not go this far, but pointed out that the kinds of experience that Hopkins dealt with were not limited to people religious in the formal sense, but could be understood by all sensitive, thinking individuals. She also put him in the same tradition as Herbert, although noting the valuable distinction that, whereas the latter's poems ended on a note of reconciliation, Hopkins's were characterised by a 'crescendo of emotion'. Interestingly, religion as subject-matter was seen as the appropriate domain of the modern poet. Michael Roberts[65] thought modern poets were searching for a system of belief and that the best of them were 'metaphysical and (in the widest sense) religious'. They were looking to the work of Eliot and Hopkins as a 'starting point'. Herbert Read (No. 57) saw Hopkins as a characteristic modern writer because he attempted to grapple with problems of faith and belief, although he had a low opinion of his explicitly religious verse, such as 'Ad Mariam': the best poetry, he thought, emerged out of a state of tension, rather than certainty (Nos. 64, 69) G.W. Stonier (No. 62) took a less purist view: it was religion that made Hopkins a poet and he wrote 'to the glory of God'.

Some writers were not sure if he was a religious poet (although one feels they were tinkering with terms, rather than making a particularly original statement). W.J. Turner (No. 51) granted him religious belief, but not a 'religious sense'. Elsie Phare (No. 67), in the first but not particularly influential book devoted to Hopkins, also thought he could not properly be called a religious poet. T.S. Eliot, in *After Strange Gods* (No. 76), preferred to use the word 'devotional' (although in 'Religion and Literature'[66] seemed willing to use the word 'religious' and to concede that Hopkins's poetry showed something more than 'limited awareness'). In the midst of such refinements it is refreshing to come across such down-to-earth enthusiasts as Dom Wulstan Gregory in the *Downside Review* who from 1933 to 1939 wrote a series of personal reviews of Hopkins in terms that made up in sincerity for what they may have lacked in ingenuity.

Despite these concessions to the existence of religious thought in Hopkins, warnings about the disproportionate importance of expression compared with content continued to be uttered. It was a cliché that died hard. Even Herbert Read (No. 64) complained that in Hopkins 'the thought...tends to be overlaid by the surface beauty'. T.S. Eliot's observation (No. 76) that Hopkins's writing 'sometimes [comes] near to being purely *verbal,* in that a whole poem will give us *more* of the same thing, an accumulation, rather than a real development of thought or feeling' certainly registered one aspect of Hopkins's art, but is an unbalanced general condemnation: 'Tom's Garland', 'That Nature is a Heraclitean Fire', are difficult because of their concentration of meaning, not for lack of it.

Despite the admission of Hopkins's uniqueness, occasional claims were made for parallels, sources, and influences. Wordsworth was occasionally mentioned. Hester Pickman detected a 'Wordsworthian lack of taste—and emotional naiveté that is embarrassing' in 'The Bugler's First Communion'.[67] Elsie Phare mentioned him, however, because she found Hopkins lacking Wordsworth's feeling for human situations. F.R. Leavis, as has already been suggested, could only see some comparison with the Metaphysical poets, none with the Victorians. More interesting was a discussion about possible classical influences that developed as a result of a review of Read's *Essays in Order* in the *Times Literary Supplement* in February 1933. In the ensuing correspondence,[68] Michael Tierney of University College, Dublin, claimed that Hopkins had adopted his metrical theory from Greek poetry. Further letters followed, including the suggestion that Sophocles had been an influence. This promising line of investigation, however, was taken no further, at least before 1940.

FAME II: AFTER THE PROSE, 1935–40

In 1935 Hopkins's Correspondence with Bridges and with Dixon was published, both volumes edited by Professor Claude Abbott. Samples from these (and the Journals) had appeared sporadically in several books and periodicals over the preceding forty years, and had drawn appeals for more. W.J. Turner wrote in December 1930 (No. 47) that 'Hopkins's eminently sane, exceptionally acute mind displays its logical power far more obviously for the general reader in his prose than in his poetry'.

The Letters offered a vivid and informative picture of Hopkins that was more absorbing than any biographical essay so far printed, and many readers must have been surprised at the quality and interest of the mind revealed. Hopkins was shown as a dedicated priest and serious poet, neither the cranky figure that Bridges had been in danger of suggesting nor the romantic individual of some over-enthusiastic apologists. The Letters and the later Journals both stimulated and were part of the increasing interest in Hopkins: the knowledge they provided deepened enjoyment of his poetry, and contributed to making it better known.

Claude Abbott had already (the *Nation and Athenaeum*, June 1930) demonstrated caution in reviewing Hopkins, who 'as a model...is likely to prove dangerous',[69] and it was surprising that he chose the Introduction (No. 79) to the *Letters to Bridges* as an opportunity for a long essay on his poetry. His critical principles were closer to those of Bridges than Leavis, to the tradition of Arnold rather than Richards, and the general tone of the Introduction, for 1935, sounded uncomfortably old-fashioned in its insistence on traditional values and suspicion of originality. Like Bridges, Abbott was not impressed by 'The Wreck of the Deutschland', which struck him as an 'academic religious subject', too much like propaganda. He enjoyed most of the poems of the middle period where he felt the religion was only incidental, and where Hopkins's 'senses, not his religion, [were] in the ascendant'. The poems of the later years were affected by the conflict between poet and priest: 'He suffered slow martyrdom as a poet.' Like the first editor, too, Abbott had little admiration for sprung rhythm and stylistic devices.

There was plenty of evidence of Abbott's affection for certain aspects of Hopkins's poetry and personality ('the poet is a classic' he remarked at one point), but just as with Bridges a crucial lack of sympathy marks the overall tone. Nevertheless, the essay seems to have had no impact on the development of Hopkins criticism, and it was on the contents of the Letters themselves that reviewers concentrated. The verdict was almost unanimous. Bonamy Dobrée in the *Spectator*[70] called them a 'permanent addition to literature'; Morton Dauwen Zabel in *Poetry*[71] declared they were 'one of the most important additions to English literature...since the war'; F.R. Leavis in *Scrutiny* (No. 87) stated, 'A classic is added to the language' and remarked on their author's remarkable rise to fame:

Developments in the last few years have been so rapid. Half a decade ago, though his name was pretty generally known, to judge him the greatest poet of the Victorian age was a perverse and laughable eccentricity. It is not, perhaps, orthodoxy today, but even in the academic world it is a debatable proposition.

For which transformation, of course, Leavis himself could take much credit.

Reviews of the prose—later to include the *Note-Books* (1937) and *Further Letters* (1938)—naturally led to discussion and judgment of the poetry, and religion remained one of the first topics. The critic in *Time and Tide*,[72] who liked the poet but condemned the letter-writer for his 'enormous dullness', reflected at some length on the disturbing dichotomy between poet and priest, and this rapidly became one of the most attractive critical themes. *Time and Tide* interpreted Hopkins as a 'split man' in whom there was an 'inner division, the pulling opposite ways of poetry and religion'. Desmond MacCarthy in a long two-column review in the *Sunday Times*[73] took a less simple view, suggesting that the two contrasting vocations led instead to a 'peculiar concentration' of Hopkins's powers, and this more sympathetic attitude was generally taken up. The poet Laurence Binyon spoke of the 'inner conflict' between the sensuous and the ascetic giving the poetry 'its peculiar intensity'.[74] *Life and Letters*,[75] describing him as one of the 'powers behind the throne' of poetry, said that his Jesuit life had both curtailed his experience and been a 'source of energy in his work'.

It is interesting to read a fellow-Jesuit's view in Fr Keating's discussion of the *Letters* in the *Month* (No. 81), where after noting the difficulties of non-Catholic writers in appreciating the import-ance of Hopkins's religious beliefs, Fr Keating emphasised the deliberateness with which Hopkins's choice had been made. It had been his decision to adapt himself as a poet to the prior calling of a priest, and if he suffered, he did so with the understanding and acceptance of a thinking and responsible individual.

Fr Keating's argument, of course, assumed the rightness of Hopkins's priorities, and it does not take into account the possibility that he might have carried out a Christian vocation of a less explicit nature by devoting himself more fully to poetry. But the question of what Hopkins might have been if he had not been a priest, and if a poet, the same or a better poet, is so speculative as to be no question at all. It is impossible to take seriously the point of view that says Hopkins 'seems to have written poetry almost in spite of himself'.[76] As Herbert Read, writing in the *Criterion*[77] put it: 'To ask for a different man is to ask for a different poet.'

Hopkins's range of experience, which might seem limited to the superficial eye, was sufficient to provide him with material and inspiration for his poetry. W.H. Shewring in *Blackfriars*[78] pointed out that a poet's experience does not need to be unusual to produce great poetry: 'Hopkins's greatest utterances, like Milton's, are the fruits of great silence.' But the precise religious nature of this subject-matter was as yet uncharted, and in the April 1935 number of *New Verse* (No. 82), which was totally devoted to Hopkins, the editor, Geoffrey Grigson, gave notice that the time had come 'to begin on the real difficulties in Hopkins, in his thought and in his life as a poet and priest'. Two of the most worthwhile contributions tackled, albeit briefly, more theological aspects of Hopkins's background: Humphry House introduced the question of the role of the Ignatian *Exercises*, while Christopher Devlin related the philosophy of Scotus to his poetry.[79] Less successfully, in 'Blood and Bran', the editor psychoanalysed Hopkins and found too much guilt, too much 'morbid exuberance': 'Hopkins would have been a more excellent poet, had he known himself better; and those who read his poems will not be good readers unless they also examine themselves.'[80]

Fr Keating replied in defence of Hopkins in the *Month* in the following September.[81] He denied the suggestion in House that the *Spiritual Exercises* had made Hopkins over-scrupulous, and rejected psychoanalysis as a way of understanding religious experience. Christopher Devlin, in a much fuller treatment of the Ignatian influence (No. 86), however, submitted that there was 'in Hopkins a strain of something narrow and almost morbid', although it was only found in the later poems. Some interest in this rather limited aspect of Hopkins was also shown by David Daiches in his *Poetry and the Modern World* (1940) (No. 102) where it was suggested that the 'psychologist rather than the sociologist must be called in'[82] if one was to understand some of the personal problems that were the source of Hopkins's revolutionary approach. Fortunately, few writers have been attracted up this perilous road.

The Devlin article, to which reference has already been made, 'The Ignatian Inspiration of Gerard Manley Hopkins', was an important contribution to Hopkins scholarship, which demonstrated that 'devotional', the word that Eliot had favoured, was too insubstantial to do justice to the Ignatian content of Hopkins's verse. Devlin maintained that the *Exercises* were the source of, and not merely incidental to, some of his best writing, and that it was his becoming a Jesuit that eventually inspired verse far superior to his earlier poetry—'anaemic verse about St Dorothea's basket'. The St Beuno's poetry exemplified the doctrine that 'the soul can love no created thing on the face of the earth *in itself*, but only in the creator of them all'; 'The Wreck of the Deutschland', he claimed, was inspired by the first two weeks of the *Exercises*. Devlin contested the view that the *Exercises* encouraged morbid subjectivism, and felt that even in the last poems there was no 'absolute tragedy' because death was not seen as the final end.

This is a convenient point at which to mention two other contributions to understanding Hopkins's religious background. W.H. Gardner's 'A Note on Hopkins and Duns Scotus', published in *Scrutiny*, June 1936 (No. 90), expanded Devlin's earlier essay,[83] and pointed out that the Scotist principle of individuation provided a religious and aesthetic base for Hopkins's life as priest and poet. In June 1937, also in *Scrutiny* (No. 97), Gardner developed Devlin's thesis that the *Spiritual Exercises* were an important inspiration of his poetry. Since Hopkins regarded the sensuous as reaching its consummation in the love of Christ, there was no 'emotional dislocation' (the phrase had been used by an earlier critic) in his twin-vocations of priest and poet. But Gardner admitted that in certain poems—'Carrion Comfort', 'To Seem the Stranger'—there was a more tortured note, and thought that Fr Keating (writing this time in the *Month*, February 1935)[84] underestimated this evidence of frustration. He came to the conclusion that the 'personality of Hopkins found in its delimited experience' an obstacle which was in fact a cause of growth.

The first of Gardner's long list of contributions to Hopkins scholarship had been his essay on 'The Wreck of the Deutschland' in *Essays and Studies* (No. 88). Gardner's enthusiasm for the poem led him to place it with 'Lycidas' and 'Intimations of Immortality', but he interestingly noted that readers were likely to be divided in the reasons for their appreciation: 'To the ardent Catholic the poem must always stand as one of the loftiest expressions of... his creed.... To others it will perhaps rather suggest the tragedy of faith and the triumph of pure poetry.' It might be said that this poem still remains an interesting test-case of appreciation of

Hopkins, its greater appeal being with the Catholic, rather than the non-Catholic reader.

Hopkins's interest in Scotus was the subject of a brief article[85] in the Dominican review *Blackfriars*, by the layman Bernard Kelly, who wrote several pieces on Hopkins in the thirties. He suggested that Scotus, by emphasising Hopkins's individualism, encouraged a highly personal response to Christ, and that this led to a greater sense of human loneliness. The poet, therefore, was 'not...an exponent of the Church's catholicity but...an individual witness to Christ'. In an earlier, popular exposition in *G.K.'s Weekly* (No. 85) he defended the religious importance of what Hopkins had to say, and justified the word theological, rather than devotional for his poetry. Dallas Kenmare[86] similarly objected to the term which Eliot had used: '[Hopkins's] approach to God, and through God to poetry, in some indefinable way transcends the devotional'; and he complained that contemporaries had concentrated on him as an 'important technical innovator', but ignored him as a 'religious poet of almost unparalleled power and significance'.

The words were written in 1939, and were really already out-of-date. By comparison with ten years, or even five years before, much more attention was now being given to this aspect of his work, and John Pick's two articles in the *Month* for January and February 1940 (No. 100) again demonstrated the importance of the *Spiritual Exercises* for his verse. The first showed Hopkins as developing an aesthetic 'in which the experience of beauty and religious experience coalesce'[87] and confirmed the importance of the *Exercises* for the poetry written after his conversion. The second article dealt with the poems of 1877–8 which revealed the contrast between 'nature as instinctively praising God, and man as sinful, failing to use nature sacramentally'.[88]

Thus, by 1940, to utilise the current distinction, Hopkins had achieved the status of religious, rather than devotional poet. Scholarship had endowed him with theological respectability: the poetry did not become automatically 'better' as a result, but by suggesting the presence of a density of argument, rather than merely personal outbursts of feeling, it contributed to the impression of an intriguing and unified personality at work behind the poems.

But if Hopkins's religion increasingly interested readers, style and metre still inspired the greatest discussion. Basil de Selincourt (No. 80) described some of his poems as 'works for performance' which required a study of their rhythm and tempi, if they were to be correctly read. G.M. Young[89] thought his verse was simply disorder and part of the general mistreatment of metre in modern poetry. Desmond MacCarthy tried to see this aspect in the wider context of Hopkins's achievement when he declared that despite his obscurity, his 'insistence on sincerity and on the importance of using living words and phrases in poetry or in prose are qualities which make Hopkins influential today. His discoveries in prosody are part of the same effort to get closer to a contemporary and natural rhythm of thought and feeling'.[90] Harris Downey (*Southern Review*, 1936)[91] also believed that Hopkins had proved the 'rhythm of speech is the rhythm of the best poetry', but reiterated the common view that his influence had been in technique, not in ideas.

C.K. Ogden's essay 'Sprung Rhythm' (No. 94) was a highly entertaining attack on the critics of Hopkins's metrical theories. Believing that the analysis of stress was crucial to the study of meaning, he was scathing at the expense of those from Bridges onwards who had shown themselves incapable of scanning 'The Wreck of the Deutschland'. 'The ineptitudes of prosodists have clearly made it impossible for most contemporary writers on verse to regard Hopkins's specific contribution to the subject as more than an aberration of genius.' He believed, with Hopkins, that the reading of verse aloud was an essential step in its understanding. W.B. Yeats, in his Introduction to the *Oxford Book of Modern Verse* (No. 91), was sceptical about Hopkins as a metricist. He complained that sprung verse made it difficult to tell where the stress should fall, and that meaning seemed submerged in mere words and rhythm. It was in reviewing this volume in the *London Mercury*[92] that G.M. Young (again) made the comment that 'much subsequent verse has run into the Hopkins siding and got stuck there, while the mainline is bare of traffic'. It was an over-generous tribute to Hopkins's influence.

But many agreed that there was far more to Hopkins than technical or linguistic bravura. In *Modern Poetry* (1936) Babette Deutsch wrote:

He never sought oddity for its own sake. It was merely that he packed his verse so closely with meaning, filled it so full of music, that he had no room for the elaborate forms required by grammatical correctness.[93]

The difficulty of his poetry, Deutsch added, was due less to his technique than to the 'complexity of the personality' behind it. David Daiches (No. 102) felt, paradoxically, that Hopkins had sacrificed intelligibility to a desire for directness; his theories about sprung rhythm came from a 'desire to achieve more direct methods of expression'.

Both Deutsch and Daiches implicitly rejected the notion that Hopkins's importance was simply that of a 'great technical innovator'. The Jesuit critic Calvert Alexander, writing in 1935,[94] claimed that Hopkins's technique was 'secondary' to his 'vision', and agreed that his difficulty arose from the fact that he 'has too much to say, rather than from his saying it in an unconventional manner'. Yet it was this 'unconventional manner' that still impressed many readers and imitators. Edith Sitwell complained that the younger poets imitated him 'from outside',[95] and in contesting C. Day Lewis's earlier claim that he was a 'naif' poet Terence Heywood, writing in *English* (No. 101), came up with a varied list of poetic ancestors to illustrate possible influences on his style. The Metaphysicals were described as sharing with him the same 'explosiveness, [and] surprise technique', while Donne and he demonstrated a 'mastery of rhetoric'. Heywood also discovered some surprising parallels with the seventeenth-century poet Edward Benlowes, with his strong rhythms and clipped style.

Hopkins's qualifications as a modern, or as an influence upon modern poets, continued to be eagerly contested by the critics. Desmond MacCarthy pointed to his sincerity and the use of 'living words and phrases' as qualities 'which make Hopkins influential today'.[96] The *Wilson Bulletin*[97] believed his influence on modern poetry was 'still in the ascendant', and that Auden, Spender, and Lewis were trying to imitate his 'tremor of expectancy'. Lewis (No. 83) confirmed this claim of Hopkins's importance and remarked that he suffered the 'more terrible exile of the man born out of his time'. One difference with the moderns suggested by David Daiches (No. 102) was Hopkins's unselfconcious lyricism: on the other hand, like poets of the thirties (and like Donne), he faced similar problems regarding the nature of his art and the audience for which he was writing. The modern poets 'faced with the splitting-up of the poetry-reading public, cannot make up their minds for whom to write'. In Ruth Bailey's *Dialogue on Modern Poetry* (1939), Hopkins appears as the type of the Modern Poet. The

Faber Book of Modern Verse (No. 92) opened with thirteen of Hopkins's poems, and Michael Roberts, although he did not see Hopkins as making a complete break with his age, admired him for creating a style which expressed himself. Bernard Kelly (No. 84) declared that he used language in ways with which 'many of the most daring modern poets are no more than experimenting', and Calvert Alexander also isolated his modernism in the fact that he had rejected 'the poetic language of the day and... invented a new one'.[98]

But many demurred from assigning a Victorian the role of good influence. G.M. Young[99] described Hopkins's views on metre as 'demonstrably wrong', and his influence 'as pernicious as it had been potent'. He labelled Eliot the 'originator' and Hopkins the 'legislator of the new mode'. Louis MacNeice repeated a common view when he deprecated Hopkins's effect on the present generation: 'A close imitation of his manner is dangerous because both his rhythms and his syntax were peculiarly appropriate to his own unusual circumstances and his own tortured but vital personality'.[100] The American academic Cornelius Weygandt also regretted that modern poets had taken him as a guide, for Hopkins 'cannot be judged a great poet on what we have of him, but only a poet with moments of greatness here and there'.[101]

Bridges's name made the occasional appearance as a stick to beat Hopkins: the *Oxford Magazine*[102] believed that nothing had been written about Hopkins's poetry 'half as good as what Bridges wrote when he introduced Hopkins to the world'. It also believed that 'extraneous causes' had exaggerated Hopkins's importance and that 'unfledged poets and unimaginative versifiers are making great play with his eccentricities'. But the respective fortunes of Bridges and Hopkins had undergone a great change since the Poet Laureate had cautiously issued his friend's poems into the world in 1918, and it was a writer in the *Nineteenth Century and After* in February 1935[103] who anticipated what had perhaps been achieved by the end of the thirties: he foresaw that it would not be Hopkins's friends who would ensure the future fame of the once obscure Jesuit poet, but that Bridges and Dixon 'by a kind of poetic justice' would 'strengthen their claim upon posterity by their friendship with this friend'.

It was well said by R.P. Blackmur writing in the *Kenyon Review* in 1939,[104] that with so much by Hopkins now published, 'any but the all-or-nothing reader should feel possessed of all the documentation, all the aids to understanding, that Hopkins, as a poet, needs'. He was warning against giving more attention to the background material than to the poetry: nothing could be more indicative of the transformation in the state of knowledge about Hopkins in the course of the thirties. Yet the rise in his reputation as a poet over a slightly longer period was surely still more astonishing. By 1940 he stood with the major English poets of the twentieth century and the Victorian period. He was discussed in company with Eliot and Auden, and compared with Browning and Wordsworth. Even Milton and Shakespeare were invoked for comparison. The tide of approval had overwhelmed the current of doubt which had its source in Bridges's criticisms—those of obscurity, awkwardness of metre and diction, narrowness of outlook. The publication of Hopkins's prose from 1935 had brought about a fuller appreciation of his poetry by providing many insights into a rich and subtle personality, and by 1940 his religious background, due to the work of members of his own Society and such sympathetic laymen as Gardner, House, and Pick, was no longer an unexplained mystery. The highly distinctive style existed not for itself but to express significant experience, and Eliot's criticism of 'an accumulation, rather than a real development of thought' seemed the verdict of impatient reading.

Was Hopkins a Victorian or a modern? First seen as an eccentric Victorian, then a displaced modern, he still remained something of an enigma: his prose brought out his nineteenth-century values, but his poetry remained obstinately distinctive. What came through all he wrote was a sensitivity of feeling and sincerity of personality that is found in the best writing of all periods. It was this sincerity that struck a number of critics, a 'unity and clarity of character'[105] that expressed itself in his verse, and was partly due, as Humphry House remarked, to a situation in which the audience did not matter: Hopkins did not write to please Bridges, satisfy a convention, or pretend what he did not feel.

Although his reputation on the verge of the forties was considerable, many aspects of his poetry had still not been explored. No one followed Bernard Groom's essay on compound epithets in English poetry[106] which pointed to their frequency in Hopkins, with more extended studies of his vocabulary or syntax.

W.H. Gardner's demonstration of Welsh literary devices in the St Beuno's poems[107] was not emulated by any serious study of Greek and Latin influence, although several reviewers had indicated there was scope for such research. Despite the evidence of Hopkins's Victorianism in the *Note-Books* and *Letters*, no one examined what features of Victorian poetry might be reflected in his verse. His painting and musical interests had hardly been noticed, either in themselves or as possible channels for study of his poetry. A good biography remained a serious need. But the thirties had finally established that he was more than a poet for the minority, that a religious poet is neither abnormal nor cripplingly restricted, that a delight in language is compatible with seriousness of thought, and that a poet who may not be to the taste of one age can re-emerge as an inspiring force in another.

There has been no diminution in the quantity of Hopkins criticism since 1940, and it is only possible to comment on a few aspects of the work produced. In 1942, John Pick's *Gerard Manley Hopkins, Priest and Poet* (see No. 100) was a persuasive if uncritical introduction to the spiritual background of the poet, underlining the importance of the *Exercises* as an intellectual source of Hopkins's work, and has continued to be reprinted. An outstanding and comprehensive study was W.H. Gardner's *Gerard Manley Hopkins: A Study of Poetic Idiosyncrasy in Relation to Poetic Tradition*, which was published in two parts, in 1944 and 1949. It remains the work to which one would direct all intending serious students of Hopkins; there are few avenues of his achievement it fails to explore, and even if Gardner does not entirely fulfil one of his main intentions, to show Hopkins as part of the European poetic tradition, he convincingly demonstrates the universal appeal of his poetry.

The publication in the United States in 1945 of a collection of essays on Hopkins from the *Kenyon Review* which balanced both criticism and praise was a sign of his mature status as a major poet. Austin Warren raised doubts about the content of his poetry (later elaborated by Yvor Winters) when he suggested that 'To try prose paraphrasing of the middle poems is invariably to show how thin the "thinking" is'.[108] Arthur Mizener dealt with 'Victorian Hopkins' and concluded that he was a poet of Victorian sensibility raised to an exceptional level. Much more on this topic appeared in

Alison Sulloway's *Gerard Manley Hopkins and the Victorian Temper* (1972), which outlined an ideological background that had been much neglected by earlier writers.

To return to the 1940s, an important work that had been delayed by World War II was *Immortal Diamond* (1949), edited by Norman Weyand. This scholarly collection of essays by Jesuits included a notable contribution by Walter Ong on sprung rhythm, but it made no attempt to interpret Hopkins critically. *Gerard Manley Hopkins*, a book by another Jesuit, W.A.M. Peters, published the previous year, should also be mentioned for the fullest treatment to date of the concepts of inscape and instress.

It was in two public lectures by Winters, printed by the *Hudson Review* in 1949, that the author uttered his doubts about the disproportion between meaning and feeling in Hopkins's verse. He also accused 'The Windhover' of being 'romantic both in its overwrought emotionalism and in its carelessness'.[109] The latter essay has been conveniently included in the *Twentieth Century Views* edition of Hopkins (1966), edited by G.H. Hartman, who himself revived the old argument that Hopkins's dual vocation of poet and priest did not successfully mix. This collection reflected the increasing interest in 'The Windhover' as a crucial text (twenty-four essays on the poem were edited by John Pick in one volume in 1969). Mention should also be made of the Hopkins volume edited by Margaret Bottrall in the 'Casebook' series (1975), which includes a certain amount of historical material, as well as a number of useful, modern critical essays.

Such collections reflect the establishment status that Hopkins has achieved in the post-war period, his poems the regular choice of A-level examining boards in England and university examiners internationally. Explanatory commentaries have become available for an increasingly wide range of readers. Donald McChesny's *A Hopkins Commentary* (1968) was 'intended for the average student', and, like Paul Mariani's *Commentary on the Complete Poems of Hopkins* (1970), principally occupied itself with a careful study of the meaning of each poem.

While these brief notes can in no way do justice to the mass of material in books, essays, and theses that his work has inspired, from 1970 to 1976 the *Hopkins Research Bulletin*, the publication of the Hopkins Society (founded 1969), both printed Hopkinsiana and kept readers in touch with Hopkins research. The Society also promoted a series of annual lectures by eminent scholars. In 1971 F.R. Leavis unwillingly added to his previous assessments of Hopkins, disputing the need for scholarship in order to appreciate him, and, at the same time, confessing that Hopkins now seemed to him a major rather than a great poet. Hopkins's supreme virtue, he thought, was his attempt to return to 'living—that is, spoken—English'.[110]

From April 1974, the *Hopkins Quarterly* (published in Canada) has become an important means to enable students to keep up with (particularly) Transatlantic research. Naturally, perhaps, its standpoint has been that Hopkins *is* a great poet, and literary criticism has played a lesser role than scholarship. Of late years it has widened its terms of reference to include some of Hopkins's contemporaries, a significant indication of a more contextual approach to Hopkins criticism.

The establishment of a definitive Hopkins text was generally recognised as having been achieved by Professor Gardner, assisted by Norman Mackenzie, for the fourth edition in 1967, but Professor Mackenzie is currently preparing a veriorum edition of the text. The same writer's *Hopkins* (1968) was a brief but independent survey of the poet, and his name has become increasingly associated with Hopkins scholarship over the last twenty years.

Reflecting the more critical vein of current Hopkins criticism, Bernard Bergonzi's *Gerard Manley Hopkins* (1977) was an incisive combination of biography and literary assessment. Hopkins's admitted greatness is, it was suggested, of a limited kind and 'The Wreck of the Deutschland' is marked by a 'love of deformation [of syntax], or pattern, for its own sake'.[111] Bergonzi concluded: 'It is evident that Hopkins sometimes deliberately imposed a great strain on the English language', and he rejected claims for his twentieth-century contemporaneity. Also illustrating this more questioning treatment was John Robinson's *In Extremity* (1978) which doubted whether the *Spiritual Exercises* could in fact be regarded as providing the primary inspiration of his verse.

Biography gives a context for sensitive criticism. Paddy Kitchen's *Gerard Manley Hopkins* (1978) probably offers more information than any other study, although it should be taken in conjunction with Fr Alfred Thomas's *Hopkins, the Jesuit* (1969), a fund of background detail on his life in the Society. Dr Norman

White of University College, Dublin, is currently preparing what may well turn out to be the definitive biography.

In the mid-eighties, the cumulative total of books, articles, theses, lectures, and conferences about Hopkins is very large, the written material (up to 1970) being scrupulously recorded in Tom Dunne's *Hopkins Bibliography* (1976), although those who stand closest have detected some slowing down over the past five years in what may be called the Hopkins industry. If this impression is accurate, it is probably all to the good. So much has been produced about Hopkins in the last twenty years alone that a period of digestion would be welcome. His reputation as an important English poet is now securely established, and more attention to other aspects and lesser figures of Victorian literature will be both welcome to students of the period at large and enrich our understanding of this very special Victorian poet within his context.

NOTES

1 *T.S. Eliot: The Critical Heritage*, ed. Michael Grant, London, 1982, I, pp. 84–5.

2 *Ibid.*, p. 75.

3 *Thomas Hardy: Poems*, Casebook Series, ed. J. Gibson and T. Johnson, London, 1979, p. 78.

4 *W.H. Auden: The Critical Heritage*, ed. John Haffenden, London, 1983, pp. 82–3.

5 T.S. Eliot, *Selected Essays*, London, 1951, p. 289.

6 *Post*, p. 141.

7 *Auden: The Critical Heritage*, p. 100.

8 Edmund Gosse, *The Future of English Poetry*, English Association, June 1913, p. 10.

9 *Letters and Notices*, Manresa Press, Roehampton, March 1890, p. 174.

10 James Sambrook, *A Poet Hidden*, London, 1962, p. 97.

11 *Post*, p. 130.

12 *Letters to Bridges*, ed. Abbott, London, 1935, p. 59.

13 *Ibid.*, p. 46. George Eliot, waiting to hear the reception for *Adam Bede*, reflects the more secular attitude to authorship: 'How is it possible to put one's best heart and soul into a book and be hardened to the result—be indifferent to the proof whether or not one has really a vocation to speak to one's fellow-men in that way?' (*Letters*, ed. G. Haight, London, 1954, III, p. 24.)

14 *Post*, pp. 176–7.

15 Humphry House, *All in Due Time*, London, 1955, p. 171, original review in *TLS*, 31 January 1935.
16 Laurence Binyon, 'Gerard Hopkins and his Influence', *University of Toronto Quarterly*, April 1936, pp. 264–5.
17 *Post*, p. 257.
18 W.H. Gardner, *Gerard Manley Hopkins: A Study of Poetic Idiosyncrasy*, London, 1944, I, p. 211.
19 Anthony Thwaite, *Twentieth Century English Poetry*, London, 1978, p. 17.
20 Quoted in Humphrey Carpenter, *W.H. Auden, A Biography*, London, 1981, p. 59.
21 In a review of Elsie Phare's *Poetry of Gerard Manley Hopkins* in the *Criterion*, April 1934, p. 497.
22 Letter from Bridges to Mrs Hopkins in 1890, quoted in Simon Nowell-Smith, 'Bridges, Hopkins and Dr Daniel', *TLS*, 13 December 1957, p. 764.
23 29 August 1893, p. 9.
24 George Saintsbury, *A History of Nineteenth Century Literature*, London, 1896, p. 294.
25 George Saintsbury, *A History of English Prosody*, Vol. III, London, 1910, p. 39.
26 *Spectator*, 8 December 1900, p. 846.
27 Edmund Gosse, *Coventry Patmore*, London, 1905, p. 169.
28 P. 144.
29 21 September 1912, p. 368.
30 *Month*, July 1909, p. 60.
31 Quoted in the *Month*, February 1935, p. 126.
32 *Poems by R.W. Dixon*, ed. Bridges, London, 1909, p. ix.
33 Pp. 241–5.
34 Preface (unpaginated).
35 Hopkins wrote of the English soldier's devotion to his country: 'Immortal beauty is death with duty,/If under her banner I fall for her honour' (*Poems*, 4th edn, London, p. 195.)
36 April 1916, p. 261.
37 5 February 1916, p. 428.
38 June 1916, p. 395.
39 P. 232.
40 *Irish Rosary*, June 1919, p. 475.
41 See the *Tablet,* 19 April 1919, p. 484, and No. 41.
42 See No. 18.
43 Louis Untermeyer, quoted in *Eliot: The Critical Heritage*, p. 126.
44 Quoted in the *Month*, February 1935, p. 130.
45 Quoted in the *Anthology of Catholic Poets*, ed. Shane Leslie, London, 1925, p. 13.

46 See the edition for 21 March 1919, p. 10. The *Universe*, 14 March, p. 2, had supported the *Gazette* under the heading, 'Improper Editing'.

47 April 1919, p. 289.

48 *Irish Ecclesiastical Record*, January 1920, pp. 83–86.

49 T. Earle Welby, *A Popular History of English Poetry*, London, 1924, p. 263.

50 Quoted in S. Hynes, *The Auden Generation*, London, 1976, p. 28.

51 September 1927, p. 547.

52 *Twentieth Century Poetry*, London, 1929, p. 8.

53 Pp. 591–603.

54 September 1930, p. 61 ('Dilly Tante Observes').

55 Pp. 118–27.

56 Elizabeth Drew, *Discovering Poetry*, London, 1933, p. 83.

57 Ernest de Selincourt, *Oxford Lectures on Poetry*, Oxford, 1934, p. 220.

58 April 1931, p. 222.

59 P. 400.

60 Michael Grant, Introduction, *T.S. Eliot: The Critical Heritage*, p. 30.

61 B. Ifor Evans, *English Poetry in the Later Nineteenth Century*, London, 1933, p. 222.

62 9 February, p. 81.

63 Dudley Fitts, writing in *Hound and Horn*, Summer 1931, quoted in *Auden: The Critical Heritage*, p. 93.

64 *New York Herald Tribune Books*, January 1934, p. 2.

65 'Notes on English Poets', in *Poetry*, February 1932, pp. 271–9.

66 In *Essays Ancient and Modern*, London, 1936, pp. 96–7.

67 *Hound and Horn*, October-December 1930, p. 127.

68 *TLS*, 16 February–9 March.

69 P. 411.

70 11 January 1935, p. 56.

71 July 1935, pp. 210–19.

72 26 January 1935, p. 127.

73 3 February 1935, p. 8.

74 *University of Toronto Quarterly, op. cit.*, p. 270 (see n. 16 above).

75 February 1935, pp. 613–19.

76 Review of the *Letters* by C.H. Warren in the *Fortnightly*, April 1935, p. 504.

77 April 1935, p. 481.

78 April 1935, p. 270.

79 'Hopkins and Duns Scotus', *New Verse*, April 1935, pp. 12–15.

80 P. 23.

81 'Fr Gerard Hopkins and the Spiritual Exercises', pp. 268–70.

82 P. 24 (this passage is not reprinted in No. 102).

83 See n. 79 above.

84 Pp. 125–36.
85 'Gerard Manley Tuncks', *Blackfriars*, June 1937, pp. 424–9.
86 Dallas Kenmare, *The Face of Truth*, Oxford, 1939, quotations from pp. 98 and 59.
87 January 1940, p. 43.
88 February 1940, p. 110.
89 'Tunes Ancient and Modern' in *Life and Letters*, February 1935, pp. 544–54.
90 See n. 73 above.
91 Vol. I, no. 4, pp. 837–45.
92 December 1936, pp. 112–22.
93 P. 189.
94 Calvert Alexander, *The Catholic Literary Revival*, Milwaukee, 1935, p. 74.
95 Edwith Sitwell, *Trio*, London, 1938, pp. 98–9.
96 *Sunday Times, op. cit.* (see n. 73 above).
97 May 1935, p. 492.
98 Alexander, *op. cit.*, p. 78.
99 *London Mercury, op. cit.* (see n. 92 above).
100 Louis MacNeice, *Modern Poetry*, London, 1938, p. 125.
101 Cornelius Weygandt, *The Time of Yeats*, New York, 1937, p. 388.
102 10 March 1938, pp. 522–3.
103 Review of the *Letters* by Osbert Burdett, p. 241.
104 Review of *Further Letters* in the Winter number, pp. 96–9.
105 Bernard Kelly, *The Mind and Poetry of Hopkins* (see *post*, p. 310).
106 Society for Pure English, Tract no. XLIX, Oxford, 1937.
107 'Gerard Manley Hopkins as Cywyddwr', in the *Transactions of the Honourable Society of Cymmrodorion*, 1940, London, 1941, pp. 184–8.
108 Reprinted in G.H. Hartman (ed.), *Hopkins, Twentieth Century Views*, Englewood Cliffs, NJ, 1966, p. 177.
109 *Ibid.*, p. 56.
110 Hopkins Society, 2nd Annual Lecture, 1971, p. 7. Leavis first modified his enthusiasm for Hopkins in the 1950 edition of *New Bearings*: see 'Retrospect 1950', pp. 237–8.
111 For this and the following quotations, see Bernard Bergonzi, *Gerard Manley Hopkins*, London, 1977, pp. 163 and 174.

ADDENDUM

In an interesting letter to Bridges, dated 30 December 1918, A.E. Housman thanks him for the poems, but takes a generally critical view of Hopkins, finding the sprung rhythm confusing and 'resenting' the 'violence' done to the English language. He concludes: 'His [Hopkins's] early poems are the promise of something better, if less original; and originality is not nearly so good as goodness, even when it is good. His manner strikes me as deliberately adopted to compensate by strangeness for the lack of pure merit' (*Letters of Housman*, ed. Henry Maas, London, 1971, pp. 158–9).

Chronology of Hopkins's Life

1844 (July) Born Stratford, Essex, of a middle-class Anglican family.

1854–63 Pupil at Highgate School, North London.

1863–7 At Balliol College, Oxford (where he first met Bridges). Double First in Greats.

1866 Becomes a Catholic.

1867–8 Teaches at Oratory School, Birmingham, under Newman.

1868 (May) Destroys his poetry.

1868 (September) Enters the Society of Jesus: nine years of training before ordination. At Roehampton, Stonyhurst, and St Beuno's (N. Wales).

1875 (December) Encouraged by his superior at St Beuno's to write 'The Wreck of the Deutschland', which led to a renewal of his poetry.

1877 (September) Ordained.

1877–8 Teaches and does other duties at Mount St Mary's, the Jesuit boarding school near Sheffield. Then, briefly, at Stonyhurst and Farm Street, Mayfair.

1878 (June) Begins correspondence with Dixon.

1878–9 Parish priest at St Aloysius, Oxford.

1879 (October–December) Parish priest at Bedford Leigh, near Manchester.

1880–1 Parish priest at St Francis Xavier, Liverpool.

1881 (August–October) Parish priest in Glasgow.

1881–2 Tertianship (part of Jesuit training) at Roehampton.

1882 (August)–1884 Teaches classics to the older students at Stonyhurst (where he first meets Patmore).

1884 (January)–1889 Holds Chair of Classics at University
College, Dublin (managed by the Jesuits).
1889 (June) Dies of typhoid.

Principal Publishing Dates up to 1940

1893 *The Poets and the Poetry of the Century*, ed. Alfred Miles, vol.
VIII (contains a selection of Hopkins by Bridges)
1916 *The Spirit of Man, an Anthology ... from the Philosophers and
Poets*, ed. Robert Bridges (contains some poems by
Hopkins)
1918 *Poems of Hopkins*, ed. Bridges
1930 *Poems of Hopkins*, ed. Charles Williams (2nd edition).
1935 *Letters of Hopkins to Bridges*, ed. C.C. Abbott
Correspondence of Hopkins and Dixon, ed. Abbott
1937 *Note-Books and Papers of Hopkins*, ed. Humphry House
1938 *Further Letters of Hopkins*, ed. Abbott

This list omits many works that included individual poems by
Hopkins (from 1863 to 1917 such poems appeared in a score or so
of mainly obscure publications; from 1925 to 1940 they appeared in
at least nine important anthologies).

Note on the Text

Extracts and omissions are indicated by ellipsis dots. Page numbers of the original book or article are indicated in the document heading: in some cases these refer to the whole of the original passage about Hopkins, and not simply the extract used. Notes are either the editor's, and indicated by 1, 2, 3, etc., or the author's (*, or, if several, a,b,c, etc.). Many reference sources have been consulted, but some of the basic ones are listed in the Bibliography at the end of the volume.

COMMENTS 1877–1918

1. Contemporary correspondence

Robert Bridges (1844–1930) had been a friend of Hopkins since their Oxford days. A doctor until 1881, he concentrated on poetry for the rest of his life, and became Laureate in 1913. Canon R.W. Dixon (1833–1900), a minor poet and church historian, had first briefly met Hopkins while teaching at Highgate School: they resumed their association, which was to be mainly in the form of letters, in June 1878. Hopkins met Coventry Patmore (1823–96), the Catholic poet, for the first time in July 1883. His correspondence with all three was continued until his death.

The mixed response to his verse, even by Hopkins's friends, will be noted. Few of Bridges's letters appear to have survived, but the nature of his criticisms can be appreciated from Hopkins's replies, of which I print a small selection: as C.C. Abbott, the first editor of the correspondence remarked: 'The contribution of Bridges to the correspondence has to be divined, but its importance may to some degree be measured by the response evoked' (*Letters to Bridges*, p. xvi).

(a) From *Letters of Hopkins to Bridges*, ed. Abbott (1935)

Hopkins to Bridges

St. Beuno's, St. Asaph. Aug. 21 1877.
... Your parody reassures me about your understanding the metre. Only remark, as you say that there is no conceivable licence I shd. not be able to justify, that with all my licences, or rather laws, I am stricter than you and I might say than anybody I know.

With the exception of the *Bremen* stanza,[a] which was, I think, the first written after 10 years' interval of silence, and before I had fixed my principles, my rhymes are rigidly good—to the ear—and such rhymes as *love* and *prove* I scout utterly. And my quantity is not like 'Fīftȳtwō Bĕdfŏrd Squāre', where fīftȳ might pass but *Bĕdfŏrd* I should never admit. Not only so but Swinburne's dactyls and anapaests are halting to my ear: I never allow e.g. *I* or *my* (that is diphthongs, for $I = a + i$ and $my = ma + i$) in the short or weak syllables of those feet, excepting before vowels, semi-vowels, or *r*, and rarely then, or when the measure becomes (what is the word?) molossic—thus: ∪ – ∪|∪ – ∪|∪ – ∪, for then the first short is almost long. If you look again you will see. So that I may say my apparent licences are counterbalanced, and more, by my strictness. In fact all English verse, except Milton's, almost, offends me as 'licentious'. Remember this.

I do not of course claim to have invented *sprung rhythms* but only *sprung rhythm*; I mean that single lines and single instances of it are not uncommon in English and I have pointed them out in lecturing—e.g. 'why should this ˙ desert be?'—which the editors have variously amended; 'There to meet with Mac ˙beth' or 'There to meet with Macbeth'; Campbell has some throughout the *Battle of the Baltic*—'and their fleet along the deep˙proudly shone'—and *Ye Mariners*—'as ye sweep˙through the deep' etc; Moore has some which I cannot recall; there is one in *Grongar Hill*; and, not to speak of *Pom pom*, in Nursery Rhymes, Weather Saws, and Refrains they are very common—but what I do in the *Deutschland* etc is to enfranchise them as a regular and permanent principle of scansion. ...

Why do I employ sprung rhythm at all? Because it is the nearest to the rhythm of prose, that is the native and natural rhythm of speech, the least forced, the most rhetorical and emphatic of all possible rhythms, combining, as it seems to me, opposite and, one wd. have thought, incompatible excellences, markedness of rhythm—that is rhythm's self—and naturalness of expression—for why, if it is forcible in prose to say 'lashed ˙ rod',[b] am I obliged to weaken this in verse, which ought to be stronger, not weaker, into 'láshed birch-ród' or something?

My verse is less to be read than heard, as I have told you before; it is oratorical, that is the rhythm is so. I think if you will study what I have here said you will be much more pleased with it and may I say? converted to it.

You ask may you call it 'presumptious jugglery'. No, but only for this reason, that *presumptious* is not English.

I cannot think of altering anything. Why shd. I? I do not write for the public. You are my public and I hope to convert you.

You say you wd. not for any money read my poem again. Nevertheless I beg you will. Besides money, you know, there is love. If it is obscure do not bother yourself with the meaning but pay attention to the best and most intelligible stanzas, as the two last of each part and the narrative of the wreck. If you had done this you wd. have liked it better and sent me some serviceable criticisms, but now your criticism is of no use, being only a protest memorialising me against my whole policy and proceedings.

I may add for your greater interest and edification that what refers to myself in the poem is all strictly and literally true and did all occur; nothing is added for poetical padding....

Stonyhurst College, Blackburn. May 13 1878.
... I must tell you I am sorry you never read the Deutschland again.

Granted that it needs study and is obscure, for indeed I was not over-desirous that the meaning of all should be quite clear, at least unmistakable, you might, without the effort that to make it all out would seem to have required, have nevertheless read it so that lines and stanzas should be left in the memory and superficial impressions deepened, and have liked some without exhausting all. I am sure I have read and enjoyed pages of poetry that way. Why, sometimes one enjoys and admires the very lines one cannot understand, as for instance 'If it were done when 'tis done' sqq., which is all obscure and disputed, though how fine it is everybody sees and nobody disputes. And so of many more passages in Shakespeare and others. Besides you would have got more weathered to the style and its features—not really odd. Now they say that vessels sailing from the port of London will take (perhaps it should be/used once to take) Thames water for the voyage: it was foul and stunk at first as the ship worked but by degrees casting its filth was in a few days very pure and sweet and wholesomer and better than any water in the world. However that maybe, it is true to my purpose. When a new thing, such as my ventures in the Deutschland are, is presented us our first criticisms are not our truest, best, most homefelt, or most lasting but what come easiest on the instant. They are barbarous and like what the ignorant and the ruck say. This was so with you. The Deutschland on her first run worked very much and unsettled you, thickening and clouding your mind with vulgar mudbottom and common sewage (I see that I am going it with the image) and just then unhappily you *drew off* your criticisms all stinking (a necessity now of the image) and bilgy, whereas if you had let your thoughts cast themselves they would have been clearer in themselves and more to my taste too. I did not heed them therefore, perceiving they were a first drawing-off. ...

St Giles's, Oxford. Feb. 15, '79.
... No doubt my poetry errs on the side of oddness. I hope in time to have a more balanced and Miltonic style. But as air, melody, is what strikes me most of all in music and design in painting, so design, pattern or what I am in the habit of calling 'inscape' is what I above all aim at in poetry. Now it is the virtue of design, pattern, or inscape to be distinctive and it is the vice of distinctiveness to become queer. This vice I cannot have escaped. ...

(b) From *Correspondence of Hopkins and Dixon*, ed. Abbott (1935)

Dixon to Hopkins

Hayton Vicarage, Carlisle. 5 April 1879.
REVEREND AND MOST DEAR SIR – I have your Poems and have read them I cannot say with what delight, astonishment, & admiration. They are among the most extraordinary I ever read & amazingly original. ...

S. Mary's Vicarage, Hayton, Carlisle, 1 Mar. 1880.
... I have read them many times with the greatest admiration: in the power of forcibly & delicately giving the essence of things in nature, & of carrying one out of one's self with healing, these poems are unmatched. The Eurydice no one could read without the

deepest & most ennobling emotion. The Sonnets are all truly wonderful: of them my best favourites are the Starlight Night, the Skylark, Duns Scotus Oxford: and the Windhover.

I am haunted by the lines—

'And you were a liar, o blue March day,
Bright, sunlanced fire of the heavenly bay.'ᶜ

which seem to me more English-Greek than Milton, or as much so, & with more passion. The Deutschland is enormously powerful: it has however such elements of deep distress in it that one reads it with less excited delight though not with less interest than the others. I hope that you will accept the tribute of my deep and intense admiration. You spoke of sending me some more. I cannot in truth say what I think of your work....

Hayton Vicarage, Carlisle. 15 Nov. 1880.
...This 'new prosody', which is your invention, exercises me greatly. I think I understand it in a general way from your poems and written explanations. But the question is whether it can be laid down or drawn out in a system of rules. Eventually, in application, I suppose it must be a matter of ear, rather than of formal rule: but still it has principles that can be expressed, and therefore might form a system. I asked Bridges whether the foundation of it did not lie in fixed quantity, and he said that it did, but that much more was involved in it. This however would in itself involve a revolution; and a great deal of work, though very valuable work, if certain terminations, e.g. or certain words also, were decided to be absolutely long or short. For instance, the word *over* is long in the first syllable, & generally so used (I owe this to Bridges, I had never thought about it): but Tennyson uses it short (I think) in the Ode to Memory.

Have you any thought of drawing it out in a system?...

Hayton Vicarage, Carlisle. 24 Jan. 1881.
...I wish you had more time for writing: it certainly does seem a great pity, however valuable the other work that you do. I like very much the two little pieces that you have sent: no one else could have written them. It seems to me that in the couplet

'Nor mouth it, no nor mind expressed
But heárt heárd of, ghóst guéssed:'[1]

it would be an improvement to bring the latter line into common
rhythm—

But heart heard of it, ghost guessed.

Just there the poem seems to want to be very plain, as it gives the
leading, a very beautiful, thought. You will pardon me, I know.
Also, in the other truly charming piece, I c^d. wish that the first
couplet finished the sense. It runs,

How lovely is the elder brother's
Love, all laced in the other's
Being—[2]

If it would go somehow,

How lovely in the elder brother
Love, all laced in the other.

Would not that be an improvement—I dont mean *that*, but
something like it, which you could do.

How lovely in the elder brother
The love, all laced in the other,
Which he bears! I watched this well; &c.

This has just occurred to me, & I write it: you w^d. get rid of 'I *have*
watched this well', which seems not the right tense, unless there be
a full stop after well. . . .

Hayton Vicarage, Carlisle. 26 Oct. 1881.
. . . I hope that you are going on with poetry yourself. I can
understand that your present position, seclusion and exercises
would give to your writings a rare charm—they have done so in
those that I have seen: something that I cannot describe, but know
to myself by the inadequate word *terrible pathos*—something of
what you call temper in poetry: a right temper which goes to the
point of the terrible; the terrible crystal. Milton is the only one else
who has anything like it: & he has it in a totally different way: he
has it through indignation, through injured majesty, which is an
inferior thing in fact. I cannot tell whether you know what I
mean. . . .

Hopkins to Dixon

Manresa House, Roehampton, S.W. Oct. 29/Nov. 2 1881.
... My vocation puts before me a standard so high that a higher can
be found nowhere else. The question then for me is not whether I
am willing (if I may guess what is in your mind) to make a sacrifice
of hopes of fame (let us suppose), but whether I am not to undergo
a severe judgement from God for the lothness I have shewn in
making it, for the reserves I may have in my heart made, for the
backward glances I have given with my hand upon the plough, for
the waste of time the very compositions you admire may have
caused and their preoccupation of the mind which belonged to
more sacred or more binding duties, for the disquiet and the
thoughts of vain-glory they have given rise to. A purpose may look
smooth and perfect from without but be frayed and faltering from
within. I have never wavered in my vocation, but I have not lived
up to it. I destroyed the verse I had written when I entered the
Society and meant to write no more; the *Deutschland* I began after a
long interval at the chance suggestion of my superior, but that
being done it is a question whether I did well to write anything else.
However I shall, in my present mind, continue to compose, as
occasion shall fairly allow, which I am afraid will be seldom and
indeed for some years past has been scarcely ever, and let what I
produce wait and take its chance; for a very spiritual man once told
me that with things like composition the best sacrifice was not to
destroy one's work but to leave it entirely to be disposed of by
obedience. But I can scarcely fancy myself asking a superior to
publish a volume of my verses and I own that humanly there is
very little likelihood of that ever coming to pass. And to be sure if I
chose to look at things on one side and not the other I could of
course regret this bitterly. But there is more peace and it is the
holier lot to be unknown than to be known.—In no case am I
willing to write anything while in my present condition: the time is
precious and will not return again and I know I shall not regret my
forbearance....

Dixon to Hopkins

Hayton Vicarage, Carlisle. 28 Jan. 1882.
... I cannot but take courage to hope that the day will come, when
so health-breathing and purely powerful a faculty as you have been

gifted with may find its proper issue in the world. Bridges struck the truth long ago when he said to me that your poems more carried him out of himself than those of any one. I have again and again felt the same: & am certain that as a means of serving, I will not say your cause, but religion, you cannot have a more powerful instrument than your own verses. They have, of course with all possible differences of originality on both sides, the quality which Taine has marked in Milton: & which is more to be noted in his minor pieces than the great ones, of admiration—I forget Taine's expression, but it means admiration (or in you other emotions also) which reaches its fullness & completeness in giving the exact aspect of the thing it takes: so that a peculiar contentation[3] is felt. ...

(c) From *Further Letters of Hopkins*, ed. Abbott (1938)

Patmore to Hopkins

Hastings, March 6, 1884.
MY DEAR MR. HOPKINS, I have just received your MSS. It may be sometime before you hear from me about them, as I expect to find in them something quite new, and I am conscious of my extreme slowness in taking fully in what is new. I suppose it comes of my all along having followed a single line of my own, that I am really the worst *off-hand* critic of really new work that I know. But, as one of the Greek poets, I believe, says, 'Slow is the wrath of Gods, but in the end not weak,' so my judgment, though hard to make up, may rank perhaps with the judgment of the best of the 'gallery-Gods' when it is made up; for it is founded on the severe and instinctive principles which I believe I owe mainly to my Father's having taught me from my early boyhood a contempt for what is meretricious and a love for all the best models within my reach....

Hastings, March 20, 1884.
...I have read your poems—most of them several times—and find my first impression confirmed with each reading. It seems to me that the thought and feeling of these poems, if expressed without any obscuring novelty of mode, are such as often to require the whole

attention to apprehend and digest them; and are therefore of a kind to appeal only to the few. But to the already sufficiently arduous character of such poetry you seem to me to have added the difficulty of following *several* entirely novel and simultaneous experiments in versification and construction, together with an altogether unprecedented system of alliteration and compound words;—any one of which novelties would be startling and productive of distraction from the poetic matter to be expressed.

System and learned theory are manifest in all these experiments; but they seem to me to be *too* manifest. To me they often darken the thought and feeling which all arts and artifices of language should only illustrate; and I often find it as hard to follow you as I have found it to follow the darkest parts of Browning—who, however, has not an equal excuse of philosophic system. 'Thoughts that *voluntary* move harmonious numbers' is, I suppose, the best definition of poetry that ever was spoken. Whenever your thoughts forget your theories they do so move, and no one who knows what poetry is can mistake them for anything but poetry. 'The Blessed Virgin compared to the Air we breathe' and a few other pieces are exquisite to my mind, but, in these, you have attained to move almost unconsciously in your self-imposed shackles, and consequently the ear follows you without much interruption from the surprise of such novelties; and I can conceive that, after awhile, they would become additional delights. But I do not think that I could ever become sufficiently accustomed to your favourite Poem, 'The Wreck of the Deutschland' to reconcile me to its strangenesses.

I do not think that your musical signs ⌒ ~ ⌒ etc. help at all. I fancy I should always read the passages in which they occur as you intend them to be read, without any such aid; and people who would not do so would not be *practically* helped by the notation.

I do not see how I can say more without going into the matter at very great length indeed; and, after all, I might very likely be wrong, for I see that Bridges goes along with you where I cannot, & where I do not believe that I ever could; and I deliberately recognise in the author of 'Prometheus' a sounder and more delicate taste than my own. You remember I only claimed to be a God among the *Gallery* Gods—i.e. the common run of 'Nineteenth Century', 'Fortnightly' & such critics. I feel *absolutely* sure that you would never conciliate *them*—but Bridges' appreciation is a fact that I cannot get over. I cannot understand his not seeing defects in your system wh. I seem to see so clearly; and when I do not understand a man's ignorance, I obey the Philosopher and think myself ignorant of his understanding. So please do not rely upon impressions which I distrust myself. ...

Hastings, April 5, 1884.

... At the very time your letter came, this afternoon, I was feeling very anxious as to how you might have received my last. My difficulty in getting at anything very new is, as I said before, greater than that of most persons; and sometimes that difficulty seems insuperable. It struck me, however, at once, on reading your poems, that the key to them might be supplied by your own reading of them; and I trust some day to have the benefit of that assistance. I do not, however, feel at all sure that, even with such aid, I shall be able to enter into your spirit. The partiality and limitation of my appreciation of art often surprises myself. I have the most acute delight in some of the best music, but it seems a mere accident. Most of Beethoven, for example, seems to me to be simply noise; but when I do understand him I understand him indeed. It was twenty years before I could learn to see anything in Wordsworth's sonnets to the River Duddon.

What you say concerning your modes of composition disposes, at once, of some of what I thought were sound critical objections against writing upon theory etc. but *how* such modes, or at least some of them, as for example your alliterations, come to be the spontaneous expression of your poetical feeling, I cannot understand, and I do not think I ever shall.

I have never met with the 'Potato Poet',[d] and I fear I have not enough in me of 'the native earth and real potato' to like him if I did. I cant help being a little amused by your claiming for your style the extreme of popular character. But after all perhaps that is the secret of my being so insensible to its peculiar merits. I never could understand 'the people'—indeed, I may say with Sir Thomas Browne, that the People is the only entity which I sincerely hate. If you succeed in pleasing them with your potato-style as much as you do me when you write in your Ambrosia-manner (as in 'Wild Air etc.') you may claim an almost incomparable universality of influence. ...

58

(d) From *Memoirs and Correspondence of Coventry Patmore*, ed. Basil Champneys, London, 1900, II, 247

Patmore to Bridges

Hastings, 2 May 1884

...I hesitate to give so absolute a verdict of dissent from some of his [Hopkins's] poetical novelties as I otherwise should give. To me his poetry has the effect of veins of pure gold imbedded in masses of unpracticable quartz. He assures me that his 'thoughts involuntary moved' in such numbers, and that he did not write them from preconceived theories. I cannot understand it. His genius is however unmistakable, and is lovely and unique in its effects whenever he approximates to the ordinary rules of composition. ...

NOTES

a *The Wreck of the Deutschland*, stanza 12.
b *The Wreck of the Deutschland*, st. 2, 1, 2.
c *Poems*, 17, *The Loss of the Eurydice*, ll. 21–2 (2nd line misquoted...).
d Identity not established.

1 Quoted from an earlier version of 'Spring and Fall'.
2 Quoted from an earlier version of 'Brothers'.
3 Satisfaction.

2. Robert Bridges, in *The Poets and the Poetry of the Century*, ed. Alfred Miles

Vol. 8, London, 1893, pp. 161–4

Miles's anthology of the major and minor poets of the nineteenth century eventually filled ten stocky volumes and is still valuable reading for students of late Victorian taste in poetry. Bridges claimed that he used his influence with the editor in order to publish this first significant selection from Hopkins's work, which, as with the other poets, was preceded by a biographical and critical introduction. It was a major step in his campaign to bring Hopkins gradually to public notice.

These were the poems on which most readers based their assessment of Hopkins until the *Spirit of Man* (1916); Charles Williams, Lascelles Abercrombie, and Roger Fry all said they first read Hopkins in Miles (Mellown, *Modern Philology*, November 1959, p. 95). The poems were: 'A Vision of the Mermaids' (part), 'The Habit of Perfection', 'The Starlight Night', 'Spring', 'The Candle Indoors', 'Spring and Fall', 'Inversnaid', 'To R.B.' Bridges also used his introduction to the Hopkins selection, reproduced here, to quote from four more poems (but nothing, predictably, from 'The Wreck of the Deutschland').

This brief account of Hopkins's life and work fulfils the requirements of what Bridges described to Mrs Hopkins in 1890 as a short preface which 'should put the poems out of reach of criticism'. Bridges's tendency, therefore, to dwell on Hopkins's 'faults', both here and in the Preface to the Notes of the *Poems* (1918), may partly be explained as a strategy to disarm public criticism.

Gerard Manley Hopkins was born at Stratford, in Essex, July 28th, 1844. He was educated at the Cholmondeley School, Highgate, when Richard Watson Dixon was a master there, which was the beginning of a poetic friendship revived in later years; thence he took an exhibition at Balliol College, Oxford, and there a classical first class in 1867, in preparation for which he enjoyed the sympathetic tuition of Walter Pater. In October of the previous year he had been received into the Roman Catholic Church, and he left Oxford, his—

> Towery city, and branchy between towers,

to be with Cardinal Newman at Birmingham, till, in 1868 he joined the Jesuits.

He never published any poems, but he took a school prize with verses, the loss of which is to be regretted, if their quality may be judged from the verses of the same date given below; and he was known as a poet at Oxford. When he entered on his novitiate in 1868 he burned what he had written, but he subsequently returned to the muse and devoted much attention to poetry. His early verse shows a mastery of Keatsian sweetnesses, but he soon developed a very different style of his own, so full of experiments in rhythm and diction that, were his poems collected into one volume, they would appear as a unique effort in English literature. Most of his poems are religious, and marked with Catholic theology, and almost all are injured by a natural eccentricity, a love for subtlety and uncommonness, well denoted by the Greek term τὸπεριττόν.[1] And this quality of mind hampered their author throughout life; for though to a fine intellect and varied accomplishments (he was both a draughtsman and musician) he united humour, great personal charm, and the most attractive virtues of a tender and sympathetic nature,—which won him love wherever he went, and gave him zeal for his work,—yet he was not considered publicly successful in his profession. When sent to Liverpool to do parish work among the Irish, the vice and horrors nearly killed him: and in the several posts, which he held in turn—he was once select preacher in London, and had for a while some trust at Oxford,—he served without distinction. Of this he was himself conscious, and in a sonnet on the words *Justus quidem tu es, Domine,* etc., he says:—

Thou art indeed just, Lord, if I contend
With thee; but, sir, so what I plead is just,
Why do sinners' ways prosper? and why must
Disappointment all I endeavour end?
Wert thou my enemy, O thou my friend,
How couldst thou worse, I wonder, than thou dost
Defeat, thwart me? Oh, the sots and thralls of lust
Do in spare hours more thrive than I that spend,
Sir, life upon thy cause. ...

In connection with which may be read the following undated
fragment of a hymn.

Thee, God, I come from, to thee go,
All day long I like fountain flow
From thy hand out, swayed about
Mote-like in thy mighty glow.

What I know of thee I bless,
As acknowledging thy stress
On my being, and as seeing
Something of thy holiness.

Once I turned from thee and hid,
Bound on what thou hadst forbid;
Sow the wind I would; I sinned:
I repent of what I did.

Bad I am but yet thy child.
Father, be thou reconciled.
Spare thou me, since I see
With thy might that thou art mild.

I have life left with me still
And thy purpose to fulfil;
Yes, a debt to pay thee yet:
Help me, sir, and so I will.

At length in 1884, he was elected Fellow of the Royal University
of Ireland, and he seems to have entirely satisfied the Society as
classical examiner at Dublin. That drudgery, however, and the
political dishonesty which he was there forced to witness, so
tortured his sensitive spirit that he fell into a melancholy state,
vividly pictured in his last sonnets, in one of which his isolation and
exile are thus told:—

To seem the stranger lies my lot, my life
Among strángers. Father and mother dear,
Brothers and sisters are in Christ not near,
And he my peace my parting, sword and strife.
  England, whose honour O all my heart wooes, wife
To my creating thought, would neither hear
Me, were I pleading, plead nor do I: I wear-
y of idle a being but by where wars are rife.

★   ★   ★   ★   ★

These lines and others written at that time were his dirge; for he was attacked shortly after by the material contagions of the city, and making no effort for life, he died of the fever in his prime, June 8th, 1889.

The octets above quoted are in his best style, the dated specimens below are from all periods of his writing. The first two of these he would not have wished to be printed, but it is necessary to give them in proof that the unusual and difficult rhythms of his later work were consciously sought after, and elaborated from the common types which he had set aside. Poems so far removed as his came to be from the ordinary simplicity of grammar and metre, had they no other drawback, could never be popular; but they will interest poets; and they may perhaps prove welcome to the critic, for they have this plain fault, that, aiming at an unattainable perfection of language (as if words—each with its twofold value in sense and in sound—could be arranged like so many separate gems to compose a whole expression of thought, in which the force of grammar and the beauty of rhythm absolutely correspond), they not only sacrifice simplicity, but very often, among verses of the rarest beauty, show a neglect of those canons of taste which seem common to all poetry.

Some syllables have been accented in the text, as a guide to the reader, where it seemed that the boldness of the rhythm might otherwise cause him to doubt the intended stress.

NOTE

1 'Out of the ordinary, unconventional'.

3. Fr John MacLeod, 'The Diary of a Devoted Student of Nature', *Letters and Notices*

April 1906, p. 390

Letters and Notices has been since 1862 the private, internal publication of the English province of the Society of Jesus. Three articles containing extracts from Hopkins's journals were published between 1906 and 1907, when the editor of the magazine, and of these extracts, was Fr John MacLeod (1826–1914), whom Hopkins knew at Roehampton (see *Journals*, 2nd edn, p. 240, December 1873). I print the opening of the first article.

Those who were acquainted with Father Gerard Hopkins in past years knew him as a man of a very original cast of mind, of very marked character, and of quaint and somewhat extravagant poetic fancy. It was often by no means easy to understand the line of his thought or the play of imagination by which he sought to give greater effect to the scenes or events portrayed by him, just as he himself in his turn was inclined to be suspicious of and to misinterpret what was passing through the minds of others. He was undoubtedly possessed of a keen intellect, enriched with many brilliant talents and varied accomplishments, for from his earliest childhood he could draw with a marvellous precision and delicacy of hand; he had a very exquisite voice, and took great interest in music, besides being devoted to the study of art and literature generally, and having an extensive acquaintance with poets and their work, with regard to which his judgments differed considerably from those formed by most persons. Indeed, in respect of all his views and opinions it may be said that his mind tended to that form of eccentricity which is closely allied to a touch of true genius. Along with the amiable and most lovable qualities of his heart and natural disposition, it has well been said that 'he had in him all the elements of an eminent artist or literary man, and that the quality of his criticism was perhaps the best of its kind, if he had not been the victim of a lengthened and overwrought critical education.' This, combined with and fostering a deeply-ingrained originality of views and tastes, while his mind was still inexperienced and unformed, gave a character of undue strain and excess to the criticisms which he passed on the persons with whom he came in contact, as well as on the different objects he observed in nature. He was intimately versed in the whole range of scientific expression, and showed a preference for such terms as were most recondite and but seldom used. ...

4. Katherine Brégy, 'Gerard Hopkins, an Epitaph and an Appreciation', *Catholic World*

January 1909, pp. 433ff

Katherine Brégy was an American writer of French descent who was born in Philadelphia and studied at the University under Cornelius Weygandt (see No. 99). She was received into the Catholic Church in 1904. She began to correspond with Louise Guiney (see No. 16), who urged her to write about Hopkins, while Fr Russell, SJ, editor of the *Irish Monthly*, warned her off the poet as a 'very odd' and 'not practical subject'.

The *Catholic World* was an American monthly of religious and general interest founded by the Paulist fathers in 1865. Brégy's reminiscences began to appear in the magazine in February 1939 and include some interesting information about personalities associated with the development of Hopkins's reputation. She died in 1967.

The full article from which these extracts are taken was later reprinted in *The Poet's Chantry*, a collection of Brégy's essays (see No. 5).

... Always the world was fresh to him [Hopkins], as it is fresh to children and to the very mature. At every turn, and by sheer force of his own vivid individuality, he was finding that 'something of the unexplored,' that 'grain of the unknown,' which Flaubert so sagely counselled de Maupassant to seek in all things; but which none of us may ever hope to find until we cease looking upon life through the traditional lenses of other eyes. Therefore was Father Hopkins Ignatian in his own very personal way. Few men have loved nature more rapturously than he; fewer still with such a youthful and perennial curiosity. There is a tender excitement in his attitude toward natural beauty (whether treated incidentally or as a parable) that is very contagious, and the exultation of that early and earthly *Vision* clung to the young monk almost with life itself. Nature, indeed, was his one secular inspiration; and that even she was not wholly secular is evinced by the characteristic music of his spring song:

[Quotes 'Spring'.]

Here at last, in one of the most hackneyed of poetic subjects, we are come upon an original vein of poetry; a spiritual motivation, a vigor of word-painting, and a metrical proficiency of very real distinction. It was written in 1877, and its existence argues for Father Hopkins more than a mere dilettante use of the poetic faculty.

Another sonnet of the same year, 'The Starlight Night', is almost equally striking in music and in metaphor. But it must be acknowledged that both of these poems bear traces of that eccentricity and occasional ambiguity which point forward to Father Hopkins' eventual excesses. Lucidity was the chief grace he sacrified as years wore on; and his fondness for uncommon words—at one moment academic and literate, at another provincial—did not help matters. 'Inversnaid' (written in 1881) is an extreme instance of his later manner: there is a certain bounding and prancing charm about it, but, in truth, the stream's highroad is sadly obstructed by Anglo-Saxon and other archaic undergrowth. *Wiry heathpacks—flitches of fern*—and the *groins of the braes that the brook treads through*, send the reader's mind back with some ruefulness to that lovely random line from the 'Vision of Mermaids':

To know the dusk depths of the ponderous sea!

We are not born original in these latter days of literature, it would seem; we must achieve originality—and often at the cost of so much complexity! Not a few of us, indeed, would appear to have been born complex, with a congenital impulse toward entangling an existence already difficult enough. But there is one ineradicable simplicity about religious men—they are always coming back upon God. To Him they reach out, and peradventure attain, through the mysteries of nature, through the mazes of science and abstract speculation, even through the fundamental intricacies of their own temperament. His Spirit they perceive brooding above the patient earth, glorifying and illumining her travail. And so we find Father Hopkins' ultimate message, clarion-clear, in this very direct and characteristic sonnet upon 'God's Grandeur':

[Quoted.]

...The poems have been permitted to speak for themselves, and if their faults are conspicuous enough, so too is their unique and magnetic attraction. No doubt this is in the nature of an acquired taste. They were not written for the public (during their maker's lifetime not one of them was put into print!) they were written for the consolation of the poet and a few chosen friends. And to such readers no concessions need be made. Father Hopkins' very delicate craftsmanship—and not less the singularity of his mental processes—might produce on some minds an impression of artificiality. Yet nothing could be further from the fact, for in all the poems of his manhood there is a poignant, even a passionate sincerity. It is quite true that his elliptical and involved expression mars more than one poem of rare and vital imagining. It is true also, and of the nature of the case, that our poet was to a certain degree self-centered in his dream of life. He was not an egoist; but it must be obvious that from first to last he was an individualist. And in our human reckonings the individualist pays, and then he pays again; and after that, in Wilde's phrase, he keeps on paying! Yet in the final count his chances of survival are excellent. Outside of the poets, Father Hopkins' work has had no recognition and no understanding; but his somewhat exotic influence might easily be pointed out in one or two of the foremost Catholic songsters of to-day. And for all its aloofness, the young priest's work struck root in the poetic past. Its subtle and complex fancifulness and its white heat of spirituality go back in direct line to that earlier Jesuit, Father Southwell; while one would wager that Hopkins knew and loved other seventeenth-century lyrists beside the very manifest Crashaw. It is by no means without significance, moreover, to note that Coventry Patmore's Odes 'To the Unknown Eros,' and Browning's masterpiece *The Ring and the Book*, both appeared in that memorable 1868 when Gerard entered upon his novitiate. Those were the days when a young poet might, almost without public comment, fling out to the world his daring and beautiful gift.

After all there is nothing sadder in the world of letters than a fragment—unless it be a fragmentary genius! And always in proportion to the magic of the fragment, and to its promise, is the depth of this sadness. We can nowise escape such a shadow of incompleteness in treating Father Hopkins' work. We cannot, as yet, gather the fundamental materials for more than a tentative criticism. His poems are scattered in a few precious anthologies, still awaiting the zeal of collector and editor. It seems probable, unless he himself destroyed them during the last years, that a number of them are still—somewhere—in manuscript form; for of those already published, about one-third have been given in this article. Merely great poetry is, of course, seldom popular; although the greatest of all poetry—that of Homer and Dante and Shakespeare—strikes a universal echo in the hearts of men. It is inclusive, and it is written not as an escape from life but as the inevitable and impassioned expression of life itself. Gerard Hopkins' artistry was not of this supreme sort. He was essentially a minor poet: he wrote incredibly little and he interpreted few phases of human experience. But, with the minor poet's distinctive merit, he worked his narrow field with completeness and intensity. And who can deny that the very quality which seemed, at worst, an eccentric and literate mannerism, proved itself in the finer passages a strikingly original and authentic inspiration?

5. Unsigned review of Brégy's *The Poet's Chantry*, Month

October 1912, p. 439

For Brégy see No. 4. The *Month* was, and still is, edited by
the English Jesuits, and described itself, when it first appeared
in 1864, as 'An Illustrated Magazine of Literature, Science,
and Art'. The illustrations soon virtually disappeared, but it
continued to print substantial articles of general as well as
religious interest. It rejected 'The Wreck of the Deutschland'
in 1876, but made belated amends from 1909 onwards by its
support for Hopkins. Fr Joseph Keating, editor from 1912,
was a great admirer.

We cannot be too grateful to the authoress for proving to us once
more that we still have poets. For the glories of Francis Thompson
have so eclipsed the rest, that we forget these; and our general level
of art is so indescribably debased that we are, in moments of
depression, capable of forgetting even Francis Thompson and even
Bentley. It is true that we are referred to rather distant years for
Southwell, Habington (about whom, we suppose, not many
people knew), and, of course, Crashaw—whose spell, however,
lies strong upon most later Catholic poetry, as the authoress sees.
And Aubrey de Vere (whom we constantly find ourselves liking
better than we were expecting) and Coventry Patmore even, have
that occasional flavour in their verses which we nickname
'old-fashioned.' But what of Patmore's contemporary and critic,
Gerard Hopkins? Is it not an appalment for heaven and earth that so
little is being done for him? Here is a writer emancipated from time
and tradition. Here is a Prophet, a Martyr, and an Apostle who is at
the same time a Poet—and which of us has the chance of reading
him? Many of his poems survive in MS., are, in fact, in the careful
and reverent keeping of another poet, Mr. Robert Bridges, and
ultimately, we trust, are destined to see the light. But will the
Catholic public really appreciate this portion of the inheritance that

falleth to them? We hear rightly, of the unique and magnetic attraction of his poems: of his *'terrible* pathos' (Dixon's words), of his 'poignant, ever passionate sincerity'; of his 'final crucifixion of mind as well as of body.' But who seems to care, or to want to make amend?

It may be that, as in 1889, he just 'let himself die,' so neither had nor has he any wish to survive even in these his secret poems, half-forecasting, it may be, their misapprehension by the multitude. ...

6. [Fr] G[eorge] O'N[eill], review of *The Poet's Chantry, Studies*

December 1912, p. 736

George O'Neill, SJ (1863–1947), was Professor of English Language at University College, Dublin, and published in the fields of both literature and religion. Judging by his criticism here, his association with Hopkins's old university did not influence his judgment, but his later comments were more favourable (see No. 24). *Studies*, founded in 1912, continues to be published by the Jesuits in Dublin.

... Father Hopkins' is a tiny harp indeed, and one which was very rarely handled with deftness. It seems strange that judging ears should be excited to any rapture by what she gives us to hear of its notes. To us most of her specimens of this writer seem curiously cacophonous. ...

7. F.E. Brett Young, *Robert Bridges: A Critical Study*

London, 1914, p. 142

This book was the result of the collaboration of Francis Brett Young (1884–1954), later to become a best-selling novelist, and his younger brother and journalist, Eric (b. 1893). The two started planning the book in 1911 and Francis stayed with Bridges in 1913. Jessica Brett Young, the novelist's widow, relates that the combined initials of the authors 'gave rise to some misunderstanding' (*Francis Brett Young*, 1962, p. 50). In a letter of thanks for his copy Bridges regretted that more had not been said 'about Hopkins's influence on his writing' (*ibid.*, p. 52). See also No. 10.

... One cannot leave this point [Bridges's mixture of stress and syllabic verse] without reference to the work of a man whose name is still quite unknown, and the bulk of whose poetry has never been published. The late Gerard Hopkins S.J. was a writer with a very real poetic gift, whose metres were consciously elaborated from common syllabic types. We have no record of the theory upon which he worked, but I believe some idea of stress–equivalence formed part of it. A great deal of his work was so obscure both in metre and diction that there is little chance of its ever becoming popular. ...

8. Unsigned review of *The Spirit of Man*, *New York Times Review of Books*

26 March 1916, p. 105

Bridges's anthology, which the editor explained in the Preface was published for the spiritual consolation of the Allies in time of war, was to achieve wide circulation, especially amongst writers at the Front. F.R. Leavis, who later unkindly described it as being designed to be 'carried round in officers' pockets', first read Hopkins in it in wartime France, and it also stimulated the interest of Auden. Ivor Gumey thought it was 'a good book, though very far below what it might be. Why all that Shelley and Dixon and Hopkins or what's his name of the crazy precious diction?' (*War Letters,* ed. R.K. Thornton, London, 1984, p. 99). Of the poems included, 'Spring and Fall' was a partial text, and 'The Wreck of the Deutschland' was represented by less than one verse.

This review was one of several brief references to Hopkins which the selection brought. The present extract follows the reviewer's remark that the anthology was valuable for bringing to light lesser-known poets, such as Digby Dolben.

... And then there is Gerard Hopkins, who was Walter Pater's pupil, a poet whose craftsmanship was as elaborate as his inspiration was genuine. No book of his poems has ever been published, and it is good to see that Mr Bridges quoted 'Spring and Fall', 'The Candle Indoors', 'In the Valley of the Elwy', 'The Handsome Heart', part of 'The Habit of Perfection', and part of 'The Wreck of the Deutschland'. But it is lamentable that only two stanzas of 'The Habit of Perfection' are given, since that poem in its entirety is Gerard Hopkins's best claim to literary immortality, and the best poetry ever written about the religious life.

9. George Saintsbury, *Cambridge History of English Literature*

Vol. xiii, Cambridge, 1916, p. 210

George Saintsbury (1845–1933) voluminous editor and critic, was one of the chief contributors to the monumental *Cambridge History*. He lived and worked in London 1876–96, and then became Professor of English Literature in Edinburgh until 1915. His friendship with Bridges may explain his interest in Hopkins, which is also demonstrated in *A History of English Prosody* (1910) and *A History of Nineteenth Century Literature* (1896), where he spoke of the 'remarkable talents of Mr. Gerard Manley Hopkins' (p. 294) and grouped him with the Pre-Raphaelites.

... A few lines must be given to a contemporary of Lang at Oxford who was, to a greater extent than is usual, a poetical might-have-been. Gerard Hopkins was not only much let and hindered in writing poetry, but never published any, and all we have consists of fragments issued as specimens from MSS. But these fragments show that he not merely might have been, but was, a poet. Unfortunately, an ingrained eccentricity which affected his whole life, first as an undergraduate and then as a Jesuit priest, helped these accidents. He developed partially acute, but not generally sound, notions on metre; and though, quite recently, broken-back rhythms like his have been often attempted, the results have scarcely been delightful. In his own case, though the process of appreciation is most like the proverbial reconstruction of a fossil beast from a few odd bones, it shows that they belonged to a poet. ...

10. E. Brett Young, 'The Poetry of Gerard Hopkins', *Today*

January 1918, pp. 191–6

For Brett Young, see No. 7. *Today*, 1917–23, was a weekly literary magazine aimed at a popular audience. The editor was Holbrook Jackson.

Most neglected of all the Victorian poets, Gerard Hopkins would have been quite content to know that his work would be forgotten by the generation that followed him. His elaborately wrought verse, with its devices of rhythm and assonance, invites applause no more than the curious decoration of a missal. But these poems have a subtlety of workmanship which makes it certain that they will not be forgotten; for their value as adventures in technique—if they were nothing more—cannot be ignored by the poets who will seek hereafter for new forms of expression. ...

When Gerard Hopkins renounced the 'natural man,' burning his poems, he reined in a poetic fancy that was almost riotous in its exuberance. His muse took, as it were, the veil. I shall quote a simile written in his boyhood, side by side with an example of his mature style. It is from 'A Vision of Mermaids,' dated 1862:

[Quotes lines 84–98.]

Here is a sonnet written seventeen years later:

[Quotes 'The Candle Indoors'.]

Here is a difference not of style only, but of orientation. There is a gulf fixed between the early verse, with what Doctor Bridges calls its Keatsian sweetnesses, and the austere accents of those other lines. His work, developing naturally from such a beginning, would never have been without sensuous beauty. A young poet whose talent was bearing such fruit, might well have been content to linger a little longer with the Hesperides. I conclude that Hopkins deliberately abandoned this easy sweetness. If he had

merely carried the repressive part of his code into his verse, he
might have been silenced altogether. But he was ascetic in the
original sense of the word; he became ascetic in his poetry as in his
life, devoting himself to the pursuit of a new technique by tireless
trial and experiment in the art which he loved too well to abandon.

Crabbed and cryptic, sometimes harsh and even ugly this later
and better verse undoubtedly is. Hopkins was both draughtsman
and poet, and I think his few critics have failed to realize how far
the verbal complexity is the outcome of a collision between the two
arts. He lavished his genius in trying to translate the delight of a
quick eye into terms that would please a subtle ear. Phrases like
'blear-all black,' 'mealed-with-yellow sallows,' 'a wind-puff bonnet of fawn-froth,' show his impatience with a language that will
not fit itself to niceties of colour and movement. He reversed
Scriabine's experiment of the colour-organ by trying to paint with
sounds, and in lines like these, he nearly achieves the impossible
end:

> Nothing is more beautiful than spring,
>   When weeds in wheels shoot long and lovely and lush;
>   Thrush's eggs look like little low heavens, and thrush
> Through the echoing timber does so rinse and wring
> The ear, it strikes like lightnings to hear him sing;
>   The glassy pear-tree's leaves and blooms they brush
>   The descending blue; that blue is all in a rush
> With richness; the racing lambs too have fair their fling.

Here even the song of the thrush—who, I think, but for the
exigence of rhyme, would have been a robin—must take its vivid
place in the picture before it can be turned again to music. Hopkins
is most like Keats in his passion for the shows of nature. But he
likes the little pageants best—the tiny, meticulous shifts of the
kaleidoscope—and seen melodies are sweetest to him. His genius
was in danger of being quite snared in a network of small lights and
shadows. We find this delight in things seen—I am tempted to call
it a lust of the eye—in the lovely sonnet (Miles's anthology, page
185), in which 'the self-remembring soul sweetly recovers its
kindred with the stars...' and again in the picture of the stream in
'Inversnaid':

[Quotes verses 1 and 3.]

He invades, too, in his restlessness, the realm of pure music. Alliteration and assonance are not for him, as for Swinburne, a means of emphasizing the rhythm of the verse. Often they run counter to it, and he blends two melodies in one line. It is not easy to deduce, from his one-sided correspondence with Coventry Patmore, precisely what theories of metre he evolved. But the ear is, after all, the only arbiter in these matters, and Hopkins's counterpoint, which impressed Patmore as 'lovely and unique,' should not alarm a generation far more alert to the attraction of subtle rhythms. The machinery of English verse is not equal to the triple strain of sound, sense, and colour which Hopkins tried to place upon it, and his effects are often won at the expense of a baffling disregard of grammar. But many even of his crabbedest lines, in which the words have been jolted out of all natural relationship, and the sense seems buried under the ruins, haunt the memory with an echo of rare loveliness.

It may be that the blossom for which he waited was only budding when his life came to an end. The unrest of mind which darkened his later years creeps everywhere into his verse. Its beauty gleams against a background of melancholy. He turns constantly— as in 'The Candle Indoors' and the 'Starlit Night'—from the poetic aspect of things, with their lovely or sad gestures, to the religious import which he conceives to lie behind them. He interprets beauty in terms of death, regeneration and resurrection. I have quoted the octave of the beautiful sonnet 'On Spring.' Here is the doctrinal appendix, the sestet:

[Quoted.]

Pope said of Herbert that he wrote 'like a gentleman, for his own amusement'. Hopkins wrote like a devotee offering a sacrifice. Sometimes he is stung by 'the fine delight that fathers thought' and poetry. But in the midst of his song, he seems to turn aside with a sigh, confessing, like an older poet and mystic,

There is no dealing with Thee in this art.[1]

NOTE

1 Line 2 of Herbert's 'Love', 'Thou art too hard for me in love', but 'this' should read 'that'.

POEMS OF GERARD MANLEY HOPKINS

edited by Robert Bridges, London, 1918

---

11. Robert Bridges, Preface to Notes, and Notes, *Poems of Hopkins*

1918, pp. 94ff

Bridges, Poet Laureate since 1913, had been planning an edition of Hopkins, with a 'memoir', in August 1889, before dropping the idea in favour of his 'anthology' policy (see Introduction, pp. 6–9). Admirers of Hopkins continued to beg, publicly and privately, for a full edition (for example, Fr Keating in the *Month*, August 1909, p. 258), but it was not until 1918 that Bridges judged the moment was right. Seven hundred and fifty copies were printed, and were only finally disposed of just before the publication of the second edition, twelve years later. The book's price—12*s*. 6*d*. a copy, and adversely commented on—contributed to its exclusiveness.

Despite the doubtfulness of Bridges's critical principles, there has often been much praise for the more technical side of his work: 'The volume of 1918', wrote Abbott, some years later, 'is a masterpiece of editing' (*Letters to Bridges*, p. xvii).

(a) From the Preface

Mannerism

... Apart from questions of taste—and if these poems were to be arraigned for errors of what may be called taste, they might be convicted of occasional affectation in metaphor, as where the hills are 'as a stallion stalwart, very-violet-sweet', or of some perversion of human feeling, as, for instance, the nostrils' relish of incense 'along the sanctuary side', or 'the Holy Ghost with warm breast and with ah! bright wings', these and a few such examples are mostly efforts to force emotion into theological or sectarian channels, as in 'the comfortless unconfessed' and the unpoetic line. 'His mystery must be unstressed stressed', or, again, the exaggerated Marianism of some pieces, or the naked encounter of sensualism and asceticism which hurts the 'Golden Echo',—

Style

Apart I say, from such faults of taste, which few as they numerically are yet affect my liking and more repel my sympathy than do all the rude shocks of his purely artistic wantonness—apart from these there are definite faults of style which a reader must have courage to face, and must in some measure condone before he can discover the great beauties. For these blemishes in the poet's style are of such quality and magnitude as to deny him even a hearing from those who love a continuous literary decorum and are grown to be intolerant of its absence. And it is well to be clear that there is no pretence to reverse the condemnation of those faults, for which the poet has duly suffered. The extravagances are and will remain what they were.

Oddity

Nor can credit be gained from pointing them out: yet, to put readers at their ease, I will here define them: they may be called Oddity and Obscurity; and since the first may provoke laughter when a writer is serious (and this poet is always serious), while the latter must prevent him from being understood (and this poet has always something to say), it may be assumed that they were not a part of his intention. Something of what he thought on this subject may be seen in the following extracts from his letters. In Feb. 1879, he wrote: 'All therefore that I think of doing is to keep my verses together in one place—at present I have not even correct copies—, that, if anyone should like, they might be published after my death. And that again is unlikely, as well as remote.... No doubt my poetry errs on the side of oddness. I hope in time to have a more balanced and Miltonic style. But as air, melody, is what strikes me most of all in music and design in painting, so design, pattern, or what I am in the habit of calling *inscape* is what I above all aim at in poetry. Now it is the virtue of design, pattern, or inscape to be distinctive and it is the vice of distinctiveness to become queer. This vice I cannot have escaped.' And again two months later: 'Moreover the oddness may make them repulsive at first and yet Lang might have liked them on a second reading. Indeed when, on somebody returning me the 'Eurydice', I opened and read some lines, as one commonly reads whether prose or verse, with the eyes, so to say, only, it struck me aghast with a kind of raw nakedness and unmitigated violence I was unprepared for: but take breath and read it with the ears, as I always wish to be read, and my verse becomes all right.'

Obscurity

As regards Oddity then, it is plain that the poet was himself fully alive to it, but he was not sufficiently aware of his obscurity, and he could not understand why his friends found his sentences so difficult: he would never have believed that, among all the ellipses and liberties of his grammar, the one chief cause is his habitual omission of the relative pronoun; and yet this is so, and the examination of a simple example or two may serve a general purpose:

Omission of relative pronoun

This grammatical liberty, though it is a common convenience in conversation and has therefore its proper place in good writing, is apt to confuse the parts of speech, and to reduce a normal sequence of words to mere jargon. Writers who carelessly rely on their elliptical speech-forms to govern the elaborate sentences of their literary composition little know what a conscious effort of interpretation they often impose on their readers. But it was not carelessness in Gerard Hopkins: he had full skill and practice and scholarship in conventional forms, and it is easy to see that he banished these purely constructional syllables from his verse because they took up room which he thought he could not afford them: he needed in his scheme all his space for his poetical words, and he wished those to crowd out every merely grammatical colourless or toneless element; and so when he had got into the habit of doing without these relative pronouns—though he must, I suppose, have supplied them in his thought,—he abuses the licence beyond precedent, as when he writes (no. 17)[1] 'O Hero savest !' for 'O Hero that savest!'.

Identical forms

Another example of this (from the 5th stanza of no. 23)[2] will discover another cause of obscurity: the line

> Squander the hell-rook ranks sally to molest him

means 'Scatter the ranks that sally to molest him': but since the words *squander* and *sally* occupy similar positions in the two sections of the verse, and are enforced by a similar accentuation, the second verb deprived of its pronoun will follow the first and appear as an imperative; and there is nothing to prevent its being so taken but the contradiction that it makes in the meaning; whereas the grammar should expose and enforce the meaning, not have to be determined by the meaning. Moreover, there is no way of enunciating this line which will avoid the confusion; because if, knowing that *sally* should not have the same intonation as *squander*, the reader mitigates the accent, and in doing so lessens or obliterates the caesural pause which exposes its accent, then *ranks* becomes a genitive and *sally* a substantive.

Here, then, is another source of the poet's obscurity; that in aiming at condensation he neglects the need that there is for care in the placing of words that are grammatically ambiguous. English swarms with words that have one identical form for substantive, adjective, and verb; and such a word should never be so placed as to allow of any doubt as to what part of speech it is used for; because such ambiguity or momentary uncertainty destroys the force of the sentence. Now our author not only neglects this essential propriety but he would seem even to welcome and seek artistic effect in the consequent confusion; and he will sometimes so arrange such words that a reader looking for a verb may find that he has two or three ambiguous monosyllables from which to select, and must be in doubt as to which promises best to give any meaning that he can welcome; and then, after his choice is made, he may be left with some homeless monosyllable still on his hands.

Homophones

Nor is our author apparently sensitive to the irrelevant suggestions that our numerous homophones cause; and he will provoke further ambiguities or obscurities by straining the meaning of these unfortunate words.

Rhymes

Finally, the rhymes where they are peculiar are often repellent, and so far from adding charm to the verse that they appear as obstacles. This must not blind one from recognizing that Gerard Hopkins, where he is simple and straightforward in his rhyme is a master of it—there are many instances,—but when he indulges in freaks, his childishness is incredible. His intention in such places is that the verses should be recited as running on without pause, and the rhyme occurring in their midst should be like a phonetic accident, merely satisfying the prescribed form. But his phonetic rhymes are often indefensible on his own principle. The rhyme to *communion* in 'The Bugler' is hideous, and the suspicion that the poet thought it ingenious is appalling; *eternal*, in 'The Eurydice', does not correspond with *burn all*, and in 'Felix Randal' *and some* and *handsome* is as truly an eye-rhyme as the *love* and *prove* which he despised and abjured;—and it is more distressing, because the old-fashioned conventional eye-rhymes are accepted as such without speech-adaptation, and to many ears are a pleasant relief from the fixed jingle of the perfect rhyme; whereas his false ear-rhymes ask to have their slight but indispensable differences obliterated in the reading, and thus they expose their defect, which is of a disagreeable and vulgar or even comic quality. He did not escape full criticism and ample ridicule for such things in his lifetime; and in '83 he wrote: 'Some of my rhymes I regret, but they are past changing, grubs in amber: there are only a few of these; others are unassailable; some others again there are which malignity may munch at but the Muses love.'

Euphony and emphasis

Now these are bad faults, and, as I said, a reader, if he is to get any enjoyment from the author's genius, must be somewhat tolerant of them; and they have a real relation to the means whereby the very forcible and original effects of beauty are produced. There is nothing stranger in these poems than the mixture of passages of extreme delicacy and exquisite diction with passages where, in a jungle of rough root-words, emphasis seems to oust euphony; and both these qualities, emphasis and euphony, appear in their extreme forms. It was an idiosyncrasy of this students's mind to push everything to its logical extreme, and take pleasure in a paradoxical result; as may be seen in his prosody where a simple theory seems to be used only as a basis for unexampled liberty. He was flattered when I called him περιττοττος,[3] and saw the humour of it—and one would expect to find in his work the force of emphatic condensation and the magic of melodious expression, both in their extreme forms. Now since those who study style in itself must allow a proper place to the emphatic expression, this experiment, which supplies as novel examples of success as of failure, should be full of interest; and such interest will promote tolerance.

The fragment, on a piece of music, No. 67, is the draft of what appears to be an attempt to explain how an artist has not free-will in his creation. He works out his own nature instinctively as he happens to be made, and is irresponsible for the result. It is lamentable that Gerard Hopkins died when, to judge by his latest work, he was beginning to concentrate the force of all his luxuriant experiments in rhythm and diction, and castigate his art into a more reserved style. Few will read the terrible posthumous sonnets without such high admiration and respect for his poetical power as must lead them to search out the rare masterly beauties that distinguish his work.

(b) From the Notes

...it was after the publication of Miles's book in 1894[4] that his co-religionists began to recognise his possible merits, and their enthusiasm has not perhaps been always wise. It is natural that they should, as some of them openly state they do, prefer the poems I am rejecting ['Rosa Mystica' and 'Ad Mariam'] to those which I print; but this edition was undertaken in response to a demand that, both in England and America, has gradually grown up from the genuinely poetic interest felt in the poems which I have gradually introduced to the public:— that interest has been no doubt welcomed and accompanied by the applause of his particular religious associates, but since their purpose is alien to mine I regret that I am unable to indulge it; nor can I put aside the overruling objection that G.M.H. would not have wished these 'little presentation pieces' to be set among his more serious artistic work. I do not think that they would please any one who is likely to be pleased with this book. ...

The labour spent on this great metrical experiment ['The Wreck of the Deutschland'] must have served to establish the poet's prosody and perhaps his diction: therefore the poem stands logically as well as chronologically in the front of his book, like a great dragon folded in the gate to forbid all entrance, and confident in his strength from past success. This editor advises the reader to circumvent him and attack him late in the rear; for he was himself shamefully worsted in a brave frontal assault, the more easily perhaps because both subject and treatment were distasteful to him. A good method of approach is to read stanza 16 aloud to a chance company. To the metrist and rhythmist the poem will be of interest from the first, and throughout. ...

NOTES

1 'The Loss of the Eurydice'.
2 'The Bugler's First Communion'.
3 'Extraordinary, subtle, over-curious'. See *ante*, p. 61.
4 In fact, 1983.

12. Unsigned review, *Glasgow Herald*

2 January 1919, p. 3

E.W. Mellown, in 'The Reception of Hopkins's Poems, 1919–1930', suggested, on the basis of information from the *Herald*, that the author was Robert Bain, 'senior English master for many years at Morrison's Academy, Crieff' (*Modern Philology*, August 1965, p. 39n).

...The book is a hard nut to crack, and a lecturer on English literature might make a week's work out of it. Browning in his most crabbed and elephantinely humorous mood was smooth compared with Hopkins, yet in the rhythms of the latter amid much that is uncouth there is such success in new movements as only the Laureate himself has paralleled. Both were daring experimenters. The crudities obscure the intellectual swiftness and the imaginative boldness which are the note of the book, but where there is not a shred of the commonplace one does not grudge digging into granite. ...

13. Arthur Clutton-Brock, unsigned review, *Times Literary Supplement*

9 January 1919, p. 19

Arthur Clutton-Brock (1868–1924) was a critic, essayist, and friend of Bridges. He had been a contributor to the *TLS* since 1904, and was art critic for *The Times* from 1908.

Hopkins himself gives an account of his prosody in the preface to his poems, which will enable anyone who reads attentively to understand it; and Mr. Bridges, in his notes, enumerates the defects of Hopkins's poetry. We shall speak, therefore, neither of his prosody, though it is a most interesting subject, nor much of his defects, which are obvious, but of his very great merits.

He was a Jesuit who died in 1889 at the age of 44, and whose first verses in this book, leaving out some extracts from school prize poems, date from 1866. In 1876 he wrote a poem, 'The Wreck of the Deutschland,' which is still more novel than the most novel poems of to-day. Mr. Bridges calls it a great dragon folded in the gate to forbid all entrance; and, indeed, it is difficult. For Hopkins poetry meant difficulty; he wrote it to say more than could be said otherwise; it was for him a packing of words with sense, both emotional and intellectual. The defect of the newest English poetry is that it says too little. Our young poets seem determined to make their art too easy, at least for themselves, to reduce it to expletives. But Hopkins went further than any other poet known to us from common speech. In all his more difficult poems there are several ordinary poems assumed, both their ideas and their metre; and on

84

these assumptions, which the reader is expected to make, he builds his own poem. It is like that modern music which assumes the conventions of older music and departs from them, still using them as the basis of departure. But Hopkins's verse is more difficult even than that music because it assumes that the reader grasps the sense of what is unsaid. He begins where most poets leave off, not out of affectation, but because he wishes to go further. Sometimes even the grammar is implied; its skeleton is not there, you have to imagine it there. The words succeed each other without it, each one bringing a new inrush of sense into the sentence, which hardly exists; and each inrush would in ordinary prose, or even verse, need a whole sentence to itself. Here is an example, not the most extreme from 'The Wreck of the Deutschland.' The subject is Christ:—

> I admire thee, master of the tides,
> Of the Yore-flood, of the year's fall;
> The recurb and the recovery of the gulf's sides,
> The girth of it and the wharf of it and the wall;
> Stanching, quenching ocean of a motionable mind;
> Ground of being, and granite of it; past all
>   Grasp God, throned behind
>
> Death with a sovereignty that heeds but hides,
>   bodes but abides.

In Hopkins's poetry words become independent, as if they were whole sentences; they bang in one after another; and this independence affects the metre. The sense emphasis of the single word is in the sound also. But the verse survives the great test of verse; it is best read aloud; then the very sense becomes clearer and anyone with an ear can hear that the method is not affectation but eagerness to find an expression for the depths of the mind, for things hardly yet consciously thought or felt. Hopkins was exploring not merely the instrument of verse, but the undiscovered regions of his own, and the universal, soul. And in this exploration he has the audacity and the good faith of the religious poet. He is like Crashaw in his extravagance and the manner in which he redeems it by good faith. His worst trick is that of passing from one word to another, like the Jewish admirer of Mr. Jaggers in *Great Expectations,* merely because they are alike in sound. This, at its worst, produces the effect almost of idiocy, of speech without sense and prolonged merely by echoes. It seems to be a bad habit, like

GERARD MANLEY HOPKINS

stuttering, except that he did not strive against it. Perhaps he
sought words that way, took shots at them, so to speak, and
enjoyed the process; but we cannot enjoy it; and yet we forgive him
all such faults and brush hastily through them in search of the
beauties that he makes us expect.

Seeking for pieces to quote, one rejects one after another,
however beautiful, because, by themselves, they are unprepared
for; and it is the whole book that prepares one for them, making the
extravagances seem not extravagant in the wild yet ordered world
of that book. But we cannot refrain from the end of the poem with
the title: "That Nature is a Heraclitean fire and of the comfort of the
Resurrection." He speaks of the fleeting life of man:—

> Manshape, that shone
> Sheer off, disseveral, a star, death blots black out; nor mark
> Is any of him at all so stark
> But vastness blurs and time beats level. Enough! the Resurrection,
> A heart's-clarion! Away grief's gasping, joyless days, dejection,
> Across my foundering deck shone
> A beacon, an eternal beam. Flesh fade, and mortal trash
> Fall to the residuary worm; world's wildfire, leave but ash;
> In a flash, at a trumpet crash,
> I am all at once what Christ is, since he was what I am, and
> This Jack, joke, poor potsherd, patch, matchwood, immortal
> diamond,
> Is immortal diamond.

There are examples of his faults, wilfully displayed: but to us, at
least, in the climax of that poem they seem no longer faults. His
passion strikes sparks out of the hard, flinty words. It is a fierce
utterance of belief fiercely won. At least it could not be said better
in other words: and that is the test of all writing. . . .

. . . But the whole book thrills with spirit, a spirit that does not
disdain sense but heightens it. The poems are crowded with objects
sharply cut, and with sounds no less sharp and clashing; you fight
your way through the verses, yet they draw you on. There is
beauty everywhere without luxury, the beauty that seems to come
of painful intense watching, the utter, disinterested delight of one
who sees another world, not through, but in this one. It is as if he
heard everywhere a music too difficult, because too beautiful, for
our ears and noted down what he could catch of it; authentic
fragments that we trust even when they bewilder us.

14. Theodore Maynard, 'The Artist as Hero', *New Witness*

24 January 1919, pp. 259–60

Theodore Maynard was born in 1890 of English parents in India, became a Roman Catholic in 1913, and from 1920 taught at American Catholic universities. His first book of poems, introduced by Chesterton, appeared in 1915. Both in *Our Best Poets* (1924) and *Commonweal* (2 August 1935) Maynard continued to show cautious enthusiasm for Hopkins.

The *New Witness*, a newspaper edited by G.K. Chesterton, with a strong interest in social reform, was published from 1912 to 1922 (later revived as *G.K.'s Weekly:* see No. 85).

Heroism may be defined as the refusal of the path of least resistance. For the soldier that path is the one that leads away from the battle, while courage calls a man to hold his ground or to charge the enemy. To the same rejection of easy things, though to heroism in another field—that of life rather than of death—the saint is girded. He must leave comfort and security, compromise and prudence, for the arduous following of his Lord. When a highly sensitive poet, Gerard Manley Hopkins, became a Jesuit at the age of 24, he accepted a threefold heroism as his vocation. He did not leave the cloisters of Oxford for the cloisters of a monastery, but for a camp and the rigid military life of the most rigid and military of religious orders. We do not know enough about his spiritual experiences to assert his heroism here, but after what has been shown to us of his capacity for decision, of his ruthless self discipline and of his agonies as an artist, it must be supposed that nothing less than an intolerable virtue would be tolerable to his strong and courageous soul. The man who burnt his poems upon joining the Society of Jesus—it could only have been to emphasise his renunciation; the poet, who, when he began writing again, reserved his poetry, a passionate secret, for the eyes of a couple of friends; the artist whose art was born in torments must have possessed the virtues of the soldier and of the saint.

I can think of Gerard Hopkins under no other figure than that of the flagellant of song. There was more than the ordinary mortification, the asceticism necessary to art in his making of poetry. Other men might save their souls in other ways, but he must draw blood. Sidney Smith once told somebody that Rogers (I think it was) had just been delivered of a couplet and would, in consequence, be confined to bed for a fortnight. I feel, in reading Father Hopkins' poems, as if every word had been born in anguish and had awoken with a cry.

The modern poets, who attempt to invent new verse forms or rhythms, generally succeed because they attempt so little. In their case, a mountain is in travail with a mouse. They find that English rhymes are limited in number, so declare that the absence of rhyme is a vast improvement. Strict metres are too much trouble, so bad prose must be chopped up into arbitrary lengths and called verse. But with Hopkins it was otherwise. His carefully concealed sonnets (none of his work was published in his lifetime) with their amazing intricacies are the result of the toils and tortures of a giant. A shy mid-Victorian priest, writing while Tennyson, Swinburne and Patmore led their various schools, was more modern than the most freakish modern would dare to be. Ezra Pound is stale set beside this poet who has been dead for thirty years. Many of our clever Georgians have done their best to invent metrical novelties, but their wildest work seems tame when we read Hopkins. He is the last word in technical development.

To say this, however, is not to give Gerard Hopkins unqualified praise. His style has its own original beauty, but it is a style no one should use again. The lyric gold is there, but as Coventry Patmore said, 'it has the effect of pure gold imbedded in masses of impracticable quartz'.[1] Mr Bridges, in his editorial notes, dwells at some length upon his friend's faults, his 'artistic wantonness' and his artistic eccentricity. These, says he, 'a reader must have courage to face, and must in some measure condone before he can discover the great beauties'. The grammatical skeleton is often absent from the body, whose spirit goes soaring up to the seventh heaven; the thoughts and words are packed too tightly into a line (too little sawdust is as bad as too much); and the oddities of rhyme and rhythm are sometimes repellently ugly. Here, for instance, are the first two stanzas of 'The Bugler's First Communion':

> A bugler boy from barrack (it is over the hill
> There)—boy bugler, born, he tells me, of Irish
>   Mother to an English sire (he
> Shares their best gifts surely, fall how things will),
>
> This very, very day came down to us after a boon he on
> My late being there begged of me, overflowing
>   Boon in my bestowing,
> Came, I, say, this day to it—to a First Communion.

Boon he on and *Communion* are bad enough, but what shall we say to the middle rhymes of the preceding stanza? '*Irish*' and '*Sire he sh-ares*,' are, I think, the worst example that can be found of ingenious barbarism in English verse. And then the poem goes on finely, though obscurely:

> Frowning and forefending angel-warder
> Squander the hell-rook ranks sally to molest him;
>   March, kind comrade, abreast him;
> Dress his days to a dexterous and starlight order.

Always obscure, Hopkins' simplest things are nearly as difficult as Browning's most complex. Browning's obscurity is generally due to the fact that one has to infer the whole story from the half that is told. 'My Last Duchess' is only difficult because there is no introduction to the speaker's remarks, and this poem is typical of Browning, being otherwise perfectly clear and direct. But I defy anyone to make head or tale of some of Hopkins' poetry— 'Spelt from Sibyl's Leaves,' or 'Tom's Garland.' Even Mr. Bridges and Canon Dixon, the poet's only literary intimates, had to confess themselves beaten by the last. Whereupon Father Hopkins wrote explaining it, concluding with the cry, 'O once explained, how clear it all is!' He probably thought it was!

Now and then, however, the poet managed to be comparatively intelligible. 'The May Magnificent,' [*sic*] 'The Habit of Perfection,' 'Morning, Midday and Evening Sacrifice,' 'The Blessed Virgin compared to the Air we Breathe,' and the sonnet on Patience, all exquisite, can be understood by those who take a very little trouble to read carefully. Even 'The Wreck of the Deutschland,' which the Poet Laureate says is 'like a great dragon folded in the gate to forbid all entrance,' can be overcome by the stout heart. Hopkins' obscurity was never an affectation, for his most impassioned work is usually his most difficult. 'Hurrahing in Harvest' was, we are told by the author, 'the outcome of half an-hour of extreme enthusiasm as I walked home alone one day from fishing in the Elwy'. The ecstatic note is in it, but the 'hurrah' is set to highly complex music.

One could go on pointing out Hopkins' defects, and the obscurity which must be as bad as a defect to all but a few readers. It is much more important to point out that there are great beauties in poems where any fool can find flaws. Perhaps this can best be done by quoting (out of many that could and should be quoted) this wonderful sonnet:—

[Quotes 'The Windhover',]

'The roll, the rise, the carol, the creation' do, like the music of Father Hopkins' thrush, 'rinse and wring the ear!' At last, after many years, during which all that we had of the poet were a few pieces included in Mr. Miles' *Anthology of Nineteenth Century Poetry,*' and a selection of them in Canon Beeching's *Lyra Sacra,* Gerard Manley Hopkins has his fitting memorial. We are already deeply indebted to Mr. Robert Bridges for his making known to us several admirable, though unfamed poets, but the greatest benefit he has conferred upon us is the opening to the world, by the publication of this book, of so rich a legacy of imperishable song.

NOTE

1 See *ante,* p. 59.

15. Michael Henry, 'The Book of the Week: Sweet Discord', *Everyman*

8 February 1919, pp. 416–17

... The Laureate was Hopkins's constant friend and the custodian of most of his work as it was completed. Only a poet could have discharged the trust with the unobtrusive completeness that makes this edition a final one. The critic must be conscious that a master has been before him with his task when he turns to the Editor's modest 'Preface to Notes' on the Poems, and learns thus in what spirit the valuation of Hopkins's achievement must be attempted.

[Quotes from 'There are definite faults' to 'part of his intention', see *ante*, p. 78.]

This frank, lucid, and just summary makes appreciation easy. Mr. Bridges notes that as a schoolboy Hopkins was writing prize-poems under the influence of Keats. In acuteness of physical perception he could sometimes draw close to this great model, and not stay far behind in the power of rendering the physical, and especially the visual impression, in words. It is not only the well-known stanza of 'The Habit of Perfection' (1866):—

> Palate, the hutch of tasty lust,
> Desire not to be rinsed with wine:
> The can must be so sweet, the crust
> So sweet that come in fasts divine!—

that would make one attend to its author. There is the phrase four lines above, 'Be shelléd, eyes, with double dark,' sufficient to show, if we had nothing else of him, that he knew the way to fetch a perfect comparison for the half-opaque, half-translucent oval which can make the windows of a face the most beautiful part of its design. He was full of such images, and he only falls short of the highest rank, the absolute success of, say,

> Plump the hazel shells
> With a sweet kernel.

because his expression does not reach identity with his conceptions, and leaves something intractable and obstinate to perplex us when we hover on the verge of complete satisfaction. But how near he comes to it, with the invocation 'to the dappled-with-damson west' ('dapple' a very favourite word which led him ultimately to coin a verb, 'to betweenpie,' the occasion of an admirable note by his Editor); with 'Look! March-bloom, like on mealed-with-yellow sallows!'; with 'crush-silk poppies aflash'; with 'Spring,' when

Thrush
Through the echoing timber does so rinse and wring
The ear, it strikes like lightning to hear him sing;

or with 'The May Magnificat':—

> When drop-of-blood-and-foam-dapple
> Bloom lights the orchard-apple,
> And thicket and thorp are merry
> With silver-surféd cherry.

An ecstatic and difficult poet, like the men of the seventeenth century whose life centered in religion, he pours forth knowledge of nature in the sestet of 'Hurrahing in Harvest' (1877), 'the outcome of half an hour of extreme enthusiasm as I walked home alone one day from fishing in the Elwy':

> These things, these things were here and but the beholder
> Wanting; which two when they once meet,
> The heart rears wings bold and bolder
> And hurls for him, O half hurls earth for him off under his feet.

Man, too, if he delights him not, fills him with the passion of the priest, and he felt like Mr. Housman some peculiar fascination in the scarlet coat which used to symbolise the soldier. 'The Bugler's First Communion' has an intensity which I must own to finding repellent; but he could indict a whole country with moderation:—

> Lovely the woods, waters, meadows, combes, vales,
> All the air things wear that build this world of Wales;
> Only the inmate does not correspond:
> God, lover of souls, swaying considerate scales,
> Complete Thy creature dear O where it fails
> Being mighty a master, being a father and fond. ...

16. L.I. Guiney, 'Gerard Hopkins: A Recovered Poet', *Month*

March 1919, pp. 205ff

Louise Imogen Guiney (1861–1920), b. Boston, came to England 1889, and gained a reputation in Catholic circles as an essayist and poet. She introduced Katherine Brégy to the poetry of Hopkins (see No. 4). Her selection of *Recusant Poets*, in co-operation with Fr Geoffrey Bliss SJ (see No. 19) was not published until 1938.

...Not since Francis Thompson have we had so disturbing, debatable, and compelling a poet. This vocabulary is almost purely Saxon, against that of the 'Latinate Englishman'; and this Muse is for harmony and for sculptural effect rather than for symbolism and for Catholic philosophy. Let there be no doubt about the worth of Father Hopkins' literary work. It has winged daring, originality, durable texture, and the priceless excellence of fixing itself in the reader's mind. The editor realizes this fully; and Father Hopkins, not out of egoism, but from sheer humorous detachment, seems also to have known it well. It is abundantly clear, then, that we all owe Dr. Bridges a debt of profound gratitude. He, with the late Canon Dixon, was Father Hopkins' chief confidant and wisest critic; and during just a quarter-century he has tentatively and sparingly, and with the nicest discretion, given some among his friend's verses to anthologies, and created for them the patrician public which will welcome them to-day. Enviable indeed are the modern men of letters who, with their own differentiated achievement, bring in also to the granaries of the future the sheaves of those reapers who have not lived to see the harvest. Mr. Bullen has salvaged his heart-delighting Campion; the late Mr. Dobell brought in, alive, the lyric musings of buried Traherne; Mr. Meynell's ever-honourable burden is nothing less than Francis Thompson; and last, in point of time, comes Dr. Bridges, an artist like few, heaping up with his own high spoils the golden young genius of Digby Dolben, and the real and noble glories of Gerard Hopkins. Of these two, lost to him long ago, he has become in some sort, the father and the angel; his sympathy with them is perfect, except indeed (not without a sigh can it be said!) where they need it most fully, and would feel it most deeply: in the definite religious idealism which was to them compass and star, life-breath and heart's blood. Dr. Bridges' annotation goes all awry there; little mists and breezes of complete misunderstanding flicker then between him and the text; and he cannot let the text stand without protests: may one be pardoned for calling them protests of the most irrelevant unwisdom? *Ma guarda e passa.* Let it be forgiven, in view of his spiritual works of mercy, not least of which is the beautiful legacy to us which this new book is and ever must be.

The book will breed debate. To quote a line from its maker,

All things counter, original, spare, strange

convene in it. Nothing is derivative: neither subject, treatment, means nor ends. From a wonderfully-formed and most attractive youthful diction which had here and there something in common with Giles Fletcher, Marvell, or Keats, Father Hopkins, after a seven years' abstention from the Muse, broke out and away into an untrammelled imagery, an uncharted metrism, a concentrated speech of such opulence and yet of such severest asceticism as English poetry had never known together, hardly had known at all separately, in any conspicuous degree. Students of prosody, and especially practitioners of it, fellow-craftsmen, will find here nuts to crack and bones to gnaw. Browning Societies, inured to long tunnels, or even super-alert Societies for Psychical Research, will lose their way, whatever lanterns they carry. Those characteristics of Father Hopkins which his editor calls oddity and obscurity, are admirably and fairly dealt with in the notes; and the challenged author, judging from the extracts from his letters, was aware of his singularities, and often rose with great spirit and humour to the defence of them....

Father Hopkins wrote a scientific proem to go with his book whenever it should be published; it stands first here, in place of a memoir, and defines his technical methods and aims. In this prelude, like Adam in Eden, he names things never named before which yet existed before him. His schemes are worthy of the closest attention. Running, rocking and falling rhythms; paeonic and counterpointed rhythms; 'sprung rhythm, the most natural of things,'—here they are in full play, with their stresses and 'rove-overs' and 'outridings,' all based on traditional trochee or dactyl, carried forward with meticulous industry and amazing art, and shot through and through with the very virtuosity of verbal melody. He would fill every stanza, Debussy-like, with accent, slur, pause, tie, syncopation: the editor has sagaciously kept the printers from following out the score as a whole. In the argument of the preface there is but one flaw. Fr. Hopkins reminds us that as in Greek and Latin verse, much old English verse is in his 'sprung rhythm,' but that 'it has, in fact, ceased to be used since the Elizabethan age, Greene being the last writer who can be said to have recognized it. For perhaps there was not, down to our days, a single even short poem in English in which sprung rhythm is employed, not for single effects or in fixed places, but as the governing principle of the scansion. I say this because the contrary has been asserted: if it is otherwise the poem should be cited.' Sprung rhythm, let it be understood, is a sequence of regular feet of from one to four syllables, using 'any number of weak or slack syllables for particular effects,' so that 'feet are assumed to be equally long or strong, and their seeming inequality is made up by pause or stressing.' Well, there is no doubt whatever that Fr. Hopkins has carried this theory into triumphant exemplification; he leaves a reader breathless, as breathless as he describes himself when watching the flight of the windhover, 'at the achieve of, the mastery of the thing'; and in that one particular it may be said that he leaves much of antiquity, and all the Elizabethans, and the vers-libres of our contemporary French and English far behind. But Greene, who died in 1592, was by no means 'the last writer' in this vein. How can it have escaped so keen a scholar that Donne, who did not die until 1631, Donne, who, as Mr. Gosse says, 'desired to develope the orchestral possibilities of English verse,' roves and revels and radiates in sprung rhythm?...

[Quotes passages from Donne.]

Has not each of these the very trick and fashion of Gerard Hopkins's formulated song? He was, in fact, a musician and a draughtsman of no mean kind: and he carried over into creative literature the hand skilled in melody and in design. Melody and design: these are his delight and his attainment. He aims deliberately at getting his pattern recognized; he sets plain to the eye 'what I am in the habit of calling *inscape* in poetry.' He also calls the silent lonely reader away from his task. He would never be looked at, only listened to. 'Read me with the ears, as I always wish to be read.' The ideal of this acutely conscious modern mind (though he does not phrase it thus) is declamation to the harp, the original purpose of lyric, alive to-day in the primitive Judaic and Gaelic corners of the world. So in some degree accepted and used, how well does Gerard Hopkins's heartfelt unique art get its justification! Gets it over against and despite of the most desperate difficulties confronting the mere reader. The very inversions whch serve for emphasis or for euphony, and for nothing else known to man, the very elisions which toss and gore the principles of English grammar, turn, in a chant, to 'woodnotes wild.' Everything in this astonishing book is singable as its Elizabethan equivalent would by nature be: from that early lilt of the saddened mermaidens who 'in a half-circle watched the sun,' and the Leaden Echo and the Golden Echo of 'Saint Winefride's Well' (spraying like a score of slenderest fountains from that powerful water), to the trampling agonies of the great sonnets where

> O the mind, mind has mountains: cliffs of fall
> Frightful, sheer, no-man-fathomed!

From end to end, in short, Gerard Hopkins is the most choral of English poets. Not that he invariably needs, as it were, transposition. As his editor does not fail to point out, in dealing with many disconcerting and some intolerable 'freaks,' he can be absolute master of 'simple and straight-forward rhyme.' In

> Thee, God, I come from, to Thee go.

one of the successful fragments, there are six stanzas, the sixth of which may be counted out as not structurally in the sequence; of the hundred and twenty-three words remaining, there are only fifteen which are not monosyllables, and the whole hymn is the perfection of directness and simplicity.

But it is time to dip into the verse itself, and put rumours of high quality to the proof. A quite random dip, to any instructed and sensitive explorer, is enough. The sparkle, the authentic tang of those least but crucial things, adjectives, here make instant appeal.

'Groundlong babyhood'; 'elmy England'; 'wiry and white-fiery and whirlwind-swivellèd snow': these are some of them. The 'lovely behaviour' of 'silk-sack clouds'; the 'bright boroughs' and 'circle-citadels' of the stars; 'heaven-gravel' flung by 'hustling ropes of hail'; 'mazy sands all water-wattled'; the swimming trout's 'rose moles all in stipple'; and (even less possible to forget)

> Those gold nails and their gay links that hang along a lime;

the èddying spume of the black pool, 'a wind puff bonnet of fawn froth'; the glen of Inversnaid where

> Degged with dew, dappled with dew
> Are the groins of the braes that the brook treads through;

and the 'burl' and 'buck' of the angry wave; the imperilled ship where

> —inboard seas run swirling and hawling,
> The rash smart sloggering brine;

(how it still bangs itself, that brine, into one's throat and nostrils here ashore!)—when did Shelley, when did Tennyson, when did Swinburne, the English poets most at home with air, landscape, ocean, give diviner report of the thing seen? In the poets' Kingdom of Nature this poet too is supreme.

We have seen Fr. Hopkins's preoccupation with water, which Thales called the fairest and first of things, and which in every land, all through the centuries, has been written about and hallowed by human genius. But of no equally familiar subject is he afraid. He can describe even a skylark, a 'dare-gale skylark' with a 'new-skeinèd score,' and

> hear him ascend,
> In crisps of curl off wild winch whirl and pour
> And pelt music, till none's left to spill nor spend!

Highly artificial as is this whole passage, one is not sure that it does not outdo Wordsworth and Meredith and even Shelley in having within it a sort of delirium cognate to that spiralling rapture, inhaled and exhaled, which is not, properly speaking, a bird's song at all. In Fr. Hopkins's spring weather,

> magic cuckoo-call
> Caps, clears, and clinches all;

and the thrush

> Through the echoing timber does so rinse and wring
> The ear, it strikes like lightnings to hear him sing.

Any comment on the felicity of such lines is superfluous.

   With the same ease with which he pictures a storm at sea, Fr. Hopkins can give us the sweetest and stillest prospect of Oxford,

> Cuckoo-echoing, bell-swarmed...river-rounded,

where old romance, and the 'rural keeping, folk, flocks and flowers' still help 'country and town' to be 'coped and poisèd powers'; but his truth carries him on to mention 'a base and brickish skirt' in 'graceless growth' (even in the 'eighties!) as threatening the 'grey beauty' so beloved. The opening of this sonnet, 'Duns Scotus's Oxford,' is such a miracle of congested wording and such another miracle of visual accuracy, sweeping a whole horizon,

> Towery city, and branchy between towers,

that it puts Arnold's 'Dreaming spires,' as a quotation, almost out of court at last. ...

17. Unsigned review, *Saturday Westminster Gazette*

8 March 1919, pp. 13–14

When Gerard Hopkins died in 1889 he was almost unknown save to a small circle of friends, among whom were Coventry Patmore and Robert Bridges. With both of these he shared an intense interest in the technique of poetry; a further bond of sympathy with Patmore being the ardent Catholic mysticism which inspired his religious verse. Patmore submitted to him all his later poems, receiving in exchange elaborate technical criticisms, which he usually accepted. Less fortunately for English literature, he also showed to Hopkins the mystical work called 'Sponsa Dei,' which he regarded as his masterpiece. Hopkins returned this to him with the words, 'That's telling secrets'; and Patmore immediately destroyed the manuscript.

This strange episode has more than a historical importance. It indicates the character of Hopkins's mysticism, his reticence, and his strong temperamental opposition to the erotic symbols of spiritual communion in which Patmore took so great a delight. His own mystical passion, almost certainly more profound and more ardent, is coloured by a deep consciousness of the greatness and terror of that Power which he feels in closest contact with his soul; so that, where Patmore aspires to intimacy and exclaims that he 'cannot dare to be reverent,' Hopkins is overwhelmed with adoration and dread:

[Quotes 'The Wreck of the Deutschland', verses 1 and 2.]

This solemn rapture and awe is one characteristic note of his mysticism. The other, not unconnected with it, is the avoidance of human imagery, the tendency to escape from the personal to the spatial. A natural Platonist, it is plain that he discovers God most easily through the beauty and life of the physical universe: Christ behind 'the piece-bright paling' of the stars, the Holy Ghost brooding on 'the bent world's brink' at dawn, even Mary in the 'world-mothering air.' This mood, this vision, appears again and again: because of it, for him, 'There lives the dearest freshness deep down things.'

> I walk, I lift up, I lift up heart, eyes
> Down all that glory in the heavens to glean our Saviour,

Or again, as in the opening of his best-known sonnet:

> The world is charged with the grandeur of God.
> It will flame out, like shining from shook foil.

He found this grandeur everywhere; not least in the concrete actual and ordinary—the 'brute beauty and valour' of the windhover, the muscles of the ploughman, the soldier's dedicated life—for he loved best vivid and energetic beauty, and the manly virtues of active types:

> ...Christ plays in ten thousand places,
> Lovely in limbs, and lovely in eyes not his.

Nature he worshipped with the peculiar intensity of the English poets; and, finding through her perpetual intimations of spirit, felt no need for imaginative escape. We see in his correspondence with Patmore the deep contempt which he felt for the 'day dreams and fairy tales' of romantic poetry. Mysticism meant for him, as it has always done for true mystics, an intensification, not a denial, of life. It gave him that child-like freshness of delight, that undimmed wonder when confronted by the world's vitality and loveliness, with which he infects us as we read his poems:

> Look at the stars! look, look up at the skies!
> O look at all the fire-folk sitting in the air!
> The bright boroughs, the circle-citadels there!

or, at the other end of the scale of perception, made him thank God for 'dappled things':

> Landscape plotted and pieced—fold, fallow, and plough;
> And all trades, their gear and tackle and trim.
> All things counter, original, spare, strange;
> Whatever is fickle, freckled (who knows how?)
> With swift, slow; sweet, sour; adazzle, dim;
> He fathers-forth whose beauty is past change:
> Praise him.

The technical side of Hopkins's poetry, which is of great interest to students of prosody and was his own chief preoccupation, cannot be discussed here. He was a skilled and daring metrical experimenter, though often betrayed by his own theories into errors of style which seriously interfere with our enjoyment, sometimes even our comprehension, of his poems. Those who are interested in this aspect of his genius will find his system fully discussed in the prefatory essay and in Dr. Bridges's notes; and demonstrated, both for good and evil, in numerous pieces which are here published for the first time.

During the thirty years which have passed since Gerard Hopkins's death he has been known only through the few poems included in Miles's *Poets and Poetry of the Century* and other anthologies. These served to attract many admirers; but it has been impossible for students of poetry to estimate the value of his work as a whole. The Poet Laureate, who now at last publishes from manuscripts in his own possession the bulk of Hopkins's mature work, observes in a dedicatory sonnet that so far these creations of his friend's genius have 'lain coy in his home'; but are now loosed upon the world to discountenance, by their loftier flights, the 'chaffinch flock' of contemporary poets. There may, of course, be good reason why it was held necessary to reserve for this long period the most important work of a distinguished writer; but there can surely be none for its publication in an incomplete form. It is true that Hopkins's poetry was extremely uneven; but the mass of it is so small, and its character is so original, that none can be spared from what is doubtless intended to be the definitive edition of his text. Dr. Bridges, however, has felt that it lay within his discretion to omit poems on two scores: first, that of immaturity; secondly, that of inferiority. An unfortunate want of sympathy with his friend's religious convictions has led him to apply this principle in a rather curious way. Under the head of immaturity he omits a number of religious pieces written between 1862 and 1868, including the beautiful 'Barnfloor and Winepress,' which was printed in Beeching's *Lyra Sacra*. Even were it correct to dismiss this poem and its like as 'religious verses worked in George Herbert's manner,' still they would be important as showing the lines along which Hopkins's genius first developed.

The poems omitted as inferior are also devotional in type. One of them, 'Rosa Mystica', was included in Shipley's *Carmina Mariana*. These pieces have long been favourites with Roman Catholic readers; of whom the Poet Laureate rather unkindly observes that 'it is natural that they should, as some of them openly state they do, prefer the poems that I am rejecting to those which I print, ... but since their purpose is alien to mine I regret that I am unable to indulge it.' No serious critic will class these omitted pieces with Hopkins's best work. Nevertheless they do represent a distinct side of his restricted literary output, and ought certainly to have their place among his collected poems. A less important but exceedingly irritating feature of Dr. Bridges's editorial methods is the total absence of any index of titles or of first lines.

18. Edward Shanks, unsigned review, 'The Prophet Unveiled', *New Statesman*

15 March 1919, p. 530

The author (see Dunne, *Hopkins Bibliography*) was Edward Shanks (1892–1953), an established poet at this date and winner of the Hawthornden Prize for Imaginative Literature, 1919. Assistant-editor of the *London Mercury* 1919–22, he was attacked, along with its editor Sir John Squire, in Osbert Sitwell's anti-Georgian *Jolly Old Squire* (1922).

It is now some thirty years since the death of Father Gerard Hopkins; and, during this time, the reluctance of Mr. Bridges to publish his manuscripts has turned him into a sort of veiled prophet, an oracle whence mysterious replies are obtained by the hierophants of prosody for the confusion of the unelect. The few pieces that appeared in anthologies or were quoted by writers who had access to his works were strange enough; and the reports of his prosodical theory and practice which gained currency were stranger still. Nevertheless, it was not unnatural that, when the veil was withdrawn, most readers should expect something a little less extraordinary than rumour had indicated. But these moderate expectations were for once below the mark. Father Hopkins's poetry is to eye, ear and mind the strangest that has been published in England—the poetry of Mr. Doughty not excepted—in modern times. The hierophants were right; and their use of Hopkins to disconcert the simple persons who imagine that prosody, deeply considered, is as easy a matter as the enjoyment of its effects was perfectly justified.

Mr. Bridges does not pretend that Hopkins is a perfectly straightforward poet, or even that his peculiarities, properly understood, are merits:

[Quotes from Bridges's Preface, 'There are definite faults' to 'part of his intention', *ante*, p. 78.]

Hopkins remarks himself, somewhat naively, in a letter:

No doubt my poetry errs on the side of oddness.... But as air, melody, is what strikes me most of all in music and design in painting, so design-pattern, or what I am in the habit of calling *inscape*, is what I above all aim at in poetry. Now it is the virtue of design, pattern, or inscape to be distinctive, and it is the vice of distinctiveness to become queer.[1]

This passage is disarmingly characteristic: the poet cannot even designate the quality which tends to queerness without using to describe it a word itself gratuitously queer. And of the queerness of his work, at first sight, before any attempt be made to analyse it, there can be no doubt. We quote at this point, for introduction, a specimen which is by no means extreme:

[Quotes first eight lines of 'Felix Randal'.]

The metrical scheme of this poem is described by Mr. Bridges on the authority of the author in the following words: 'Sonnet: sprung and outriding rhythm; six-foot lines.' But these strange terms are not made much clearer by the preface in which the poet elucidated them. Here he explains that Running Rhythm is 'the common rhythm in English use' and is measured by feet, each having a stress and one or two additional syllables called the Slack. He adds that poems in this rhythm may be 'counterpointed' by substituting here and there a new arrangement of feet for that already established, so that the ear perceives two rhythms at once. This is comprehensible, even if the truth of the assertions be disputed. But Hopkins's definition of Sprung Rhythm, which is measured by feet of one stress and containing ordinarily up to three 'slack' syllables and for particular effects as many as may be desired, is much more difficult to follow. When he adds that Sprung Rhythm has two licences, one rests (which again is comprehensible), the other *hangers* or *outrides*, the reader might be excused for being puzzled. *Hangers*, he says, are

one, two, or three slack syllables added to a foot, and not counting in the nominal scanning. They are so-called because they seem to hang below the line or ride forward or backward from it in another dimension than the line itself, according to a principle needless to explain here.[2]

We confess frankly that we do not follow this explanation, that it has not helped us to understand the scansion of 'Felix Randal', and that we have nowhere succeeded with certainty in identifying a hanger. The darkness is made more obscure by the fact that Mr. Bridges has not reproduced the peculiar signs which Hopkins adopted to indicate these and other phenomena.

But many excellent poets have had strange or eccentric prosodical theories, which have not injured their work and which it has not been necessary for their readers to understand. The likelihood here is that a good many readers will identify Father Hopkins with this class and will imagine that only an effort to master his curious metrical system is necessary before gaining access to the great beauties which Mr. Bridges proclaims in his works. We are of opinion, however, that this is not the case. Hopkins's rhythmical peculiarity was only one expression of a general and pervading eccentricity. His treatment of English syntax was surprising beyond measure, as when he wrote:

> Squander the hell-rook ranks sally to molest him,

and meant the word 'that' to be understood before the fifth word of the line. His adjectives are commonly so chosen that, not only at the first reading but also at the tenth or twentieth, they distract the mind altogether from their meaning by their strangeness. 'Silk-sack clouds,' 'azurous hung hills... majestic as a stallion stalwart, very-violet-sweet,' 'mild night's blear-all black' and the like are traps for the attention, not aids to visualisation.

There is no doubt that the aim of his rhythmical innovations and experiments, whether conscious or not, was to approach as nearly as possible to the effect of music. This was responsible for alliterations, assonances, jingles and repetitions which would have delighted the heart of the late lamented Max Nordau.[3] Sometimes it has its own curious success, as in the conclusion of 'The Leaden Echo':

[Quotes last eight lines.]

Sometimes, as in 'Binsey Poplars,' it entrapped the poet into what perhaps he did not recognise as a very close resemblance to the choruses of musical comedy:

> Ten or twelve, only ten or twelve
> Strokes of havoc unselve
>   The sweet especial scene,
> Rural scene, a rural scene,
> Sweet especial rural scene.

In the first of these instances a certain effect was achieved. In the second Hopkins showed that he did not realise that words, having meanings, cannot be used for musical purposes without reference to those meanings; and here his common-sense and his sense of humour were clearly at fault. In both cases it was music at which he aimed; and this is perhaps the most consistent aim discoverable in his work. But the aim unfortunately does not guarantee the capacity; and it cannot be said that Hopkins's ear for sound and sense of rhythm were invariably impeccable.

Would he, as he himself hoped, have acquired in time 'a more balanced and Miltonic style'? It seems improbable: for his last poems have the same eccentricities and obscurities as those of earlier date. Will English readers, as Mr. Bridges hopes, surmount the difficulties which Hopkins opposes to them and become free of the beauties that do undoubtedly exist in his work? This too seems improbable. The beauties are not a sweet kernel with a rough husk. They are scattered and they are never far from extravagant uglinesses. A perfect line is exceedingly rare; and a poem which is good as a whole, even in spite of faults, is hard to discover. It seems more likely that a few poets will discover, absorb and render again the little which Hopkins had to offer to English verse, either in new rhythms or the free and vigorous use of epithet. They perhaps will extract the gold from the quartz and put it into circulation. It is too rare and too difficult to work for the ordinary reader to make much of it.

NOTES

1 Bridges's Preface, *ante*, p. 78.
2 Author's Preface, *Poems of Hopkins*, 4th edn, p. 48.
3 (1849–1923) Austrian writer and philosopher.

19. Fr Geoffrey Bliss, unsigned review, *Tablet*

5 April 1919, pp. 420–2

The author of this lengthy and discriminating article was Fr Geoffrey Bliss, SJ (1874–1952), an ex-pupil of Stonyhurst and a teacher in Jesuit schools, who later became editor of a devotional magazine. His obituary (*Our Dead*, Manresa Press, 1954–6, p. 336) described him as a poet 'of no mean order' and a 'discerning critic' with a special interest in Hopkins, but he published little. See also No. 89.

The *Tablet* had been an important Catholic weekly since the previous century.

The poems of Gerard Manley Hopkins, S.J., have had to wait long for publication. It may be longer still before the public at large are likely to realize the value of the slender volume now presented to them, though the beauty of its printing and the laboured and loving care of the editing will be conceded by everyone. All poets, however, even if the commendation of their Laureate were lacking, must be interested in this book. For Hopkins was one of those poets who hold high and conscious ideas on the craftsmanship of their art. He had mighty belief in the power of words—in the power of the *sound* of words; and strong faith has here beaten a way to very remarkable achievement.

Mr. Bridges labels these poems not altogether unjustly (despite his capital letters, of which he is more than chary in the text) with the two words Oddity and Obscurity. The obscurity is nearly always verbal, and usually resolvable when the reader will give a little patience to the study of his author's style. Those, and there are numbers about, who consider clearness of meaning at a glance to be an essential mark of all good poetry, had better not buy this book even if they have twelve-and-sixpence to throw away on 124 pages of delightful paper! Yet poetry, which attempts to speak the deepest thoughts of the soul, will surely be obscure at times, and not verbally alone; if some fancies can break through language and escape, others will leave but gold feathers in the net of words.

As to oddity, new things are apt to seem odd at first, and this poetry is a new poetry. It is new in this, that it attempts to do continuously what other poets have been content to achieve by rare moments, and in virtue of what must generally seem to the poet a kind of miraculous luck—I mean that entire 'wedding of the term to its import,' not only by way of the term's notation and connotation in meaning, but also by way of its very sound and cadence. This identity of sound and sense all poets compass, seemingly unawares, with greater or less frequency; Hopkins believed that they should aim at it as a constant element of their verse. Does he justify his belief in this book? Not fully, of course. Mr. Bridges wrote of his work in Miles' *Poets of the Century* that it attempted 'an unattainable perfection of language.' The phrase is disheartening from such a master-craftsman, but we think that Hopkins has made the beginning of a breach in the walls of the impossible. Let it be for others to break through.

The newness, then, of this poetry is not the newness of the 'futurists' in painting; not a break with established canons, but rather a new degree of fidelity to their precepts, a new faith in the possibility of such close adherence. And it is the same with the means here employed. The author's preface sets forth a somewhat elaborate justification of his metrical method which will not, we think, be of any great help to the reader. That method might be expressed roughly as a precise counting of the *stressed* syllables in each line, while allowing the others to take care of themselves. Thus one line will consist almost alone of the prescribed number of accented syllables, while in the next these will be largely outnumbered by syllables that are not accented. And the stresses may come anywhere in the line, boldly emphasising its beginning, scattered equally through it, or massed towards its close. Such lines can nearly always be analysed into an orthodox succession of mixed iambs and anapaests (or alternatively of trochees and dactyls) if you will allow pauses when necessary to take the place of the unaccented portion of a foot. There is nothing very new in this. As applied to blank verse, at any rate, the beginnings of it are at least as old as Shakespeare. And, of course, Father Gerard Hopkins does not really allow the non-stressed syllables 'to take care of themselves.' Rather he marshals them with most meticulous and sensitive art to endow his line with emphasis, or speed, or hesitation, or airiness, or clamour.

The other devices, also, here displayed are but old devices used more freely than other poets have ventured; more freely and perhaps with a more conscious intention. Alliteration, for instance, called by someone an artful aid, is of the very texture of Hopkins' verse; but he employs it in no timid or secretive fashion, and with him it is no mere stringing of initial consonants; median syllables and vowels too, most of all, are compelled to the chime. This from a craftsman's point of view may well be the most interesting and fruitful of the author's experiments. For alliteration as a mere grace or trick is common in all writing, and may be found (as R.L. Stevenson has pointed out) in grave prose authors who will repudiate the charge with vigour till it is brought home to them. What comes so readily must have a deep, natural basis, and in the artist's hands should be capable of far elaboration.

> And flock-bells off the aerial
> Downs forefalls beat to the burial.

I hardly know anything in English literature more haunting to the ear than these lines from Hopkins' 'Loss of the Eurydice.' (The vessel foundered close in to the shore.) Here the alliteration might be described as a series of 'o' and 'e' (struck sharp at the beginning, and varied thereafter) with another, strictly subordinate, of dental-labials. One other example in lighter vein, and of less subtle texture—a breath of lime-tree blossom:

> When the air was sweet-and-sour of the flown fineflower of
> Those goldnails and their gaylinks that hang along a line.

Only a tinkle is intended; but note how skilfully the 'n's' are led from the outset to a crescendo at the close.

Of rhyme, again, Father Hopkins is a frank lover, and he is not content to rhyme only at the verse's end, but matches all convenient opportunities. Those assonances, too, and vowel-rhymes which more plodding workers are troubled to avoid he makes to serve his purpose. Here are two lines from a fragment titled 'Moonrise':

> I awoke in the Midsummer not to call night, in the white and
> walk of the morning:

The moon, dwindled and thinned to the fringe of a finger-nail
  held to the candle...

The first of these verses illustrates another characteristic of all
these poems, one which carries us a little beyond purely technical
matters. It is the readiness to make use of the suggestions conveyed
by words beyond what their bare meaning can carry. Who ever
heard of 'the white of the morning'? Yet readers of this line know
that they have seen it in its ghostliness; and 'walk' is even more
effective, if more elusive, in its suggestiveness of the silent oncome
of the light. Like a certain hero of dream-land Gerard Hopkins
works his words hard, but he 'pays them extra' in the revelation of
what they can be made to accomplish. He accomplishes much with
them because he is no rhetorician. He will have nothing to do with
a word simply because it is a fine-sounding word or a 'poetical'
word. Either Matthew Arnold or Pater said of Flaubert that with
him 'the search, the unwearied search, was quite simply and
honestly for the adjustment of word to meaning,' and it is the same
with Hopkins. No word is for him too homely or too outlandish if
it will help him, by what it means or by what it connotes, to
express his thought—and not his thought only, but something at
least of the emotion that goes with it, 'the fine delight that fathers
thought.'

With so many special preoccupations it is to be expected (though
not, perhaps, to be condoned) that the poet is impatient at times
under his art's more primary limitations of grammar and syntax—
that he jettisons relatives, banishes pronouns too far from their
principals, leaves prepositions a-dangle in mid-air, and shuts his
eyes to the plentiful ambiguities of accidence with which our
uninflected speech abounds. These faults make verbal obscurities
which require some little study to resolve and occasionally (to the
present writer, he confesses) yield no solution. It is evident, indeed,
from what has been said that this new poet—who died twenty-nine
years ago—makes large demands upon his readers; but a pioneer
can no otherwise. Doubtless the first writer of verse (or of prose,
for which came second?) was decried as a troublesome fellow who
could not say a plain thing in a plain way. Those who are content to
serve a brief apprenticeship to Hopkins will not judge wasted the
time required to gain acquaintance with the mystery (if such it
seem) of his craft.

For it is a fine spirit that dwells behind the arabesque-wrought tapestries of these poems, a sensitive and a strong soul wherein three devotions and delights are here revealed, their objects God and Man and Nature. All poets, of course, serve these shrines, but each in his own manner, and each with his special insight into their arcana. For this poet it is in God's *mastery*, his creator-hood, above all, that he finds at once terror and joy. Yet he has also a most intimate sense of God's fatherly tenderness, and can speak to Him with the direct simplicity of a son to an earthly father. In man it is, well, just humanity that he loves, its frailness, its beauty, the frailness of its beauty, so easily, so piteously brought to foulness and corruption. Yet this in no minor key. There is a most refreshing strength and manliness in this, the principal side of Hopkins' poetry; and his recurrent word is that the labile fairness of human things becomes immutable as diamonds if it is rendered to the Giver. In nature it was her pied raiment (his own adjective) that he loved best, her contrasts, her million-fold play of light and colour, gleam and gloom, sally and recovery: 'Glory be to God for dappled things!' It is a love that is reflected in the form of his poetry.

Lastly, we find here a trace of that pain of soul which poets must pay down for their vision and which in one so eager and so sensitive we should have divined had it found no record. These last sonnets, found among the papers of Father Hopkins after his death, are called 'terrible' by Mr. Bridges. But suffering is not terrible where it does not overcome. Here it was nobly vanquished. These poems discover (far wide of their author's aim) such qualities of courage and of humility and of idealism as are the makings of sanctity.

20. F.C. Moore, unsigned review, *Spectator*

10 May 1919, p. 598

According to information from the *Spectator* (March 1985) the author was F.C. Moore. Those reviewed along with Hopkins included Edward Thomas, Sassoon, and Newbolt, leading the writer to exclaim: 'How much excellent poetry has been written in an age when the verse form of expression is supposed to be at least obsolescent.' When he turned to Hopkins, however, he could only praise Bridges's editorship (Mellown claims that he had only read the Preface).

... The poems themselves, despite occasional flashes of the illuminating fire, are on the whole disappointing; they are too often needlessly obscure, harsh, and perverse. The metrical effects which Mr. Hopkins studied with such assiduity do not seem to us to be worth the pains bestowed on them; many of his verses have to be elaborately accented in order to give the reader the clue to the rhythm, and lyrics which do not sing themselves would, in our opinion at least, be better in prose.

Mellown suggests that this was written by one of the senior members of the University.

The first feeling of a reader on dipping into this book will probably be one of surprise; for these poems are almost all immediately incomprehensible, and in some cases strike the ear with a discordant defiance of verbal beauty actively unpleasant. But if a sense of the real poetical authority of Father Hopkins's editor lead him to explore more deeply, then, although he may remain unconverted, he cannot fail to be interested.

The author of these poems died in 1889, and for thirty years Mr. Bridges has kept this volume at his side, waiting for the psychological moment in which to publish it. Whether he has chosen that moment well may be doubted; for we are still afflicted, though less than we have been of late, with an intolerable deal of verse which is unintelligible through sheer indiscipline and carelessness. And the desultory reader might well confuse with these the work of a poet who is rather too much given to one form of discipline and to a too constrained selection. But Mr. Bridges will answer that this book is not for the desultory reader, but for the genuine lover of the beautiful, however hardly come by; he himself at any rate has so great a conviction of the ultimate beauty of these poems that he is at no pains to gloss over the real defects which conceal it.

These defects indeed force themselves upon us. Father Hopkins was a very careful student and inventor of unusual rhythms, and in his eagerness to exercise his powers in this direction he too often forgets that the highest art uses rhythm only as one of many aids to poetical beauty. The very fact that nearly all these rhythms need stressing in the text and explanation in the notes reveals their artificiality; the vision only too often is forced into and not expressed by them. It is true that these experiments will be greeted with great interest by rhythmical enthusiasts, but no poet of Father

Hopkins's quality should write only or chiefly for specialists. His use of rhyme, again, is not above criticism, and finds indeed no mercy at Mr. Bridges's hands: in places, it is true, he shows a real mastery of it, yet in others the rhymes are either in themselves harsh and even grotesque, or else mere obstructions to a metre which is intolerant of them.

But it is probably the obscurity of the poems which most provokes criticism, for it is this that goes farthest to destroy their beauty. This obscurity, the editor says, was not sufficiently realized by the poet himself; though we recollect one passage where he writes, referring to one of his sonnets, 'The sonnet (I say it snorting) aims at being intelligible': and we would suggest that thirty years' familiarity has reconciled the Laureate himself to it more than he realizes. The violent breaches of grammar and syntax, the strained artificial expression, the sense of labour almost everywhere evident, will for many completely discount enjoyment. We will resist the temptation to give isolated quotations, and will content ourselves with giving one complete poem, 'Harry Ploughman' (by no means the least intelligible), of which Father Hopkins wrote: 'This is a direct picture of a ploughman, without afterthought. ...I want Harry Ploughman to be a vivid figure before the mind's eye. If he is not that, the sonnet fails.'

[Quoted.]

There are many who will turn with relief to, say, Masefield's sketch of the ploughman at the end of 'The Everlasting Mercy'; all those at any rate who believe in the inevitable quality of real poetry. The fault is not, as we have indicated, one of lack of power or vision; on the contrary, the poet has impatiently discarded all but the highest-toned words to express his meaning, and in so doing has lost all sense of proportion. He cannot see the wood for the trees.

But in spite of all the obscurities—avowed and elaborated by the editor in his preface—there is real beauty in many of the poems: beauty at its simplest in the early poems written at school and college; the picture of the mermaidens in the school prize poem; the high purpose of the nun, familiar to us (like most of Father Hopkins's finest work) in 'The Spirit of Man':

[Quotes first two verses of 'The Habit of Perfection'.]

Beauty again in his poems of children: 'The Brothers,' 'Spring and Fall,' 'The Handsome Heart': beauty struggling out of elaboration in 'God's Grandeur,' 'The Caged Skylark,' 'Inversnaid,' 'Felix Randal': beauty emerging now and then triumphant, as in 'At the Wedding March' and the first stanza of 'The Wreck of the Deutschland.'

[Quoted.]

But, here at least, how quickly is that beauty obscured by the violence and confusion of the stanzas which follow!

But, whatever be our final decision as to the ultimate value of these writings as poetry, there can be no two opinions as to the quality of Mr. Bridges's editorship. He has taken up his long-delayed task with an affectionate and minute care, and a deep yet not uncritical devotion which in themselves demand for the poems a corresponding measure of our attention and appreciation. It has indeed been to him a labour of love; only it seems that the Laureate is trying to breathe life into that which cannot live save by its own vitality, by the virtue of some more direct vision and more complete expression than it was given to Gerard Hopkins to attain.

22. '161', review, *Methodist Recorder*

29 May 1919, p. 9

In the first part of the review, the writer had been dealing—at greater length—with another book, a life of Joel Harris, the creator of Uncle Remus.

...In a very different order is a volume from the Cambridge[1] University Press, *Poems of Gerard Manley Hopkins*, edited by Robert Bridges (12s. 6d.). These choice poems have been waited for through years, by studious readers of current poetry and lovers of it. It is scarcely likely the book will have a very wide circulation. It is quite certain to find its place on the shelf of the discerning. For the rest there are not more than half-a-dozen selections likely to be popular. This is the best candidate for universal favour—and it has already been published in various forms, as in various anthologies:—

[Quotes 'Heaven-Haven'.]

The poet was a Jesuit Father. He set himself, resolutely, to keep silence, save under the command or direction of his superiors. He studied the techniques of poetry and mastered them as few men have ever done. He left practice for the study of form, the mastery of the knowledge of all the laws of poetic and rhythmic expression. Possibly that provoked in him a kind of Browning obscurity when he rose up to sing; not only obscurity, but verbal violence and mystic glooms. The two verses quoted were written when young, before the poet became a Jesuit. Art did not fail of simplicity, but seldom remained so direct, large, and gracious. Yet the book is a book that will count; for the author's influence on other poets the book must be consulted. It would have been fortunate had we been permitted a biography, however brief. There is none. But readers in the literary reminiscences of the last fifty years will recall more than one reference to the influence of this chaste, devout, and passionate soul, who was the revered friend of Canon Dixon, and of the present Laureate. Few volumes so slight have received so close and so pious care.

NOTE

1 In fact, Oxford.

23. Unsigned review, *Dial*

31 May 1919, p. 572

This unsympathetic review seems surprising in a journal that was to become one of the most influential and progressive literary magazines in the United States, but, as William Wasserstrom points out (*The Time of the Dial*, Syracuse,

1963), its editorial policy was still in process of reorganisation in 1919. Along with the *Criterion* in England, the *Dial* gave first publication to Eliot's *The Waste Land* in November 1922.

The chief interest in these posthumous poems lies in their metrical eccentricities.... The subject matter of Father Hopkins' poetry is too prevailingly theological to gain a wide reading.... His style possesses a teasing quaintness, and antique tone oddly incongruous with the time of publication. The poems frequently are obscure, excessively so, as if the writer deliberately strove to mystify his readers. The lack of intelligibility usually results from unwise condensation, or from the omission of relative pronouns, as in the line

> Squander the hell-rook ranks sally to molest him.

These poems, seen in manuscript by only two or three persons during the author's lifetime, and published thirty years after his death, show a kinship with the roughness and obscurity, as well as with the force of Browning and Meredith. They express a strange talent, but will claim few readers.

24. [Fr] G[eorge] O'N[eill], review, *Studies*

June 1919, pp. 331–5

For George O'Neill see No. 6.

The critics in general have been at one as to the difficulty and strangeness, the 'obscurity and oddity' (his editor's words) of this new-old poet. His work has baffled their endeavours to arrive at general judgments, and the central reason for this seems to be a curious lack of judgment on the poet's own part. Gerard Hopkins had an exquisitely refined literary sense, but it permitted him to lapse into nearly every literary fault. He was a cultivated scholar, but this did not stay him from fantastic misuse of the English language. Most delicate perceptions were associated in him with a most untrustworthy sense of fitness and proportion. His metrical notions as here expounded in an 'Author's Preface,' are a mixture of simplicities, unintelligibilities, and one or two illuminating suggestions. His poetry in general has—to use the words of Coventry Patmore—'the effect of veins of pure gold embedded in masses of unpracticable quartz'; and there is evidence enough that he misjudged the golden and quartzian elements and their mixtures. He is a proof (by no means the first) that a *crassa Minerva*, not a subtly-poised discernment, is the surest preserver against the misadventures of genius.

With regard to the being and doing of the author whom he introduces to the literary world Mr. Bridges is almost wholly silent. It is clear enough (indeed there are incidental evidences) that his telling of the tale of one who, besides being a poet, was a convert to Catholicism, a priest, a Jesuit, and a soul tried by severe interior struggles, would have been somewhat lacking in sympathy, and that, therefore, we may put down his reticence entirely to the credit of good feeling and discretion. The general reader, however, will probably feel somewhat impatient under the *disciplina arcani* to which he is thus subjected. We would recommend him to seek the bibliographical information he desires in the sympathetic study of the poet found in Miss K. Brégy's volume, *The Poet's Chantry*.[1]

But if the editor thus keeps his counsel as regards the life and the man, he is not silent as to the poet and the poems. There are few causes of the latter's 'oddity and obscurity' which he does not touch on and exemplify. He notes the occasional bad or ludicrous rhymes, the 'mixture of passages of extreme delicacy and exquisite diction with passages where, in a jungle of rough root-words, emphasis seems to oust euphony'; the erring quest of euphony itself with an outcome of mere jingle. Although thus sternly judicial, and although—as already hinted—unsympathetic to the thought and feeling of not a few poems, yet, on the other hand, he has an abiding belief in the genius of his friend and in 'the rare masterly beauties that distinguish his work.' After a dedication (couched, oddly enough, in Latin) to the poet's aged mother, who still survives in her ninety-eighth year, he addresses Gerard Hopkins himself in a sonnet which lacks nothing of reverential affection and esteem.

It would, indeed, be difficult to find a volume which justifies so many different impressions and comments. It is chiefly, we think, in matters of form that Fr. Hopkins's poetry defies precedent and invites attack. It would be an easy, but also an ungrateful and tedious task to quote long passages or entire poems in which meaning which we fain would gather is hidden beneath a cloud-mirage of far-fetched phrases and queerly-assorted vocables, or tangled up in hard-knotted and sometimes quite insoluble syntax. Euphonious verse beguiles us over some difficult passages, but too often we are bumped over stylistic ruggednesses without the relief of any perceptible rhythm. Sometimes, too, the author's passion for verbal assonances, echoes and jingles of all kinds leads him off into oblivion of both sense and tune.

It is in this way that 'Binsy Poplars' quite misses the elegiac effect intended:—

[Quotes twelve lines.]

A sort of breathless hunt after assonant monosyllables is one of this poet's amusements. Thus:—

> Let life, waned, ah, let life wind
> Off her once skeined stained veined variety
>   Upon, all on two spools; part, pen, pack
> Now her all in two flocks, two folds—black,
>   White; right, wrong; reckon but, reck but, mind
> But these two; etc.

This excerpt may serve also to illustrate the wilful oddities of Fr. Hopkins' grammatical constructions. So, again, instead of 'end your roaming round me' he will say, 'your round me roaming end'; instead of 'to my own heart' he writes, 'to own my heart' (he always seems to ignore the ambiguities of English monosyllables like 'own,' 'part,' 'still,' 'well'). Again, in his 'Andromeda':—

> With not her either beauty's equal or
> Her injury's,

where the meaning is sufficiently guessable; or in this question, which certainly 'might admit of a wide solution':—

What being in rank-old nature should earlier have that breath been
That here personal tells off these heart-song powerful peals?

In the formation of compound words Fr. Hopkins goes easily beyond all precursors in his audacity. Not merely two or three, but up to half-a-dozen elements will he juggle with. We hear of 'come-back-again things,' and 'O-seal-that-so feature,' 'to heaven-pie,' 'a fallowbootfellow,' 'wind-lilylocks-laced' (meaning apparently 'lilylocks laced by the wind'), and a

Tatter-tassel-tangled and dingle-a-dangled
Dandy-hung dainty-head!

To the poet's prosodic notions we have already devoted a passing word. He provides some of his poems or else lines here and there with marks intended to help scansion and reading, and duly retained by the editor. Most readers will feel, we think, that they add bewilderment rather than elucidation. Of what use are the marks in this line:—

And éyes, héart, what looks, what lips yet gave you a?

Why a stressed preposition in this:—

Her Perseus linger and leave her tó her extremes?

On the other hand, we *should* be glad of some help towards making rhythmical such a stanza as this:—

The Eurydice—it concerned thee, O Lord:
Three hundred souls, O alas! on board,
Some sleep unawakened, all un-
warned, eleven fathoms fallen.

Logical completeness might perhaps require that we should follow up these remarks on our poet's peculiarities of form with some notes on certain (perhaps corresponding) idiosyncrasies of thought and feeling. But the quotations already made, though brief, will dispense us from any further stressing of the less admirable aspects of this volume. Its unusual merits well deserve that we should at least conclude on a note of praise. Unjust it would be not to acknowledge distinctly and illustrate—if but imper-

fectly—the very genuine poetic gift which shines in originality and beauty from many of these pages. The magic of expression
in some is as marked as the freakish word-play in some others.
Catholic readers and critics have already noted with pleasure that
some of the purest gems of Fr. Hopkins' works are crystallizations
of Catholic thought and feeling. Of this kind is the longish poem,
'The Blessed Virgin compared to the Air we Breathe,' which is
beautiful with scarcely a flawlet from beginning to end. Such,
again, is the brief lyric on a nun taking the veil, entitled
'Heaven-Haven':—

[Quoted.]

Nor must we omit to notice the poems, mostly sonnets, which
are an expression of deep personal sorrows, of the triumph after
fierce struggle in a soul at once childlike and strong of faith and
hope over anguish and despair. They are very characteristic and
their painfulness and beauty are in a kind of linked proportion. Not
many expressions of human suffering have been at once so
poignant and so profound as the sonnet beginning, 'No worst,
there is none'; with its sestet:—

[Quoted.]

Very beautiful, with a milder beauty, are the sonnets on Patience
and that entitled 'In the Valley of the Elwy.' They require, but they
repay, more than one reading—three or four perhaps; and we fancy
many generations of readers will be willing to take them and a few
of their companion-pieces at that price and that valuation.

NOTE

1 See headnote to No. 4.

25. Peter McBrien, review, *Irish Rosary*

June 1919, pp. 473–8

The *Irish Rosary* was a monthly printed in Dublin, and this review was the main article of the Literary Supplement.

...His poetry is laden down with a wealth of concrete, but intensely significant, pictures, as here, where he describes those who are satisfied to pass through life sans care and sans ideal once they are well fed and have a bed to sleep on:

[Quotes 'Tom's Garland'.]

...We have quoted 'Tom's Garland' in full, not because it is by any means the best of Fr. Hopkins' poems, but because brought together in its small compass are nearly all the characteristic virtues and vices of this great poet. Most people, very cultured people, too, will not understand it for a start. Even if they did understand it they might not appreciate it. Appreciation of art is a fitful thing, to some extent dependent on the mood one is in. It requires nearly as much inspiration to appreciate a great poem as to create one....

It is only when the subject is inherently subtle and difficult that this obscurity of diction arises. When the subject is homely and elemental, then his meaning is perfectly plain. It would be quite unjust to the memory of this great Jesuit not to give an idea of the sweetness, the childlikeness even, of those of his poems that deal with friendship and with nature, two themes that came out of Eden with the only two persons then in the world.

His love of nature is a very personal thing. He loves it exactly as a child loves its mother. Her moods are well known to him. Into them he reads none of the high and dry philosophy of Wordsworth, or the gorgeous and unsettling anarchy of Shelley. He just loves her, and no more. He dreads that any extrinsic harm shall be done her. To cut down a tree is like the amputation of the arm of a friend. Here we will quote 'Binsey Poplars,' a simple little thing, in full:

[Quoted.]

If Cowper had been a man he might have written like that. Nature, and friendship, and things that unite in themselves innocence with divinity, as in 'The Bugler's First Communion' or 'The Wreck of the Deutschland,' these are the things his inspiration lingers about, and, with two exceptions in the whole book, two fragments, the thought and inspiration are true, unforced, and in good taste, if we may be permitted to use such a phrase of wings that beat so close to the starry feet of Urania.

It cannot be said that the form this inspiration is found in is always in such good taste. In some of his best poems there are strange infractions of what the world of conventional literary art regards as *de rigueur*. (We have not space to examine the question of poetical convention: we regard Yeats, Pomairols, Browning, Swinburne, as conventional poets; we regard Walt Whitman as unconventional and deficient in artistic expression. That will give an idea of our point of view).

The hard, harsh, short words, advancing in file like a line of Red Indians, suit the masculinity of his thought; but they are too long kept up and too frequently recurring to be musical. 'Shivelights and shadowtackle in long lashes lace, lance and pair,' is one verse. Another runs: 'Now her all in two flocks, two folds—black, white; right, wrong; reckon but, reck but, mind.' The quality, as you have noticed in 'Tom's Garland,' is dramatic rather than lyrical, as in Browning. Sometimes the two notes crash together, like an intricate harmony in *Tristan and Isolde*. When, as in 'Binsey Poplars,' the dramatic note is absent, the music is as sweet as a Moskowski valse. On the whole the difficult poems have neither harmony of line or paragraph. The ruggedness and vividness of the hybrids he evolves out of Anglo-Saxon and modern words add to their harshness, and the burlesque combination-rhyming and splitting of end words will hurt the aesthete.

The elaborate contrapuntal effects, for which he got a hint from *Samson Agonistes* are carried so far that he lets what might be called the ground or basal rhythm drop altogether, and the effect is sometimes as if it were prose instead of poetry. Mr. Maynard differs from us in this verdict.[1] At any rate, what the poems lose in smoothness they gain in vividness and fire. They are indeed thought-compelling.

These are incidentals. But the man has poetry of the highest order in him. It is plainer to be seen, perhaps, because it is not

cloyed over with the niceties and sweetnesses that are inseparable
from the average verse of the magazines. It demands stern thought,
and cleanness of heart, for its appreciation. He has white-clear
vision. Any boy or girl can see it in the simple melodies, 'Penmaen
Pool,' and 'What shall I do for the land that bred me?'...

NOTE

1 See No. 14.

26. J[ohn] M[iddleton] M[urry], review, *Athenaeum*

6 June 1919, pp. 425–6,

This once highly respected but by this time declining literary
weekly was edited by John Middleton Murry (1889–1957)
from 1919 to 1921. Murry was opposed to the Georgians, but
his interests, as in this article, often seem more aesthetic
than specifically literary. This essay also appeared in the
author's *Aspects of Literature* (1920).

Modern poetry, like the modern consciousness of which it is the
epitome, seems to stand irresolute at a crossways with no signpost.
It is hardly conscious of its own indecision, which it manages to
conceal from itself by insisting that it is lyrical, whereas it is merely
impressionist. The value of impressions depends upon the quality
of the mind which receives and renders them, and to be lyrical
demands at least as firm a temper of the mind, as definite and
unfaltering a general direction, as to be epic. Roughly speaking, the
present poetical fashion may, with a few conspicuous exceptions,
be described as poetry without tears. The poet may assume a
hundred personalities in as many poems, or manifest a hundred
influences, or he may work a single sham personality threadbare or
render piecemeal an undigested influence. What he may not do, or

do only at the risk of being unfashionable, is to attempt what we may call, for the lack of a better word, the logical progression of an *oeuvre*. One has no sense of the rhythm of an achievement. There is an output of scraps, which are scraps, not because they are small, but because one scrap stands in no organic relation to another in the poet's work. Instead of lending each other strength, they betray each other's weakness.

Yet the organic progression for which we look, generally in vain, is not peculiar to poetic genius of the highest rank. If it were, we might be accused of mere querulousness. The rhythm of personality is hard, indeed, to achieve. The simple mind and the single outlook are now too rare to be considered as near possibilities, while the task of tempering a mind to a comprehensive adequacy to modern experience is not an easy one. The desire to escape and the desire to be lost in life were probably never so intimately associated as they are now; and it is a little preposterous to ask a moth fluttering round a candle-flame to see life steadily and see it whole. We happen to have been born into an age without perspective; hence our idolatry for the one living poet and prose writer who has it and comes, or appears to come, from another age. But another rhythm is possible. No doubt it would be mistaken to consider this rhythm as in fact wholly divorced from the rhythm of personality; it probably demands at least a minimum of personal coherence in its possessor. For critical purposes, however, they are distinct. This second and subsidiary rhythm is that of technical progression. The single pursuit of even the most subordinate artistic intention gives unity, significance, mass to a poet's work. When Verlaine declares 'de la musique avant toute chose,' we know where we are. And we know this not in the obvious sense of expecting his verse to be predominantly musical; but in the more important sense of desiring to take a man seriously who declares for anything 'avant toute chose.'

It is the 'avant toute chose' that matters, not as a profession of faith—we do not greatly like professions of faith—but as the guarantee of the universal in the particular, of the *dianoia*[1] in the episode. It is the 'avant toute chose' that we chiefly miss in modern poetry and modern society and in their quaint concatenations. It is the 'avant toute chose' that leads us to respect both Mr. Hardy and Mr. Bridges, though we give all our affection to one of them. It is the 'avant toute chose' that compels us to admire the poems of

Gerard Manley Hopkins; it is the 'avant toute chose' in his work which, as we believe, would have condemned him to obscurity to-day, if he had not (after many years) had Mr. Bridges, who was his friend, to stand sponsor and the Oxford University Press to stand the racket. Apparently Mr. Bridges himself is something of our opinion, for his introductory sonnet ends on a disdainful note:

> Go forth: amidst our chaffinch flock display
> Thy plumage of far wonder and heavenward flight!

It is from a sonnet written by Hopkins to Mr. Bridges that we take the most concise expression of his artistic intention, for the poet's explanatory preface is not merely technical, but is written in a technical language peculiar to himself. Moreover, its scope is small; the sonnet tells us more in two lines than the preface in four pages:

> O then if in my lagging lines you miss
> The roll, the rise, the carol, the creation. . . .

There is his 'avant toute chose'. Perhaps it seems very like 'de la musique'. But it tells us more about Hopkins' music than Verlaine's line told us about his. This music is of a particular kind, not the 'sanglots du violon,' but pre-eminently the music of song, the music most proper to lyrical verse. If one were to seek in English the lyrical poem to which Hopkins' definition could be most fittingly applied, one would find Shelley's 'Skylark'. A technical progression onwards from the 'Skylark' is accordingly the main line of Hopkins' poetical evolution. There are other, stranger threads interwoven; but this is the chief. Swinburne, rightly enough if the intention of true song is considered, appears hardly to have existed for Hopkins, though he was his contemporary. There is an element of Keats in his epithets, a half-echo in 'whorlèd ear' and 'lark-charmèd'; there is an aspiration after Milton's architect tonic in the construction of the later sonnets and the most lucid of the fragments, 'Epithalamion.' But the central point of departure is the 'Skylark'. The 'May Magnificat' is evidence of his achievement in the direct line:

[Quotes from 'May Magnificat'.]

That is the primary element manifested in one of its simplest most recognizable, and some may feel most beautiful forms. But a melody so simple, though it is perhaps the swiftest of which the English language is capable without the obscurity which comes of the drowning of sense in sound, did not satisfy Hopkins. He aimed at complex internal harmonies, at a counterpoint of rhythm; for this more complex element he coined an expressive word of his own:

But as air, melody, is what strikes me most of all in music and design in painting, so design, pattern, or what I am in the habit of calling *inscape* is what I above all aim at in poetry.[2]

Here than, in so many words, is Hopkins' 'avant toute chose' at a higher level of elaboration. 'Inscape' is still, in spite of the apparent differentiation, musical; but a quality of formalism seems to have entered with the specific designation. With formalism comes rigidity; and in this case the rigidity is bound to overwhelm the sense. For the relative constant in the composition of poetry is the law of language which admits only a certain amount of adaptation. Musical design must be subordinate to it, and the poet should be aware that even in speaking of musical design he is indulging a metaphor. Hopkins admitted this, if we may judge by his practice, only towards the end of his life. There is no escape by sound from the meaning of the posthumous sonnets, though we may hesitate to pronounce whether this directness was due to a modification of his poetical principles or to the urgency of the content of the sonnets, which, concerned with a matter of life and death, would permit no obscuring of their sense for musical reasons.

[Quotes 'I wake and feel', ll. 1–8.]

There is compression, but not beyond immediate comprehension; music, but a music of overtones; rhythm, but a rhythm which explicates meaning and makes it more intense.

Between the 'May Magnificat' and these sonnets is the bulk of Hopkins' poetical work and his peculiar achievement. Perhaps it could be regarded as a phase in his evolution towards the 'more balanced and Miltonic style' which he hoped for, and of which the posthumous sonnets are precursors; but the attempt to see him from this angle would be perverse. Hopkins was not the man to feel, save on exceptional occasions, that urgency of content of which we have spoken. The communication of thought was seldom the dominant impulse of his creative moment, and it is curious how simple his thought often proves to be when the obscurity of his language has been penetrated. Musical elaboration is the chief characteristic of his work, and for this reason what seem to be the strangest of his experiments are his most essential achievement. So, for instance, 'The Golden Echo':

[Quotes ll. 17–29.]

Than this, Hopkins truly wrote, 'I never did anything more musical.' By his own verdict and his own standards it is therefore the finest thing that Hopkins did. Yet even here, where the general beauty is undoubted, is not the music too obvious? Is it not always on the point of degenerating into a jingle—as much an exhibition of the limitations of a poetical theory as of its capabilities? The tyranny of the 'avant toute chose' upon a mind in which the other things were not stubborn and self-assertive is apparent. Hopkins' mind was irresolute concerning the quality of his own poetical ideal. A coarse and clumsy assonance seldom spread its snare in vain. Exquisite openings are involved in disaster:

[Quotes 'Peace', ll. 1–5.]

And the more wonderful opening of 'Windhover' likewise sinks, far less disastrously, but still perceptibly:

[Quotes ll. 1–7.]

We have no doubt that 'stirred for a bird' was an added excellence to the poet's ear; to our sense it is a serious blemish on lines which have 'the roll, the rise, the carol, the creation.'

There is no good reason why we should give characteristic specimens of the poet's obscurity, since our aim is to induce people to read him. The obscurities will slowly vanish and something of the intention appear; and they will find in him many of the strange beauties won by men who push on to the borderlands of their science; they will speculate whether the failure of his whole achievement was due to the starvation of experience which his vocation imposed upon him, or to a fundamental vice in his poetical endeavour. For ourselves we believe that the former was the true cause. His 'avant toute chose' whirling dizzily in a spiritual vacuum, met with no salutary resistance to modify, inform and strengthen it. Hopkins told the truth of himself—the reason why he must remain a poets' poet:

I want the one rapture of an inspiration.
O then if in my lagging lines you miss
The roll, the rise, the carol, the creation,
My winter world, that scarcely yields that bliss
Now, yields you, with some sighs, our explanation.

NOTES

1 'Thinking', 'reasoning'.
2 Bridges's Preface, *ante*, p. 78.

27. Henry A. Lappin, 'Gerard Hopkins and his Poetry', *Catholic World*

July 1919, pp. 501–12

...In power and charm of expression it is less obviously easy to demonstrate his very real distinction. Some of his metres are woven with such tortuous subtlety, with such tremulous ingenuity, that the endurance of most readers will faint and fail before the task of penetrating through them to what lies beyond; one must tear oneself through thorns and briars, as it were, and not many suffer willingly so stern a trial of onset. Sometimes so opulently obscure is his imagery that only the most painstaking lovers of poetry can hope to win their difficult way to his thought. But these things, too, had their purpose and their justification.

28. [Fr] C[lement] B[arraud], 'Reminiscences of Father Gerard Hopkins', *Month*

August 1919, pp. 158–9

Clement Barraud (1843–1926) was educated at Stonyhurst, entered the Society of Jesus in 1862, and studied at St Mary's Hall and St Beuno's with Hopkins. In the *Journal*, Hopkins wrote that on 8 October 1874 he walked with Barraud over to Holywell where they bathed, 'and returned very joyously' (2nd edn, p. 261). Barraud later worked in the West Indies, returning to be Spiritual Father at St Beuno's in 1910.

Having had the joy of his friendship, I will jot down here a few personal reminiscences of this odd but gifted man with whom I was in constant intercourse whilst we studied philosophy and theology together.

Gerard Hopkins was a slight man, with a narrow face, prominent chin and nose, brown hair and—what may surprise those who know him only by his poetry—a somewhat girlish manner. He was a delightful companion, full of high spirits and innocent fun. One instance of his wit I recall. Once, while in Ireland, he called on a certain parish priest, the Rev. Father Wade, and was hospitably pressed to stay for dinner. Father Hopkins, an exact observer of discipline, replied that he had no leave to dine out. 'Is that all?' said Father Wade. 'Well now, I'll take the whole responsibility upon myself.' 'Ah, yes,' said Father Hopkins, 'you may be Wade; but *I* shall be found wanting'.

He was a very close observer of Nature, and had a marvellous power of recording his impressions. He has left behind him in his Diaries some glowing descriptions of sky scenery, real triumphs of delicate word-painting, which I hope may some day be given to the public.

That he had the soul of a poet is obvious; but his poems

themselves, with some happy exceptions, are like leaves from the sketch-book of a Michael Angelo, full of tremendous power, yet rough and often rudely grotesque, mere suggestions of perfect thoughts and striking turns of expression, which should have been worked up and finished off at leisure in the studio.

But somehow or other the grotesque had an overbearing attraction for this Michael Angelo of verse—and such he ought to have been, had he but condescended to write plain English. As it was, he wilfully set all tradition at defiance, and so the more he laboured at his subject the more obscure it became. Yet he did not repent. It was of his poem on St. Alphonsus Rodriguez that, as recorded in Miss Guiney's luminous appreciation in *The Month* for March,[1] he writes to his old friend, Mr. Bridges:—'The sonnet (I say it snorting) aims at being intelligible'.

Not that he was unable to appreciate a simple style. He once showed me certain early poems of that other lifelong friend of his, Canon Dixon, which I thought very lovely; and Father Hopkins admired them as much as I did. In truth, he himself wrote at times with charming directness.

It has been said—he used to say it himself—that his verses need for proper appreciation to be read aloud by one who has mastered their eccentricities. Well, I heard the bard himself read parts of 'The Wreck of the Deutschland,' which he was writing at the time, and could understand hardly one line of it.

Is it not strange that this and 'Penmaen Pool' should have come from the same workshop?

The wildest of all his wild freaks is that, with a notably pure Saxon vocabulary, he chooses to cast his sentences and phrases into Latin order, the fanciful order of Latin verse. Thus—

> The rolling level underneath him steady air

means

> The steady air rolling level underneath him.
> In wide the world's weal

stands for

> In the wide world's weal,

or

> In the world's wide weal.

It may perhaps be a question whether this highly artificial arrangement is a beautiful feature even in Latin verse. Still there one always has unmistakable inflections as a clue to the meaning, whereas in English one is left floundering in a bog.

I once wrote to my friend from Demerara, describing the Feast of Lanterns, as celebrated there by the resident Chinese. His reply was a learned disquisition on Chinese music, God save the mark! discussing its peculiar tonality, and claiming for it merits which had certainly escaped my observation. Everything bizarre had a charm for this whimsical genius. But the pure gold in his work, to use Patmore's image, more than reconciles us to the plentiful and unlovely quartz.

NOTE

1 See No. 16.

29. The Editor, 'Fr Gerard Hopkins S.J. and his Poetry', *Irish Monthly* (Dublin)

August 1919, pp. 441–8

The *Irish Monthly* was a magazine of religious and general interest, founded 1873 and edited until 1912 by Fr. Matthew Russell, SJ, who was well known for his encouragement of younger writers. He had printed two Latin translations of Shakespeare songs by Hopkins in 1886–7 (see *Letters to Bridges*, p. 230), as well as 'Rosa Mystica' in 1898.

... The poetry of Father Hopkins, for all its strangeness and its tangled passages, stands out in refreshing contrast to the derivative, groove-confined verses which make up a large part of the output of modern English poets. He is essentially original, strikingly original in his expressions and rhythm, original, too, in the freshness and individuality of inspiration which give him kinship to the Elizabethan lyricists....

30. Fr George O'Neill, *Essays on Poetry*

Dublin, 1919, pp. 117–38

The author repeats some of his review material from *Studies* (see No. 24) in this essay. Consequently, I have reprinted only a little.

...The poet's impatience of every word or syllable that is merely constructive and his eagerness to pack every phrase and line with meaning and colour lead him to omissions of the relative pronoun which out-Browning Browning. An inserted 'that' is the key to many a strange line like the following:—

> Squander the hell-rook ranks sally to molest him.

In the building up of compound words Hopkins is again audacious beyond all precursors. Not merely two or three but half-a-dozen elements will he juggle with. We hear of 'come-back-again things,' an 'O-seal-that-so feature,' 'to heavenpie' (*i.e.* to make pied with bits of heaven), 'a fallowbootfellow' (?) 'wind-lilylocks-laced' (*i.e.* apparently 'lilylocks laced by the wind') and a

> Tatter-tassel-tangled and dingle-a-dangled
> Dandy-hung dainty head!

But—when we have rejected, in the name of all the orthodoxies, such 'derangements of epitaphs' and topsy-turveydoms of grammar—it remains impossible, in fairness, to deny his striking successes. They are to be met with on many a page, constantly intermingled (to their detriment, alas!) with some of his least happy inventions. We cannot admire as a whole the harsh force of 'The Wreck of the Deutschland,' but it has not a few lines as fine as these:—

Wiry and white-fiery and whirlwind-swivelled snow
Spring to the widow-making, unchilding, unfathering
deep.

What life again in those picturing Oxford:—

Towering city and branching between towers;
Cuckoo-echoing, bell-swarmèd, lark-charmèd, rook-
racked, river-rounded.

What magic in such phrases as these:—'hoar-hallowed shrines,' 'a crimson-cresseted dawn'; what power in these—'Christ, our passion-plungèd giant risen,' 'womb-of-all, home-of-all, hearse-of-all Night!' Such poems in miniature make us regret more the ill-setting of the gems, the perverse unthrift of so wealthy a brain.

However we may estimate the poet's failures or successes, beyond question his audacities made him a true pioneer. His belated appearance should not be allowed to obscure his notable originality. In his passion for Teutonic monosyllables, in his hatred of convention or meretricious ornament, in the free swing of his rhythms and the running over of his lines, in the restless novelty of his forms, of his rhymes following all manner of schemes or no-schemes, of his sonnets varied in some half-dozen ways, he was quite ahead of his own generation and anticipated doings still far off in the twentieth century. Many a poem of Walter de la Mare, of Sandburg, Untermeyer, W.W. Gibson, James Stephens, Joseph Campbell, could be fitted without any incongruity into the slender volume of this shy recluse who passed from earth long before Victoria or Tennyson.

When we turn our attention to the spirit and substance away from the body and form of this poetry one finds much that may (for many readers) redeem the less-happy ventures and peradventures of the 'rare ill-brokered talent'—to quote a phrase from his editor's verse-tribute. Subtle penetration of thought and kindly human feeling are both found and sometimes in happy combination. Sympathy with the poor and simple, with children and boys, is often breaking out: would it were always with unmixed charm!'Tom's Garland (upon the Unemployed)' and 'Harry Ploughman' are among the author's most freakish and bewildering inventions, and 'The Bugler's First Communion' has fantastic twists and queer rhymes; but very beautiful are 'Spring and Fall (to a young child)' and 'In the Valley of the Elwy'.....

31. Edward Sapir, review, *Poetry*

September 1921, pp. 330–6

Poetry, published in Chicago and edited by Harriet Monroe, was one of the most enterprising of American literary magazines. It published 'The Love Song of J. Alfred Prufrock' in June 1915.

Edward Sapir (1884–1939) was an authority on anthropology and linguistics. From 1910 to 1925 he was chief of the anthropology division of the Canadian National Museum. He wrote *Language, an Introduction to the Study of Speech* (1921).

When the author's preface and the editor's notes are eliminated, we have here but a small volume of some eighty-five pages of poetry, and of these only a scant sixty-three consist of complete poems, the rest being fragments assembled from manuscripts in the Poet Laureate's possession. The majority of them date from the years 1876 to 1889; only three earlier poems are included. Hopkins is long in coming into his own; but it is not too much to say that his own will be secure, among the few that know, if not among the crowd, when many a Georgian name that completely overshadows him for the moment shall have become food for the curious.

For Hopkin's poetry is of the most precious. His voice is easily one of the half dozen most individual voices in the whole course of English nineteenth-century poetry. One may be repelled by his mannerisms, but he cannot be denied that overwhelming authenticity, that almost terrible immediacy of utterance, that distinguishes the genius from the man of talent. I would compare him to D.H. Lawrence but for his far greater sensitiveness to the music of words, to the rhythms and ever-changing speeds of syllables. In a note published in *Poetry* in 1914, Joyce Kilmer speaks of his mysticism and of his gloriously original imagery.[1] This mysticism of the Jesuit poet is not a poetic manner, it is the very breath of his soul. Hopkins simply could not help comparing the Holy Virgin to the air we breathe; he was magnificently in earnest about the Holy

134

Ghost that

> over the bent
> World broods with warm breast and with ah! bright wings.

As for imagery, there is hardly a line in these eighty-odd pages that does not glow with some strange new flower, divinely picked from his imagination.

Undeniably this poet is difficult. He strives for no innocuous Victorian smoothness. I have referred to his mannerisms, which are numerous and not always readily assimilable. They have an obsessive, turbulent quality about them—these repeated and trebly repeated words, the poignantly or rapturously interrupting *oh's* and *ah's*, the headlong omission of articles and relatives, the sometimes violent word order, the strange yet how often so lovely compounds, the plays on words, and, most of all, his wild joy in the sheer sound of words. This phonetic passion of Hopkins rushes him into a perfect maze of rhymes, half-rhymes, assonances, alliterations:

> Tatter-tassel-tangled and dingle-a-dangled
> Dandy-hung dainty head.

These clangs are not like the nicely calculated jingling love-linesses of Poe or Swinburne. They, no less than the impatient ruggednesses of his diction, are the foam-flakes and eddies of a passionate, swift-streaming expression. To a certain extent Hopkins undoubtedly loved difficulty, even obscurity, for its own sake. He may have found in it a symbolic reflection of the tumult that raged in his soul. Yet we must beware of exaggerating the external difficulties; they yield with unexpected ease to the modicum of good will that Hopkins has a right to expect of us.

Hopkins' prosody, concerning which he has something to say in his preface, is worthy of careful study. In his most distinctive pieces he abandons the 'running' verse of traditional English poetry and substitutes for it his own 'sprung' rhythms. This new verse of his is not based on the smooth flow of regularly recurring stresses. The stresses are carefully grouped into line and stanza patterns, but the movement of the verse is wholly free. The iambic or trochaic foot yields at any moment to a spondee or a dactyl or a foot of one stressed and three or more unstressed syllables. There is, however, no blind groping in this irregular movement. It is nicely adjusted to the constantly shifting speed of the verse. Hopkins' effects, with a few exceptions, are in the highest degree successful. Read with the ear, never with the eye, his verse flows with an entirely new vigor and lightness, while the stanzaic form gives it a powerful compactness and drive. It is doubtful if the freest verse of our day is more sensitive in its rhythmic pulsations than the 'sprung' verse of Hopkins. . . .

NOTE

1 See *ante*, p. 9.

32. T.S. Omond, *English Metrists*

Oxford, 1921, p. 263

Omond (d. 1923) had been a Fellow of St John's College, Oxford. The title-page describes *English Metrists* as a 'Sketch of English Prosodical Criticism from Elizabethan Times to the Present Day'. The passage on Hopkins appears in a 'Postscript' covering the twentieth century.

. . . 1918 brought also the *Poems* of Gerard Hopkins, with introduction and notes by the Poet Laureate. Readers who enjoy fantastic new would-be developments of metre will study these poems and their author's teaching about 'Sprung Rhythm' and other mysteries, and will find ample material in the one poem entitled 'The Wreck of the Deutschland'; others, neither intolerant of nor unhopeful for new experiments, will turn from them with repugnance. The Editor's introduction and notes are, as always, clear and helpful, expounding his friend's metrical theories, and not infrequently registering dissent from his eccentricities, especially in rhyming. The double rhymes in 'The Loss of the Eurydice' are simply atrocious, and curiously enough the Editor has singled out for special censure one of the least offensive of these. I cannot

believe that these poems deserve or will receive attention from even
the most determined seeker after novelties.

33. George Shuster, *The Catholic Spirit in Modern English Literature*

New York, 1922, pp. 115–21

Shuster (1894–1952) was an American Catholic writer. The
brief extract below is an example of his rhetorical and not
very farsighted treatment of Hopkins.

. . . It seems impossible that poetry should ever follow the direction
of his teaching, no matter how different its form may come to be.
He was the elf-child playing with the fringe of the sober modern
sea, and such children are rare and even unpopular. . . .

34. Alan Porter, 'Difficult Beauty', *Spectator*

13 January 1923, p. 66

According to Mellown, Porter wrote this essay shortly before
becoming literary editor of the *Spectator*. It was Porter and
Edmund Blunden who helped to revive the reputation of
John Clare.

Gerard Manley Hopkins, a Jesuit priest, died in 1889. His poems
have been anthologized, sparingly and perhaps not wisely: four
years ago they were collected and edited by the Poet Laureate.

They are known mainly to students of prosody and to the youngest generation of poets. Readers who meet them for the first time and attempt them casually often make neither head nor tail of them; here and there they may be astounded by some audacious phrase—'the dappled-with-damson east,' 'a dare-gale skylark scanted in a dull cage,' or, of the stars, 'O look at all the fire-folk sitting in the air!'—but, without persistence, they may dismiss most of the poems as quaint and perverse or account it disproportionate to spend much labour on one poet, a poet not canonized among the great. Indeed, Gerard Hopkins may well be taken as a test-case in obscurity.

His poems repay study. He was, like all true poets, 'the first poet in the world for some things.' And his difficulties are necessary: they are the impress of himself. He was a man of heightened, almost hysterical, acuteness of sense. To him, the thrush:—

> Through the echoing timber does so rinse and wring
> The ear, it strikes like lightnings to hear him sing;

and, when a cuckoo calls:—

> The whole landscape flushes on a sudden at a sound.

Coincident with this quickening of sense was a fierce variability of mood. He was subject often to the 'carrion comfort, despair,' and he spoke truly when he described himself as:—

> this tormented mind
> With this tormented mind tormenting yet.

Like most other true poets he had little of that sense of humour which makes our humanity half laughable, that minor blasphemy through which we alleviate the stress of life. And, naturally with such a temperament, what most affected him in fact and art, his ideal beauty, was a moodlessness, a suddenly-seized, abrupt finality, a flash off an architypical perfection. His torment came from the conflict between his belief in this absolute and the acknowledged rarity in the world of evidence for belief. His quickened sense gave him also an original pattern of music for his verse and original theories in metric. It was a music sometimes too sweet:—

> In coop and in comb the fleece of his foam
> Flutes and low to the lake falls home.—

but more generally nerved by clash and resolved inconsonance, knit close and made virile. He never betrayed it for the sake of meaning; but he was fastidious, too, to match sense with music. For this reason he was compelled often to use obscure words or curious new coinages. And in his determination to have sense and music at one, to reconcile emphasis and euphony, he took other liberties with languages. He refused to give prominence to words that are not visual and dynamic, to stress articles, pronouns, or conjunctions. He would tuck them away in unheard-of places or entirely omit them, and his scholarship in Latin made him forget that an uninflected language has need of such words. He wrote for no public, he hoped for no fame, he made no compromise. His qualities had thus the fullest room for development. He was, as Mr. Robert Bridges remarks, αυήρπεριττατος, and his 'arch-especial spirit' comes nakedly from his poems.

These are the causes of his obscurity: briefly, he created an idiom of his own. The poems are not so hard of comprehension as at first sight they seem. Read slowly and, as it were, tonelessly, but with alert intelligence, they will soon shape themselves and cohere....

NOTE

1 See *ante*, p. 82.

35. Shane Leslie, Introduction, *An Anthology of Catholic Poets*

London, 1925, pp. 12–13

Shane Leslie (1885–1971) wrote on a wide range of (usually) Catholic subjects, and also taught for some time in American Catholic universities. This anthology included seven poems by Hopkins.

...Gerard Hopkin's poems remained hidden like violets, while his whole life became a passion-flower in the Jesuit Conservatory. ...For [Patmore and Thompson] the broad-pinioned Ode, but Hopkins only essayed broken metres and disappearing sevenths to express the thoughts of an ascetic too reserved in his inner life to burst into flame. Technically he seems a casualty to his own cadences. He arranged his words sometimes like coloured counters of mosaic and sometimes like the notes in a harmony of music. His poems are handed down by the initiated not like candles of flame or glowing coals, but like enamels that have run into each other with intensity of heat upon a reliquary. He has remained hidden except for the little-known collections revealed by Canon Beeching and Robert Bridges....

36. I. A. Richards, 'Gerard Hopkins', *Dial*

September 1926, pp. 195–203

I. A. Richards (1893–1979), apostle of the new criticism, was an influential teacher at Cambridge in the twenties, where Empson (No. 43) was a pupil. His *Principles of Literary Criticism* (1924) and *Practical Criticism* (see No. 39) became key texts.

This essay is reprinted in *A Dial Miscellany*, ed. W. Wasserstrom (Syracuse, 1963).

Modern verse is perhaps more often too lucid than too obscure. It passes through the mind (or the mind passes over it) with too little friction and too swiftly for the development of the response. Poets who can compel slow reading have thus an initial advantage. The effort, the heightened attention, may brace the reader, and that peculiar intellectual thrill which celebrates the step-by-step conquest of understanding may irradiate and awaken other mental activities more essential to poetry. It is a good thing to make the light-footed reader work for what he gets. It may make him both more wary and more appreciative of his reward if the 'critical point' of value is passed.

These are arguments for some slight obscurity in its own right. No one would pretend that the obscurity may not be excessive. It may be distracting, for example. But what is a distraction in a first reading may be non-existent in a second. We should be clear (both as readers and writers) whether a given poem is to be judged at its first reading or at its nth. The state of intellectual enquiry, the construing, interpretative, frame of mind, so much condemned by some critics (through failure perhaps to construe the phrase 'simple, sensuous, and passionate') passes away once its task is completed, and the reader is likely to be left with a far securer grasp of the whole poem, including its passional structure, than if no resistance had been encountered.

Few poets illustrate this thesis better than Gerard Hopkins, who may be described, without opposition, as the most obscure of English verse writers. Born in 1844, he became a Jesuit priest in 1868, a more probable fate for him then—he was at Oxford—than now. Before joining the Order he burnt what verses he had already written and 'resolved to write no more, as not belonging to my profession, unless it were by the wish of my superiors.' For seven years he wrote nothing. Then by good fortune this wish was expressed and Hopkins set to work. 'I had long had haunting my ear the echo of a new rhythm which now I realized on paper. . . . However I had to mark the stresses . . . and a great many more oddnesses could not but dismay an editor's eye, so that when I offered it to our magazine . . . they dared not print it.' Thenceforward he wrote a good deal, sending his poems in manuscript to Robert Bridges and to Canon Dixon. He died in 1889 leaving a bundle of papers among which were several of his best sonnets. In 1918 the Poet Laureate edited a volume of poems with an introduction and notes of great interest. From this volume comes all our knowledge of his work.

Possibly their obscurity may explain the fact that these poems are not yet widely known. But their originality and the audacity of their experimentation have much to do with the delay. Even their editor found himself compelled to apologize at length for what he termed 'blemishes in the poet's style.' 'It is well to be clear that there is no pretence to reverse the condemnation of these faults, for which the poet has duly suffered. The extravagances are and will remain what they were... it may be assumed that they were not a part of his intention.'[1] But too many other experiments have been made recently, especially in the last eight years, for this lofty tone and confident assumption to be maintained. The more the poems are studied, the clearer it becomes that their oddities are always deliberate. They may be aberrations, they are not blemishes. It is easier to see this to-day since some of his most daring innovations have been, in part, attempted independently by later poets.

I propose to examine a few of his best poems from this angle, choosing those which are both most suggestive technically and most indicative of his temper and mould as a poet. It is an important fact that he is so often most himself when he is most experimental. I will begin with a poem in which the shocks to convention are local and concern only word order.

[Quotes 'Peace'.]

Hopkins was always ready to disturb the usual word order of prose to gain an improvement in rhythm or an increased emotional poignancy. *To own my heart* = to my own heart; *reaving* = taking away. He uses words always as tools, an attitude towards them which the purist and grammarian can never understand. He was clear, too, that his poetry was for the ear, not for the eye, a point that should be noted before we proceed to 'The Windhover', which, unless we begin by listening to it, may *only* bewilder us. To quote from a letter: 'Indeed, when, on somebody's returning me the Eurydice, I opened and read some lines, as one commonly reads, whether prose or verse, with the eyes, so to say, only, it struck me aghast with a kind of raw nakedness and unmitigated violence I was unprepared for: but take breath and read it with the ears, as I always wish to be read, and my verse becomes all right.' I have to confess that 'The Windhover' only became all right for me, in the sense of perfectly clear and explicit, intellectually satisfying as well as emotionally moving, after many readings and several days of reflection.

[Quotes 'The Windhover'.]

The dedication[2] at first sight is puzzling. Hopkins said of this poem that it was the best thing he ever wrote, which is to me in part the explanation. It sounds like an echo of the offering made eleven years ago when his early poems were burnt. For a while I thought that the apostrophe, 'O my chevalier!' (it is perhaps superfluous to mention that this word rhymes strictly with 'here' and has only three syllables) had reference to Christ. I take it now to refer only to the poet, though the moral ideal, embodied of course for Hopkins in Christ, is before the mind.

Some further suggestions towards elucidation may save the reader trouble. If he does not need them I crave his forgiveness. *Kingdom of daylight's dauphin*—I see (unnecessarily) the falcon as a miniature sun, flashing so high up. *Rung upon the rein*—a term from the *manège*, ringing a horse = causing it to circle round one on a long rein. *My heart in hiding*—as with other good poets I have come to expect that when Hopkins leaves something which looks at first glance as though it were a concession to rhyme or a mere pleasing jingle of words, some really important point is involved. Why in hiding? Hiding from what? Does this link up with 'a billion times told lovelier, more dangerous, O my chevalier!'? What is the greater danger and what the less? I should say the poet's heart is in hiding from Life, has chosen a safer way, and that the greater danger is the greater exposure to temptation and error than a more adventurous, less sheltered course (sheltered by Faith?) brings with it. Another, equally plausible reading would be this: Renouncing the glamour of the outer life of adventure the poet transfers its qualities of audacity to the inner life. (*Here* is the bosom, the inner consciousness.) The greater danger is that to which the moral hero is exposed. Both readings may be combined, but pages of prose would be required for a paraphrase of the result. The last three lines carry the thought of the achievement possible through renunciation further, and explain, with the image of the ash-covered fire, why the dangers of the inner life are greater. So much for the sense; but the close has a strange, weary, almost exhausted, rhythm, and the word 'gall' has an extraordinary force, bringing out painfully the shock with which the sight of the soaring bird has jarred the poet into an unappeased discontent.

If we compare those poems and passages of poems which were conceived definitely within the circle of Hopkins' theology with those which transcend it, we shall find difficulty in resisting the conclusion that the poet in him was often oppressed and stifled by the priest. In this case the conflict which seems to lie behind and prompt all Hopkins' better poems is temporarily resolved through a stoic acceptance of sacrifice. An asceticism which fails to reach ecstasy and accepts the failure. All Hopkins' poems are in this sense poems of defeat. This will perhaps become clearer if we turn to

[Quotes 'Spelt from Sibyl's Leaves'.]

Elucidations are perhaps less needed. The heart speaks after 'Heart you round me right' to the end, applying in the moral sphere the parable of the passing away of all the delights, accidents, nuances, the 'dapple' of existence, to give place to the awful dichotomy of right and wrong. It is characteristic of this poet that there is no repose for him in the night of traditional morality. As the terrible last line shows, the renunciation of all the myriad temptations of life brought no gain. It was all loss. The present order of 'black, white; right, wrong' was an afterthought and an intentional rearrangement; the original order was more orthodox. *Let life, waned*—the imperative mood carries through to the end; let life part, pen, pack, let life be aware of. *All throughther* = each through the other.

I cannot refrain from pointing to the marvellous third and fourth lines. They seem to me to anticipate the descriptions we hope our younger contemporary poets will soon write. Such synaesthesis has tempted several of them, but this is, I believe, the supreme example. Hopkins' technical innovations reach out, however, into many fields. As a means of rendering self-consciousness, for example, consider this:

> Only what word
> Wisest my heart breeds dark heaven's baffling ban
> Bars or hell's spell thwarts. This to hoard unheard,
> Heard unheeded, leaves me a lonely began.

Or this:

> Soul, self; come poor Jackself, I do advise
> You, jaded, let be; call off thoughts awhile
> Elsewhere; leave comfort root-room; let joy size
> At God knows when to God knows what; whose smile
> 's not wrung, see you; unforeseen times rather—as skies
> Betweenpie mountains—lights a lovely mile.

My last quotations must be the sonnets which most I think, represent the poet's inner conflict.

[Quotes 'Carrion Comfort', and 'No worst, there is none'.]

Few writers have dealt more directly with their experience or been more candid. Perhaps to do this must invite the charge of oddity, of playfulness, of whimsical eccentricity and wantonness. To some of his slighter pieces these charges do apply. Like other writers he had to practise and perfect his craft. The little that has been written about him has already said too much about this aspect. His work as a pioneer has not been equally insisted upon. It is true that Gerard Hopkins did not fully realize what he was doing to the technique of poetry. For example, while retaining rhyme, he gave himself complete rhythmical freedom, but disguised this freedom as a system of what he called Sprung Rhythm, employing four sorts of feet (–,– ˬ,– ˬˬ,– ˬˬˬ). Since what he called *hangers* or *outrides* (one, two, or three slack syllables added to a foot and not counting in the nominal scanning) were also permitted, it will be plain that he had nothing to fear from the absurdities of prosodists. A curious way, however, of eluding a mischievous tradition and a spurious question, to give them a mock observance and an equally unreal answer! When will prosodists seriously ask themselves what it is that they are investigating? But to raise this question is to lose all interest in prosody.

Meanwhile the lamentable fact must be admitted that many people just ripe to read Hopkins have been and will be too busy asking 'does he scan?' to notice that he has anything to say to them. And of those that escape this trap that our teachers so assiduously set, many will be still too troubled by beliefs and disbeliefs to understand him. His is a poetry of divided and equal passions—which very nearly makes a new thing out of a new fusion of them both. But Hopkins' intelligence, though its subtlety with details was extraordinary, failed to remould its materials sufficiently in attacking his central problem. He solved it emotionally, at a cost which amounted to martyrdom; intellectually he was too stiff, too 'cogged and cumbered' with beliefs, those bundles of invested emotional capital, to escape except through appalling tension. The analysis of his poetry is hardly possible, however, without the use of technical language; the terms 'intellectual' and 'emotional' are too loose. His stature as a poet will not be recognized until the importance of the Belief problem from which his poetry sprang has been noticed. He did not need other beliefs than those he held. Like the rest of us, whatever our beliefs, he needed a change in belief, the mental attitude, itself.

NOTES

1 See *ante*, p. 78.
2 'To Christ Our Lord'.

37. Laura Riding and Robert Graves, *A Survey of Modernist Poetry*

1927, pp. 90–4

Graves (1895–1985) was already a published poet at this date. Laura Riding, b. 1901 in New York City, also a poet, came to England in 1926, and worked with Graves in publishing and writing. In a letter to the *Times Literary Supplement*, 29 April 1955, Graves claimed that this book really began the Hopkins influence, since it prompted Empson and other academics to take an interest in the poet. However, the distinction could equally well be argued for Richards's essay in the *Dial* (No. 36), whose importance was acknowledged by both Leavis and Empson.

... One of the first modernist poets to feel the need of a clearness and accuracy in feelings and their expression so minute, so more than scientific, as to make of poetry a higher sort of psychology, was Gerard Manley Hopkins, a Catholic poet writing in the 'eighties. We call him a modernist in virtue of his extraordinary strictness in the use of words and the unconventional notation he used in setting them down so that *they had to be understood as he meant them to be, or understood not at all* (this is the crux of the whole

question of the intelligibility of 'difficult' poetry). Hopkins cannot
be accused of trying to antagonize the reading public. In 1883 he
wrote about the typographical means he used in order to explain an
unfamiliar metre and an unfamiliar grammar: 'There must be some
marks. Either I must invent a notation throughout, as in music, or
else I must only mark where the reader is likely to mistake, and for
the present this is what I shall do.' In 1885 he wrote again: 'This is
my difficulty, what marks to use and when to use them: they are so
much needed and yet so objectionable. About punctuation my
mind is clear: I can give a rule for everything I write myself, and
even for other people, though they might not agree with me
perhaps.' These lines from a sonnet written in his peculiar metre
will show to what an extent he is a modernist.

> Soul, self; come, poor Jackself, I do advise
> You, jaded, let be; call off thoughts awhile
> Elsewhere; leave comfort root-room; let joy size
> At God knows when to God knows what; whose smile
> 's not wrung, see you; unforeseen times rather—as skies
> Betweenpie mountains—lights a lovely mile.

First of all *Jackself*. The plain reader will get no help from the
dictionary with this, he must use his wits and go over the other uses
of *Jack* in combination: jack-screw, jackass, jack-knife, Jack Tar,
Jack Frost, Jack of all trades, boot-jack, steeple-jack, lumber-jack,
jack-towel, jack-plane, roasting-jack. From these the central
meaning of 'jack' becomes clear. It represents a person or thing that
is honest, patient, cheerful, hard-working, undistinguished—but
the fellow that makes things happen, that does things that nobody
else would or could do. (Tom in English usage is the mischievous,
rather destrcutive, impudent and often unpleasant fellow—
tomboy, tomcat, tomfoolery, tomtit, peeping Tom, etc.). 'Jackself', then, is this workaday self which he advises to knock off
work for awhile; to leave comfort or leisure, crowded out by work,
some space to grow in, as for flowers in a vegetable garden; to have
his pleasure and comfort whenever and however God wills it, not,
as an ordinary Jackself would, merely on Sundays (Hopkins uses
'God knows when' and 'God knows what' as just the language a
Jackself would use). God's smile cannot be forced from him, that
is, happiness cannot be postponed until one is ready for it. Joy
comes as suddenly and unexpectedly as when, walking among

mountains, you come to a point where the sky shines through a cleft between two mountains and throws a shaft of light over a mile of ground thus unexpectedly illumined for you. We must appreciate the accuracy of the term *Betweenpie*. Besides being again just the sort of homely kitchen language that the Jackself would use to describe how sky seems pressed between two mountains (almost as a smile is pressed between lips) it is also the neatest possible way of combining the patching effect of light—as in the word 'pied' (The Pied Piper of Hamelin) or in 'magpie'—with the way this light is introduced between the mountains.

Of Hopkins, who carefully observed so many rules, his editor, Dr. Robert Bridges, who postponed publication of his poems for thirty years, thus making Hopkins even more of a modernist poet, writes:

> Apart from faults of taste…affectations such as where the hills are 'as a stallion stalwart very-violet-sweet' or some perversion of human feeling, as, for instance, the 'nostrils' relish of incense along the sanctuary side', or 'the Holy Ghost with warm breast and with ah! bright wings', which repel my sympathy more than do all the rude shocks of his purely artistic wantonness—apart from these there are faults of style which the reader must have courage to face. For these blemishes are of such quality and magnitude as to deny him even a hearing from those who love a continuous literary decorum.[1]

Why cannot what Dr. Bridges calls a fault of taste, an affectation, in the description of hills as 'a stallion stalwart very-violet-sweet' be, with the proper sympathy for Hopkins' enthusiasm, appreciated as a phrase reconciling the two seemingly opposed qualities of mountains, their male, animal-like roughness and strength and at the same time their ethereal quality under soft light for which the violet in the gentle eye of the horse makes exactly the proper association? What Dr. Bridges and other upholders of 'literary decorum' object to most in a poet is not as a matter of fact either 'faults of taste' or 'faults of style' (in Hopkins supposedly consisting chiefly in the clipping of grammar to suit the heavily stressed metre) but a daring that makes the poet socially rather than artistically objectionable….

NOTE

1 A free rendering of the Preface, *ante*, pp. 77–8.

38. Alec Brown, 'Gerard Hopkins and Associative Form', *Dublin Magazine*

April–June 1928, pp. 6–20

...The matter of obscurity as an advantage can not enter here, although I might suggest that the weakness of modern verse is in part due, not so much to its lucidity, as to the small flight our successful modern poets (culminating a technically fruitful, but otherwise distressingly sterile, few centuries of adolescence), allow themselves—to the trifling matter and manner they wish to give us. It may be that the most perfect, ambitious and recondite poem will be, in spite of its appearance, and in spite of its not conveying meaning through the ordinary logical machinery of speech, a most translucent thing.

In fact, Hopkins, fumbling in the dark, his brain tortured by the religious phantasies by which he sublimated his remarkable sensuality, became (which is noteworthy in an innovator), even facile in what at first glance appear to be some of his most precious and tortured moments. If we read, say, the first stanza of 'Binsley Poplars', we look perplexedly for the grammatical sense, we are baffled and annoyed. Yet, if it is read slowly and deliberately (and unmetrically), by someone else, and the words, without analysis, are allowed to drip on the ear, a cogent picture accompanied by rich suggested comment can be obtained. Here is the stanza:

> My aspens dear, whose airy cages quelled,
> Quelled or quenched in leaves the leaping sun,
> All felled, felled, are all felled;
>> Of a fresh and following folded rank
>> That dandled a sandalled
> Shadow that swam or sank
> On meadow and river and wind-wandering weed-winding bank.

In the first place it is clear that if, not merely we analyse and make grammatical sense of this stanza—but that if Hopkins himself were there to explain himself—the task could be performed without departing from the ordinary logical speech-structure of language. It runs that 'my aspens, whose airy cages quelled or quenched the leaping sun with their leaves, are all felled—the aspens which stood in a fresh and folded (is it a compact?) rank, and which let hang down a sandalled shadow which floated on the surface, or vanished by moments (sank) on meadow, or river etc.'

But to force this logic into it is, however, to mistake the very nature of developed poetry, and if this were the only way of taking in the stanza the stanza would be a failure, for is not such confused, undecided thought, such an overladen and grotesque picture, much too obscure and tortuous to be beautiful?

Let us, then, take it the other way—as it falls on an ear from which the interference of arguing reason has been removed. We may assume that the separate lines form, to all intents, sense-units—for us. Separate images fall on our minds, which we strip of all mechanism to connect and explain. 'My aspens dear, whose airy cages quelled'—we have the airy bunchy bird-haunted tops of the aspens, whch are involved in a quelling; quelled or that quell—let that be, for once, no matter to our logic-empested minds. Float on the buoying sea of images. Where are we? We end the line on *quelled*; what of the quelled, we ask, not logically but rhythmically—because the first line has borne us upwards on a curve, and we look for the resolution. All artistic units are, after all, at bottom presentation of a rhythm and the resolution of it; epitomes of our own lives.

Quelled, quelled, rings in our brain; and the response comes: quelled—or, if you prefer it, quenched—(and perhaps he uses both words because quelled is abstract, quenched a shift to the concrete, or even because this flame and water concept will be necessary to the picture—all that, in suspension in our memory, will be clear later), 'in leaves the leaping sun'; then it is, perhaps not the aspens quelled—it is the sun quenched, quelled in the leaves. The apprehension which the first complex image may have given (that the sense was 'O my dear aspens, whose airy cages are quelled'— for we are told at the beginning that the poem is to Binsley Poplars, which were felled such and such a date), is thus resolved; but, as the stanza goes further, which it must do (unless it is imperfect, or really part of a larger stanza), the scene changes.

The stanza has to go further, because other unresolved elements have been started; the water concept of *quenched*, and the *leaping* aspect of the sun. We listen, however, and in place of any reference to water, or any more of the sun, we have a sudden lament, in startling opposition to the triumph of the aspens quelling the sun, and the relief of the second line that it is not the aspens that are quelled, but that quell. The effect is most poignant; and (most important), the poignancy does not depend on grammar, but results from a succession of words, calling up varied associations, exciting both a series of states, and a cumulative, affective state in us. This is the ultimate structure of poetry, which I will call that of cumulative association.

But we have not yet finished the stanza. We have, in the preceding lines, merely a lamentative statement; to complete the rhythm of a unit there must be a responsive part. How does Hopkins get it? Let us not forget the two possible tail-ends to develop on—aspens as water, and sun as a leaping thing. The aspens quench—likely then they are fresh—so 'of a fresh and following folded rank' we begin; a suggestive, inconclusive line. How are we to react to 'a following folded rank'?

Rank suggests something military and ordered, and as the poem is unmilitary the sense of ordered is presumably dominant; *folded*, we can only presume, as we have not yet the enlightenment of the remainder of the poem, is to suggest the aspect of the aspens, with their leafy branches folded to the trunk; *following*—obviously one will say, because they are planted in a regular row; following and rank each playing with the same idea, each a little redundant. Yet, after the image clarity of the first three lines, one finds (and especially in so far as conscious of the nature of rhythmic units, by which this line, in the response to the first 'question and answer,' is only the 'question,' the rising section of the rhythm), something inconclusive in these elucidations. The words are awkard if they are meant to mean merely the above; so awkward that they suggest a further content. We are still presuming the stanza is in good verse; we therefore expect more; and get it.

'Not spared, not one'—not one, them of these, of a fresh and following folded rank, the poplars, then, that are felled, has been spared—not one... 'that dandled a sandalled'—and, like little natural trains of tinderdry grass in a fire on the moors, the images burst into running channels of flame, of light—'that dandled a sandalled'—the images leap, Greek dancing, Greek vase, (even *folded*, for their robes), *rank*. But now it is the metre sweeps us on:—

Dandled a sandalled
Shadow that swam or sank.

the swaying up and down of the aspens, the water suggestion—'on meadow and river and wind-wandering (cf. *airy cages*), weed-winding bank,' and the stanza is complete.

Words, after all, are, mainly, but complex sounds, partly musical, partly noise, which, when heard by another person acquainted with the conventional meanings of any system (*i.e.*, any language), result in the imagination by that person of some arbitrary unit of perception (ideas or things). There is a small number of words which indicate interrelationships of what other words denote; but these, (articles, prepositions and the like), are of little real importance for conveying a complicated realisation of some aspect of the universe. They supply the grammatical structure, but they are of less relative importance in conveying to another a sense of the actual concretenesses (physical or mental) which are the principal content of poetry. Thus it is not surprising that we may understand a poem without any real reference to the grammatical structure; it is not surprising, either, that one of the chief elements even of the most reasoned pseudo-classical 'poetry' is the introduction of characteristics entirely unnecessary to the argument—words associated by sound, rhyme, assonance, alliteration.—or even by mere metrical position. It is only curious that it has needed so long for this fundamental associative understructure of poetry to become evident as what it is....

39. I. A. Richards, *Practical Criticism*

1929, pp. 80–90

Richards called this celebrated volume 'A piece of field-work in comparative ideology', publishing, with commentary, the responses—called protocols—of his students to little-known and anonymous poems that were placed before them. Richards's main thesis was the need for close, objective reading, and the Hopkins poem 'Spring and Fall' (printed in a faulty version) evoked a response which was as revealing, from this point of view, as any in the book.

> Margaret, are you grieving
> Over Goldengrove unleafing?
> Ah! as the heart grows older
> It will come to such sights colder
> By and by, nor spare a sigh
> Tho' world of wanwood leafmeal lie;
> And yet you will weep and know why.
> Now no matter, child, the name.
> Sorrow's springs are the same.
> Nor mouth had, no, nor mind express'd,
> What heart heard of, ghost guess'd:
> It is the blight man was born for,
> It is Margaret you mourn for.[1]

Both response and opinion here divide with a pleasing neatness. Furthermore, all stages of the cleavage are well shown. If some of the other protocol sets have something of the wildness and unexpectedness, the untidiness and bizarrity, of industrialised hill-country, or the variety of a rich but ill-tended garden, this set, on the other hand, has the soothing simplicity of a demonstration in elementary geology.

The incipient crack—to pursue the metaphor a little way—and the forces that provoke it appear in 6.1 This writer might, later on, be found on either side of the gulf. He is sufficiently susceptible and sufficiently impatient to have landed himself anywhere.

6.1. Has a decided *fascination* for me, but it is *an irritating rather than a satisfactory fascination*. I can't be quite sure I have grasped the meaning. One reading I really feel I do understand it, but at the next reading I am not sure that I am not completely on the wrong tack after all. Part of the fascination is the balanced alliterative rhythm and rhyme scheme but at the same time that is part of the irritation because I find myself attending exclusively to the sound and general feel of the word-pattern regardless of the sense. Finally *I cannot make up my mind whether or not I understand it or whether or not I like it.*

Rather more pertinacity, and perhaps more intelligence, carry 6.12 over to the positive side. He shows a prudent awareness of some of the dangers of this poetic theme and a due sense of what their avoidance implies.

6.12. I have not had time to 'attack' this poem as much as I should like to. It conveyed little to me on the first reading, but now I like it, and think the sentiment as good and genuine as that of No. 8 is spurious and false. I think it is a beautiful expression of a mood often expressed in poetry—that of the poet watching a child, and thinking of its future, and I think that, as *the mood is one that particularly lends itself to false sentiment,* it is a triumph for a poet to give us a new and impressive rendering of it.

Since so many readers did not succeed in applying their intelligence, a paraphrase kindly supplied by one writer may be inserted here. It will help moreover to bring out an interesting double-reading that the seventh line of the poem lends itself to.

6.13. It is difficult to understand this poem at first. After thinking about it a good deal I have come to the conclusion that this is the meaning of it—an elderly man, experienced in such matters, has found a girl grieving at the falling of leaves in autumn.

He shows that she will not longer have the same quick sensitiveness when she is old—she will no longer be able to grieve for such things (Cf. lines 2–4). Then she will weep, but this time, not for such things as the falling leaves in autumn, but because she can no longer have such feelings—the feelings of youth. (Cf. 'And yet you will weep and know why'). Even now in weeping at the transience of all things she enjoys in autumn, she is really weeping for the transience of all things. She is mourning among other things, for the fleetingness of her own youth.

The other and the preferable reading of the line is indicated in 6.2 where an admirable power of detailed analysis is displayed.

6.2. This poem shows great skill and I think it is by far the most difficult of the four. The more I read it the more I find in it; I did not really grasp its whole meaning till I had made about three attacks on it and even now I am not sure I thoroughly understand it. *I do not think this is because it is obscure, but because it requires a special reading*; the accenting of the seventh line is particularly important—the accent falls on 'will weep' and 'know why'.

The way the poem is written I admire greatly. I like the simple opening and closing couplet, *the one answering the other.* The first six lines begin at a low pitch and then rise at 'Ah! as the heart grows older', only to fall again in the sixth line. I like the even accentuation of the sixth line. Then there is great control of vowel music, the more open vowels where the voice rises in the third and fourth lines; the vowel 'i' introduced in 'sights' is made much of in the next line, and a triple rhyme made on it. There is *a breathing sigh* in 'By and by, nor spare a sigh'.

I like the whole idea of the poem, and I think the last couplet is excellent, giving the poem universal application and making this specially refer to Margaret.

That the author of the poem was aware of the possible alternative readings of the seventh line is shown by an accent-mark he originally placed on 'will'.

And yet you will weep and know why.

This mark I omitted, partly to see what would happen, partly to avoid a likely temptation to irrelevant discussions. Without it, 'will' may be read as giving the future tense, as 6.13 in fact reads it. Then the accents may fall on 'weep' and on 'and'; the sense being that in the future she will know the reason for a sorrow that is now only a blind grief. When 'will' is accentuated it ceases to be an auxiliary verb and becomes the present tense of the verb 'to will'. She persists in weeping and in demanding the reason for the falling of the leaves, and perhaps also for her grief. The rhythmical difference made by the change of sense is immense. Both the sense and the movement rejected by the poet are very good, however, and doubtless some readers will privately retain them. But because the authentic version is perhaps better still the hint given by the accent-mark ought to be retained. The swing over from one reading to another (without perhaps sufficient appreciation of the first) is remarked upon in 6.21

6.21. I like this best of all. *What looks like preciosity*—'Golden grove unleafing' and 'world of wanwood leafmeal lie'—is *really a means of compression*. I was puzzled at first reading because I took 'will' in 'and yet you will weep and know why' to be future. Wistfulness without sentimentality: the pang of transience well conveyed.

How much the poem conveyed to those who admitted it will appear from the next two protocols. It will be noticed that few of our chosen poems evoke praise of such quality even when most admired.

6.22. Excellent, the emotions of sorrow and forlornness lose nothing in communication; I have never experienced them more poignantly, and could not imagine myself doing so, than in reading the poem. Rhyme words are the (intellectually and emotionally) important ones both separately and in their pairs.

$$\left.\begin{array}{l}\text{Grieving}\\\text{Unleafing}\end{array}\right\} \text{very stong associations.}$$

$$\left.\begin{array}{l}\text{nor mind expressed}\\\text{ghost guessed}\end{array}\right\}$$

Rhythm and 'sense' (scientific) inseparable. Contrast lilt of

'By and by nor spare a sigh'

with

'Tho' world of wanwood leafmeal lie'.

The last two lines stick in the throat like real sorrow.

The praise here of the rhymes is worth noting, for our rhymesters, as indeed always happens whenever the least opportunity occurs, were not slow to pounce upon the opening and the close, though I am not, this time, illustrating these antics.

6.23. *Unless really soaked in, would pass unnoticed. Sounds* all way through. 'Margaret' strikes note, colour and sadness. 'Golden grove unleafing' full, soft. 'Tho' world of wanwood leafmeal lie'—gloriously melancholy (worthy of Keats' 'La Belle Dame Sans Merci'). Last two lines especially rhyme. Metre: 7, 9, 11, jar unless read *most sympathetically*: they can be made to sound in perfect keeping with rest. Sound, sense, rhythm and rhyme really wonderfully interwoven. Freedom of words (wanwood leafmeal, unleafing) and the newness of the whole: with its strange simplicity, lend distinction, intimacy, spontaneity. Not the least particularising detail, therefore its appeal is universal: yet subtle strokes like 'Golden grove', 'Margaret', remove any suggestion of the 'airy nothing'. Perfect melancholy, perfect artistry. It has conveyed to me a sentiment as completely as very few poems have ever done before.

This reader is mistaken in his opening remark. Many who by no means 'soaked in' the poem, yet had plenty to say about it.

Another paraphrase at this point may make the poem seem more confusing and so assist us.

6.3. It took me a long time to find out what was being said, and *even now I am not sure that my solution is correct*. The poem reminds me of Browning's remark of one of his poems—'When I wrote this God and I only knew what it meant, now, God only knows.'

Margaret is grieving over the falling leaves, and she is told that *there are other sights colder than this, meaning death,* which when she gets older *she will not even sigh for;* yet she will weep when she realises that all of us like leaves must die. Her mouth and her mind had neither expressed this idea of death which she felt at heart in a vague way. Man was born to die, and she is mourning for herself. The poem might have been expressed far more intelligibly without loss of any charm or impression. *A great contrast to No. 5 where death is made light of—here it is regarded dismally.*

6.31. I read this ten times without finding any meaning in it and very little attraction. Either I am, or the writer is, more than usually idiotic, but I really am quite unable to digest this doughy, heavy, obscure, indigestible and unsustaining piece of whatever it is meant to be.

We may remind ourselves here that these are the opinions of serious and professed students of English.

6.32. The thought is worthless, and hopelessly muddled. *A nonsensical conglomeration of words.* Expressed in jerky, disconnected phrases, *without rhythm.*

Blank bewilderment and helpless inability to comprehend either the sense or the form of the poem naturally gave rise to irritation.

6.33. This is difficult to read and difficult to understand, and not worth the effort to understand it. I find it impossible to recreate the poet's experience: the poem merely annoys me when I try.
There doesn't seem to be the least vestige of a metrical scheme. It is most difficult to scan or to read. Such lines as

> 'Nor mouth had, no, nor mind expressed
> What heart heard of, ghost guessed'

are enough to put anybody off from reading it a second time. I certainly shouldn't have done except for this test.

Excuses were suggested:

6.34. *If this is an extract we ought to have more of it* to judge from. If not, there is probably *some biographical information needed.* I frankly don't understand it.

And many explanations offered:

6.35. This, to me, is a jumble of ideas, most badly expressed. The poet is apparently sermonising in words, *in order that the reader shall exercise his ingenuity.* The whole thing is cramped in thought and expression. It is not surprising that a poet of this kind considers himself born for a 'blight'. It is very annoying being told that 'the name' in the 8th line does not matter. It would be so delightful to know. *It might be a part of a dialogue, in which one lunatic addresses another.* I presume this is typically modern-born in the little philosophy which I can gather. And in the style, the only aim of which seems to be to baffle the reader.

6.36. What does all this mean? Margaret *has apparently been jilted* and is, very sensibly, *finding solace* in the autumn tints of golden-grove. Whereat the poet tells her, by way of comfort, that as she gets older she will get accustomed to sorrow, 'nor spare a sigh'. 'This has only been a dream. But naturally you're feeling it a bit. Never mind, my dear. You'll get over it. We all do'.

But I *should* like to know precisely *what* is the 'blight man was born for'.

Tenderness for Margaret prompted further complaints:

6.37. This is the worst poem I have ever read. It is vague and incoherent, and does not appeal to any of my senses, except my sense of humor. The *parent or whoever it is* who is advising Margaret *is a bitter, hard individual* who seems to be trying to take away all the hope and happiness of the child. I don't think that *any really kind person* would feel so little sympathy for a child's trivial sorrow, and make her unhappy by telling her that the worse is yet to come. As for the line

'Tho' world of wanwood leafmeal lie'

I have looked up both 'wanwood' and 'leafmeal' in four dictionaries, and I cannot find their meanings. I see no excuse for making a poem so vague.

The 'family-constellation' may have its part in this as another personal situation may have in 6.36. Another intrusion of something not easily to be found in the poem is made in 6.38 and seems also to voice some personal reverberation.

6.38. *An average reader* will probably not get anything out of this poem—it is much too complicated and symbolical. *The melancholy reproachful voice from a wasted life.* It is true—with exception of the last line but one—but not sound.

The note of conscious superiority rings out clearly in many of the protocols as the indignation swells:

6.40. This seems to me to be a remarkably bad attempt to put into poetry *a thought that possibly the author imagined* was original. Namely, that Margaret, though she thinks she is grieving for Goldenbrook, is really mourning for herself. The poem appears to me to be disconnected and rather pointless; *the few sane remarks in it are trite.* An extra line seems to have dropped into the middle of the poem as it were by mistake; thus making three rhyming lines instead of two as in the rest of the poem. Why the line

'And yet you will weep and know why'

is there at all I don't know.
Trite thought, somewhat incoherently and badly expressed.

The unfortunate readers bray, snort, and bleat, so overmastering is their contempt.

6.41. This is extraordinarily bad poetry, embodying the trite philosophy that the world is 'a vale of tears'. Winter, as so often, reminds the speaker of the desolation and sorrows of life. In putting his doggerel together, *the poet mixes his verbs and his metaphors hopelessly*. The *grave air of the thing adds to the laughableness* of it.

6.42. *Pish-posh!*

6.43. Sentamental. It is very remeniscent of Hardy in language and form, but Hardy was not in the least sentamental, he plunged in the depths for truth and felt it to be sad. I find this poem *quite unintelligible and useless*.

'Sentamentality' was certainly invited by the poem, and the invitation was not refused. As so often happens the reader's own revulsion at his own devious excesses is counted against the poet.

6.5. The poet has used his technical perfection *to express a common human failing* to which he is subject, in veiled language; *he is ashamed of it* and only wishes to be understood by fellow sufferers (or cowards). That is that form of egotism which allows a person to identify himself with the changes of the seasons and to live autumn as well as see it—to read Sir Thomas Browne, Ibsen and the profounder Russian pessimists and *imagine that he is depressed*. Usually he realises that it is a form of self-satisfaction before he commits suicide for haply he may hit upon Aldous Huxley:

'If, O my Lesbia, I should commit
Not fornication, dear, but suicide,'
K.T.L.

The 'Obscurity—Ah!—Browning' association must be very widely and firmly established. It is not surprising that here it is accompanied by inability to apprehend form.

6.6. The communication of this is bad. Thoughts are packed together, half-evolved, and the sentences are consequently ruthlessly clipped. It is *a sort of combination of* A.S.M. Hutchinson *and* Browning. It is very difficult to untangle the real points. I don't think it would lose as much as it would gain by a prose paraphrase.

I like the ideas implied, except that of the last couplet, which *denies the existence of disinterestedness*. The other ideas are worth expressing better than they are here.

6.61. This is either an imitation of Browning, or Browning in one of his worst moments. The thought expressed is a fairly simple one, and there does not appear to be any reason why it should be expressed in so complicated a manner. We guess the general meaning of the sixth line. The other lines are inharmonious, and rather flat. *The poet adopts rather a patronising attitude towards Margaret*, in order to explain a quite elementary truth, *i.e.* that when we weep for the past we are only weeping for the death of ourselves. He is earnest and *evidently likes his idea*. He *even shows some emotion* in the expression of it.

How near a reader may come to an understanding of both aspects of a poem, only to be deprived of it by a false expectation of what a poet should do with a given subject appears in 6.7.

6.7. This is clearly an experiment in sound and in striving after effect the sense suffers considerably. The style is jerky, *like convulsive sobbing, throughout*: and suffers from lack of clarity. In fact the later part of the piece is so cramped that it takes quite a long time to make out the sense, though the meaning is there right enough. The ingenious arrangement of *l*s and *w*s, *m*s and *s*s seems rather a misdirection of energy, though the result goes far to justify the attempt. This is *no mournful and majestic dirge;* but a very passable whimper.

Finally, a long and very subtle analysis of the rhythm (giving perhaps a third reading to line seven, for 6.21 may have stressed 'and') will round the discussion off, as in such a case justice requires.

6.8. Love at first sight. Perfect in *its sonnet-like di-partite valvular structure; in its 'whole' and 'local' rhythms;* in its emotion content (the poignancy with which it brings home, from its objective Pathetic Fallacy, the subjective 'Tragedy'); and *in the intellectual articulation that contrasts with its formal economy*. A fusion, in the culmination of the last 2 lines, of tragic disclosure with a Katharsis that unites the individual to the universal fate.

The symmetry on either side the crucial, rhythmically broken, central line is admirably managed. Less obvious, *qua* symmetry, is the lilt, and subtly contrasted change in it, as between the groups of six lines on either side the lilt-breaker (1.7). This, it seems to me, should be read in two portions:

And yet you will weep (gap) and know why

the emphatic words 'know why' receiving strong but long-drawn stresses, that on know being slightly stronger on an uptake and upward inbreathe of pitch, 'why' being on an, equally slight, down outbreath of pitch. *Nowhere, I think, should the speed-tempo be as slow as here.* If read like this the element of slightly more argumentative disturbance differentiating the last half from the first is more likely to be demasked and the rhythmical rendering *invested with a certain distractedness,* which expressing itself in lines 11 and 12 (11 especially) disturbs the continuity of the rhythmic sighing which characterises all but the central line, and never so exquisitely as in 4th, 5th, and 6th lines of the piece.

Particularly admirable is the relation of the first and last couplets and their manner of functionally framing the intermediate arguments that draws the veil of illusion from ineluctable disillusion. They frame the remorselessly remorseful disclosure between two solicitudes—a solicitude presaging disclosure that must dispel the enchanting premise of naïvety, and a solicitude that must make what amend it can for *this exquisite vandalism,* by consolatory merging of the individual in the common fate.

(Of course I don't mistake this for overt dialogue. It is no more—and no less—than *meditated dialogue,* an imaginary conversation between young mind and old, between old and youthful 'Ego.')

NOTE

1 This is the version printed by Bridges in *The Spirit of Man.* Lines 3 and 4 of the full version are omitted.

40. Fr G.F. Lahey, *Gerard Manley Hopkins*

London, 1930

The first biography of Hopkins, by the American Jesuit Fr Lahey (1903–69), was greeted with respect by most reviewers, but its deficiencies have become more apparent with time. However, it included much new material from the letters and journals, and became the usual reviewing companion of the 2nd edition of the *Poems*.

... Every poetic distinctiveness has at first a certain obscurity, and any appreciation commensurate with poetic values will always postulate many 'second readings', much intellectual meditation—the 'salt of poetry'. Hopkins's oddness lies mainly in his verbal and rhythmic obscurity. But even this may please. His peculiar interest comes from the perennial source of surprises which meet any reader however well-informed; his peculiar greatness lies in the amazing union of intellectual profundity with great emotional intensity and imaginative power, under the control of a highly developed faculty of expression and structural perfection. It is well to remember, however, that these qualities may not be predicated indiscriminately to all his work. In fact before the 'Deutschland' in 1875 his poetry has but slight aesthetic interest other than youthful precocity and a certain idyllic sweetness. Later poems, such as 'Rosa Mystica' and 'Ad Mariam', are also of this category, though 'Rosa Mystica' has a simple beauty that would only be blemished by aesthetic self-consciousness. 'Ad Mariam' is an entirely remarkable poem in the style of Swinburne, which may indeed have eclipsed its model. It is a poem of five octets written in rather breathless tetrameters; the first two stanzas will illustrate its competence sufficiently for our purpose:

[Quotes first two verses of 'Ad Mariam'.]

'Winter in the Gulf Stream', written in 1871,[1] is interesting because it stands like a lonely flower amid the fallow land of his seven years poetical silence. It reminds us somewhat of the magic of Mr. De la Mare, and yet simultaneously it faintly foreshadows that castigation and white-hot austerity which characterizes his later work....

NOTE

1 In fact, 1862.

41. Isidor Schneider, 'A Great Poet', *Nation* (New York)

16 April 1930, pp. 456–8

Isidor Schneider (1896–1977), b. in the Ukraine, came to the United States in 1902, worked in publishing, and wrote novels and poetry. His literary criticism also appeared in the *New Republic*.

This article is a review of *A Vision of the Mermaids* and Lahey.

Two hundred and fifty copies,[1] I have heard, made up the whole edition in which for the first time the few but wonderful poems of Gerard Manley Hopkins were published. That was in 1918. Their extraordinary author had been dead twenty-nine years. Save for occasional publication chiefly in religious periodicals and anthologies, on whose reluctant editors they had almost to be forced, the poems were known only to a handful of impressed but not always understanding friends. They knew the man to be remarkable and respected the poetry as his utterance. These friends included Coventry Patmore, who esteemed Hopkins enough to take his advice in revising his own work, but who gave up the effort of following Hopkins's bewildering innovations, and Robert Bridges, who in his understanding and will to understand becomes an example of a good friend. It was to Bridges that Hopkins intrusted his manuscripts to be published after his death. Victorian timidity no doubt, and later the war, lengthened the delay; finally the book was published in the carefully and conscientiously annotated edition of 1918, which is being reprinted within a few months with additional poems. To precede this reprinting we have now a useful biography and a facsimile of one of the longer Hopkins manuscripts.

Bridges may seem to have been a hesitant sponsor; but the temper of Hopkins's generation and the general impatience with experiment will account for his hesitation. He may seem to be too defensive in his editorial notes, to dwell too submissively on the defects and too shyly on the excellences. But in 1918 matters were different. Today we have become not so much tolerant of as styled to experiment. Mr. Bridges could not have anticipated the quick acceptance of this poetry, and still less its immediate and increasing influence.

In the twelve years since their publication the 250 small books have been searched out and become scarce. Five English booksellers in a year's time could not locate a copy for one insistent purchaser. Among poets the possessors' names were exchanged and the copies were borrowed oftener perhaps than those of any book in recent years. With the publication of the forthcoming new edition of the poems it will probably be observed that in some recent poetry influences attributed to other poets are in reality Hopkins's. The Poet Laureate's work owns it, and Hart Crane's 'The Bridge,' unquestionably a great poem and one of the few of our generation, shows the present benefits of Hopkins's liberating and enriching experiments.

This influence cannot, I think, be attributed mainly to his many and extraordinary contributions to English versification, although they are the first to be noticed and both in quality and in quantity constitute probably the greatest addition made by a single poet. Today we are inclined rather to imitate an attitude of mind than a form; and for that reason a T.S. Eliot exerts more authority than an E.E. Cummings. In Hopkins, however, it is not so much an attitude of mind—else we should all seek some individual form of asceticism—as the virtue of an example. Here is a poet who was not afraid to write exactly as he wished, who dared to take the risk of a crabbed and queer appearance, of obscurities into which readers would not follow him.

Such independence has always been rare in literature. Few poets seem to have been so indifferent to or disciplined against the pleasure of publication. It is the only form of his asceticism that it would be profitable for us to imitate, though devout Catholics may think differently. Hopkins was even content after his admission to the Soceity of Jesus to give up writing poetry altogether.....

He wrote, as he said elsewhere, to satisfy a love of design; but he wrote, too, out of a love and understanding of words, of their sound and of their sense, that is unrivaled in our literature. He played almost boisterously with them, running them out in delightful repetitions, in transformations and substitutions. This freedom with words is even more characteristic than his rhythms or his marvelous imagery. This and the exigencies of his bold rhythmic scheme led to the oddities for which Bridges apologizes too much, and of which the author was fully conscious....

The elements of Hopkins's originality are bewildering. He is astonishingly bold with words and with forms of speech; he is free with ellipses, coins new words, breaks them in two, transfers the parts of combined words, as when 'brimful in a flash' becomes 'brim in a flashful'; rhymes internally, alliterates, omits that's and which's to have every word dynamic, and displaces prepositions so that their very movement in the sentence adds to their force; combines words to sharpen their rhythm, quicken their meaning, and harmonize their sound.

Such a procedure is inimitable; it is his poetic personality, which will certainly stimulate and encourage other poets along the paths of their own individuality, but which it would be very dangerous to copy. It is his prosody that is his main contribution....

...Beyond question Hopkins belongs among the great poets of English literature. The experiments may be taken as evidence of the subtlety and diversity of one of the greatest minds to express itself in poetry in his generation....

NOTE

1 In fact, 750.

42. Unsigned review, 'A Victorian Who Has Come into Fashion', *New York Times Book Review*

27 July 1930, p. 12

The reviewer saw the interest in Hopkins as little more than a modern fad. His review of Lahey's biography brought some stinging comments from the poet Stanley Kunitz in the *Wilson Bulletin* in September: see Introduction, p. 21.

...One cannot accept Mr. Lahey's view that Hopkins's later work—as revealed in the examples which he presents—shows any of the signs of greatness; and while the writer's unpretentious earlier productions do manifest an undeniable poetic talent, one is inclined to wonder whether the verse of his later years, with its impossible rhythms and its air of freakishness and affectation, would not have been more kindly treated had it been allowed to remain in that oblivion to which Hopkins's contemporaries seemed content to consign it?

43. William Empson, *Seven Types of Ambiguity*

London, 1930, (a) pp. 186–9, (b) pp. 284–6

William Empson (1906–84), poet and critic, taught during the thirties in China and Japan. He was an early admirer of Auden. *Seven Types* was his first book.

The extracts need some introduction. An ambiguity is 'Any consequence of language, however slight, which adds some nuance to the direct statement of prose' (*Seven Types*, p. 1).

'An ambiguity of the fourth type occurs when two or more meanings of a statement do not agree among themselves, but combine to make clear a complicated state of mind in the author' (p. 168).

'An example of the seventh type of ambiguity...occurs when the two meanings of the word, the two values of the ambiguity, are the two opposite meanings defined by the context, so that the total effect is to show a fundamental division in the writer's mind' (p. 244).

(a)

...The meaning of an English sentence is largely decided by the accent, and yet one learns in conversation to put the accent in several places at once; thus the poem[1] can be read so as to combine these two ways of underlining it.

These cases are curious in that the different versions demand to be read aloud in different ways, and apparently cannot be united into a single vocal effect. One may be intended, while reading a line one way, to be conscious that it could be read in another; so that if it is to be read aloud it must be read twice; or one may be intended to read it in some way different from the colloquial speech-movement so as to imply both ways at once. Different styles of reading poetry aloud use these methods in different proportions, but I should take my two last examples from Donne as respectively demanding the two methods in isolation. The following example from Hopkins shows the first case being forcibly included in the second.

[Quotes, incorrectly, 'Spring and Fall'.]

Will weep may mean: 'insist upon weeping, now or later,' or 'shall weep in the future.' *Know* in either case may follow *will*, like *weep*, 'you insist upon knowing, or you shall know,' or may mean: 'you already know why you weep, why you shall weep, or why you insist upon weeping,' or thirdly, may be imperative, 'listen and I shall tell you why you weep, or shall weep, or shall insist upon weeping, or insist upon weeping already.' Mr. Richards, from whom I copy this (*Practical Criticism*, p. 83)[2], considers that the ambiguity of *will* is removed by the accent which Hopkins placed upon it; it seems to me rather that it is intensified. Certainly, with the accent on *weep* and *and*, *will* can only be the auxiliary verb, and with the accent on *will* its main meaning is 'insist upon'. But the future meaning also can be imposed upon this latter way of reading the line if it is the tense which is being stressed, if it insists on the contrast between the two sorts of weeping, or, including *know* with *weep*, between the two sorts of knowledge. Now it is useful that the tense should be stressed at this crucial point, because it is these two contrasts and their unity which make the point of the poem.

It seems difficult to enjoy the accent on *are*, which the poet has inserted; I take it to mean: 'Sorrow's springs, always the same, independent of our attitude to them and of our degree of consciousness of them, exist,' permanently and as it were absolutely.

The two sorts of knowledge, intuitive and intellectual, form ambiguities again in the next couplet; this may help to show they are really there in the line about *will*. *Mouth* and *mind* may belong to *Margaret* or somebody else; *what heart heard of* goes both forwards and backwards; and *ghost*, which in its grammatical position means both the profundities of the unconsciousness and the essentially conscious spirit, brings to mind both immortality and a dolorous haunting of the grave. 'Nobody else's mouth had told her, nobody else's mind had hinted to her, about the fact of mortality, which yet her own imagination had already invented, which her own spirit could foresee.' 'Her mouth had never mentioned death; she had never stated the idea to herself so as to be conscious of it; but death, since it was a part of her body, since it was natural to her organs, was known at sight as a portent by the obscure depths of her mind.' My point is not so much that these two are mixed up as that the poet has shown elsewhere, precisely by insisting that they were *the same*, that he knew they were distinguishable. ...

(b)

... I shall end this chapter with a more controlled and intelligible example from George Herbert, where the contradictory impulses that are held in equilibrium by the doctrine of atonement may be seen in a luminous juxtaposition. But in such cases of ambiguity of the seventh type one tends to lose sight of the conflict they assume; the ideas are no longer thought of as contradictory by the author, or if so, then only from a stylistic point of view; he has no doubt that they can be reconciled, and that he is stating their reconciliation. So I shall first consider a Sonnet by Gerard Manley Hopkins, 'The Windhover, to Christ our Lord,' as a more evident example of the use of poetry to convey an indecision, and its reverberation in the mind.

[Quotes 'The Windhover'.]

I am indebted to Mr. Richards for this case; he has already written excellently about it.[3] I have nothing but some grammatical points to add to his analysis, and repeat it here merely because it is so good an example.

Hopkins became a Jesuit, and burnt his early poems on entering the order; there may be some reference to this sacrifice in the *fire* of the Sonnet. Confronted suddenly with the active physical beauty of the bird, he conceives it as the opposite of his patient spiritual renunciation; the statements of the poem appear to insist that his own life is superior, but he cannot decisively judge between them, and holds both with agony in his mind. *My heart in hiding* would seem to imply that the *more dangerous* life is that of the Windhover, but the last three lines insist it is *no wonder* that the life of renunciation should be the more *lovely*. *Buckle* admits of two tenses and two meanings; 'they do buckle here,' or 'come, and buckle yourself here'; *buckle* like a military belt, for the discipline of heroic action and *buckle* like a bicycle wheel, 'make useless, distorted, and incapable of its natural motion.' *Here* may mean 'in the case of the bird,' or 'in the case of the Jesuit'; *then* 'when you have become like the bird,' or 'when you have become like the Jesuit.' *Chevalier* personifies either physical or spiritual acivity; Christ riding to Jerusalem, or the cavalryman ready for the charge; Pegasus, or the Windhover.

Thus in the first three lines of the sestet we seem to have a clear case of the Freudian use of opposites, where two things thought of as incompatible, but desired intensely by different systems of judgments, are spoken of simultaneously by words applying to both; both desires are thus given a transient and exhausting satisfaction, and the two systems of judgment are forced into open conflict before the reader. Such a process, one might imagine, could pierce to regions that underlie the whole structure of our thought; could tap the energies of the very depths of the mind. At the same time one may doubt whether it is most effective to do it so crudely as in these three lines; this enormous conjunction, standing as it were for the point of friction between the two worlds conceived together, affects one rather like shouting in an actor, and probably to many readers the lines seem so meaningless as to have no effect at all. The last three lines, which profess to come to a single judgment on the matter, convey the conflict more strongly and more beautifully.

The metaphor of the *fire* covered by ash seems most to insist on the beauty the *fire* gains when the ash falls in, when its precarious order is again shattered; perhaps, too, on the pleasure, in that some movement, some risk, even to so determinedly static a prisoner, is still possible. The *gold* that painters have used for the haloes of saints is forced by alliteration to agree with the *gash* and *gall* of their self-tortures; from this precarious triumph we fall again, with *vermilion*, to bleeding. . . .

NOTES

1 Donne's 'The Apparition'.
2 See No. 39.
3 In the *Dial*: see No. 36.

POEMS OF GERARD MANLEY HOPKINS

Second edition, edited, with an introduction, by Charles Williams,
London, 1930

---

44. Charles Williams, Introduction,
Poems of Hopkins

1930, pp. x–xvi

This new edition contained a further sixteen (relatively unimportant) poems. Charles Williams (1886–1945) worked for the Oxford University Press, but also did much writing and lecturing. He was a devout Anglican, whose books and personality seem to have had a profound effect on a number of people, including W.H. Auden. (His obituary in the *Dictionary of National Biography* was written by Gerard W.S. Hopkins, a nephew of the poet.) Williams's more sympathetic tone, compared with Bridges's Preface which continued to be printed, reflects the change in attitude of the poetry-reading public since 1918.

A good deal of attention has been paid to Gerard Hopkins's prosody, to his sprung-rhythms and logaoedic, his paeons and outrides; not so much has been spent on those habits, especially alliteration, to which English verse is more accustomed. Yet the alliteration so largely present in his poems is significant; especially if it be compared with that of another notable Victorian,

Swinburne. It is of course a habit prevalent in all poets, but in general it is unintentionally disguised; the inexpert reader will not easily believe how much of it is in Shakespeare. But there have never been two poets who employed it more than Hopkins and Swinburne; and the astonishing thing about Swinburne is not its presence but its uselessness, as the admirable thing about Hopkins is not its presence but its use. In verse after verse words beginning with the same letter hurry to Swinburne's demand; and all that can really be felt about them is that they do begin with the same letter. There is thought in Swinburne—more than it has of late been the fashion to admit—but the diction does not help it. The two things run almost parallel, so separate are they; they often divide at the opening of a poem, and when they come together it is by chance. The result is that Swinburne's alliteration will not usually stand close examination. Even the famous 'now folded in the flowerless fields of heaven' leaves the reader with the feeling that 'flowerless' which might—there—have been so remarkable an epithet, was as a matter of fact an accidental one. He was the child of the English vocabulary.

But Gerard Hopkins was not the child of vocabulary but of passion. And the unity of his passion is seen if we consider his alliteration: 'nor soul helps flesh more there than flesh helps soul.' The first stanza of the first poem, after the early ones, 'The Wreck of the Deutschland', may serve as an example. It is enough to suggest here that the curious reader might separate such almost inevitable 'poetic' alliterations as 'Lord of the living' from those in which the intense apprehension of the subject provides two or more necessary words almost at the same time. 'Thou hast bound bones... fastened me flesh.' It is as if the imagination, seeking for expression, had found both verb and substantive at one rush, had begun almost to say them at once, and had separated them only because the intellect had reduced the original unity into divided but related sounds. A line like 'And cast by conscience out, spendsavour salt' ('The Candle Indoors') is one in which that intellect goes speeding to sound the full scope of the imaginative apprehension, and yet all the while to keep as close to its source as possible. It is true we cannot make haste when we are reading him, but that is what helps to make him difficult. The very race of the words and lines hurries on our emotion; our minds are left behind, not, as in Swinburne, because they have to suspend their labour until it is wanted, but because they cannot work at a quick enough rate. 'Cast by conscience out' is not a phrase; it is a word. So is 'spendsavour salt'. Each is thought and spoken all at once; and this is largely (as it seems) the cause and (as it is) the effect of their alliteration. They are like words of which we remember the derivations; they present their unity and their elements at once.

The work of the intellect is in the choice of the words. One may compare again 'Maiden and mistress of the months and years' with 'Why tears! is it? tears; such a melting, a madrigal start' ('Wreck of the Deutschland'). Madrigal is the last word expected, but it is justly chosen. So in 'Stigma, signal, cinquefoil token', 'lettering of the lamb's fleece', 'the gnarls of the nails', and many another. For all the art of the impulse and rush, 'the roll, the rise, the carol, the creation,' it is very evident that the original impulse was to most careful labour as well as to apparent carelessness. The manuscripts confirm this by their numerous alterations, deletions, and alternative readings; they are what we might expect to find in the work-book of a good poet.

Of the same nature are his interior rhymes—as in 'The Lantern Out of Doors', 'heart wants, care haunts', 'first, fast, last friend', or the three last lines of the next poem; and his mere repetitions—'and hurls for him, O half hurls earth for him', 'lay wrestling with (my God!) my God'. Alliteration, repetition, interior rhyme, all do the same work: first, they persuade us of the existence of a vital and surprising poetic energy; second, they suspend our attention from any rest until the whole thing, whatever it may be, is said. Just as phrases which in other poets would be comfortably fashioned clauses are in him complex and compressed words, so poems which in others would have their rising and falling, their moments of importance and unimportance, are in him allowed no chance of having anything of the sort. They proceed, they ascend, they lift us (breathlessly and dazedly clinging) with them, and when at last they rest and we loose hold and totter away we are sometimes too concerned with our own bruises to understand exactly what the experience has been.

It is arguable that this is not the greatest kind of poetry; but it is also arguable that the greatest kind of poetry might easily arise out of this. Robert Bridges has said that he was, at the end, abandoning his theories. But his theories were only ways of explaining to himself his own poetic energy, and if he were abandoning them it was because that energy needed to spend no more time on explanation, because, that is, it was becoming perfectly adequate to its business, 'without superfluousness, without defect'. While it was capable of producing lines like 'Or to-fro tender trambeams truckle at the eye', it may very well have felt that it ought to do a certain amount of explanation, though it did not (as it could not) explain that. It is perfectly possible to smile at the line, but hardly possible to laugh; or only sympathetically, as at the wilder images of the metaphysicals, the extremer rhetoric of Marlowe, the more sedate elegances of Pope, the more prosaic moralities of the Victorians, or the more morbid pedestrianisms of Thomas Hardy. Such things are the accidents of genius seriously engaged upon its own business, and not so apt as the observer to see how funny it looks.

The poet to whom we should most relate Gerard Hopkins, however, is perhaps none of these—not even the Metaphysicals nor the other Victorians—but Milton. The simultaneous consciousness of a controlled universe, and yet of division, conflict, and crises within that universe, is hardly so poignantly expressed in any other English poets than those two. Neither of them is primarily a mystic in his poetry, though Gerard Hopkins might easily have become one, or rather mysticism might very well have appeared in it. But such poems as 'The Blessed Virgin compared to the Air we breathe' hardly suffice to mark his verse with that infrequent seal, any more than the 'Hound of Heaven' alone would seal Francis Thompson's. Both poets are on the verge of mystical vision; neither actually seems to express it. But if the sense of division and pain, of summons and effort, make mysticism, then Hopkins was a mystic, but then also Milton was. The suffering in 'Thou art indeed just, Lord' is related to the suffering of Milton's *Samson Agonistes*, though Milton, under the influence of an austerer religious tradition, refused to 'contend' with God as Gerard Hopkins was free to do. Both their imaginations, nevertheless, felt the universe as divided both within them and without them; both realized single control in the universe; and both of them fashioned demands upon themselves and upon others out of what they held to be the nature of that control. This was the nature of their intellect.

Gerard Hopkins's experience of this is expressed largely in continual shocks of strength and beauty. Strength and beauty are in all of the more assured poets; it is therefore on the word 'shocks' that emphasis must be laid. Any poet when he is not at his greatest is preparing us for his greatest; it is by that approach to him that we can discern the elements which go to make up the unity of his achievements. We can find in this poet's work the two elements which have been mentioned: (*a*) a passionate emotion which seems to try and utter all its words in one, (*b*) a passionate intellect which is striving at once to recognize and explain both the singleness and division of the accepted universe. But to these must be added a passionate sense of the details of the world without* and the world within, a passionate consciousness of all kinds of experience. 'The Bugler's First Communion' is unsurpassed in its sense of the beauty of adolescence, as 'A Handsome Answer'[1] or 'Brothers' of the beauty of childhood or 'Spring and Fall' of its sadness, the 'Windhover' or the 'Starlight Night' of the beauty of Nature, or certain of the sonnets of the extreme places of despair.

Yet perhaps, in the poems as we have them, the most recurrent vision seems to be that of some young and naked innocence existing dangerously poised among surrounding dangers—'the achieve of, the mastery of the thing!' Had he lived, those dangers and that poise might have been more fully analysed and expressed. As it is, his intellect, startled at the sight, breaks now into joy, now into inquiry, now into a terror of fearful expectation, but always into song. Other poets have sung *about* their intellectual exaltations; in none has the intellect itself been more the song than in Gerard Hopkins. In this he was unique among the Victorians, but not because he was different from them in kind—as they indeed were not different in kind from us or from their predecessors—only because his purely poetic energy was so much greater.

His poetic tricks, his mannerisms, his explorations in the technique of verse, are not in the earlier poems and they are disappearing from the later. Had he lived, those tricks might have seemed to us no more than the incidental excitements of a developing genius. Since he did not live they will probably always occupy a disproportionate part of the attention given him. But that that attention must increase is already certain: poets will return to him as to a source not a channel of poetry; he is one who revivifies, not merely delights, equivalent genius. Much of his verse is described in that last line which in 'Felix Randal' brings in the outer world with such an overmastering noise of triumph over the spiritual meditation of the other lines; he himself at his poetry's 'grim forge, powerful amidst peers' fettled for the great gray drayhorse of the world 'his bright and battering sandal'. Some of his poems are precisely bright and battering sandals. But some again are like another line—'some candle clear burns somewhere I come by'. He is 'barbarous in beauty'. But he is also 'sweet's sweeter ending'. This again is the result of and the testimony to his poetic energy. He is integral to the beauty and storm without as to the beauty and storm within. But it will take a good deal of patience in us before we are integral to his own.

NOTES

* He is usually so exact in his outward detail that one slip which is certain to be remarked sooner or later by a student of such things may as well be noted here. It will be observed that the stranger in the most lovely 'Epithalamion'—admirable fellow!—in preparing to bathe, takes off his boots *last*.

1 Actually 'The Handsome Heart: at a Gracious Answer'.

45. M[orton] D[auwen] Z[abel], 'Poetry as Experiment and Unity', *Poetry*

December 1930, pp. 152–61

Morton Dauwen Zabel (1901–64) was Professor of English at Chicago and associate editor of *Poetry*. He wrote again on Hopkins in the number for July 1935.

This is a review of *Poems*, 2nd edn, *A Vision of the Mermaids* and Lahey.

... To describe this poetry [*Poems*, 2nd edn] is to discover a counsel of idealism for poets. In it is arrested, with almost unrivaled intensity, the essence of the highest creative passion. Disclosed by the phrases of these sonnets and lyrics is a spiritual entity which has already begun, however fugitively, to impress the imaginative thought of our time. Hopkins' labors were wholly divorced from the commercial and personal influences of the literary market, and from the politics of esthetic schools. He wrote under no stimulus of clerical or public approbation. If an enthusiasm for experiment colors, sometimes indecisively, most of his mature works, it is free from exhibitionism, any threat of which is instantly nullified by the persuasive humility of his ascetic avowals. His interest in novelty is nowhere betrayed as specious, nor his stylistic courage as arrogant. He wrote poems whose rewards and defects ('oddnesses') for the most part delighted or reproached himself alone. On his death his note-books were committed to a friend who did not publish them for thirty years.

Hopkins thus appears as a poet in isolation. Emily Dickinson alone, among poets of his rank, presents a comparable figure. Doubtless she surpassed him in experiential range as in volume, and perhaps inaccuracy of intuitive logic, but she did not approach the ingenuity of his stylistic resources. The present biography leaves unanswered many problems long postulated to readers of the poetry—notably in regard to Hopkins' religious and emotional development—but concerning the purity and singleness of his moral dedication it verifies, by the necessarily limited means of letters and personal testimony, the implications of the poems themselves.

To seek beyond Hopkins' work, therefore, for a gauge of integrity in contemporary poetry would merely lead to confusion among the relative values of the three or four modern poets who share his distinction. Nor would their styles prove as significant as Hopkins', for no modern poet in English has undertaken with equal conviction the three modes of experiment—symbolic, prosodic, and verbal—which have marked the progress of poetry during the last seventy years. If Bridges' confidential publication of the poems in 1918 hindered the application of that gauge, its use is now rendered both convenient and imperative. For Hopkins' work is at once the measure of his own genius, and of the worth of the reforms and innovations which, for better or worse, have occupied the poets of two generations.

Hopkins' poetry is, first of all, a created poetry. It is devoid of echo and reference. It resists the importunities of analogy and comparison. Occasional parallels with other poets may be established in images and phrases, only to be cancelled by unpredictable elements in the next line or stanza. Hopkins' originality is organic.

His innovations in imagery, meter, and diction are integral and indispensable components of his style. By this unity he rivals the more prodigal (though often vicarious) brilliance of great contemporaries like Baudelaire and Rimbaud. However, his conception of poetry as dynamic, like theirs, was supported by creative passion and authority in every detail. It is necessary to examine the tenets of this authority if one is to approach his work with sympathy and intelligence.

Experiment in poetry since 1860 has proceeded largely on assumptions fostered by psychological and social research. The liberalizing, and subsequently the reform, of meter and metaphor grew with an increasing flexibility in dogma, scientific as well as moral. By their modification of conventional meters and classical forms, poets agreed that the standard prosody offered no adequate harmony with the libertarian and creative spirit of science and social progress. ...

... Unless flawlessly used, the free form merely becomes a slovenly garment for unpoetic material, insignificant as an instrument of analysis. To attempt to relate it to any valuable esthetic experience ends in the same fog of confusion and duplicity which originally surrounded the poet himself. The revolution of the word is fraught with similar evils of arbitrary and unprincipled association. Mr Joyce's apologists have supplied many clues to his new vocabulary, and indicated the immense courage of his project, but they give little hint that a logic based on linguistic principle persists in his reforms. Obscurity in poetry, where unjustified, usually involves this failure in principle, this inability of poetic language and content to withstand the test of realistic sublimation.

Hopkins is usually considered a poet of unprecedented obscurity. But from this point of view he is scarcely obscure at all. His ineluctability diminishes as one defines the sources of his allusions in minute observation, of his comparisons in exact and logical translation of physical or theological ideas, and of his rhythms in modulations of thought and feeling which always derive immediately from the subject-matter and tone of the poem. Unquestionably his poetry remains complex, but his obscurity is only the measure of impatience and lagging intelligence in the reader. ...

Hopkins' security as a poet exists in spite of (perhaps because of) his avoidance of the rigid intransigence which usually marks religious verse. His humility and despairing doubts, even a certain frailty in moral courage, are overweighed by an uncanny accuracy in his use of stylistic instruments, and in his attacks on concepts of awesome magnificence. His symbols, as I have said, derive from an observation of reality at once bold and patient. For example: his notes on celestial and astronomical phenomena (included in Lahey's book) explain his mastery of the imagery of clouds, birds, trees, sunlight, and stars. Infused into this imagery, however, is a vast range of associations, often very difficult to trace. These mnemonic values lie not only in his paraphrasis and word-coinages, but in the historical or liturgical allusions they conceal.

> I caught this morning morning's minion, king-
> > dom of daylight's dauphin, dapple-dawn-drawn Falcon,
> > in his riding
> > Of the rolling level underneath him steady air, and striding
> High there, how he rung upon the rein of a wimpling wing
> In his ecstasy!

Here in the opening lines of 'The Windhover', there is an extraordinary synesthesia induced by the alliterative series and the flowing 'outrides' of the sprung rhythm. And in addition may be found in single combination the natural phenomena of the theme, the double-image of minion and dauphin (with hints both chivalric and theological), and the movement described in terms of horsemanship—ringing on a rein. But a fusion is completely and brilliantly achieved. A similar resolution of complexities appears in many separate lines. In 'Spelt from Sybil's Leaves':

> Earnest, earthless, equal, attunable, vaulty, voluminous,
> > ... stupendous,
> Evening strains to be time's vast, womb-of-all, home-of-all, hearse-
> > of-all night.

The single progression encompasses man's life-cycle with order and fluidity, only to proceed to two lines of overwhelming cumulative beauty:

> Her fond yellow hornlight wound to the west, her wild,
> > hollow hoarlight hung to the height
> Waste; her earliest stars, earl-stars, stars principal, overbend us,
> > Fire-featuring heaven.

'The Leaden Echo' reveals an intricacy of suggestion none the less real for being based on more obvious external effects. In simpler lyrics like 'Inversnaid', 'Morning Midday and Evening Sacrifice', and 'Binsey Poplars', the clear descriptive intention will not prevent an acute reader from seeking the exquisite implications hovering over the details. These implications are perhaps more obvious in the first four lines of the sonnet, 'Duns Scotus' Oxford:'

> Towery city and branchy between towers;
> Cukoo-echoing, bell-swarmèd, lark-charmèd, rook-racked,
>   river-rounded;
> The dapple-eared lily below thee; that country and town did
> Once encounter in, here coped and poisèd powers.

While in 'Peace' the shapely unity of the concept does not exclude a rare evocation and interplay of tenuous emotional states—fatigue, querulous despair, fortitude, and finally abnegation to Providence:

[Quotes 'Peace'.]

In the ten sonnets which constitute Hopkins' last work, the sublimation of these states is more fully achieved, and the control of suggestion and implication more absolute. Yet neither the sublimation nor the control is final. Hopkins' poems remain an incomplete document. They bear, both in their finished parts and in their total sum, clues to infinite extension. Like the greatest poetry which M. Valéry has defined, they come to us at a very advanced stage of realization, but the final phrasing, the ultimate rhythmical finish, and the completed meaning still hover—alluring though intangible—beyond the grasp of the reader. Finality of a different order is to be found within these poems, only a dozen of which may perhaps be laid aside as mediocre or tentative. It is the finality of unflinching honesty in craftsmanship, and of courage and vision in motive. It may be traced in the strength of every symbol, rhythm and word as an esthetic reality, and in the synthesis of these to an irreducible poetic substance. The difficulties in his verse will probably never disappear, but as long as they confront readers they will elicit the creative effort which is never exacted by the innocuous competence and glibness of the essentially mediocre, but which remains the first demand of absolute art. As long as they encourage that effort, Hopkins will teach the future poet those ideals of integrity and pure creative ardor whereof his poems are the embodiment.

46. 'E.O.', review, *Tablet*

6 December 1930, pp. 767–8

This is a review of *Poems*, 2nd edn, *A Vision of the Mermaids* and Lahey.

Not long ago, a pert young verse-maker was frisking under the delusion that he and his contemporaries were pioneers in rhythm. He firmly believed that 'they were the first who ever burst' into a new sea of poetical effects. After being advised to acquaint himself with Gerard Manley Hopkins, this youngster came back to make a surprising report. Only one G.M. Hopkins, he said, is mentioned in the latest edition of the *Encyclopaedia Britannica*, namely, the G.M. Hopkins who invented something or other to improve gyroscopes. He added that Mr. Humbert Wolfe's article in the *Britannica* on Modern Poetry punctiliously mentions Mr Humbert Wolfe himself, but has no word to say about Gerard Manley Hopkins, the Jesuit poet. Yet the works and theories of Hopkins have been keenly discussed by indisputable poets for nearly fifty years, and have been well known in literary circles since the Poet Laureate of that day brought out an annotated selection from the poems twelve years ago. ...

Lest we should be raising in any simple bosom the hope of finding in Hopkins' poems a new treasure-trove of crystal-clear lyrics and easily scrutable sonnets, we had better run up a red light, here and now. Putting aside the Juvenilia and a very few later pieces, there is little in Gerard Hopkins for those readers who must have either fluent and translucent poetry or none at all. He is nearly always difficult, and often obscure. His worst faults are so bad that they will forever disable him from popularity. Take, for example, his disdain of relative pronouns. It is true that such pronouns can often be omitted. We can say 'the book which he wanted,' or 'the book he wanted,' or (with less clearness) 'the book wanted.' But Hopkins omitted relative pronouns when they were indispensable. His 'O Hero savest' meant 'O Hero who savest'; his 'Creep, wretch, under a comfort serves in a whirlwind ' meant 'a comfort that serves'; and his, 'the beauty been' meant 'the beauty that has been.'

In rhyme, Hopkins fondly believed that 'the Muses loved' such horrors as 'behaviour' rhyming with 'gave you a.' Here are the opening stanzas of 'The Bugler'.

> A bugler boy from barrack (it is over the hill
> There)—boy bugler, born, he tells me, of Irish
>   Mother to an English sire (he
> Shares their best gifts surely, fall how things will),
>
> This very, very day came down to us after a boon he on
> My late being there begged of me, overflowing
>   Boon, in my bestowing,
> Came, I say, this day to it—to a First Communion.

In the second and third lines above, 'Irish' is supposed to rhyme with 'sire he sh—'; that is to say, with the two words 'sire' and 'he', plus the first hiss of 'shares.' 'Boon he on' rhymes with 'communion'. Such doings make one wish to be with Longfellow under a spreading chestnut-tree.

Here is the opening of a sonnet, 'The Windhover', of which Hopkins thought highly:

> I caught this morning morning's minion, king-
>   dom of daylight's dauphin, dapple-dawn-drawn Falcon
>   in his riding.

In short, we warn off all indolent readers, and many attentive ones, from Gerard Hopkins. And when it comes to picking out specimens with which to bait our hooks and to angle for more Hopkinites we hesitate. The only complete poems brief enough for quotation would not reveal the essential Hopkins. But we risk copying out the little piece, 'Pied Beauty'.

[Quoted.]

This poem, like all truly Hopkinsy Hopkins, is for ear-reading, not for eye-reading; indeed, it must be read aloud several times over, with two stresses on the words 'all trades', and with no skimping at the line-ends. But we repeat that Hopkins is not to be known by stray extracts. Nor are there many detachable single lines. Readers must begin at the beginning of 'Felix Randal, the

Farrier,' in order to get the anvil-music of its ending:

> Didst fettle for the great grey drayhorse his bright
> and battering sandal.

We suspect that if Father Hopkins, who died at the age of forty-five in Dublin, had lived ten years longer, he would have diminished his oddity and would have clarified his self-expression. But he died on the very eve of the adventurous 'nineties, and is only now coming into his own. Some of us think less highly than does Father Lahey of Robert Bridges in this matter. We feel that the poetical theories and experiments of Hopkins ought to have been allowed to speak for themselves long before the year 1918. Bridges, we are afraid, allowed his anti-Catholicism to influence him. His Notes on Hopkins' 'co-religionists', and 'particular religious associates' are far from gracious; and his exclusion of 'Margaret Clitheroe' from the 1918 selection must surely have been on sectarian rather than poetical grounds. . . .

47. W.J. Turner, unsigned review, *Times Literary Supplement*

25 December 1930, p. 1099

According to the editor of the *TLS*, November 1984, the author of this review of *Poems*, 2nd edn, and Lahey, was W.J. Turner (1889–1946), the Australian-born poet. He had come to Europe in 1907 and his verse established him as a prominent member of the Georgian movement. He wrote a good deal of literary and musical criticism for periodicals. For a further piece by Turner on Hopkins, see No. 51.

Gerard Manley Hopkins himself wrote:—

It is a happy thing that there is no royal road to poetry. The world should know by this time that one cannot reach Parnassus except by flying thither.

Yet from time to time more men go up and either perish in its gullies fluttering excelsior flags or else come down again with full folios and blank countenances. Yet the old fallacy keeps its ground. Every age has its false alarms.[1]

Hopkins was not an example of the 'old fallacy,' for he flew straight to the top of Parnassus and characteristically kept it so secret that his generation and the generation that followed him after his death in 1889 never knew of his achievement. Not until his friend the late Poet Laureate, Robert Bridges, edited the first volume of Hopkins's poems in 1918 did the world know that the second half of the nineteenth century had possessed another major poet whose achievement in bulk and quality can perhaps best be compared with Matthew Arnold's. This first volume went out of print, and for the last few years it has been impossible to obtain it. It is now reissued intact with an appendix of additional poems with notes and an introduction by Mr. Charles Williams, to whom Robert Bridges had confided the task of preparing a second edition.

It must be said that none of the additional poems here first collected are of prime importance, thus proving how thoroughly Robert Bridges did his work. The majority of them are early poems written from 1860 to 1866, and the best of them show very markedly the influence of Keats, not only in metrical form but in imagery. Nevertheless, 'A Vision of the Mermaids,' written in 1862, when Hopkins was eighteen years old, and with the sensuous opulence of the young Keats, could only have been written by a boy of genius. Even the most acute literary sense fostered by intensive culture will not enable a young undergraduate out of his study of poetry to produce such lines as:—

[Quotes 'A Vision of the Mermaids', ll. 84–98.]

Yet Hopkins was not to develop along the lines that this poem indicates. He was received into the Roman Catholic Church while still an undergraduate, although on Cardinal Newman's advice he finished his studies at Oxford, taking a double-first in Greats in 1867. That vein of rich sensuousness then flowed into another channel; and the early examples of this later preoccupation are far less felicitous than those modelled on Byron (for example, 'The Escorial,' dated 1860) or Keats.

The poem 'Ad Mariam' is so thoroughly Swinburnian (*cf.* its opening line, 'When a sister born for each strong month-brother') that on internal evidence it could only be classed as a juvenile production. Bridges omitted it because he could find no autograph. Mr. Williams, however, includes it because it appeared in the *Stonyhurst Magazine* 'under a letter from a correspondent signed "O.S.J.," in which they are said to have been written in 1884.' Mr. Williams might have been less obscure. To what does his 'they' refer? What evidence is there that this poem is by Hopkins? It is to us almost inconceivable that this wholly derivative and feeble production could have been written by Hopkins as late as 1884. Thoroughly characteristic, however, are 'Lines for a Picture of St. Dorothea', 'Winter with the Gulf Stream' and 'Margaret Clitheroe'—the final lines of the latter may be quoted as an example of Hopkins's vitality in plain speech:—

> Within her womb the child was quick.
> Small matter of that then! Let him smother
> And wreck in ruins of his mother.

It would hardly be an exaggeration to say that Hopkins was the most original of the poets of the second half of the nineteenth century. It is true that Tennyson, Browning, Arnold and Swinburne are all truly individual, speaking with distinct and unique voices; but none of them broke down so violently as Hopkins the old rhythmic forms. They were all inventive and each added something new to English poetry—as indeed did the two Rossettis and Francis Thompson—but, no poet writing to-day feels that he can learn technical secrets from these poets, whereas Hopkins is full of strange powers (and an unexhausted technical prowess) which he feels he must assimilate and possess.

Technically Hopkins is a great liberating influence in English verse. Poetry is made up of many elements, and it is only the greatest poets who possess all the elements; but what poetry has been weakest in since the seventeenth century is rhythm. The eighteenth century only heard music in a regular pattern, and in spite of Blake and the Romantic revival this is largely true of the nineteenth century. Thus it came about that a metrist like Swinburne was hailed as a great master of music, partly because nobody could fail to scan his verses. Arnold was far finer rhythmically, and there is nothing in Swinburne to match the rhythmic beauty of the famous lines beginning:—

> Far, far from here,
> The Adriatic breaks in a warm bay...

Hopkins is one of the great masters and innovators of rhythm in the English language. The best analysis of his poetry in this respect is in the chapter entitled 'The Craftsman' in Father Lahey's monograph on Hopkins published this year, which reveals the complexity and logic of his technique. The analysis of such a sonnet as 'The Windhover' into 'sprung rhythm, falling paeons, outrides, rocking rhythm, monosyllabic feet, catalectic inflections,' may confound the reader, but to anyone with a sensitive ear Hopkins is as easy as he is beautiful to read. Those who find such lines as the opening of the sonnet 'Windhover' difficult must ask themselves whether their ear is not as yet imperfectly trained to poetic rhythm as distinct from metrical scansion.

Of Hopkins's other poetic qualities there is hardly space left to speak. He had the true poetic power of phrase. Such lines as:—

> Didst fettle for the great grey drayhorse his bright
> and battering sandal!

his comparison of a ploughman's furrows:—

> Cragiron under and cold furls—
> With-a-fountain's shining-shot furls.

this description of Oxford:—

> Towery city and branchy between towers;
> Cuckoo-echoing, bell-swarmèd, lark-charmèd, rook-
> racked, river-rounded;

suffice to illustrate his felicity and originality; but the white-hot intensity of his greatest work can be felt only as a whole in such poems as 'That Nature is a Heraclitean Fire and of the comfort of the Resurrection.'

The letters quoted by Father Lahey in his all too short biography of Hopkins are of such quality as to make it desirable that an edition of his letters and a selection of his prose should be published. Father Lahey quotes a description of Hopkins as a young man by a college friend, who writes:—

His conversation was clear and incisive, and perhaps critical in excess. As to the quality of this criticism I thought much at the time and have thought much since, that it was the best of the kind to be had in England. ... His acquaintance with poetry was extensive, and his judgments differed upon various poets considerably from what most people entertain. ...[2]

If any written criticism by Hopkins exists it ought to be printed. There are critical passages of great interest in the letters written to Coventry Patmore from which Father Lahey quotes extensively; but these letters ought to be printed in full. In a letter from the Royal University of Ireland dated June 4, 1886, Hopkins writes to Patmore:—

What marked and striking excellence has England to show to make her civilization attractive? Her literature is one of her excellences and attractions, and I believe that criticism will tend to make this more and more felt; but there must be more of that literature—a continued supply, and in quality excellent. This is why I hold that fine works of art...are really a great power in the world, an element of strength even to an empire.[3]

There is a letter to Patmore dated Dublin, 1888, containing a magnificent criticism of Keats, which is far too long to quote here. Hopkins's eminently sane, exceptionally acute mind displays its logical power far more obviously for the general reader in his prose than in his poetry. This is an additional reason why his prose should be collected and published; for everything possible should be done to make Hopkins's work more generally known and to spread the fame of this poet of true genius.

NOTES

1 Quoted by Lahey, p. 125. See *Journals*, 2nd edn, p. 23.
2 Lahey, pp. 125–6.
3 *Ibid.*, pp. 70–1. *Further Letters*, pp. 367–8.

48. Morris U. Schappes, review, *Symposium*

January 1931, pp. 129–36

Morris Schappes, b. 1907 in the Ukraine, came to the USA in 1914, and taught in the English Department of the City College of New York from 1928.

The *Symposium* was a critical review published at Concord, New Hampshire, 1930–3. Like *Hound and Horn* (see No. 61) its tone and approach were much influenced by Eliot's *Criterion*. This review is of *Poems*, 2nd edn, and Lahey.

The contemporary biography reading public had to wait for a study of the life of Gerard Manley Hopkins before it could evince the crescendo of interest in his poetry that makes possible this belated edition of his work. But so self-sufficient are these poems that Hopkins is less in need of a biography than most other writers. Least of all did he merit the blunt, badly written, and actually misleading work here given us. Father Lahey has little of the ability to digest and organize gathered material, of the art of presenting the product in a unified and clear fashion, or of the insight into character that would make Hopkins something more than a wooden target for admiring adjectives. Suffice it to say that one third of the 150 pages of text are little more than a reprinting of letters to Hopkins written by Newman, Patmore, and Richard Watson Dixon, with a sentence or two of connection by Father Lahey himself. Exactly the same thing had already been accomplished, however, by Father Keating in the Jesuit periodical, *The Month* (July–September, 1909), of whose work this section is almost a paraphrase. The opening chapters on Hopkins' early life and Oxford companions consist of long letters from the poet's friends—letters that might easily have been summarized in a short paragraph—and the printing of some very long and very early verses. The only attractions are the few portions from Hopkins' own letters. Suddenly Father Lahey becomes peculiarly selective and *refers* to the fact that in 1860 'He astonished his friends at home with a remarkable letter written from Nuremberg, and enclosing [sic!] some first-rate sketches of Bavarian peasantry.' *This* letter is not quoted. After a discussion of the Craftsman and the Artist (to which we shall return) Father Lahey concludes his presentation with a chapter on The Man, in which, among tributes by Hopkins' friends, we find an occasional revealing passage from a brilliant letter by the poet. At the close, the biographer makes a categorical, undocumented denial of Hopkins' own testimony that his experience in Ireland was one of spiritual torment. And, pursuing the strain of apologetics begun when we were informed that the pain of Hopkins' conversion was compensated by 'the inexpressible peace and exhilarating happiness that he afterwards experienced' (p. 44), Father Lahey explains the last sonnets as follows: 'The celebrated "terrible" sonnets [Bridges' phrase] are only terrible in the same way that the beauty of Jesus Christ is terrible. Only the strong pinions of an eagle can realize the cherished happiness of such suffering. It is a place where Golgotha and Thabor meet. Read in this light his poems cease to be tragic' (p. 143). This seems mere logomachy.

The treatment of Hopkins as a craftsman would be negligible were it not typical of the failure of so many reviewers and critics to examine point by point the poet's own statements. But before turning to the weakness Father Lahey shares with others, I ought to indicate that his own contributions are invalidated by either ineptitude or carelessness. How else can one explain the thirty more or less important mistakes in quotations from the poems? In one instance Hopkins is even scolded for a misquotation! He had written: 'Majestic—as a stallion stalwart, very-violet-sweet!' Father Lahey changes this to: 'Majestic—as a stallion stalwart, *very violet, sweet!*' and brands it as a 'discordant image'! And what credence can we place in any analysis that so misunderstands Hopkins' ideas as to offer as examples of other poets' use of Sprung Rhythm, work of Green, Beaumont and Fletcher, Donne, Herbert, Herrick, and Milton, that is severely trochaic or iambic?... Thanks are due the biographer, however, for including twenty pages of Hopkins' remarkable prose in an appendix.

What neither Father Lahey nor any other critic of Hopkins has as yet indicated is that the poet's metrical *theories* are contradictory and unimportant. Hopkins' error is fundamental, for it is based upon inaccurate analogies with painting and more frequently with music. This confusion appears in the constantly quoted statement of his goal: 'But as air, melody, is what strikes me most of all in music and design in painting, so design, pattern or what I am in the habit of calling *inscape* is what I above all aim at in poetry.' To imply, even, that melody is analogous to design in painting is to blunder radically. The second such error occurs in the definition of Counterpoint Rhythm, which is caused by the reversal of two consecutive feet of an already established rhythm: '...and since the new or mounted rhythm is actually heard and at the same time the mind naturally supplies the natural or standard foregoing rhythm ...two rhythms are in some manner running at once and we have something answerable to counterpoint in music, which is two or more strains of tune going on together...' (Author's Preface to *Poems*). The difference is, however, that counterpoint actually presents two simultaneous tunes whereas in verse one is merely remembered. If a musical term must be sought, Variation would be the nearest. But the naming of it is unessential if we understand that he means only that the poet may introduce certain changes into any standard rhythm. Hopkins further complicates the matter by the idea of Sprung Rhythm, which 'is measured by feet of from one to four syllables, regularly, and for particular effects any number of weak or slack syllables may be used. It has one stress, which falls on the only syllable...or...on the first,[a] and so gives rise to four sorts of feet, a monosyllable and the so-called accentual Trochee, Dactyl, and the First Paeon.' The question now arises as to how one is to distinguish between, say, a Counterpointed or Reversed Iambic and a Sprung Dactyl plus a Sprung Monosyllable. Especially when Hopkins has poems written in all combinations of these, as in 'Walking by the Sea,' which is in 'Standard rhythm, in parts sprung and in others counterpointed'.[b] Had his critics tested his canon and applied it to the poems they could not but have discovered that as theory it was only verbalism. The variations that Hopkins tried to combine into a metrical system have been so commonly used that every device, from counterpoint to paeon, is to be found in the first four lines of 'Tintern Abbey.' His prosody, then, is merely an attempt to rationalize for the benefit of Bridges and Dixon what he had already accomplished in practice. Challenged because of the irregularity of his verse, he replied with these no less erratic theories. A contemporary reader, however, should disregard them and concentrate all his powers on the poems themselves.

And much persistence is necessary before one apprehends the might and the music of these poems. If they are difficult, they are difficult because of originality, not because of vagueness or confusion in structure. Hopkins consciously ripped open the conventional eighteenth century metrics that dominated the Victorian era, not by theory, but by a fine and subtle practice that justifies all his defiance of rules. Nor is his originality confined to his rhythms and melodies, for it extends even more bewilderingly to his compressed, precise, and hammered diction. In his early work, included in the appendix to this Second Edition, he reveals an ability to use effectively the conventional patterns of his day. He can be Swinburnian in 'Ad Mariam,' Wordsworthian in 'The Nightingale,' more Keatsian than Keats in 'The Vision of Mermaids.' But his was not an imitative genius. 'The effect of studying masterpieces,' he wrote to Bridges in 1888, a year before his death, 'is to make me admire and do otherwise. So it must be on every original artist to some degree, on me to a marked degree.' Since originality is always difficult, Hopkins' has been an 'ill-broker'd talent'. But now that we have his work, mere difficulty should not repel us, no more certainly than does the complexity and crabbedness of the verse in *Antony and Cleopatra*.

The key to an understanding of the poetry lies, to my mind, in the grasp of Hopkins' concreteness. He had a naïvely literal mind, and the most common objects often evoked from him an intensity of observation that resulted almost in a transformation of the object into something alien. So precise was his vision that it is only by an effort on our part to strain our own focus that we can discern the inevitability of his expression. The poet whom an Irish hostess found stitching his waistcoat, absorbed in the movement of the thread, or who, to illustrate the dragging of Hector, made a student lie on his back to be drawn through the room—such a man inhabits a world of concreteness that cannot easily be comprehended by our more complacently vague imaginations. The same literalness that made him admit to his friend Addis that he 'never can believe that the Song of Solomon is more than ordinary love-song', (Lahey, p. 19) led him to assert in 'The Bugler's First Communion' that he 'Forth Christ from cupboard fetched.' And the same hypnotic concentration on the immediate situation moved him, in an

argumentative sonnet with the Lord, to address God as 'sir'.[c]
Applied to descriptions of nature, such a quality produces: 'The
moon, dwindled and thinned to the fringe of a finger-nail held to
the candle,' or '...rose-moles all in stipple upon trout that swim.'
In short, here is a poet and man whose distinction consists of a
transmogrifying intentness of observation and a literalness that
transcends in acuteness the most conventionally daring imagination.

With this element understood, we can observe that all his troublesome rhythmical devices are a means for expressing as compactly as
possible his exact thought. There is seldom any flabbiness of
diction or rhythm caused by the need to adhere to cramping rules.
The cement of connectives, relatives, and transitional words is
consciously excised from his structures; the parts, instead of being
soldered, are welded together. In the following lines, for example,
the words in parentheses were cut from an earlier existing version.

> (Then) Í say móre: the just man justices;
> Keéps gráce (and); thát keeps all his goings graces;
> (In God's eye acts) etc.
> Acts in God's eye, etc. ...

What is decoration in other poets is with him always a structural
element, necessary to the sense and the rhythm, inevitable in the
fusion of both. Alliteration, so soporific in Swinburne, attains
novel importance.

> Thou mastering me
> God! giver of breath and bread;
> World's strand, sway of the sea;
> Lord of living and dead;
> Thou hast bound bones and veins in me, fastened me flesh...
> ('The Wreck of the Deutschland')

The crescendo of adjectives, a constant device of Hopkins, is used
with stunning precision:

> Wiry and white-fiery and whirlwind-swivellèd snow
> Spins to the widow-making unchilding unfathering deeps.
> ('The Wreck of the Deutschland')

> Earnest, earthless, equal, attuneable,│vaulty voluminous,...[d]
>   stupendous

Evening strains to be tíme's vast, | womb-of-all, home-of-all,
   hearse-of-all night.   ('Spelt from Sibyl's Leaves')

In diction he is equally impressive: desiring accuracy above all he
batters it into his own shape. He combines words, breaks them,
transposes the parts of speech, forges them anew so that the
meaning, if it is to be understood at all, will be understood *his* way.
His vocabulary is earthy, full of words used in accepted but
uncommon senses that demand the aid of an unabridged dictionary, but the perception of the meaning and the perception of the
rightness of the word are usually simultaneous.

But since the conventional critical terms merely travesty such a
poet without adequately conveying much more than enthusiasm, I
must in this brief space turn to a skeletal statement of the temper of
the poet's mind, especially in its relation to God.

The two poles of his attitude towards his God may be indicated
by contrasting his statement that God is 'Ground of being, and
granite of it,' with the reference to 'dark heaven's baffling ban.'
Joined, these extremes produce a line like 'Father and fondler of
heart thou hast wrung.' His faith was ecstatic in acceptance of pain
and joy (if only for this reason the common attempt of his critics to
compare him with Milton would be abortive, without considering
the difference between their styles):

        I did say yes
     O at lightning and lashed rod;
Thou heardst me truer than tongue confess
    Thy terror, O Christ, O God;...

Representation of eager bewilderment before the Lord has seldom
surpassed this passage, descriptive of the vision that appeared to the
nuns who sank on the *Deutschland* in 1875:

    But how shall I...make me room there:
    Reach me a...Fancy, come faster—
  Strike you the sight of it? look at it loom there,
    Thing that she...there then! the Master,
Ipse, the only one, Christ, King, Head:...

When the poem is read through the effect is tremendous, especially
because of the leaping *Ipse*.

This joy in God, however, was tempered by the incursions of a
questing mind, and his mood, especially in the poems written in

the last four years of his short life (he was only forty-five when he died), hurtles down until it plumbs a depth as utter as his former beatitude.

> O the mind, mind has mountains; cliffs of fall
> Frightful, sheer, no-man-fathomed. Hold them cheap
> May who ne'er hung there. Nor does long our small
> Durance deal with that steep or deep. Here! creep,
> Wretch, under a comfort serves in a whirlwind: all
> Life death does end and each day dies with sleep.

In these later years his art became even more sure, more chastened. He was master of a pliable technique that facilitated the complete presentation of his tempestuous but subtle feeling. The result was the series of 'terrible sonnets' already mentioned (34 out of 65 complete poems we have are in the sonnet form). At least one of them is—and I say this after prolonged thought but with no hesitation—unsurpassed in the nineteenth century, unsurpassed until we return to Milton's sonnet 'On the late Massacre in Piemont'.

[Quotes 'Carrion Comfort'.]

Hopkins was a genius of repelling originality. But the weighty adjective 'great' cannot, I feel, be any longer denied him. He tapped the 'bower of bone' for his materials, and fused them with incredible lyricism. 'The Wreck of the Deutschland', 'The Leaden Echo and the Golden Echo', the sonnets—but why list names?—the bulk of his achievements forms a glorious pinnacle of poetry.

NOTES

a Hopkins had already asserted that 'for purposes of scanning it is a great convenience to follow the example of music and take the stress always [sic!] first.' This isolation of scanning as no more than a pedantic device is self-vitiating.

b Hopkins' utter confusion in thought is seen in his example of the classic use of Counterpoint Rhythm: 'Of this kind of verse Milton is the great master and the choruses of *Samson Agonistes* are written throughout in it—but with the disadvantage that he does not let the reader clearly know what the ground rhythm is meant to be and so they have struck most readers as merely irregular.' How Hopkins could perceive a counterpointing in the absence of an established rhythm, I do not know.

c It is noteworthy that in all his religious poems Hopkins seldom capitalizes *thee* or *he* or any religious symbol except Lord or God, and these not always. But most of his Catholic critics insist on distorting his intention by a liberal use of capitals.

d Indicates a pause; note the breathless emphasis on the next word.

49. Unsigned review, *Glasgow Herald*

1 January 1931, p. 4

...The impression gathered from all of these [recommended poems] is that of a superabundant energy and a love of quixotic rhythm and phraseology, while everywhere an amazing beauty flashes its wings. Hopkins' system of scansion is interesting to specialists, but lack of knowledge of it is no deterrent to enjoying these poems. The oddities and obscurities of the style...are part of the fascination; without them, indeed, Hopkins would not be Hopkins.

50. Unsigned review, *Nation*

28 January 1931, p. 105

Commenting on the brevity of the review, the writer points out that the *Nation* had already reviewed Hopkins the previous April: see No. 41.

...In the interval since 1918 Hopkins has won recognition as a major English poet. His few detractors accuse him of overcultivating verbal dexterity. However, a study of even his obscurest poems reveals that his experiments in internal rhyme, in counterpointed rhythm, and in word transposition have always a justified intention, and his failures are remarkably few. No other poet in the entire range of English literature has bought sense and sound into so perfect or beautiful a unity.

51. W.J. Turner, 'Some Modern Poetry', *The Nineteenth Century and After*

February 1931, pp. 243–52

For Turner, see No. 47. As well as Hopkins's *Poems*, the author discussed work by Eliot, and by Edith and Sacheverell Sitwell, in this article.

... Although the three critics whose reputation stands higher than any others in English literature are all fine poets—I refer to Dryden, Coleridge, and Arnold—yet I doubt if a poet can ever be the best critic of contemporary work. He may easily be the most profound and say the most illuminating things, but he is bound to have a bias; and, further, the creative and the critical functions are distinct, and I am not sure that they need appear together in the same man. Speaking personally, I have to admit that I can rarely see any faults in the poetry I like, while the poetry I dislike seems to me to be just one huge mistake from beginning to end, and in no way a mixture of good and bad. I may be an extreme case, but to me criticisms of grammar, of punctuation, of vocabulary, of metre, of rhythm always seem completely beside the point. Either the poet is a master or he is not. If he is a master, then all his infringements of rules and precedents are part of his idiosyncratic expression, and cannot be criticised adversely unless from the *a priori* standpoint that the whole effect of his poetry is bad. But, if he is recognised as a master, this is absurd; so I would conclude that criticism of this sort can only be an analysis of his procedure in the light of past procedure and a comparison of his methods with the methods of others without any pronouncement of value as method, but only a pronouncement on the value of the end. That is to say, I deny that we can ascertain the value of a poem (or, for that matter, of any work of art) by a technical analysis. I submit that we can only tell the value of a poem by assessing it as a whole by an act of poetic judgment analogous to the act of vision by virtue of which we see the person who stands opposite us and can remember him again. I do not believe that this impression, or any subsequent total impression, is the result of an analysis, nor that different people's impressions of the same object are due to their different analyses. It is rather a matter of selection and emphasis, and different people select differently and put the emphasis in different parts. One might explain difference in selection by difference in analysis, but hardly a difference in emphasis when the analysis is identical. There are people who are irritated almost to the point of madness by too many commas, others by too few; are we to suppose that in the one case the critic sees more commas than in the other? Surely we can get an agreement upon the analysis without agreement upon the effect of the whole?

The poetry of Gerard Manley Hopkins offers an admirable illustration of my principle. Either you can swallow this poet whole or you cannot swallow him at all; bit by bit he will surely stick in the grammarian's or the prosodist's throat and be spat out either with dislike or contempt. And not only these, but the man of taste or of academic habit is likely to be so offended as to be unable to understand and enjoy Hopkins. Nevertheless, I am bound to add that his first editor, the late Robert Bridges, who was more a poet of fine taste than of natural genius, although he animadverts on Hopkins's 'errors of taste,' succeeded in largely understanding and admiring his work. And if we examine Bridges' condemnations of Hopkins on the ground of 'taste' we will find that they are too personal to be valid. This is the danger in all matters of taste. A classic example in criticism is Matthew Arnold's diatribe against Keats's sensuousness in his poetry and his letters. This age is grown more detached than that of the constrained and inhibited Arnold; we are not shocked to-day by what shocked him, and we realise that Arnold's 'moral' implications were in this instance of no more value than those of some sex-suppressed seaside town councillor

who finds mixed bathing an error in 'taste'. So when Robert
Bridges condemns certain expressions they reveal, to my mind,
some finickiness in Bridges and make me rather doubtful whether
he really appreciated the poem in which they occur, and of which
they are so intrinsic a part that to take out one of these offending
expressions would be to destroy the character of the poem. For
example, take the poem 'Hurrahing in Harvest':

[Quoted.]

I quote the whole of this sonnet, of which Bridges only criticises
adversely the metaphor 'as a stallion stalwart, very violet-sweet,'
because, while I can conceive a criticism of this poem as a whole as
the expression of a too peculiar emotion that, intense as it is,
impoverishes rather than enriches, yet a mere criticism of this
metaphor as an 'affectation' seems to me not only to miss the mark
completely, but shows a lapse of poetic sensibility, for—given an
acceptance of the meaning of the sonnet—the compound metaphor
is as fine as it is bold.

Then, again, Bridges demurs to 'the naked encounter of
sensualism and asceticism which hurts the "Golden Echo,"' when
this encounter is an essential element in the poem. To say it 'hurts'
the poem is saying that Hopkins ought to have written a different
poem altogether. As this poem is one of Hopkins's triumphs, and
was something entirely new in English poetry when it was written,
I will quote the second part of it. The full title is 'The Leaden Echo
and the Golden Echo,' and it is a maidens' song from an
uncompleted play, 'St. Winefred's Well.' The first part of the song,
'The Leaden Echo,' begins thus:

> How to keep—is there any any, is there none such, nowhere
> known some, bow or brooch or braid or brace, lace, latch or
> catch or key to keep
> Back beauty, keep it, beauty, beauty, beauty,...from vanishing
> away

and this first part ends with the lines:

> So be beginning, be beginning to despair.
> O there's none; no no no there's none:
> Be beginning to despair, to despair,
> Despair, despair, despair, despair.

Then begins 'The Golden Echo,' and its beginning is most characteristic of Hopkins, for he starts with an echo, thus connecting beautifully the second part of his poem to the first:

[Quotes 'The Golden Echo' section.]

This seems to me a perfect expression of the poet's meaning, and in its immense sweep of rhythm, intensity of expression, felicity of inner rhyming, superb compound adjectives, yet simplicity and truth, an inseparable whole. I cannot see anything for criticism to cavil at in the detail of this poem, for all its exuberance is essential. If we are to criticise it at all we must criticise the whole conception of the poem, not the detail. And this, I contend, is always the case with a genuine artist. It is only the imitators, the pseudo-artists, whose work is necessarily a pastiche, that can be analysed into their incongruous and common parts. Whatever defects Hopkins had (and he is certainly deficient in some of the elements of poetry), his mature work was for the most part congruous and had the perfect integrity of a poet of genius.

In his early work there are imitations of Keats and Swinburne. In these we can pick out the bits of Hopkins, for they stick out of the rest like a natural interjection in a prepared speech; but the 'Vision of the Mermaids,' in spite of its derivation, is an astonishing production for a boy of eighteen. Yet, although this poem shows a sensuousness and a sensibility of language comparable to that of the early Keats, Hopkins, who died in 1889 at the age of forty-five, remained to the end more sensuously enmeshed than Keats was in the later years of his much shorter life. This is one of the limitations of Hopkins, who, a fine scholar, taking a Double first in Greats at Oxford before becoming a Jesuit priest, and later, as a Jesuit, filling the chair of Greek at the Royal University, Dublin, nevertheless never showed in his work the intellectual powers of Keats, who did not possess a tenth of his erudition. Among the fragments of Hopkins's work there is an unfinished 'Epithalamium,' which is one of his most self-revealing poems. The sensuousness is here beautifully dissipated into a vivacity of exquisite words, but it remains purely physical. He sees boys bathing in a river. I quote a few lines only:

[Quotes ll. 19–28.]

This gift of physical concreteness is one of the primary elements of great poetry. Shakespeare, Milton, Keats, and Donne had it in abundance, but all these had also another realm of feeling to the expression of which they brought a similar genius of word-imagery. This was, as far as I can see, lacking in Hopkins, and may be best described as the supersensuous. We get it married to sensuousness in Shakespeare (above all others!), and we get it divorced from sensuousness in Coleridge and Wordsworth. By the supersensuous I emphatically do not mean the intellectual. Hopkins had a fine intellect, and his poetry is extraordinarily logical and close-knit, without any vagueness or incoherence. Indeed, he is a model in this respect. But he is that particular type which the great lawyer and the great priest may be—keen senses, a keen intellect, and the scrupulousness of a high-minded, conscientious man—but which the great poet never is, for the great poet is, in the phraseology of Hopkins's church, always a sinner. Not a sinner in the sense that all men are sinners, but in the sense that he is outside the law. Hopkins was within the law and needed the law:

> Bad I am, but yet thy child
> Father, be thou reconciled.
> Spare thou me, since I see
> With thy might that thou art mild.
>
> I have life before me still
> And thy purpose to fulfil;
> Yea a debt to pay thee yet:
> Help me, sir, and so I will.[1]

We are told that when a young man of twenty-one he visited the Benedictine Monastery at Belmont and had a long conversation with Canon Raynal, afterwards Abbot. His friend Addis writes:

I think he [Canon Raynal] made a great impression on both of us and I believe that from that time our faith in Anglicanism was really gone. He insisted that Anglican orders were at least of doubtful validity; that some grave and learned men questioned or denied their validity and that this being so, it was unlawful till the doubt was cleared by competent authority to accept Anglican orders or even to participate in the Anglican Communion. So far as I knew, Father Raynal was the first priest whom Hopkins had ever spoken to.[2]

This reveals clearly the mental character of Hopkins in all its logical literalness; but his was not the love of casuistical ratiocination for its own sake or with the detachment of a man sharpening an intellectual instrument. His was a passion for the law and his mind reflected his temperament, which demanded a rule to live by, and found delight in carrying out the logical consequences of his premisses to the smallest detail. The Catholic Church satisfied his temperamental, and consequently his intellectual, needs, and he soon became a member of it, so that in Lent, 1866, he writes:

> No pudding on Sundays. No tea except to keep one awake, and then without sugar. Meat only once a day. No verses in Passion Week or on Fridays. Not to sit in armchair except I can work in no other way. Ash Wednesday and Good Friday bread and water. . . .

One must not be misled by the particular form of his 'rule' of life. The form was less important than the rule, but it had to be a form which gave an outlet to his senses. Perhaps any form of strict ascesis would have done that, but the ritual of the Catholic Church was the only one in Western Europe that could possibly have satisfied Hopkins's demands:

> Pure fasted faces draw into this feast
> God comes all sweetness to your Lenten lips.

he writes; and what this form of sensuousness reveals is, I believe, not inaccurately described as lack of a certain creative vigour. Subtlety and ingenuity one might expect from Hopkins rather than creative originality. But so complex is man and the creative power that superficially Hopkins does not seem to fail in creative originality, but even to possess it exceptionally. This impression he gave to some of his friends. Father Lahey—whose short memoir is the only source of information about his life—quotes a friend writing:

> Of his ability I need hardly speak. He had a distinct dash of genius. His opinion on any subject in Heaven and earth was always worth listening to and always fresh and original. . . . If I had known him outside, I should have said that his love of speculation and originality of thought would make it almost impossible for him to submit his intellect to authority.

This shows how easily one may be misled, for, judging from Hopkins's work, one would not be able to find any great creative originality of thought in his genius. All his originality and creative power is in his rhythm and his sensuousness. Otherwise his work is ingenious, inventive, full of mental conceits; resembling the 'metaphysical' poets of the sixteenth century and with none of the power of philosophic thought possessed by Shakespeare, Milton, Coleridge, Blake, Keats, or Shelley. ...

... The visual sense would seem, as with Hopkins, to be the strongest in all these poets,[3] excluding Mr. T.S. Eliot, who is primarily moved, not through his senses, but through an emotional disappointment akin to disillusion and despair. If one were to borrow an old phraseology, one might say that Hopkins and, of course, the Sitwells were pagan writers without the religious sense, whereas Mr. Eliot at least possesses the loss of it. This may seem a strange thing to say of Hopkins, a sincere Jesuit priest, but I am referring to a religious sense, not a religious belief or a devotional ideal, and I find none of Blake's or Shelley's or Spinoza's religious sense in Hopkins. If I were asked to define what I mean by 'religious sense' I could best do so by naming the artists who I think possess it. It is possessed in music by Beethoven, Mozart and Schubert, but not by Wagner, Liszt or Saint-Saëns. It is possessed in painting by Rembrandt, but not by Rossetti or Burne-Jones. We may find it harder to discover in literature than in the other arts which have the advantage of being free from verbal ideas, but without it a writer loses the most vitalising of all human forces.

NOTES

1 See *Poems*, 2nd edn, p. 91, and 4th edn, p. 194 (a slightly different version).
2 This passage and the three subsequent ones are all taken from Lahey: see pp. 21–2 and 132.
3 The poets reviewed.

52. Hildegarde Flanner, review, *New Republic*

4 February 1931, pp. 331–2

Hildegarde Flanner (b. 1899) was an American poet and playwright. This is a review of *Poems*, 2nd edn, *A Vision of the Mermaids*, and Lahey.

His varied destiny to go uncomprehended or ignored, condescended to or sincerely but cautiously admired, alternately reverenced as a radical experimenter or a religious mystic, regarded by still others as a mouthpiece for inspirational insanity, Gerard Manley Hopkins has now come into his own. The growing interest in his work has resulted in a second edition of his poems, augmented by some not included in the scarce 1918 volume edited by Robert Bridges, to whom credit must always be due for the original and painstaking presentation of his friend's work. These new poems contribute nothing to what has already been known of the quality of his writing, but serve by contrast to illustrate the progress of his experimenting. The introduction, written by Charles Williams, is one of the most discerning estimates of certain values in Hopkins that has yet appeared. ...

His inventive views on verse rhythm and his simple elaboration of them should be sought in his own statement in the Author's Preface. He was aware of the obstacles to printing poetry with the directions and notations he desired, though he felt the need of having 'a notation applied throughout as in music.' It should be kept in mind that both in theory and in the practice of his new rhythm Hopkins dreamed of a functional similarity to music. To summarize—as a means of scanning he preferred falling to rising feet, took the stress first, and thus had two basic feet, the Trochee and the Dactyl, and a corresponding logaoedic rhythm, a mixture of the two. The reversal of feet, employed to avoid monotony, produces Counterpoint Rhythm, an attempt to superimpose one rhythm on the one already established, thus affording a contrapuntal effect, again a musical analogy. Since consistent counterpointing destroys the ground rhythm, we have, instead, Sprung Rhythm, measured by feet of from one to four syllables and using any number of slack syllables.

The effect, found in reading aloud, of emphasis or prolongation caused by the thrust of monosyllables, Dactyls, Trochees and Paeonic feet injects into an accentual language an element of time different from the ordinary time-equality of identical feet in orthodox verse, and similar to the prolongation of sound in music and the singing voice. That Hopkins meant to go this far is conjecture, but it is certainly possible to read some of his poems with such an effect, and he himself repeated the advice, 'take breath and read it with the ears, as I always wish to be read, and my verse becomes all right.' Further, he used every device he could find to break down the interference of line-ends and carry the poem as a continuous whole without divisions. Though he insisted that 'design, pattern or inscape,' in writing as in painting, was his main concern, he has no affinity for later experimentalists who have brought a visual element into modern rhythm, and whose rhythms need not always be read aloud to be enjoyed, but must certainly be seen where they lie to be appreciated. His rhythms, while they may suggest the subject, neither imitate nor parody it.

We heard much some years ago of the rhythms of common speech and of music and their superior merit for verse, but even in polyphonic prose, which made a definite attempt to be contrapuntal, there has been no modern poetry attaining to the amazing effect of lines in Hopkins. His mind discarded ordinary word sequences and grammatical arrangements, creating for itself an original order which has its own habits of ingenious displacement and irregularity, making sometimes grace and sometimes grandeur. He can halt a sentence, a verse, retard it with a broken preposition, then set it spinning with a participle to gather momentum until it collects its own climax. Verbal indulgences, so easily faults of diffuseness, are here less faults than a curious, purposive colliding and jamming, an overlapping and telescoping of images and words in an effort toward sustained music and sense. Extravagance of a kind is the inevitable result, but extravagance so integrated, so disciplined to intention, that the accomplishment never sinks to mere lavishness. The will is never relaxed.

Hopkins' poetry, as in 'The Leaden and the Golden Echo' and
'The Windhover,' is instrumental. He tried to make it so without
loss of intelligibility and wrote relatively few lines that require
exegesis. He failed to understand why poets laureate and canons
of the Church found his verses difficult. He revealed fresh
potentialities in the musical employment of words, a music that
being organic is, in its fundamental relation to actual movement, of
much significance for future poetry. His alliteration, a thing quite
apart from a superficial use of sound, is dynamic:

[Quotes 'The Golden Echo', ll. 7–13.]

Among the early verses and Marian lyrics are poems of deft
charm, containing no hint of the more orchestral and original
manner except a few hyphens and a few verbal economies—that
persistent habit of saving a pronoun to purchase a Niagara at some
later moment.

His poetry, having its roots in faith, owes some of its finest fruit
to mortal doubt. His mind was too subtle, too composite to be
consistently the rhapsodist in worship, too objective and observant
to maintain undisturbed the trance of identification between self
and whole. Acceptance would break away into defeat and crisis.
Whatever the mystical association of his writing, whatever the
reference of symbol drawn directly from theology, those sonnets
sometimes called 'the terrible,' Hopkins' most personal religious
poems, remain not mystical but psychological, in the sense that
they are not sublimated beyond sight, but are definitions of a state
of mind, of frustration and doubt common to life. 'We hear our
hearts grate on themselves':

> I am gall, I am heartburn. God's most deep decree
> Bitter would have me taste: my taste was me;
> Bones built in me, flesh filled, blood brimmed the curse.
> Selfyeast of spirit a dull dough sours. I see
> The lost are like this, and their scourge to be
> As I am mine, their sweating selves; but worse.

There is a predictable strain of asceticism which continually
returns, but prevailing with the courageous hunger of the spirit is a
remarkable excess in another direction—things seen, heard, the
shape of the world, the weight and color and taste of whatever the
curious senses can grasp. It is a transformation of facts into

something never untrue, but as surprising as a prophecy in its revelation. Never merely sensuous, his is yet a writing of sensation and of fascinated pleasure in the beauty and strangeness of matter. There is not a timid or neutral or really sober poem. So absorbing, however, was Hopkins' interest in the surface of earth that the result is in places an eloquence depending much on the seeing and assertive word. A further congestion is evident in the extreme concentration and the baffling austerity of style, which show a bright side in the lyrics and a dramatic simplification in the sonnets, but cannot always carry the burden of the close-packed thought.

Inevitably original and mutinous, his audacity betrayed him into awkward locutions: 'Our heart's charity's hearth's fire, our thought's chivalry's throng's Lord.' An almost violent translating of one form and object into terms of another, coupled with a continual liberating of sense and concept, make of this an oddly agitated poetry. Yet the strenuous lines clear suddenly under a stroke of sorcery, a flash of 'wild hollow hoarlight,' or resolve into heartiness with 'long live the weeds and the wilderness.'

Aside from its authenticity and its independent beauty, his poetry is fundamentally and deeply important because it is the expression of an inventive mind having something to add to the sum and method of creative writing. Thirty years before free verse was a recognized incident, he had already taken the next logical steps in the analysis of liberated verse forms. It is interesting to see that in at least one very noticeable use of the participle he even anticipated Miss Stein. Upon the sonnet he conferred a dignity grim beyond any it had known before, and the particular deformities he practised on his lyrics gave them an undeniable and new grace. Haunted by the impossible—to carry on two rhythms simultaneously—he at least came as near to it as verse can without verging upon delirium. He never achieved, in his experimental verse, the acute delicacy of later writers, but he did something more difficult—although, among the poet-theorists who came after him, there was repeated mention of the precedent of the choruses to *Samson Agonistes* and very little said about a Jesuit who claimed to write Sprung Rhythm better than Milton had.

He feared that he was 'Time's eunuch,' contriving nothing that could survive; but his poetry was essentially enlightened, honest and rebellious, and made to last. His loyalty as a priest was to emblem and heaven, but his choice as an artist was matter and mind. That common but most vital instinct of poetry—to fix things in their intensity and reality by recreating them in terms of other known things—entrusts the poet with identifying life by signs enduring past his own to a further day. This is not the work of fancy but of veracity. The cumulative effect of Hopkins' writing is of such veracity and reality, a priest true to heaven, a poet true to earth.

53. Geoffrey Grigson, 'A Poet of Surprise', *Saturday Review*

14 February 1931, pp. 237–8.

Geoffrey Grigson (1905–85), a much-respected writer and poet, was at the beginning of his long career in 1931. For his editorship of *New Verse*, see No. 82.

The reviewer's job, it seems to me, in reviewing this second and long awaited issue of Gerard Hopkins's poems, is to cater not for those few serious and sensitive readers of verse who already know them, but for the majority who may have read without realizing Hopkins's importance the two or three poems which occur in anthologies, who may shy at Hopkins as a pass-word of the parlour 'modernist', or may be wholly unblessed with his acquaintance. In fact the reviewer ought to indulge not in criticism but in town crying. He ought, if he has it, to expound his conviction that Gerard Hopkins was a great poet. I have that conviction; and let me start to expound it, as I must continue, by quotation:

[Quotes 'A Vision of the Mermaids', ll. 84–101.]

Those luscious but obviously original lines represent far from the best of Hopkins, but he wrote them in 1862 when he was eighteen—they are part of his 'Vision of the Mermaids'—and so from the outset his verse justifies Mr. Charles Williams's remark (he was talking in the same breath of Swinburne) that 'Hopkins was not the child of vocabulary, but of passion.' It is passion which distinguishes his verse. He developed a mastery over words out of which he combined miracle after miracle of passionate description. No poet of his or any other century exulted more, for instance, in the world around him, in the colour of skies and clouds, the colour, shape, movement and sound of birds and plants and water. Wordsworthian tranquillity of reflection is alien to him just as much as the namby-pamby naturism from which we have just recovered.

'Flake-doves sent floating forth at a farmyard scare' and 'fresh-firecoal chestnut-falls' are good samples of this side of Hopkins's work taken from the two usual anthology poems. Poppies to him are 'crush-silk poppies aflash' (does not 'crush-silk' blend colour, sight and touch?) and that most delicate of potato patch weeds he describes to perfection:

> ...lace-leaved lovely
> Foam-tuft fumitory.

...I know no other poet who achieves so often such wonders of the essence of description, or in whom, bulk for bulk, there is such a continuity of surprise; but by no means is he a poet only of natural beauty. He felt it and described it in some of his best work, but he is also a poet of intellectual inquiry into man and matter, of religious ecstasy and spiritual suffering, who was always forced willingly into song, a reader feels, under terrific and irresistible pressure, yet was always self-controlled by exacting aims and difficult metrical schemes of his own devising.

In one phase he produces that terrible sonnet:

> Not; I'll not, carrion comfort, Despair, not feast on thee;
> Not untwist—slack they may be—these last strands of man
> In me or, most weary, cry *I can no more.* ...

and in another the leaping exultant flames which end his poem 'That Nature is a Heraclitean Fire and of the Comfort of the Resurrection':

[Quotes ll. 15–23.]

These quotations I have given are meant only as bait, only to show that Hopkins possessed a style which at its best, with its strong rhythms, its links of bold alliteration and internal rhymes, was an instrument fit for poetry of the first and most exciting order. They do not show all his difficulties, his innovations of metre, diction and notation of which, as of his life and the delayed appearance of his work (most of it was first published by his friend Robert Bridges in 1918), there is information ready to hand in this book and in G.F. Lahey's short life of Hopkins which was published last year.

All that need be added is that his verbal obscurities are often the boldest compressions of fine thought that, once explained (as they are in Bridges's notes), provoke, most of them, respect rather than impatience.

The other blemishes that come out of the strength of his style Bridges frankly recognizes and perhaps overcondemned in his preface, which it is essential to read. What should never be forgotten in considering them is the way Hopkins himself spoke of his more wanton rhymes:

Some of my rhymes I regret, but they are past changing, grubs in amber.

That amber is so rare, so rich in colour, the resin of so noble a tree that to feel a need of excusing the occasional grubs in it or to emphasize them hypercritically would be ungrateful and impertinent.

54. Edward Thompson, review, *Observer*

15 February 1931, p. 5

Edward Thompson (1886–1946), formerly a Wesleyan missioner in India, was lecturer in Bengali at Oxford 1923–33. He wrote many books on India and was also a poet. He was the author of a critical memoir of some distinction about Bridges (1944), near whom he lived on Boar's Hill, Oxford.

Gerard Hopkins's best critic and praiser is still his first, Robert Bridges, whose notes are a perfect example of his bluff yet delicate gift. Mr. Bridges, both in speech and writing, excelled in packed and downright phrasing, which was also marvellously exact. He has marked down Hopkins's eccentricities, and all we need do is to agree. Practically nothing of the experimental side of our 'left-wing' modern movement was not tried out by Hopkins fifty years ago; and Hopkins had a predecessor, the writer whose influence has been so deep on the younger poets of today, John Donne. Verse is buffeted and made to wrestle, in Donne's 'Batter my heart, three-personed God,' just as in every poem Hopkins wrote. All simplification of a good writer's aim is an injustice. But Hopkins's work may be said to have been governed by two purposes, to bring immediacy of phrasing and perception into verse, and to express his mystical love of Christ. The two purposes often clash, and he undoubtedly suffers from an oddity, vexing because deliberate; his elaborate artlessness is often arch and artful (in the Cockney's, not the poet's, sense). He made an unnecessary mystery about his effort to put speech-rhythms into verse; but he was a genuine pioneer here, as also in his attempt to recover our lost freedom in adjective-making. Nevertheless, because it made such 'heavy weather' about what it tried to do, his verse is marred by restlessness, by effort, and tug and puffing. The Muse is always out of breath and straining up the hill of rhythm. Any page will illustrate.

> Yes. Why do we all, seeing of a soldier, bless him? bless
> Our redcoats, our tars? Both these being, the greater part,
> But frail clay, nay but foul clay. Here it is: the heart,
> Since, proud, it calls the calling manly, gives a guess
> That, hopes that, makes believe, the men must be no less.

There can be no question of Hopkins's originality, or continual renewal of delight, his own first and then his reader's. How vivid are his compound epithets! 'This darksome burn, horseback brown'; 'A windpuff-bonnet of fawn-froth.' To show how he can fill his page with colour and blowing airs, let me quote an early passage, written before eccentricity had become a religion. It is flawed by repetition of 'crowd'; but this does not matter, in his infectious zest of seeing.

[Quotes 'A Vision of the Mermaids', ll. 84–98.]

55. 'A.L.', review, *Studies*

March 1931, pp. 165–7

. . . The second edition is as scholarly and efficient as the first and is more worthily produced. Mr. Charles Williams in a suggestive introduction describes Hopkins' characteristic as an effort 'to recognise and explain both the singleness and the division of the accepted universe.' It is a pity that he did not explain this sentence, for in it he seems to detect just the dominant quality of the poet. Gerard Hopkins did indeed try to relate all things to One, and has left us the record in his poems of those mole-like burrowings after God with which his thoughts tunnelled the universe. And it was the very intensity of his desire to find that made him concentrate so raptly upon the slightest external detail of his subject; for he gathered tidings of his quest from all things. The zeal that the scholastics applied to the exact analysis of the subtlest concepts, was only equal to that with which he endeavoured to appreciate in its finest shades his emotional experience, and to specify it to others in his expression. Hence his neologisms, his contorted grammar, his startling and baffling metric. He required new instruments to express new discoveries, reactions of the mind to which no predecessor amongst men had ever adverted. One example will suffice. The following is a stanza from 'The Wreck of the Deutschland', a poem of the same order as 'Adonais' (I dare not say more lest I scandalise the large band of the unfaithful).

> I am soft sift
> In an hourglass—at the wall
> Fast, but mined with a motion, a drift,
> And it crowds and it combs to the fall;
> I steady as water in a well, to a poise, to a pane,
> But roped with, always, all the way down from the tall
> Fells or flanks of the voel, a vein
> Of the gospel proffer, a pressure, a principle, Christ's gift.

It portrays the poet, reflecting in repose on the wreck, his recoiling mind curbed by the thoughts of faith to accept the tragedy. 'Voel' we are told is a proper name used generically, as who should say a parnassus or an etna. Now let us by some additions and transpositions make prose of the last four lines: I steady to a poise as water in a well steadies to a pane, but yet I proffer a principle, Christ's gift, always swayed (roped), as I am by the gospel that presses upon me like a stream (vein); as water all the way down from the steep sides of the hill [may flow into the depths of the well without shattering its outward stillness]. Now this is clearer than the poetry and keeps some of the charm, but in removing the grammatical disorder of the expression, it must be evident that I have removed the vehement, staccato movement, the sense of thoughts and feelings crowding too fast for coherent utterance. In short I keep the words but lose the passion; I clarify the thought, but spill the poetry. After all it pays to struggle over Gerard Hopkins, as it always pays (as Jacob found) to wrestle with an angel.

The new poems here published will not add to his reputation, but they reveal his origins. His mature work is markedly nonderivative, its echoes few and faint. But in these *juvenilia* there are echoes discernible, echoes of Swinburne:—

> When a sister, born for each strong month-brother.

Of Shelley:—

> Break the box and shed the word (cf. Break the dance and
> scatter the song).

Of Keats:—

> Down that dank rock o'er which their lush long tresses weep.

Of the eighteenth century:—

> Since trampled Spain by royal discord torn
> Lay bleeding, to Madrid the last they bore.

Of Wordsworth:—

> Thus Frances sighed at home, while Luke
> Made headway in the frothy deep.
> She listened how the sea-gust shook
> And then lay back to sleep.

And all that only proves the paradox that the most original poets must be rooted in the aboriginal, and draw the sap of their song from the healthy soil of tradition.

56. Malcolm Cowley, 'Resurrection of a Poet', *New York Herald Tribune Books,*

8 March 1931, pp. 1 and 6

Malcolm Cowley (b. 1898), literary editor of the *New Republic* 1929–40, was later to achieve a distinguished position as writer and critic.

This review of *Poems*, 2nd edn, *A Vision of the Mermaids,* and Lahey appears as the leading article of the Books supplement.

...Hopkins could never become popular. His poems are difficult, partly because his ideas themselves are difficult, partly because he adopted a difficult style, and partly because, within the limits of this style, he was sometimes awkward in expression. His Anglo-Saxon vocabulary abounds in monosyllables, and one cannot always be sure whether a given word is an adjective, a verb or a noun. Moreover, as Robert Bridges said, 'he needed in his scheme all his space for his poetical words, and he wished those to crowd out every merely grammatical colourless or toneless element'[1]; he, therefore, omitted most of his relative pronouns, with the result that some of his lines are at first sight completely baffling. There is also a curious contrast between the deliberate logic of his ideas and the breathless gallop of his emotions, so that to appreciate any given poem one has to read it twice: once slowly and silently to understand it, once rapidly aloud to appreciate its movement and music. Indeed, one can hardly catch the full force of any poem without committing it to memory; and the reader is justified in asking whether the enjoyment will be worth the trouble.

The answer is that Hopkins is a poet who rewards one's effort. He is to be studied first of all, I think, because he is individual, a source for other poets and not a cistern filled from distant springs. He is admirable, too, because of a style rich in devices of every sort: repetitions and elisions, internal rhyme and alliterations, extraordinary metaphors alternating with flat and effective statements of fact. He is capable of compressing a shipwreck into seven monosyllables—'Too late; lost; gone with the gale'—or of endowing his favourite Oxford with five headlong adjectives in a single line:

> Towery city and branchy between towers;
> Cuckoo-echoing, bell-swarmèd, lark-charmèd, rook-
> racked, river-rounded.

He uses old words in unfamiliar senses. He invents new words, and usually to good effect. He transposes the order of all his words as freely as if he were writing in Latin. Sometimes this adds to the difficulty of his style; more often it helps him to achieve a magnificent emphasis:

> Mine, O thou lord of life, send my roots rain.

But if Hopkins is to be regarded as a great poet, it is chiefly because of a fierce conviction and emotion which struggle for expression in everything he writes. In those four 'terrible' sonnets, which record a spiritual crisis and are perhaps his final work, he often achieves an effect to be envied by other artists: that of a man stuttering from the intensity of his feeling; then again, in the same poems, he attains a Miltonic majesty without forsaking his own style:

[Quotes last six lines of 'I wake and feel the fell of dark'.]

NOTE

1 See *ante*, p. 79.

57. Herbert Read, review, *Criterion*

April 1931, pp. 552–9

T.S. Eliot was editor of the *Criterion* from 1922 to 1939. This review, the first of several essays by Read about Hopkins, reappeared virtually unchanged in *Form in Modern Poetry* (1932), and is reprinted as No. 64 below. It covers *Poems*, 2nd edn., and Lahey.

58. Justin O'Brien, review, *Bookman* (New York)

April 1931, pp. 206–8

Justin O'Brien (1906–68) taught French at Harvard 1929–31, and then at Columbia. He later wrote on Gide and Camus. His review of Lahey's life of Hopkins appeared in the *Bookman*, July 1930.

Small wonder it is that the poems of Gerard Manley Hopkins have already aroused the enthusiasm of a small but very select and extremely ardent group of admirers, for they create a language, make use of rhythms, and draw upon themes to which, shockingly new as they would have been in Hopkins's day, we have been introduced and in some cases accustomed by our contemporary idols. Among the first to welcome the work of this English Jesuit must be counted those who had earlier rallied to the support of T.S. Eliot, James Joyce, and Gertrude Stein. For this reason it is perhaps fortunate that these poems did not appear until almost thirty years after their author's death. Robert Bridges's publication of his friend's verses in 1918—and to a lesser degree this second edition—is a literary event of almost equal importance to Paul Valéry's emergence from his twenty-years' silence with *La Jeune Parque*.

Of Hopkins's obscurity too much has already been said, first by himself and his friends who discouraged publication during his lifetime and more recently by his critics. Like many another great writer he merely had to wait for the world to catch up with him. True, he distorts language constantly to pack his thought more densely or to meet the requirements of his metre or rime, using words in their secondary meanings, omitting conjunctions, pronouns, or verbs; but a careful reading and re-reading (such as all poetry is entitled to and contemporary poetry in particular has been obliged to *force* upon us) yields at once the poet's thought and the justification of his tortured syntax. Beginning with the more direct verses in 'The May Magnificat', 'Binsey Poplars', or 'The Blessed Virgin Compared to the Air We Breathe' and progressing through the more compact sonnets to such overwhelmingly radical experiments as 'Spelt from Sibyl's Leaves' and 'The Leaden Echo and the Golden Echo', no one of discernment could fail to be won over to Hopkins. It is altogether advisable, besides, to ignore at first (if not forever) his own remarks on his metrical innovations, for when not downright misleading they are most often confusing. One can easily feel throughout his poems a conscious striving for musical effects: an intelligent if not always successful use of devices peculiar to music to achieve certain relations of sounds and rhythms that will create a given emotion. And this effort really calls for no technical explanation.

Hopkins's customary 'devices', such as alliteration, repetition, and interior rime, almost always have an air of inevitability about them, as if demanded by the thought he is expressing. Their source lies often obviously in a free association of ideas; they are never useless and very rarely recherché. ...

No Jesuit poet could escape being labelled a mystic; Chesterton might say that if Hopkins is a mystic he is indeed a Jesuit among Franciscans. The 'dark night of the soul' is here in abundance, but there is very little of that serene and expansive communion with God and nature which marks the mystic's goal. A large number of these poems reflect the same problem with which Paul Valéry has

grappled—with this great difference: that Hopkins is more passionate, less urbane, than the French poet. The suffering is invariably
psychological: the poet plunges into his innermost mind and
endures the horror of seeing himself see himself (*je me voyais me
voir*). ...

This preoccupation with his own introspection and his constant
intellectual frustration is the keynote of Hopkins's poetry, explaining his stiff technique, his tangled syntax, and his cumulative
cacophony which often surpasses that of Browning's 'Popularity'.
He considered himself 'soft sift in an hourglass' or 'time's eunuch'
building nothing to endure. There lies the tragedy of his short life
and, though it is barely hinted at in Father Lahey's biography, it can
clearly be read in his verses. His experiments often led to
'queerness' (as he referred to his obscurity); sometimes they even
resulted in clumsiness. Wherever we place him, we cannot but
recognize that he was 'barbarous in beauty' and admire heartily 'the
achieve of, the mastery of the thing!'

59. Alan Pryce-Jones, 'Gerard Manley Hopkins', *London Mercury*

May 1931, pp. 45–52

The *London Mercury* was the anti-modernist review founded
and edited by Sir John Squire 1919–34. Alan Pryce-Jones
(b. 1908), writer and critic, was assistant editor 1928–32.

...Hopkins at a glance is maddening. The glance shows the most
individual of all English poets; that alone makes something in his
favour. And against him the equally obvious torture of words,
torture of meaning and rhythm, wilfulness, sometimes childishness, all packed into no more than fifty complete poems, make no
less strong an objection. What, the reader asks, is the test? What is
the possibility of fishing anything out of this truculent water?

The poetical tests do not take stock enough of the duality of poets. In every poet there is the man who composes and the man who writes down. True poetry is the quickest thing in the world; written poetry catches as much as it can of the true poem. This may seem a pretentious or roundabout statement to those who imagine that the writing of poetry is a purely mechanical labour, a treaty between convenient syllables; but, in fact, the difficulty of poetry lies in the exactness with which the true poem stands to the mind's eye, at war with the toughness of words in refusing to record the picture. Therefore a poet of so personal a bent as Hopkins is under a second disadvantage. Already we suspect him, knowing that he writes to a theory, doubly we suspect him when we notice the wilfulness of his manner, and consequently the chance of his poems being translated from the page to the mind instead of from the mind to the page.

Unfortunately it is impossible to say that a poem ought to *be* anything; for there is no quality or degree which separates a poem from nonsense. For poems it is impossible to make any general statements, to set any criterion. Nevertheless, it is possible to say that a poet ought to *be* something, and that is, to be one who, in his sphere, has the athlete's capacity of grasp, reserve, violence, and those other obvious powers necessary to conveyance, whether physical conveyance or mental. In other words, we can leave the work out of court until we are satisfied with the worker; our first energies must be spent alone on the poet; if we can find the great beauty in him, we can find it, at ease, in his work, and if his work seem to lack it, we can counter the lack by a confidence that he would not have written so without excellent cause, however dark to us.

This is the method of approach to Gerard Hopkins, and it becomes almost too neat when I declare that his manhood was his work, his work his life, so that it does not matter on which we begin. Take for analysis an early sonnet, 'The Starlight Night':

> Look at the stars! look, look up at the skies!
> O look at all the fire-folk sitting in the air!
> The bright boroughs, the circle-citadels there!
> Down in dim woods the diamond delves! the elves'-eyes!
> The grey lawns cold where gold, where quickgold lies!
> Wind-beat whitebeam! airy abeles set on a flare!

Flake-doves sent floating forth at a farmyard scare!—
Ah well! it is all a purchase, all is a prize.

Buy then! bid then!—What?—Prayer, patience, alms, vows.
Look, look: a May-mess, like on orchard boughs!
    Look! March-bloom, like on mealed-with-yellow sallows!
These are indeed the barn; withindoors house
The shocks. This piece-bright paling shuts the spouse
Christ home, Christ and His mother and all His hallows.

You have never read anything like that before; still less had you in 1877. It needs at once a characteristic giving-up of any sense of humour, and therein it differs from many similar poems of the Metaphysicals, whose conceits, however comic, were contrived to bring the reader into their confidence. They enlarged a solemn subject: Hopkins narrows our response by forcing us to make an effort not to think him laughable. Now the greatest poetry treats the sense of humour in a peculiar and a much more subtle way, than this. The reader must keep it in the background as one of innumerable, untouched, friendly, essential links between himself and the poet; it must bring their intellectual equation right in an odd, subterraneous sort of way, not because of the necessity of jokes in life or art, but because of the necessary fusion of mind between reader and poet, a fusion nearly spoiled by the knowledge, which we have of Hopkins, that the poet has no idea of his lack. Perhaps I should be more clear if I said that it is fatal for a poet to be a solemn dog; which absolves Milton for one and absolves Vergil. Yet of how great that lack is, Goethe is a perfect example, who, had he only possessed the leaven—had some trivial alkaloid helped, some squalid adjustment of the glands—would have been first, perhaps, instead of among the first.

But once prepared to be solemn too, before Hopkins's sonnet makes any impression we must try, what is a worse imposition, to be conversationally-minded at the same time. For in the first line he button-holes the reader three times with three 'looks', and in what, by a common construction of Hopkins is really the second line of the sonnet—I mean the first of the sestet—the reader is dragged right inside the poem by a 'What?' forced on his own lips. Thus, dismissing the usual manner of poets, which is to let the reader come up as if to a monument, and substituting a condescension to the reader in a serious, poetical-informal display of passion without any relief but alacrity, Hopkins demands a wholly artificial attitude of mind, as strange as if a street notice were worded: Keep the, oh, left; yes, the left to, keep, keep, keep. This sonnet makes an excellent type of all Hopkins: there is an 'Ah well' in the eighth line, for an example of his habit of interjecting sighs and apostrophes—in scarcely one poem is there not a vocative *O*; and throughout the octet an explosion of phrases, cumulatively rarer, like a fountain jet narrowing more and more towards the rose, to heighten the final escape; shameless alliteration—*bright boroughs, circle-citadels*—so profusely, so half-significantly used that, useless at last, they all cancel out; and the paring of verbs to a minimum. . . .

. . . It is not idle to compare Hopkins's prosodic achievements with Stravinsky's musical achievements. Each of them brings conversation into art, an alliance not before attempted, and each finally reaches a point—Hopkins frequently, and Stravinsky in *Petrouschka*—where feet of one syllable are allowed, and bars of one note; a point where feet are feet, and bars are bars, no longer.

We have only to take any line of Hopkins and attempt to scan it, to see how unrelated is his system to our language.

> I caught this morning morning's minion, kingdom of daylight's dauphin, dapple-dawn-drawn Falcon, in his riding,

begins 'The Windhover'; and Fr. Lahey scans it thus:

$$\cup\text{-}|\cup\text{-}|\cup\text{-}|\cup\text{-}|\cup\text{-}|\text{-}|\text{-}\cup\cup\cup|\text{-}\cup|\text{-}\cup\cup\cup|\text{-}\cup\cup\cup|\text{-}\cup|.$$

But the lines could equally well be scanned in twenty different ways, for the first line at once offends against the poet's rule of taking the stress first in a foot. Furthermore, I cannot admit in the second line the First Paeonic variation of the movement; the whole rush of the rhythm is destroyed if the initial accent is placed on the first and not on the fifth syllable, if the first syllable of *dapple* is emphasized and the words *dawn-drawn* are lightly run over. Then the division into feet is quite arbitrary. Hopkins intended his poems to be read aloud; the surety of a sensitive reader overrides any doubtful scissoring, since on no poem in our language can a unique pattern be imposed. For its principal glory is the fresh beauty which every fresh mind brings to whatever it absorbs, the fresh rhythm which every tongue can set on our broad numbers—a glory which we share only with the Greeks, whose ebullience breaks over the exactness of their scansion. In Greek alone would it be possible for Hopkins to write, if not in English, for only in Greek could the supple composites, *dapple-dawn-drawn, O-seal-that-so, no-man-fathomed, wind-lilylocks-laced* (the last a tmesis) be built into the language.

But technicalities are not the most practical approach to poetry; and it must be easy to swallow every fault in this small book of poems when so much intact beauty remains. For at a first reading of any one, there is a scattered impression of beauty, and first there is the assertive beauty of splendour, the striving after which is the excuse for most of the faults. Hopkins exults in syllables, in movements of lip and throat not less than of mind, and especially in driving all-but-precious images back to nature by the Saxon force of an everyday word. The triumphant end of 'That Nature is a Heraclitean Fire' is an example of this:

[Quotes ll. 9 to the end.]

The weight of images is lifted by *blots black out*, and later by *This Jack*, even if rather consciously odd; the use of such words is a brake on rhythmic speed which might otherwise make the whole poem topple over, a speed already dangerous because of the perpetual neglect of the usual moments for deceleration—caesura or end of line—and its rush forward to the conclusion. That is why the hideous rhyme of *deck shone* and *dejection* is allowed —because they are not to be set one against the other as full rhymes, but to be noticed like the milestones during a furious journey, for a mark only and not for a halt. 'The Loss of the Eurydice' is the best instance of this leaping progress; in that poem, each four-line stanza is to be treated as one line, so that Hopkins allows himself such rhymes as *wrecked her he C-* and *electric*, and thereby, from a foolish desire to push licence as far as possible, exceeds his effect. (But the poem is already a failure, and perhaps notable only for as bathetical a couplet as ever a religious poet confected:

> A life-belt and God's will
> Lend him a lift from the sea-swill.)...

60. Harman Grisewood, review, *Dublin Review*

October 1931, pp. 213–26

Harman Grisewood (b. 1906) was a Catholic educated at Ampleforth, who joined the BBC in 1929 and eventually became Chief Assistant to the Director-General.

The *Dublin Review*, a quarterly published in London since 1836 (until 1968), printed scholarly articles and reviews of Catholic interest. This article covers *Poems*, 2nd edn, and Lahey.

... The appreciation of Hopkins' poetry has become more than the curious interest of literary scholarship appraising one last candidate who might have qualified for Victorian poet-hood. Indeed, the critic may well be discouraged from this way of scrutiny by the example of those with whom the attempt has usually ended in the safety-first admonition, 'a poet's poet'. It is with this phrase that the critic, on finding the work too exacting for his taste, has protected his own inadequate understanding against the prying of those outside his hastily drawn pentacle. Certainly Hopkins is exacting.

> Brute beauty and valour and act, oh, air, pride, plume, here
>   Buckle! AND the fire that breaks from thee then, a billion
> Times told lovelier, more dangerous, O my chevalier!
>   No wonder of it: shéer plód makes plough down sillion
> Shine, and blue-bleak embers, ah my dear,
>   Fall, gall themselves, and gash gold-vermilion.

But it is one of his most excellent qualities that he made poetry difficult at a time when it had become deadly easy.

Il y a trop peu d'écrivains obscurs en français; ainsi nous nous habituons lâchement à n'aimer que des écritures aiseés et bientôt primaires.★

It was during the prevalence of a similar *lâcheté* in England that Hopkins was writing those 'obscurities' and 'oddities' which made his friend Robert Bridges so uneasy.

That shrewd observer, the late Sir Edmund Gosse, in an address delivered in 1913, in speaking of the Future of Poetry, said:

If we could read his [the modern poet's] verses which are still unwritten, I feel sure that we should consider them obscure. That is to say, we should find that in his anxiety not to repeat what has been said before him, and in his horror of the trite and the superficial, he will achieve effect and attach interest—*obscuris vera involvens*—wrapping the truth in darkness. . . . He will be tempted to draw farther and farther away from contact with the world. He will wrap his singing robes not over his limbs only, but over his face and treat his readers with exemplary disdain.[1]

It is significant that what is in some ways a far-seeing forecast of poetry now, serves also as something of an explanation of Hopkins' poetry that had been written thirty years before. And it is, in fact, the poets of to-day, the heirs of this predicted obscurity, who are the natural companions of Hopkins. Much poetry, and his with it, has had to wait till our times for poets to justify and again insist upon the necessary quality of troubling the reader. . . .

. . . Mr. Charles Williams, in the preface to his excellent second edition of Bridges' original edition of 1918, makes a sensible distinction in saying:—

Other poets have sung *about* their intellectual exaltations; in none has the intellect itself been more the song than in Gerard Hopkins. In this he was unique among the Victorians.[2]

And it is this quality which associates him naturally with poets to-day. Hopkins would have agreed with Rimbaud that 'poetry will no longer sing of action; it will be in advance'. 'There will be such poets!. . .' Rimbaud goes on. Hopkins was one. And it is perhaps in this quality of being 'in advance', this quality, not of celebrating, but of being itself the most extreme limit of the consciousness of living, being 'in advance' of life, that most surely links Hopkins to the Rimbaud succession and to its present developments.

Poetry 'in advance' may not be easy. It must, however, be sincere. And we can learn from the notes in this edition how natural it was for him to write in this difficult manner. Mr. Williams has added examples of his early work which show that he could make fine use of traditional styles. Even when he was developing his later technique he could write, for instance, the poem 'May Magnificat'; but this was not the poetry he wrote to please himself, and in comment on it Hopkins says, 'A May piece in which I see little good.' Of his sonnet in honour of St. Alphonsus Rodriguez, he says, 'The sonnet (I say it snorting) aims at being intelligible.'

Father Lahey's *Life of Gerard Manley Hopkins*—an *apéritif*—quotes enough of his letters to show that Hopkins was very far from desiring to make converts to any new school of experiment. He showed his work only to a small group of friends: Robert Bridges, Coventry Patmore and Canon Dixon. And one cannot but admire with what charm he preserved himself technically aloof from these poets and yet never lost sympathy with their writing in the least degree. His style was purely the outcome of his poetic sensibilities, and, in the nature of things, entirely above the suspicion of desiring to attract attention. It is characteristic that he stretched the sonnet form to its utmost rather than broke it, that he invented a new, though not a rebellious, system of prosody rather than denied prosodicality. And it is the inevitability of his new and strange phrases and the certainty that here at least is no literary humbug that compels the attention of the reader, who may feel the style a rebuff. For Hopkins is one who not so much turns his back upon but simply avoids the thinning ends of the Romantic and Humanist tradition....

NOTES

* Rémy de Gourmont, *De Stéphane Mallarmé*.

1 P. 10 of the pamphlet published by the English Association, June 1913.
2 See *ante*, p. 175.

61. Yvor Winters, 'An Appreciation of Robert Bridges', *Hound and Horn*

January–March 1932, pp. 321–7

Yvor Winters (1900–68) taught at Stanford from 1928. His plain-spoken and judicial criticism has been a cause of both irritation and admiration. He developed his doubts about Hopkins at much greater length in the *Hudson Review* in 1949.

...Dr. Bridges has been so often and so angrily compared to his friend Gerard Hopkins that I may perhaps be pardoned for a word on this subject. Hopkins seems to me to have been a truly great poet, though I cannot carry my enthusiasm as far as do his most violent admirers. The qualities that have won Hopkins almost immediate recognition during the past few years are, I fear, the very reasons for his limitations and his definite inferiority to Bridges. The mere fact that a man is a radical technical innovator does not render him a greater poet than the man who is less an innovator; extreme originality of method almost always involves extreme departure from the norm of experience, involves specialization and limitation of feeling. The greatest technical experimenter in English literature is, I suppose, Milton, and he is muscle-bound by his magnificence and the intricacy of his syntax. When he is not grand, he is grandiloquent; there is no transition between the two in Miltonic blank verse; and he killed English blank verse for two centuries. So with Hopkins: he can express with his violent rhythms an extremely special kind of excitement arising from religious experience, but he can express little else, and even the religious experience is incomplete, for if he does not deal wholly with the resultant excitement, he certainly throws his emphasis very heavily upon it. We are told, for instance, in superbly impassioned verses that the mind has mountains, but the nature of those mountains is never wholly clear. In Bridges the nature of the mountains is absolutely clear—that is, the experience is rendered whole—and the terror of the mountains is not isolated from all other experience but is seen in firm proportion. There is in the metrical experimentation in the present volume of Bridges[1] quite as much originality of thought as in the experiments of Hopkins, coupled with a much more thorough knowledge of English meters and the complexities of feeling involved in their history. Bridges' technique, if the less obviously original of the two, is the more sensitive and the more widely applicable instrument of perception. In saying this, I do not wish it to be thought, let me repeat, that I am blind to the sensitivity or the power of Hopkins, a poet who moves me very deeply.

This limiting effect of the elaborately original may be one reason for the extreme shortness of so many of the most brilliant of contemporary careers: a narrow vein of feeling only can be explored, and once it is finished, the author has got himself so far from a fresh starting point that he lacks either the courage or the vigor to do anything about it; he has systematically deadened himself through specialization. If there is any truth in this supposition, extreme originality of style would appear to be one of the shortest cuts to that condition of atrophy, from which its most fanatical devotees seek, by its means, to escape. On the other hand, traditionalism is not equivalent to dullness. ...

NOTE

1 *Shorter Poems.*

62. G.W. Stonier, review, *New Statesman and Nation*

25 June 1932, pp. 836–8

George Stonier (b. Sydney, 1903) helped to build up the *New Statesman's* high reputation for reviewing in the twenties and thirties. He was assistant literary editor to Raymond Mortimer from 1928 to 1945. This essay also appears in Stonier's *Gog Magog and Other Critical Essays* (London, 1933). For another review by him of Hopkins, see No. 95.

... An instance of grave critical insufficiency is the harm done to a poet, Gerard Manley Hopkins, even by critics whose intention has been to recommend him. Hopkins was born in 1844 and died in 1889. His first critic, Robert Bridges, recognised Hopkins as a fine poet and proved his admiration by keeping his poems in cold storage for thirty years, releasing at last, in 1918, a selection of Hopkins's poetry, which was enlarged twelve years later by another editor. He was thus given a false position from the start. Between 1918 and 1932 these criticisms were made of Hopkins: (1) that he was the most difficult English poet, in whom religion stilled art (I.A. Richards);[1] (2) that he was difficult and at times incomprehensible, and that wilfulness and a 'naked encounter between sensualism and asceticism' spoilt much of his best work (Robert Bridges);[2] (3) that he was a pseudo-Shelley whose 'central point of departure' was the 'Ode to the Skylark' (J. Middleton Murry);[3] (4) that Hopkins was on the one hand fundamentally Miltonic, and on the other fundamentally Shakespearean (various writers; two groups), and (5) that he was a post-war poet, the leader of a new school of poets. The last view is popular with anthologists.

Such a jumble of nonsense would seem to me incredible if I had not read it with my own eyes. Where did Mr. Murry find his skylark poet? Hopkins wrote two sonnets on the skylark, neither of which has any connection with Shelley beyond subject-matter. Two of his longest poems describe shipwreck: perhaps then Hopkins is repeating 'The Wreck of the Hesperus'? The argument whether Hopkins is Miltonic or Shakespearean has more interest because he was actually influenced by both; but he was also influenced by Swinburne and the author of *Beowulf*: why not admit that Hopkins is fundamentally himself? The criticisms of Bridges and of Mr. I.A. Richards are worth answering. But there are two facts about Hopkins—that he was a Victorian in style, outlook and feeling, and that he was a Catholic priest who wrote poetry to the glory of God—these facts have been recognised by no critic whom I can trace.

The most important event in Hopkins's life was his conversion in 1866, at the age of twenty-two. Till then he had been, on the surface at least, another Swinburne, precocious, sensitive, less diffused, more meticulous, but sowing his sweet pastoral oats and slipping back through sunsets and books of Cavalier verse into

Greek mythology. He began by imitating Keats, but afterwards disliked what he called the unmanly qualities in Keats's character, and wrote in a letter to Coventry Patmore:

It appears that he said something like 'O for a life of impressions rather than thoughts.'...His contemporaries, as Wordsworth, Byron, Shelley, and even Leigh Hunt, right or wrong, still concerned themselves with great causes, as liberty and religion; but he lived in mythology and fairyland, the life of a dreamer: nevertheless I feel and see in him the beginnings of something opposite to this....[4]

(Is not that the very accent of a Victorian?) From an early age he had felt and seen 'the beginnings of something opposite to this' in *himself*. At the age of twelve, he described a school-fellow in his diary as 'a kaleidoscopic, parti-coloured, harlequinesque, thaumotropic being': a note not heard in his poetry till twenty years later. A vein of resistance ran counter to the delights of the poet's boyhood, which was otherwise Swinburnian, and found outlet in an occasional prank like fasting or abstention from drinking liquids. His artistic sensibilities, even as a child, were so various that, while he allowed them to develop, his instinct hardened against submission to them.

That brings me to the third fact which critics have overlooked: Hopkins was in sensibility not only a poet but a musician and a painter. This can be seen plainly enough in his poetry. He was fond at different times of composing songs and fugues, and his skill as a painter was sufficient for his biographer to record that 'had his career not been shaped by other incidents he would undoubtedly have adopted painting as a profession.'[5] Some degree of ambidexterity in the arts is perhaps common among poets, particularly minor poets; but in Hopkins we have the unusual case of a great poet who could use his sensibilities as a musician and painter, not merely in the by-practice of these arts, not merely as an enrichment or addition to his poetry, but as an integral part of his poetic genius. The 'difficulty' of his work lies in the inaccessibility of critics to the range of his artistic feeling. By some process of critical winking they ignored his religion, his worship of God in nearly everything he wrote; and they have ignored the modes and channels of his art. ...

One other essential of Hopkins's poetry remains to be mentioned, the vision (foreshadowed in his schoolboy phrase) of the world as 'dappled, parti-coloured.' This texture, the artist's sense of life-texture as he works in his medium, is seen most strongly in poems like 'Glory be to God for dappled things,' of which it is the theme, but it is present everywhere in his later work, in the verbal texture of the poems.

There is one important date in this poet's life, which divides boyhood from maturity and early poems from great poems—the date of his conversion, 1866. Religion hardened him morally and intellectually, provided him with a background infinitely better to his genius than Greek myth, and brought into his poetry the polyphony of style, parti-colour of pattern, and expanding, realistic and passionate force of his great work. In the face of this it seems to me absurd to speak of damage done to him by conflicts of art and religion, sensuousness and asceticism. The interaction of these forces produced much of his best poetry. A friend wrote of him: 'His mind was too delicate a texture to grapple with the rough elements of life',[6] and this is true. But it is true also that no other poet has so grappled reality into his imagination, mixing earth with his words. He employed native words, root-words of old stock, rhythms of speech, and compelled them, as did Hardy, by the sheer poetic force and integrity of his mind; but while with Hardy the words remain sometimes awkward, local or antique, like tough old bits of furniture, in Hopkins they are knocked together, swept along in the one rush of his passion. 'Take breath,' he said, 'and read.' The advice is worth a lot of criticism. He was a great poet, how great I shall not venture to guess until I have read him a dozen times more, and a lonely one; like Berlioz and Van Gogh, alone in his art, demonic, and yet characteristic of his time.

NOTES

1 See *ante*, pp. 143–4.
2 See *ante*, p. 78.
3 See *ante*, p. 125.
4 Lahey, p. 73. And see *Further Letters*, p. 386.
5 Lahey, p. 2.
6 Lahey, p. 133.

63. F.R. Leavis, *New Bearings in English Poetry*

London, 1932

Frank Leavis (1895–1978) was at the beginning of a long and influential teaching and writing career when *New Bearings* was published. Whether Chapter V, on Hopkins, stimulated or irritated readers, its definite moral tone and close analysis seemed to reflect a real movement in critical taste. I have reprinted the second half of the chapter, pp. 180–93, where Leavis turns from attacking Bridges and appreciating 'The Wreck of the Deutschland', to an estimate of some of the later poems.

...But remarkable as 'The Wreck of the Deutschland' is it does not put his technical skill to the utmost stretch. This skill is most unmistakably that of a great poet when it is at the service of a more immediately personal urgency, when it expresses not religious exaltation, but inner debate. 'The Windhover' is a poem of this kind. Since not only Mr. Richards, in the essay[1] already mentioned but Mr Empson also, in *Seven Types of Ambiguity*,[2] have dealt admirably with this poem, there is no need to analyse it here. Mr Empson's book is one that nobody interested in English poetry can afford not to have read. It is an implicit commentary on Bridges' complaint that 'ambiguity or momentary uncertainty destroys the force of the sentence' and imposes on the reader a 'conscious effort of interpretation'.[3] The kind of ambiguity that Mr Empson finds to be the essence of 'The Windhover' is suggested here: 'Thus in the first three lines of the sestet we seem to have a clear case of the Freudian use of opposites, where two things thought of as incompatible, but desired intensely by different systems of judgments, are spoken of simultaneously by words applying to both; both desires are thus given a transient and exhausting satisfaction, and the two systems of judgment are forced into open conflict before the reader'. It is in place at this point to observe that

Hopkins's genius was as much a matter of rare character, intelligence and sincerity as of technical skill: indeed, in his great poetry the distinction disappears; the technical triumph is a triumph of spirit.

The inner friction expressed in the equivocal burden of 'The Windhover' comes out more explicitly in 'Spelt from Sibyl's Leaves,' which, if it represents a less difficult undertaking, is more indubitably a complete success. It is one of the finest things that he ever did, and since it exhibits and magnificently justifies most of the peculiarities of his technique, I will (though Mr Richards has analysed it) venture a brief commentary:

Earnest, earthless, equal, attuneable, | vaulty, volu-
    minous, . . stupendous
Evening strains to be tíme's vást, | womb-of-all,
    home-of-all, hearse-of-all night.
Her fond yellow hornlight wound to the west, | her
    wild hollow hoarlight hung to the height
Waste; her earliest stars, earl-stars, | stárs principal,
    overbend us,
Fíre-féaturing heaven. For earth | her being has
    Unbound, her dapple is at an end, as-
tray or aswarm, all throughther, in throngs; | self
    ín self steepèd and páshed—qúite
Disremembering, dísmémbering | áll now. Heart,
    you round me right
With: Óur évening is over us; óur night | whélms,
    whélms, ánd will end us.
Only the beak-leaved boughs dragonish | damask
    the tool-smooth bleak light; black,
Ever so black on it. Our tale, O óur oracle! | Lét
    life, wáned, ah lét life wind
Off hér once skéined stained véined varíety | upon,
    áll on twó spools; párt, pen, páck
Now her áll in twó flocks, twó folds—black, white; |
    right, wrong; reckon but, reck but, mind
But thése two: wáre of a wórld where bút these |
    twó tell, each off the óther; of a rack
Where, selfwrung, selfstrung, sheathe- and shelter-
    less, | thóughts agaínst thoughts ín groans grínd.

The poem opens with evening deepening into night. We are not merely told that evening 'strains', we feel evening straining, to become night, enveloping everything, in the movement, the progression of alliteration, assonance and rime. This progression is associated with and hardly distinguishable from, the development of meaning in the sequence of adjectives: evening is first sweetly solemn, serene, etherealizing and harmonizing, then becomes less tranquillizing and more awful, and finally ends in the blackness of night.

> Her fond yellow hornlight wound to the west, her
>   wild hollow hoarlight hung to the height
>   Waste...

—The 'yellow hornlight' is, of course, the setting moon; 'fond'—tender, soft, sympathetic, clinging as if reluctant to go, the slow gentle sinking being felt in the movement and modulation of the verse. The 'hoarlight' is the cold, hard starlight, 'wild' and 'hollow'—remote, inhuman, a kind of emptiness in the hollow vault—in contrast to the 'fond yellow' moonlight. The verse-movement itself, with the inevitable rest upon 'height', seems to hang. The 'dapple' of earth, the rich coloured variety that Hopkins loved so much (cf. 'Pied Beauty'—'Glory be to God for dappled things') has gone, merged ('throughter'—each through other) into neutrality. That he is not concerned with 'pure description' the introduction of 'self' intimates, together with the unexpected strength of 'steepèd and páshed' and 'dismembering'.

He suddenly realizes the whole thing as a parable, not meditatively worked out, but immediate: he sees the outward symbol and the significance as one, in a kind of metaphor. It is Blake's 'Sun-flower' rather than Matthew Arnold's 'Yes: in the sea of life enisled.'

> Heart, you round me right
> With: Our évening is over us; oúr night
>   whélms

—the heavy stress that his rhythm enables him to put upon 'our' brings home the poignant realization. His heart 'rounds' him, i.e. whispers (as in the ballads), and 'rounds upon him' with, the thought that he has sacrificed the 'dapple' of existence for the stark dichotomy of right and wrong.

> Only the beak-leaved boughs dragonish|damask
> the tool-smooth bleak light; black,
> Ever so black on it.

—The trees are no longer the beautiful, refreshing things of daylight; they have turned fantastically strange, hard and cruel, 'beak-leaved' suggesting the cold, hard light, steely like the gleam of polished tools, against which they appear as a kind of damascene-work ('damask') on a blade. Then follows the anguished surrender to the realization:

> ...Oúr tale, O oúr oracle! | Lét life, wáned, ah
> lét life wind
> Off hér one skéined stained véined variety | upon,
> áll on twó spools; párt, pen, páck
> Now her áll in twó flocks, twó folds—black, white; |
> right, wrong...

—The run of alliterations, rimes and assonances suggests the irresistible poignancy of the realization. The poem ends with a terrible effect as of unsheathed nerves grinding upon one another. The grinding might at first be taken to be merely that of 'right' against 'wrong', the inner conflict of spirit and flesh, and the pain that which the believer knows he must face, the simple pain of renunciation. Yet we are aware of a more subtle anguish and a more desperate plight. And if we look closely we find that Hopkins is explicit about it:

> black, white; right, wrong...

—The first draft had 'wrong, right,' but he deliberately, and significantly, reversed the order. If he were merely 'ware of a world where but these two tell' his torment would be less cruel. But his consciousness is more complex; his absolutes waver and change places, and he is left in terrible doubt.

In comparison with such a poem of Hopkins's as this, any other poetry of the nineteenth century is seen to be using only a very small part of the resources of the English language. His words seem to have substance, and to be made of a great variety of stuffs. Their potencies are correspondingly greater for subtle and delicate communication. The intellectual and spiritual anaemia of Victorian poetry is indistinguishable from its lack of body. Hopkins is a very different poet from Dante, but a remark that Mr Eliot throws out in the discussion of Dante has a bearing here: 'that Hell, though a state, is a state which can only be thought of, and perhaps only experienced, by the projection of sensory images; and that the resurrection of the body has perhaps a deeper meaning than we understand.' The critical implications of this (they can be generalized and discussed apart from any theological context) deserve pondering. They relate to another remark of Mr Eliot's that has been quoted already and applies also to Hopkins: in his verse 'the intellect is at the tip of the senses.' And along with the qualities indicated by this phrase goes a remarkable control of tempo and modulation.

The poems of Hopkins that stand in best hope of general acceptance (after 'Margaret') are the group of intensely personal sonnets that he wrote towards the end of his life. 'The Windhover' and 'Spelt from Sibyl's Leaves' are in sonnet-form, but the late sonnets are immediately recognizable as such. Moreover they lack anything in the nature of

> The roll, the rise, the carol, the creation,

for the pressure of the personal anguish was too strong; and consequently they do not present so formidable an appearance as where the Hopkins technique is more copiously elaborated. As Bridges put it,[4] when Hopkins died 'he was beginning to concentrate the force of all his luxuriant experiments in rhythm and diction, and castigate his art into a more reserved style.' The austerity was rather, perhaps, the effect of that cruel inner friction expressed in 'The Windhover' and 'Spelt from Sibyl's Leaves'. In spite of the terrible import of these poems there is still a certain magnificent buoyancy in the handling of the technical problems. But when he wrote those last sonnets Hopkins had no buoyancy left. They are the more interesting from the point of view of this study in that they bring out more plainly the relation of his medium to speech. More obviously here than in the more canorous[5] poems the ruling spirit is that of living idiom; we can hear the speaking voice:

> I wake and feel the fell of dark, not day.
> What hours, O what black hoürs we have spent
> This night! what sights you, heart, saw; ways
>   you went!

And more must, in yet longer light's delay.
  With witness I speak this. But where I say
Hours I mean years, mean life. And my lament
Is cries countless, cries like dead letters sent
To dearest him that lives alas! away.

Yet this is characteristic Hopkins in its methods of compression and
its elimination of all inessential words. There is the familiar use of
assonance: 'feel' becomes 'fell,' i.e. feeling becomes an obsessing
sense of the overwhelming darkness (the adjectival homonym is
felt in 'fell,' which is therefore the smothering coat of a fell beast);
and the sequence 'night,' 'sights,' 'light's' suggest the obsessing
horror of the night.

There are a few difficulties; notably, for instance, in the sestet of
the sonnet that begins: 'My own heart let me have more pity on.'
This is admirably dealt with in *A Survey of Modernist Poetry*★ by
Laura Riding and Robert Graves (p. 90 ff.). But the difficulty will
mainly be, not to get the sense, but to realize the full effect
intended, to get the 'oddities' into focus. Some of the effects are
extremely subtle and original. One of the most remarkable has
already been quoted:

            Only what word
  Wisest my heart breeds dark heaven's baffling ban
  Bars or hell's spell thwarts. This to hoard unheard,
  Heard unheeded, leaves me a lonely began.

This conveys the very process of frustration, the very realizing of
failure. No poet with a respect for literary decorum could have
accepted that 'Began' even if it had come; but it is magnificently
justified. The passage, with all its compression, achieved by
characteristic means, suggests the speaking voice using modern
idiom: 'word wisest' has nothing in common with ordinary poetic
inversion. And it would be hard to illustrate better the difference
between Hopkins's use of alliteration and assonance and Swinburne's: in Hopkins they serve to call the maximum attention to
each word.

Another particularly remarkable effect, is the close of the sonnet
called 'Carrion Comfort':

              That night, that year
  Of now done darkness I wretch lay wrestling with
        (my God!) my God.

This, as the sonnet is read through, is completely successful: it represents fairly the control, the sureness of touch, and the perfection of essential decorum that accompany Hopkins's audacities.

Yet training in the other decorum may cause a great deal of boggling. For example, the sonnet 'The Candle Indoors' (not one of the 'terrible' ones) begins:

> Some candle clear burns somewhere I come by,
> I muse at how its being puts blissful back
> With yellowy moisture mild night's blear-all black,
> Or to-fro tender trambeams truckle at the eye.

Of the last line the editor of the second edition of the *Poems* remarks:

> It is perfectly possible to smile at the line, but hardly possible to laugh; or only sympathetically, as at the wilder images of the metaphysicals, the extremer rhetoric of Marlowe, the more sedate elegances of Pope, the more prosaic moralities of the Victorians, or the more morbid pedestrianisms of Thomas Hardy. Such things are the accidents of genius seriously engaged upon its own business, and not so apt as the observer to see how funny it looks[6].

And yet, once the meaning has been taken, there should be nothing funny about the line. The image is so just, the expression of it, far from producing any accidental effect, so inevitable and adequate, that we hardly see the words as such; the image replaces them. Hopkins is describing the lines of light (caused, I believe, by the eyelashes) that, in the circumstances specified, converge upon the eye like so many sets of tram-rails. But 'tram' unqualified would suggest something too solid, so he adds 'tender'; and 'truckle' conveys perfectly the obsequious way in which they follow every motion of the eyes and of the eyelids.

Bridges, again, boggled at the second couplet of 'Margaret,' and, in printing this poem (probably Hopkins's best-known) in *The Spirit of Man*, left it out. I have heard him commended for the improvement. The sonnet addressed to him perhaps he may be excused for venturing to correct. It opens (as printed by him and Mr. Williams):

The fine delight that fathers thought; the strong
Spur, live and lancing like the blowpipe flame,
Breathes once and, quenchèd faster than it came,
Leaves yet the mind a mother of immortal song.
Nine months she then, nay years, nine years she long
Within her wears, bears, cares and moulds the same:

—Bridges notes: 'In line 6 the word *moulds* was substituted by me for *combs* of original, when the sonnet was published by Miles; and I leave it, having no doubt that G.M.H. would have made some such alteration.' Others will have considerable doubt. To use so weak a word as 'moulds' in this place is most unlike Hopkins. The objection to 'combs' seems to be based on nothing better than a narrow conception of metaphor—the same misconception that prompts editors to emend the 'To-morrow and to-morrow and to-morrow' passage in *Macbeth*: '. . . having regard to the turn of thought and the necessary continuity of metaphors, I am convinced that Shakespeare's epithet was *dusky*.' Good metaphor need not be a matter of consistently worked out analogy or point-for-point parallel; and the shift represented by 'combs' imposes itself as 'right' on the unprejudiced sensibility, and is very characteristic of Hopkins. Perhaps the term *prolepsis*, suitably invoked, would suffice to settle any qualms.

The strength and subtlety of his imagery are proof of his genius. But Victorian critics were not familiar with such qualities in the verse of their time. The acceptance of Hopkins would alone have been enough to reconstitute their poetic criteria. But he was not published in 1889. He is now felt to be a contemporary, and his influence is likely to be great. It will not necessarily manifest itself in imitation of the more obvious of his technical peculiarities (these, plainly, may be dangerous toys); but no one can come from studying his work without an extended notion of the resources of English. And a technique so much concerned with inner division, friction, and psychological complexities in general has a special bearing on the problems of contemporary poetry.

He is likely to prove, for our time and the future, the only influential poet of the Victorian age, and he seems to me the greatest.

NOTES

* This is a very uneven book. The authors, for instance, discuss Hopkins and E.E. Cummings with equal gravity.

1 In the *Dial* (1926). See No. 36.
2 See No. 43.
3 See *ante*, pp. 80 and 79.
4 See *ante*, p. 82.
5 'Melodious', 'musical'.
6 See *ante*, p. 174.

64. Herbert Read, *Form in Modern Poetry*

London, 1932, pp. 44–54

The Preface by the editor of the series 'Essays in Order', of which this volume formed a part, explained that its intention was to relate the modern world and the Catholic view of things, but Read's essay is literary, not religious. Herbert Read (1893–1968), Professor of Fine Art at Edinburgh, 1931–3, wrote much on the modern movement in both art and literature; his contribution to Hopkins criticism is confused by his habit of using the same material under different titles (see Nos 57, 65, and 69).

... The course of poetry in the nineteenth century was determined by Wordsworth. Not one poet—not Shelley not Keats, not Landor nor Tennyson, not even Swinburne—but was affected by the revolution in poetic diction originated by Wordsworth. They were affected, but did little to develop the situation as Wordsworth left it. Against the magnitude of Wordsworth's experiment, all the minor tinkerings of the nineteenth century are as nothing—until we come to Browing and Gerard Manley Hopkins. Browning had no particular theory of diction: he wanted his verse to be expressive, and expressive it was—of his personality. But what he did do was considerably to enlarge the scope of poetry by adding certain categories of content to it, such as those embodied in his dramatic monologues and his psychological studies generally. His influence is important because its tendency is to encourage an objective attitude in the poet. Matthew Arnold should perhaps not be passed over; he adds little to Wordsworth's achievement, but he did experiment in free verse, and the originality that is claimed for contemporary writers, of free verse is excessive unless 'The Strayed Reveller' is borne in mind. But that graceful experiment bore little fruit. Hopkins's experiments, however, were of far greater potential influence, and must be considered in more detail.

Gerard Manley Hopkins was born in 1844, and died in 1889. He may therefore be reckoned as a contemporary of Swinburne, by whom he was perhaps momentarily influenced. But while Swinburne has had his fiery ascension, and now scarcely smoulders, Hopkins is only just emerging from the darkness to which his original genius condemned him. It is a familiar story; nothing could have made Hopkins's poetry popular in his day: it was necessary that it should first be absorbed by the sensibility of a new generation of poets, and by them masticated to a suitable pulp for less sympathetic minds. That process is going on apace now, and when the history of the last decade of English poetry comes to be written by a dispassionate critic, no influence will rank in importance with that of Gerard Manley Hopkins.

Hopkins himself was aware of the quality of his genius, and therefore knew what to expect from his contemporaries. Even in his undergraduate days at Oxford, he could write:

It is a happy thing that there is no royal road to poetry. The world should know by this time that one cannot reach Parnassus except by flying thither. Yet from time to time more men go up and either perish in its gullies fluttering excelsior flags or else come down again with full folios and blank countenances. Yet the old fallacy keeps its ground. Every age has its false alarms.[1]

The most obvious false alarm, as I have already suggested, was Swinburne; but he was of the number who perish in the gullies of Parnassus. More false, because more seeming-fair, are those who come down again with full folios and blank countenances, and among these can be numbered some of Hopkins's closest friends. Probably the only one of his small circle who understood him fully was his fellow-poet, Richard Watson Dixon. Dixon, writing to Hopkins to urge him to write more poems, refers to their quality as 'something that I cannot describe, but know to myself by the inadequate word *terrible pathos*—something of what you call temper in poetry: a right temper which goes to the point of the terrible: the terrible crystal. Milton is the only one else who has anything like it, and he has it in a totally different way; he has it through indignation, through injured majesty, which is an inferior thing. ....' Here is a full understanding which we do not find in the published letters and writings of others who knew Hopkins—not in Coventry Patmore, who floundered in deep astonishment, and not in his closest friend and final editor, the late Poet Laureate. To contend that Dr. Bridges did not understand the poetry of Hopkins would not be quite fair; he understood the craftsmanship of it, and was sensible to the beauty. But there seems to have been an essential lack of sympathy—not of personal sympathy, but of sympathy in poetic ideals. The Preface to the notes which Dr. Bridges contributed to the first edition of the poems (reprinted in the new edition of 1930) is marked by a pedantic velleity which would be excusable only on the assumption that we are dealing with a poet of minor interest. That is, indeed, the attitude: 'Please look at this odd fellow whom for friendship's sake I have rescued from oblivion.' The emphasis on oddity and obscurity is quite extraordinary, and in the end all we are expected to have is a certain technical interest, leading to tolerance, and the discovery of 'rare masterly beauties.' Hopkins is convicted of affectation in metaphor, perversion of human feeling, exaggerated Marianism, the 'naked encounter of sensualism and asceticism which hurts the "Golden Echo"', purely artistic wantonness, definite faults of style, incredible childishness in rhyming—at times disagreeable and vulgar and even comic; and generally of deliberate and unnecessary obscurity. Everything, in such an indictment, must depend on the judge's set of laws, and in criticising Dr. Bridges's treatment of Hopkins, I am wishing to say no more than that the Poet Laureate applied a code which was not that of the indicted. The lack of sympathy is shown precisely in this fact. Hopkins was a revolutionary; that is to say, his values were so fundamentally opposed to current practices that only by an effort of the imagination could they be comprehended. Once they are comprehended, many apparent faults are justified, and there is no reason to dwell on any of them.

Hopkins was serene and modest in his self-confidence. He could admit the criticism of his friends, and yet quietly persist in his perverseness. To one of them he wrote, in 1879.

No doubt my poetry errs on the side of oddness. I hope in time, to have a more balanced and Miltonic style. But as air, melody is what strikes me most of all in music and design in painting, so design, pattern, or what I call *inscape* is what I, above all, aim at in poetry. Now it is the virtue of design, pattern, or inscape to be distinctive, and it is the vice of distinctiveness to become queer. This vice I cannot have escaped.[2]

And again, a little later:

Moreover, the oddness may make them repulsive at first sight and yet Lang might have liked them on second reading. Indeed, when, on somebody returning me the *Eurydice*, I opened and read some lines, as one commonly reads whether prose or verse, with the eyes, so to say only, it struck me aghast with a kind of raw nakedness and unmitigated violence I was unprepared for: but take breath and read it with the ears, as I always with to read, and my verse becomes all right.[3]

A full exposition of Hopkins's theories would take us far into a discussion of the historical development of poetry. Let me briefly indicate their main features. There is in the first place a metrical theory, of the greatest importance. Hopkins's poems are written in a mixture of what he called Running Rhythm and Sprung Rhythm. Running rhythm, or common English rhythm, is measured in feet of either two or three syllables, and each foot has one principal stress or accent. Hopkins preferred to take the stress always first, for purposes of scanning; but obviously that is only a question of convenience. To vary this running rhythm, poets have introduced various licences, of which the chief are reversed feet and reversed rhythm. If you pursue these variations far enough, the original measure will seem to disappear, and you will have the measure called by Hopkins sprung rhythm. In this measure each foot has one stress, which falls on the only syllable, if there is only one, or on the first if there are more than one. Normally there should not be more than four syllables to a foot, and the feet are regular, measured in time. Their seeming inequality is made up by pause and stressing.

In general, sprung rhythm, as Hopkins claimed, is the most natural of things. He tabulated the reasons:

(1) It is the rhythm of common speech and of written prose, when rhythm is perceived in them.

(2) It is the rhythm of all but the most monotonously regular music, so that in the words of choruses and refrains and in song closely written to music it arises.

(3) It is found in nursery rhymes, weather saws, and so on; because, however these may have been once made in running rhythm, the terminations having dropped off by the change of language, the stresses come together and so the rhythm is sprung.

(4) It arises in common verse when reversed or counterpointed, for the same reason.

These reasons need no further comment; but there are two historical considerations to note. Sprung rhythm is not an innovation; it is the rhythm natural to English verse before the Renaissance. It is the rhythm of *Piers Ploughman* and of Skelton. Greene was the last writer to use it, and since the Elizabethan age, as Hopkins claimed, there is not a single, even short poem, in which sprung rhythm is employed as a principle of scansion. The other observation Hopkins could not make, because it is part of our history since his time. It is that the principles contended for by Hopkins on the basis of scholarship and original tradition (but only *contended* for on that basis: he actually wrote as he felt, and then went to history to justify himself) are in many essentials identical with the principles contended for by those modern poets already mentioned (whose advocacy and practice of 'free verse' is also based on feeling and intuition rather than historical analysis).

A second characteristic of Hopkins's poetry which while not so original, is yet a cause of strangeness, may be found in his vocabulary. No true poet hesitates to invent words when his sensibility finds no satisfaction in current phrases. Words like 'shivelight' and 'firedint' are probably such inventions. But most of Hopkins's innovations are in the nature of new combinations of existing words, sometimes contracted similes, or metaphors, and in this respect his vocabulary has a surface similarity to that of James Joyce. Examples of such phrases are to be found in almost every poem: 'the beadbonny ash,' 'fallowbootfellow,' 'windlaced,' 'churlsgrace,' 'footfretted,' 'clammyish lashtender combs,' 'wild-worth,' and so on. Commoner phrases like 'beetle-browed' or 'star-eyed' are of the same kind, made in the same way, and freely used by him. Here again an explanation would take us far beyond the immediate subject; for it concerns the original nature of poetry itself—the emotional sound-complex uttered in primitive self-expression. Mr Williams, whose more graceful and appreciative introduction to the second edition of the poems is a fair corrective to the pedantic undertones of Dr. Bridges, has an excellent description of the phenomenon as it appeared in the composition of Hopkins's verse:

It is as if the imagination, seeking for expression, had found both verb and substantive at one rush, had begun almost to say them at once, and had separated them only because the intellect had reduced the original unity into divided but related sounds."

Poetry can be renewed only by discovering the original sense of word formation: the words do not come pat in great poetry, but are torn out of the context of experience; they are not in the poet's mind, but in the nature of things he describes.

You must know, [said Hopkins himself], that words like *charm* and *enchantment* will not do: the thought is of beauty as of something that can be physically kept and lost, and by physical things only, like keys; then the things must come from the *mundus muliebris*; and thirdly they must not be markedly old-fashioned. You will see that this limits the choice of words very much indeed.[4]

Of Hopkins's imagery, there is not much in general to be said, but that 'not much' is all. He had that acute and sharp sensuous awareness essential to all great poets. He was physically aware of textures, surfaces, colours, patterns of every kind; aware acutely of earth's diurnal course, or growth and decay, of animality in man and of vitality in all things. Everywhere there is passionate apprehension, passionate expression and equally that passion for form without which these other passions are spendthrift. But the form is inherent in the passion. For, as Emerson remarked with his occasional deep insight, 'it is not metres, but a metre-making argument, that makes a poem—a thought so passionate and alive, that, like the spirit of a plant or an animal, it has an architecture of its own, and adorns nature with a new thing'.

The thought in Hopkins's poetry tends to be overlaid by the surface beauty. But the thought is very real there, and as the idiom becomes more accepted, will emerge in its variety and strength. There is no explicit system, nor need there be in great poetry. Perhaps the only essential quality is a sense of values, and this

Hopkins had in a fervid degree. He was a convert to Roman Catholicism, and might have ranged widely in intellectual curiosity had he not preferred to submit to authority. One of his contemporaries at St. Beuno's Theological College wrote of him:

I have rarely known anyone who sacrificed so much in undertaking the yoke of religion. If I had known him outside, I should have said that his love of speculation and originality of thought would make it almost impossible for him to submit his intellect to authority.[5]

Perhaps in actual intensity his poetry gained more than it lost by this step, but one cannot help regretting the curtailment it suffered in range and quantity. After joining the Church, he applied to himself a strict ascetic censorship, and apart from what he may have destroyed, deliberately refrained from writing under every wayward inspiration. His remarkable criticism of Keats, in a long letter to Coventry Patmore published by Father Lahey, shows what a high standard of intellectual and moral rectitude be expected in a poet:

It is imposiible [he says of Keats] not to feel with weariness how his verse is at every turn abandoning itself to an unmanly and ennervating luxury.[6]

In another kind of critic such a judgment would be excessively priggish; but in Hopkins it was a principle he lived by. His poetry is nothing if not intellectually tempered, virile, masculine, 'the terrible crystal,' the very opposite of the sentimental and romantic. . . .

NOTES

1 *Journal*, 2nd edn, p. 23.
2 *Letters to Bridges*, p. 66. (See *ante*, p. 52.)
3 *Ibid.*, p. 79.
4 *Ibid.*, p. 161.
5 Hopkins's obituary in *Letters and Notices*, XX, 1889–90, pp. 175–6.
6 Lahey, p. 73, and *Further Letters*, p. 386.

65. Herbert Read, 'Poetry and Belief in Gerard Manley Hopkins', *New Verse*

January 1933, pp. 11–15

The material of this article reappeared in Read's 'The Poetry of Gerard Manley Hopkins', 1933: see No. 69.

66. Unsigned article, 'Poetry in the Present', *Times Literary Supplement*

9 February 1933, p. 81

This article, which appeared as the leader, discusses several books, including Herbert Read's *Form in Modern Poetry*, and disagrees with Read's critical attitude towards Bridges.

... The poetry of Hopkins moves in waves of natural turbulence; it yields so much to the jet and impulse of each moment's tossing, that grammar and syntax are jettisoned and he will recast the language, rather than his breakers should not curl as the wind drives them. Such creative energy is admirable, but it is ingenuous. Hopkins chooses to forget that he is using a language which has expressed itself in literature for four centuries. Bridges does not. ...

67. Elsie Elizabeth Phare, *The Poetry of Gerard Manley Hopkins*

Cambridge, 1933

In 1933 the author married Professor Austin Duncan-Jones of the Department of Philosophy, University of Birmingham; reviewers sometimes referred to her by her married name. This was the first full-length book on Hopkins and received a number of polite reviews, but it seems to have had little critical influence.

In the extract below (pp. 46ff), Phare develops a comparison between Hopkins and Wordsworth.

...Wordsworth says, in the preface to the *Lyrical Ballads*, that it was his aim in some of his poems to 'choose incidents from common life and make them interesting by tracing in them the primary laws of our nature'; and so, curiously enough, we have Wordsworth, in some ways the most egotistical of poets, entering into the feelings of little girls feeding lambs, mothers who have lost their sons, wives deserted by their husbands, peasants living in cities as exiles from their own country. Wordsworth's power of sympathy is of a kind that might well draw strictures from Mr. Irving Babbitt. It is not by grace or anything like it that he is enabled to step into the shoes of poor Susan or afflicted Margaret: the process of tracing in their actions the primary laws in our nature is not an intellectual one. He arrives at sympathy with them by falling back on a sort of blood-bond which links the whole human race together. If he had been a contemporary of our own, Wordsworth would very likely have been denounced by Mr. Wyndham Lewis for conniving at the return to the Primitive which was said three or four years ago to be making havoc in our society. As it was he was denounced as a barbarian by Peacock in his *Four Ages of Poetry*. 'While the historian and philosopher are advancing and accelerating the progress of knowledge, the poet is wallowing in the rubbish of departed ignorance, and raking up the ashes of dead savages to find gewgaws and rattles for the grown babies of the age.'

There is little in Hopkins's poetry which the most inveterate anti-romantic would think it his duty to denounce as primitive or barbarian or infantile; he is a singularly mature and, in a good sense of the adjective, a singularly conscious poet: but the little group of poems in which he tried to enter sympathetically into the hearts of other human beings to trace the primary laws of human nature working in incidents chosen from his everyday experience contains several which are inferior to the rest of his own poetry and very inferior to most of Wordsworth's works which deal with similar themes. It looks as though the workings of a subrational kind of sympathy can on occasion make better poetry than those of a sympathy which is the result of intellectual labour and aspiration after divine grace.

The poems of Hopkins to which I refer were most of them written at one time: they are 'The Bugler's First Communion,' 'Felix Randal,' 'Brothers,' 'The Handsome Heart' and the poem which though unfinished is by far the best of the group, with the exception of 'Spring and Fall,' 'On the Portrait of Two Beautiful Young People.' The task which Hopkins sets before him is not, it must be admitted, as simple as Wordsworth's. Usually his aim is not merely to trace the primary laws of human nature but to trace them in relation to, or as they are under the influence of, divine grace. 'The Bugler's First Communion' is praised by one critic as 'unsurpassed in its sense of the beauty of adolescence'. The sense of the beauty of adolescence was certainly part of what Hopkins wished to convey: in all these poems he deals with a particular incident which has a general import. But I must admit that this particular poem leaves me very uncomfortable. Though it contains many felicitous lines and phrases,

> dress his days to a dexterous and starlight order,

or

> that brow and bead of being,

for example, it is as a whole discordant and somehow false.

Hopkins is as minutely and unnecessarily circumstantial in his description of the incident as Wordsworth in the description of the old sea-captain who tells the story of the mad mother. He tells us that the boy comes from a barrack, which is over the hill there: that his father is English and his mother Irish (here the metaphysical poet who is always present in Hopkins lifts his head and tries to rationalise the introduction of this not very significant piece of information by venturing a conjecture as to the probable effects of this mixture of nationality on the boy's character). The next verse reads as though Hopkins were trying to prolong the excitement which he felt when the incident occurred.

> This very very day came down to us after a boon
>   he on
> My late being there begged of me, overflowing
> Boon in my bestowing,
> Come, I say, this day to it—to a First Communion.

But the flatness of the second line suggests that his attempt to recapture the sensation has failed.

> Here he knelt then in regimental red.
> Forth Christ from cupboard fetched, how fain I of
>   feet
> To his youngster take his treat!
> Low-latched in leaf-light housel his too huge god
>   head.

In the third verse the fact that the boy was in uniform is given a portentous air which is scarcely justified: the emotion which it presumably inspired in the poet is not reproduced in the reader. The would-be directness and simplicity of 'youngster' and 'treat' reach the reader as a forced heartiness: and in poetry so sophisticated as that of Hopkins the very picture given here of the way in which Christ is present in the wafer is odd and to me disagreeable. It is not the fact that they contain doctrine of Transubstantiation which makes these lines repugnant; there is nothing repugnant in St Thomas Aquinas's *Rythmus ad SS. Sacramentum*, 'Adoro te supplex latens deitas', nor in Hopkins's translation of it. It is, I think, the unsuccessful attempt at childlike simplicity in the description of the doctrine—Christ dwelling in the wafer as in a little house of which the door is locked—which repels. The sham heartiness of which I have spoken reappears in 'slips of soldiery'; and the apparently unconscious sensuousness of

> Limber liquid youth, that to all I teach
> Yields tender as a pushed peach,

and

> Fresh youth fretted in a bloomfall all portending
> That sweet's sweeter ending,

jars in a poem which contains praises of chastity (if this is a fault, it is one which is constantly occurring in Crashaw's work; but faults which are not grave in Crashaw's work may be so in that of Hopkins, which is much more conscious and sophisticated), besides suggesting that the Deity is a kind of ogre, waiting to swallow-up-alive.

Destructive criticism of this kind is not very valuable; perhaps all that needs to be said is that Hopkins's attempt at simplicity and directness fails; the poem recovers when he is beginning to consider his own complicated reactions to the incident, the mixture of faith and misgiving with which he looks forward to the child's future:

> Recorded only, I have put my lips on pleas
> Would brandle adamantine heaven with ride and
>   jar, did Prayer go disregarded;
> Forward-like, but however, and like favourable
>   heaven heard these.

If 'The Bugler's First Communion' fails in simplicity 'Felix Randal', though a much better poem, fails to some extent in sympathy. On the other hand, against these failures there may be set two great successes: the now well-known 'Spring and Fall: to a Young Child' is a successful poem of the same kind as 'The Bugler's First Communion': 'On the Portrait of Two Beautiful Young People' would if finished have been a great poem and it is one of which the mainspring is that sympathy with other and remote human microcosms which in 'Felix Randal' seems a little forced and artificial. In 'Spring and Fall' Hopkins traces such of the 'primary laws of human nature' as are at work in the figure of a young child crying at the sight of a golden grove whose trees are growing bare and leafless. He does not fall back on a sort of racial sympathy in his effort to enter into the child's mind, as Wordsworth does in 'Alice Fell,' and 'Barbara Lewthwaite': he is all the while a person quite separate from the child, made remote from her by his age and experience and calling, although like her he is one of the doomed human race whose fate is foreshadowed in that of the trees. The process by which he arrives at the solution of the question—what is she grieving for?—is largely an intellectual one; he uses the subtlety and shews the insight of a good confessor. Tenderness in this poem as in all Hopkins's best poems, is well under control; here it is subordinated to the impulse towards unsparing candour—he will not leave the child in ignorance, much as he would perhaps like to do so—; and to the free play of the intellect, which hovers round the slight, mysterious incident, at last to pounce and link it up with the history and the future of the whole human race. There is no false simplicity here, no spurts of sentimentality nor excessive sensuousness; the poem is everything which 'The Bugler's First Communion' might have been and was not.

'Felix Randal' is another poem in which the poet reminds the reader that he is a priest. But it is a poem which lacks entirely the sane, solemn tenderness of 'Spring and Fall'. The loose, almost uncontrolled rhythm and the exaggerated phraseology,

> When thou at the random grim forge, powerful
> amidst peers,
> Didst fettle for the great grey drayhorse his bright
> and battering sandal,

alike suggest that the poet is abandoning himself to an unchecked emotionalism over which the intellect exercises no censorship. There is a suggestion too that by force of will he is working himself up to a pitch of grief for Felix Randal which normally he would not reach.

> This seeing the sick endears them to us, us too it
> endears.
> My tongue had taught thee comfort, touch had
> quenched thy tears,
> Thy tears that touched my heart, child, Felix, poor
> Felix Randal.

That is a verse which seems to me to read as though the poet were encouraging his emotions to take more sway over him than they would normally: he is trying by repeating the man's name, by rehearsing the circumstances of his illness to work himself up to a frenzy of compassion. Finally he has recourse to the thought of the heedlessness of his coming death which characterised the blacksmith Randal in his prime; and the poem ends with a clangorous reconstruction of the smith at work at his forge; a reconstruction which by force of contrast with the picture of the wasted invalid, now a corpse, which Hopkins has in his mind, ought to be extremely moving. But the poet's intention is too overt; and the reader, if I am to speak for myself, recoils before so evident an attack on his tender feelings: his tears retreat like the eyes of the snail

> into the shelly caverns of his head.

If 'Spring and Fall' and 'Felix Randal' were to be paraphrased, there would be no more reason to think 'Felix Randal' an unsuccessful poem than to think 'Spring and Fall' so: but as it stands, considered as an organic whole, 'Felix Randal' fails, though it is difficult to say why, and the rather peevish fault-finding in which I have been indulging does not make clear why it should be so. It seems that the motion of accepting or rejecting a poem comes from the very quick of the will; it is rarely possible to give a wholly satisfactory account of one's reasons for doing one or the other. ...

Hopkins's poetry does not appeal only to touch and taste and smell, as that of Keats does; it also excites strong muscular responses. There are poems of his—the first octave of 'The Windhover' for example, 'Tom's Garland', 'Harry Ploughman,' which leave the reader feeling almost as though he had been exercising himself in a gymnasium. 'Harry Ploughman' is the poem which illustrates this most clearly.

> Hard as hurdle arms, with a broth of goldish flue
> Breathed round; the rack of ribs; the scooped flank;
>   lank
> Rope-over thigh; knee-nave; and barrelled shank—
>   Head and foot, shoulder and shank—
> By a grey eye's heed steered well, one crew, fall to;
> Stand at stress. Each limb's barrowy brawn, his thew
> That onewhere curded, onewhere sucked or sank—
>   Soared or sank—,
> Though as a beachbole firm, finds his. as at a roll-
>   call, rank
> And features, in flesh, what deed he each must do—
>   His sinew-service where do.
> He leans to it, Harry bends, look. Back, elbow,
>   and liquid waist
> In him, all quail to the wallowing o' the plough—

The poet is considering Harry with something of the admiration with which a boy expert in mechanical toys looks at an engine. He observes the ploughman limb by limb, feature by feature, until the thrilling moment comes when this marvellous assemblage of parts is put into action, made to 'stand at stress'. The muscular strength of his whole body is brought into play: the thews of each limb, hard as they are, adapt themselves to the demands made upon them with the alertness and regularity of trained soldiers. The next two lines excite a particularly strong muscular response: the phrase 'liquid waist' especially.

Harry Ploughman, like the Windhover and the stormfowl in the Purcell sonnet, is a creature who is intent on exercising all the powers with which he is endowed and who merely as a by-product flashes off beauty, unknown to himself, giving intense pleasure to the eye of the beholder, as well as giving satisfaction to the Creator who sees his creature using its faculties to their utmost. This image is one which seems to give Hopkins at once aesthetic pleasure and spiritual comfort. His own poetry, if he had been able to see it dispassionately, might have pleased him no less than Harry's ploughing and the Windhover's flying; for it evidently engaged all his faculties; it strikes the reader as involving to a peculiar degree all the energies of mind and body.

Wordsworth's poetry is written by a poet living very much out of the body; he is never acutely conscious of the different parts of his anatomy, as Hopkins is.

> How a lush-kept, plush-capped sloe
> Will, mouthed to flesh, burst
> Gush!—flush the man, the being with it, sour or sweet,
> Brim, in a flash, full.

provokes and records a singularly intense consciousness of the process of drinking a delicious juice, as

> man, the scaffold of score brittle bones

points to an unusually vivid realisation of the spillikins-like structure of the skeleton.

> Thou hast bound bones and veins in me, fastened
> me flesh

is another line which shews how curiously aware Hopkins is of the

body in which he lives. The eye is an organ which he is particularly
fond of considering anatomically. In 'Elected Silence' he describes
the descent of the two eyelids on the two eyeballs

> Be shellèd, eyes, with double dark.

(There is also a reference here, of course, to the inner darkness,
double dark conveys the idea that the novice is to preserve not only
his eyes but his soul from impressions of the physical world.) In
'Binsey Poplars' he compares the havoc made by the removal of the
trees to the effect of a single prick on the eyeball:

> O if we but knew what we do
>   When we delve or hew—
> Hack and rack the growing green!
>   Since country is so tender
> To touch, her being só slender,
> That, like this sleek and seeing ball
> But a prick will make no eye at all,
> Where we, even where we mean
>   To mend her we end her.

While in the first version of the poem on St. Dorothea his
consciousness of the convex surface of the eyeball makes him
compare the reflection which the miracle has left on the retina to
the curved rind of a fruit:

> My eyes hold yet the rinds and bright
> Remainder of a miracle.

These examples of Hopkins's consciousness of his body are not
drawn from his best poems: there is something a little inharmonious
about all of them, in the contexts in which they occur: because it is
disagreeable to be made so intensely and exclusively aware of the
particular part of the anatomy to which he refers. But on the
whole, considering it especially in its less extreme forms, the poet's
consciousness of bodily existence and the resulting appeal to
physical sensation which is consequently to be found in his poetry
are very much to the good. His devotional poems in particular gain
by being written, so to speak, with the whole man: he never
separates soul and body, never casts off his flesh like a garment in
an attempt to emerge all spirit. In describing the most painful kind
of spiritual desolation he will use a metaphor which brings in the
body:

I am gall, I am heartburn, God's most deep decree
Bitter would have me taste: my taste was me.

It was perhaps the same humility which made the Psalmist refer so freely to his bowels and his reins.

Hopkins's insistent remembrance of his physical existence might be taken as a symptom of his peculiar adequacy to experience. For all his unhappiness, spiritual and mental, and judging from his poetry he suffered and was moreover very conscious of suffering a great deal, he never makes any attempt to escape from the discomfort or the danger which confronts him by taking refuge in an imaginary world, nor even in a world purely of the spirit: he never turns to the anodyne of dreams. Religion is sometimes described by those unfriendly to it as a drug: it was certainly not that to Hopkins. It would be difficult too to accuse Hopkins of falling back on his religion instead of using his own inner resources: his poetry affords no means of distinguishing between the two.

Wordsworth, as I have already said, does not give the impression of being conscious in any unusual degree of physical existence; he is interested in the mind's eye rather than in the anatomy of the eye-ball: he never praises, never rests in the physical sensation, the sound as it strikes the ear, the sight as it strikes the eye, as Hopkins does. Wordsworth would never have written such a passage as this:

When drop-of-blood-and-foam-dapple
Bloom lights the orchard-apple
  And thicket and thorp are merry
  With silver-surfèd cherry
And azuring-over greybell makes
Wood banks and brakes wash wet like lakes
  And magic cuckoo call
  Caps, clears, and clinches all—

a passage which does not go beyond sensuous apprehension. Wordsworth like his own cuckoo turns the earth into an unsubstantial faery place: he communicates to all the sights and sounds that he describes, the air of things seen and heard in a vision and by a man who for the time is made all spirit. A vision not a dream. He does not escape from the world of sense, but sees it as though it were transfigured. ...

68. Unsigned review of Phare, *Notes and Queries*

25 November 1933, p. 378

...Roughly speaking, up to (and of course also past) Hopkins, poetry has retained what has become normal occidental sentence-construction, based, indeed, on classical Greek and Latin sentence-construction but using prepositions and auxiliary verbs, and a conventional order in place of inflexions. Hopkins in many of his obscure lines—by some half-conscious aversion, possibly, to a tediousness in auxiliaries—may be thought of as attempting sentence-construction proper to inflected words. If he had but an accusative or dative ending to use some of his obscurity would vanish. As it is, he produces something of the serried unencumbered effect we know in Latin poetry, though he has to impose a certain discipline on his reader before he gets the response upon which this can be made to tell.

69. Herbert Read, 'The Poetry of Gerard Manley Hopkins', *English Critical Essays of the Twentieth Century*

London, 1933, pp. 351–74

Read's most weighty piece on Hopkins devotes the first few pages, not printed here, to a biographical introduction. I have also omitted some other passages. The essay was reprinted in Read's *In Defence of Shelley* (1936), but also repeats earlier material.

I

...A consideration of Hopkins's poetry brings us close to a problem which has agitated modern criticism a good deal—I mean the relation of poetry to the poet's beliefs. The problem has been discussed in relation to Dante by Mr. Eliot, and more generally by Mr. Richards in his book on 'Practical Criticism'. These critics are mainly occupied in discussing whether it is necessary to share a poet's beliefs in order fully to enjoy his poetry. The aspect of the problem that arises in the case of Hopkins is even more vital—the precise effect of a poet's religious beliefs on the nature of his poetry.

II

In Hopkins's poetry, as perhaps in the work of other poets, we can distinguish (1) poetry which is the direct expression of religious beliefs, (2) poetry which has no direct or causal relation to any such beliefs at all, and (3) poetry which is not so much the expression of belief in any strict sense but more precisely of doubt. All Hopkins's poems of any importance can be grouped under these three categories. When this has been done, I think that there would be general agreement that in poetic value the second and third categories are immensely superior to the first. Indeed, so inferior are such strictly religious poems as 'Barnfloor and Winepress,' 'Nondum', 'Easter', 'Ad Mariam', 'Rosa Mystica', and one or two others, that Robert Bridges rightly excluded them from the first edition of the Poems. Of the Poems published by Dr. Bridges, one or two might conceivably be classified as poems of positive belief, like the exquisite 'Heaven-Haven' and 'The Habit of Perfection'. 'The Wreck of the Deutschland', the long poem which Hopkins himself held in such high regard, is a poem of contrition, of fear and submission, rather than of the love of God:

> Be adored among men,
> God, three-numberèd form;
> Wring thy rebel, dogged in den,
> Man's malice, with wrecking and storm.
> Beyond saying sweet, past telling of tongue,
> Thou art lightning and love, I found it, a winter and
> warm;
> Father and fondler of heart thou hast wrung:
> Hast thy dark descending and most art merciful then.

This is the beauty of terror, the 'terrible pathos' of the phrase in which a friend so perfectly defined Hopkins's quality.

Of the poetry which has no direct or causal relation to beliefs of any kind, poems such as 'Penmaen Pool,' 'The Starlight Night', 'Spring,' 'The Sea and the Skylark,' 'The Windhover,' 'Pied Beauty,' 'Hurrahing in Harvest,' 'The Caged Skylark,' 'Inversnaid,' 'Harry Ploughman,' and the two 'Echoes', the poetic force comes from a vital awareness of the objective beauty of the world. That awareness—'sensualism' as Dr. Bridges calls it—is best and sufficiently revealed in original metaphors such as 'mealed-with-yellow sallows', 'piece-bright paling', 'daylight's dauphin', 'a stallion stalwart, very violet-sweet', and many others of their kind, in which the poet reforges words to match the shape and sharpness of his feelings. Dr. Bridges, in the context I have already quoted from,[1] speaks of 'the naked encounter of sensualism and asceticism which hurts the "Golden Echo"'—a phrase I cannot in any sense apply to the poem in question; for while I appreciate the magnificent sensualism of this poem, I fail to detect any asceticism. But that in general there was a conflict[2] of this sort in Hopkins is revealed, not only by the fact that he destroyed many of his poems whch he found inconsistent with his religious discipline, but most clearly in his curious criticism of Keats:

[Quotes *Further Letters*, pp. 386–7.]

The implication of this criticism is that the poet, by nature a dreamer and a sensualist, only raises himself to greatness by concerning himself with 'great causes, as liberty and religion'. In what sense did Hopkins so sublimate his poetic powers? In a poem like 'Pied Beauty' we see the process openly enacted. After a catalogue of dappled things, things which owe their beauty to contrast, inconsistency, and change, Hopkins concludes by a neat inversion—an invocation to God who, fathering forth such things, is Himself changeless. In 'Hurrahing in Harvest' again we have an extended metaphor: the senses glean the Saviour in all the beauty of summer's end. 'The Windhover' is completely objective in its senseful catalogue; but Hopkins gets over his scruples by dedicating the poem 'To Christ our Lord'. But this is a patent deception. It does not alter the naked sensualism of the poem; and there is no asceticism in this poem; nor essentially in any of the other poems of this group. They are tributes to God's glory, as all poetry must be;

but they are tributes of the senses; and a right conception of God and of religion will not be hurt by such tributes.

In the third section, poems expressive not so much of belief as of doubt, I would place those final sonnets, Nos. 40, 41, 44, 45, 46, 47, and 50[3] in the published *Poems*. These all date from the last years of Hopkins's life—the first six from 1885, the other from 1889, the actual year of his death. But even earlier poems express at least despair: 'Spring and Fall'—the blight man was born for; the 'Sibyl's Leaves'—the self-wrung rack where thoughts against thoughts grind. But the sonnets themselves are complete in their gloom, awful in their anguish. ...

III

... We might say that Hopkins is eager to use every device the language can hold to increase the force of his rhythm and the richness of his phrasing. Point, counterpoint, rests, running-over rhythms, hangers or outrides, slurs; end-rhymes, internal rhymes, assonance and alliteration—all are used to make the verse sparkle like rich irregular crystals in the gleaming flow of the poet's limpid thought.

The other aspect of his technique is one which, to my way of thinking, is still more central to the poetic reality: I mean his fresh and individual vocabulary.[4] No true poet hesitates to invent words when his sensibility finds no satisfaction in current phrases. Words like 'Shivelight' and 'firedint' are probably such inventions. But most of Hopkins's innovations are in the nature of new combinations of existing words, sometimes contracted similes, or metaphors, and in this respect his vocabulary has a surface similarity to that of James Joyce. Examples of such phrases are to be found in almost every poem: 'the beadbonny ash', 'fallowbootfellow', 'windlaced', 'churlsgrace', 'footfretted', 'clammyish lashtender combe', 'wildworth', and so on. Commoner phrases like 'beetle-browed' or 'star-eyed' are of the same kind, made in the same way, and freely used by him. Here again an explanation would take us far beyond the immediate subject; for it concerns the original nature of poetry itself—the emotional sound-complex uttered in primitive self-expression. Mr. Williams, whose graceful and appreciative introduction to the second edition of the poems is a fair corrective to the pedantic undertones of Dr. Bridges in the first edition, has an excellent description of the phenomenon as it appeared in the composition of Hopkins's verse. 'It is as if the imagination, seeking for expression, had found both verb and substantive at one rush, had begun almost to say them at once, and had separated them only because the intellect had reduced the original unity into divided but related sounds'. Poetry can only be renewed by discovering the original sense of word-formation: the words do not come pat in great poetry, but are torn out of the context of experience; they are not in the poet's mind, but in the nature of the things he describes. 'You must know', said Hopkins himself, 'that words like *charm* and *enchantment* will not do: the thought is of beauty as of something that can be physically kept and lost, and by physical things only, like keys; then the things must come from the *mundus muliebris*; and thirdly they must not be markedly old-fashioned. You will see that this limits the choice of words very much indeed.'[5]

Of Hopkins's imagery, there is not much in general to be said, but that 'not much' is all. He had that acute and sharp sensuous awareness essential to all great poets. He was physically aware of textures, surfaces, colours, patterns of every kind; aware acutely of earth's diurnal course, of growth and decay, of animality in man and of vitality in all things. Everywhere there is passionate apprehension, passionate expression, and equally that passion for form without which these other passions are spend-thrift. But the form is inherent in the passion. 'For', as Emerson remarked with his occasional deep insight, 'it is not metres, but a metre-making argument, that makes a poem—a thought so passionate and alive, that, like the spirit of a plant or an animal, it has an architecture of its own, and adorns nature with a new thing.'

IV[6]

...To contend that Dr. Bridges did not understand the poetry of Hopkins would not be quite fair; he understood the craftsmanship of it, and was sensible to the beauty. But there seems to have been an essential lack of sympathy—not of personal sympathy, but of sympathy in poetic ideals. The Preface to the notes which Dr. Bridges contributed to the first (1918) edition of the poems, reprinted in the new edition, is marked by a pedantic velleity which would only be excusable on the assumption that we are dealing with a poet of minor interest. That is, indeed, the attitude: please look at this odd fellow whom for friendship's sake I have rescued from oblivion. The emphasis on oddity and obscurity is quite extraordinary, and in the end all we are expected to have is a certain technical interest, leading to tolerance, and the discovery of 'rare masterly beauties'. Hopkins is convicted of affectation in metaphor, perversion of human feeling, exaggerated Marianism, the 'naked encounter of sensualism and asceticism which hurts the "Golden Echo",' purely artistic wantonness, definite faults of style, incredible childishness in rhyming—at times disagreeable and vulgar and even comic; and generally of deliberate and unnecessary obscurity. Everything, in such an indictment, must depend on the judge's set of laws, and in criticizing Dr. Bridges's treatment of Hopkins, I am wishing to say no more than that the Poet Laureate applied a code which was not that of the indicted. The lack of sympathy is shown precisely in this fact. Hopkins was a revolutionary; that is to say, his values were so fundamentally opposed to current practices, that only by an effort of the imagination could they be comprehended. Once they are comprehended, many apparent faults are justified, and there is no reason to dwell on any of them. ...

V

It would be natural to conclude with some estimate of Hopkins's influence on modern poetry. But let us first ask what we should look for under this heading. The influence of a poet can be either technical, affecting the practice of other poets; or it can be spiritual, affecting the point of view, the philosophy of life, of poets and readers alike. I do not pretend to estimate this second kind of influence in Hopkins's case; and in any case I think it is irrelevant to our strictly poetical inquiry. The acute sensibility of Hopkins has undoubtedly sharpened the perceptive faculties of all who are familiar with his verse; and there may be a few who have felt the profounder truths which he expresses with so much intensity. But such effects would be difficult to estimate. Nor can we come to any very definite conclusion about a technical influence. If by that we mean a mimetic affectation of Hopkins's mannerisms, then the less said about it the better. But the true influence of one poet on another does not show itself so baldly. It may be that in the return to sprung rhythm, in the extended use of alliteration, Hopkins has made a calculable impression on the poets who have been writing during the last ten or fifteen years. But we must remember that although Hopkins's poetry was written fifty years ago, it was not published until 1918. A few of his poems appeared in anthologies a few years earlier, but they were given no prominence, and received no particular attention. The *patent* influence of Hopkins has therefore hardly had time to work itself into the body of English poetry. But the *latent* influence—that is a different question. It is a question of an impregnating breath, breathed into the ear of every poet open to the rhythms of contemporary life, the music of our existence, and the tragedy of our fate. Hopkins is amongst the living poets of our time, and no influence whatsoever is so potent for the future of English poetry.

NOTES

1 Preface to Notes, *ante*, p. 78.
2 Read later wrote to W.H. Gardner: 'In so far as I have, in my essay on Hopkins, implied that there was an open conflict between the poetic impulse and the theological faith in Hopkins, I confess I was wrong (*Gerard Manley Hopkins: A Study of Poetic Idiosyncrasy*, I 1944, p. 237).
3 Nos. 64, 65, 66, 67, 68, 69 and 74 in 4th edn.
4 For the rest of this section cf. pp. 242–3, 'No true poet hesitates' to 'with a new thing.'
5 *Letters to Bridges*, pp. 61–2.
6 For this section cf. p. 240.

70. R.L. Mégroz, *Modern English Poetry*

London, 1933

Rodolph Louis Mégroz (1891–1968), b. in London, claimed 'Pyrenean bandits and East Anglian farmers as ancestors'. He was a poet and critic with many books to his name, some of a

Catholic-modernist interest, *Walter de la Mare* (1923), *The Three Sitwells* (1926), *Francis Thompson* (1927). The following extracts occur between pp. 241 and 244.

... The freedom of the rhythm in 'The Windhover' owes its beauty of course not to the mere addition of syllables and ever-shifting stresses, but to the poet's mind working in a congenial medium. The rhythm is to be thought of as an additional opportunity for expression. Hopkins's peculiarities of diction are often such as nobody else could safely imitate, and occasionally injure his own work, but one frequent characteristic which seems surprisingly to have its fitting place in this verse that is built on speech rhythm is the undisguised prosaicism of phrases, usually idiomatic, which the poet finds useful to complete or to emphasize statements. Prose comes into its rightful due as the vehicle of ideas which may be necessary to the poet's evocation of a mood because it can be absorbed more easily into the flexible movement of sprung rhythm. 'The Wreck of the Deutschland', Hopkins's longest and greatest poem, contains the two extremes of his peculiar style—the prosaic and the intensely poetic....

... The poem must stand or fall, however, as an elegy, and it seems to me that as such, for its beauties of perception, sustained emotion, brilliant and exciting imagery, and sometimes perfectly marvellous music, to rank with the greatest English poems of its kind, with 'Lycidas', 'Adonais', 'Thyrsis', and 'Ave Atque Vale'. But the unaccustomed diction and endlessly surprising rhythm must be absorbed until they can be regarded as essentially belonging to the texture of the poem, or the cumulative effect will be dissipated in delight or bewilderment at details.

... Thanks to Hopkins, we know that sprung rhythm renders the discarding of rhyme, stanza, and other prosodic resources of poetry quite an unnecessary means to freshness of expression. There cannot be any doubt that the influence of Hopkins's *Poems* will reach far in the coming English poetry....

71. Humphry House, unsigned review of Phare, *Times Literary Supplement*

25 January 1934, p. 59

Humphry House (1908–55), after a year as English Fellow and Chaplain at Wadham College, Oxford, retired (1932) into lay life and taught classics at the University of Exeter, 1933–4. He eventually returned to teach at Oxford. He edited the Notebooks of Hopkins (1937) and was apparently writing a biography of Hopkins's early life at the time of his death.

The text used here is that of the reprint of the article in House's collection of essays, *All in Due Time* (London, 1955), which excluded the final paragraph of the original review.

The policy which Robert Bridges adopted in publishing at first only selections from Hopkins's poetry and delaying the greater part of it for thirty years has at least ensured it a full recognition in our own time. But many critics have inferred, from the fact that we are able to appreciate him in ways in which some of his contemporaries were not, that there is a special affinity between his poetic character and that of writers who live long after him and are in fact essentially different. He has been wrenched out of his context and distorted by ephemeral and propagandist judgment.

Miss Phare, whose book is the first detailed study of his poetry to be published, has felt the pressure of such criticism and partly associates herself with it by calling Hopkins a 'Modernist-Victorian'; but she does not make clear her reasons for choosing this title. She recognises that Hopkins's work is unlike much contemporary poetry in that it is not allusive, and that it does not employ what have been called 'private symbols'; but she does not press on to the conclusion, for which there is much evidence in her book, that in the whole structure of his thought and imagery Hopkins does not belong to our generation at all, and that his adoption into it is excessively misleading. He would not have understood what was meant by a 'poetic logic' or a 'logic of imagery'; for him the connection between images was controlled by the same logic as he applied in a lecture on Homer or a sermon on the Passion. This is not the method of contemporary poetry nor the cause of its occasional obscurity. Hopkins wrote in ever-more-detailed refinement on a theme, not to suggest the subtle connections between one theme and another in a system of images related only in the scheme of the poem itself. If, therefore, as Miss Phare suggests, 'the publication of his poetry in 1918 has left English poetry in a condition which seems to have many new possibilities', it would seem that when once the superficial likenesses between his poetic vocabulary and the poetic vocabulary of the present time have been fully understood, his most powerful effect will be to check the development of many prevailing poetic habits. But it is more likely that he, like Milton, will be found to have made so fine a language for himself and brought it within its limits to such perfection that his influence will be widest in pale imitation and most valuable in plagiarism. Hopkins's own attitude to great work was 'to admire and do otherwise'.

The first five sections of Miss Phare's book are loosely built round comparisons of Hopkins with other poets, and from these comparisons her own opinions develop. The longest and most fruitful for her purposes is an unexpected comparison with Wordsworth. She finds first a common pantheism, but nowhere in the poems or prose does Hopkins fail to make the wide, and for him portentous, difference between creature and Creator. The relationship is made clear in the sonnet 'Spring', in the octet of which is described the beauty of created things that in the sestet are shown in their present divergence from the first purity of creation. Knowledge of this double removal from Deity saves Hopkins always from pantheism. The work which is next compared to Wordsworth's is 'the little group of poems in which he tried to enter sympathetically into the hearts of other human beings, to trace the primary laws of human nature working in incidents chosen from his everyday experience'—'The Bugler's First Communion', 'Felix Randal,' 'Brothers', 'The Handsome Heart,' 'Spring and Fall,' and 'On the Portrait of Two Beautiful Young People.' She finds in all these poems except the last two some kind of emotional failure. In 'Felix Randal' Hopkins is 'encouraging his emotions to take more sway over him than they would normally'; in 'The Bugler's First Communion' he affects the reader with a 'forced heartiness', and 'his attempt at simplicity and directness fails'. Miss Phare herself notices that her 'rather peevish fault-finding' does not explain the 'failure' of these poems. The explanation of them is in Hopkins himself.

He knew very little about other people except as they fitted into the context of his own thoughts or became by chance the object of his affections. As a priest he had little mission experience, and perhaps could hardly have borne more; in his friendships, valuable as they were to him, there seems to have been a curious lack of real personal intimacy, and his family affections were not immediate:

> To seem the stranger lies my lot, my life
> Among strangers. Father and mother dear,
> Brothers and sisters are in Christ not near.

He could win and give affections of a kind, but not such as to satisfy him:

> I am in Ireland now; now I am at a third
> Remove. Not but in all removes I can
> Kind love both give and get.

These feelings were not due merely to his living in Ireland nor to the particular mood of frustration in which this sonnet was written. All his most intense experience was solitary. He wrote that in looking at beautiful things even one companion spoiled his ecstasy. This solitude was extremely sensitive to every invasion from outside and was perhaps intensified by the knowledge that his affections, once moved, were almost overpowering in their effects on him; for he suffered the maximum feeling from the slightest incident, and drew the fullest inference from a single word. One small occasion filled him 'brim, in a flash full'. Men were to him a source of wonder and physical delight, as in 'Harry Ploughman', when he articulated all the members of their beauty; or else were a sudden stimulus, in their moral life, to most complex states of intense feeling. It is possible to see that real intimacy might have been too much to bear. He marks the novelty of the special affection roused in him by the dying blacksmith:

> This seeing the sick endears them to us, us too it endears.

His emotions here certainly 'take more sway over him than they would normally', but they do not have to be encouraged. This occasion, as that of the bugler, rushes on him with power, and the complex thoughts, fears and comments with the images that attend them are inevitably caused by it. The feeling is no more forced and exaggerated than his involuntary tears at the accounts of the Agony in the Garden and the conversion of de Rancé.

Two similar charges are brought against 'The Wreck of the Deutschland'. 'Hopkins is not sure enough of himself, not certain enough that the traits which he is expressing are those of his own individuality', and here also he has artificially intensified his feelings. It is not clear which parts of the poem are included in the first of these censures: the second is explicitly applied to the twentieth and twenty-second stanzas. Hopkins's own account of the origin of the poem makes it clear that it was the fact that he was himself affected by the wreck which led his Rector to make the suggestion of a poem. He had written nothing of importance for over seven years, and it would seem that the first ten stanzas, in which there is no mention of the shipwreck, though they use a few images which belong to it, work in a concentrated way upon a vein of experience from those seven years as painfully personal as that of the 'terrible sonnets' themselves. The straining and oddity which one must recognise are parallel to the straining and oddity of the experience: there is no gap between the thought and the expression. To reject the first ten stanzas of the poem is to reject the whole state of mind which produced them. Miss Phare then turns to the curious emphasis which Hopkins lays on the facts that the drowned nuns numbered five and that they came from Protestant Germany; but both these facts are prominent in the newspaper accounts from which Hopkins derived his knowledge of the wreck. The magnificent narrative passages in the poem which Miss Phare praises so rightly follow these accounts with astonishing fidelity—at the crisis of the poem almost word for word. If these points had impressed themselves on the journalists, why should not Hopkins interpret them symbolically without being insincere?

In an interesting part of her book Miss Phare explains Hopkins's love of wildness, unaccountableness and pied things as a kind of revulsion from 'the tidy, cut-and-dried mental world of the Jesuit', 'an antidote to the dullness and flatness which one imagines would characterise a world which had been made entirely comprehensible', as, for instance, it is made comprehensible by Duns Scotus, whom he loved. She posits an alarmingly divided mind. But surely the reason why he was so fond of changing and irregular things was not that he wanted to retain their confusion fully confounded, but that it was exactly such things as these which exerted his intellectual passion for minute distinctions to the utmost, and many of his finest poems are poems of this passion. The being of everything is to be found exactly in its dappling. It is to this that his reading of Scotus is most relevant. The peculiar individuality which Scotus called *haecceitas,* and the *distinctio formalis a parte rei* are to be directly connected with his love of objects between which minute distinctions can be made. And Scotus further allows that the concrete individuality of each object can be known in at least a confused way intuitively. In a later part of her book Miss Phare gives a quotation from Gilson on the Scotist theory of individuation, and quotes one of the sonnets in which it is most explicit: it is therefore curious that she should have interpreted the love of what is dappled and pied as an *escape* from the mental habit implied by a concurrent love of Scotism. Again, when she says that Hopkins's imagery is almost entirely motile or dynamic, Miss Phare wisely adds: 'There is little to be said, I think, in favour of attempting to classify poets according to the motile or static nature of the imagery which they use.' Hopkins's love of actual movement (which is a very different thing from 'motile imagery') is to be found in nearly all his finest poems: 'Meaning motion fans fresh our wits with wonder,' he says in the sonnet on Purcell. It is to be noted that in the Scotist philosophy of Nature every body has not merely a material form, but also a vital form. A special element of its being is its activity and movement. Scotism made articulate to him in its own language many things which had been life-long preoccupations from the unaided bent of his mind.....

72. William Rose Benét, 'The Phoenix Nest', *Saturday Review of Literature* (New York)

24 February 1934, p. 508

Benét (1886–1950), poet and Pulitzer Prize winner (1941), was poetry critic of the *Saturday Review*.

...Those who are now making a cult of Gerard Manley Hopkins will welcome E.E. Phare's *The Poetry of Gerard Manley Hopkins*. ... Miss Phare considers Hopkins a major poet. I do not. He was a fine eccentric poet for the few, but there is certainly a lack of proportion in canonizing him. However, his name is at present the Open Sesame to poetic converse with the intelligentzia, if you wish to meet the 'right people'. To me Hopkins's style almost constantly offends against every principle I have painfully learned of a sound English style. His occasional felicities and gorgeous sparkling do not recompense for his churning method and his squirming mannerisms. It is all very quaint and delightful that a Roman Catholic priest should have written so; and those who join the church for artistic and esthetic reasons may bask in the cult; but I cannot help thinking that Hopkins's mind was one of the most confused that ever persuaded men to call it great....

73. M[ichael] R[oberts], review of Phare, *Adelphi*

April 1934, pp. 76–7

For Michael Roberts see No. 92. The reviewer leads up to the extract printed here by suggesting that the book will help those already appreciative of Hopkins, but not probably those who would like to enjoy him, but can't.

... The difficulties of such readers are not intellectual (intellectually Hopkins was quite a simple person) but arise from a mental habit. The poetry of Hopkins is valid only for those readers who organise their most profound experiences through the use of verbal images. Miss Phare traces in Milton curious parallels to Hopkins's use of puns and similar-sounding words, and she might have traced some of his other apparent innovations through Herrick, Herbert, and even the unlikely Tupper[1], but the problem involved in the relationship between Hopkins's imagery and use of sound, on the one hand, and the emotional states with which his poems deal, on the other, remains unexamined. For criticism, the problem is important, because the poetry of Hopkins is valued as Miss Phare values it with that of Shakespeare and Milton, by many who would not assent to any prose statement of the religious view upon which his poetry is based. Perhaps the fact is that a belief is not, for such people, something self-consistent and permanently in force, like a legal code, but rather a weapon, a means of dealing with particular situations. It may even be questioned whether it is justifiable to talk of beliefs at all as if they were expressible in logical, unpoetic language, and were laid up in reserve when we are not acting upon them.

NOTE

1 Martin Tupper was a nineteenth-century poet whose facile verse gained him great popularity, but critical disapproval.

74. Edith Sitwell, *Aspects of Modern Poetry*

London, 1934, pp. 51–72

Edith Sitwell (1887–1964) was a poet, critic, and personality of the twenties and thirties. Editor of the anti-Georgian anthology *Wheels* 1916–21; 'in early youth took an intense dislike to simplicity' (*Who's Who*, 1933). She became a Catholic in 1955. Hopkins was also discussed by her in *Trio* (1938).

Aspects of Modern Poetry is an idiosyncratic commentary on modern poets and critics, with a good deal of mockery at the expense of Geoffrey Grigson and, especially, F.R. Leavis ('the only difference between them lies in Dr Leavis' gift for wincing').

...In the threadbare minor poetry of the later Victorian and the Edwardian eras, though the technique of the art had recently been enriched by the innovations of Father Gerard Manley Hopkins, these had not yet had time to sink into the consciousness. But now, where these examples have been followed, they have not been understood, and Hopkins has met with the fate of nearly all innovators. It is a fact that Hopkins should never be regarded as a model, since he worked his own discoveries to the uttermost point; there is no room for advancement, for development along his lines. But leaving this truth aside it is a melancholy fact that his imitators have misunderstood his examples, and, ignorant that his rhythmical impetus, his magnificence of texture, are the results, at once natural and cultivated, of the properties of his material acted upon by the impact of his personality, they have produced poems with superimposed rhythms instead of rhythms inherent in the properties of the material. For not only have these poets lost their tactile sense, but (perhaps because of this loss) to them the resonance of all things are the same, they do not hear the difference in resonance between that of iron and of copper, as they do not feel the difference in texture between marble and stone, and, as for that, between the different marbles. Partly as a result of this insensitiveness, they produce exterior, and therefore unliving, rhythms, instead of rhythms which live in, under, and over, the lines. Imitations of Hopkins have resulted, too, in a complete loss of melody, arising from falsified, clumsy, or too-thick vowel-schemes, clumsy and huddled-up assonance patterns, useless alliterations, and a meaningless accumulation of knotted consonants.

Yet great (though incapable of further development) are the technical wonders from which these imitations have sprung—these slandered originals are full of significance. Not, perhaps, since Dryden and Pope have we had such mountains and gulfs, such raging waves, such deserts of the eternal cold, and these are produced not by a succession of images alone, but by the movement of the lines, by the texture, and by Hopkins' supreme gift of rhetoric. It should be realized that rhetoric is not an incrustation, a foreign body which has somehow transformed the exterior surface of a poem, distracting the mind from the main line; it is, instead, an immense fire breaking from the poem as from a volcano. Sometimes it is smooth, sometimes it is fierce; but the manner in which it is born is the same. 'Decoration' in poetry does not exist; either the physical beauty has arisen from the properties of the material, or the poem is a bad poem. . . .

Hopkins' rhythmical principles, which are based on scholarship, arose, actually, from his feeling, his instinct, and are thus in many ways the same as those of such modern poets as Ezra Pound, Wilfred Owen, and T.S. Eliot, men whose free verse arises from feeling and intuition, but is guided by learning; this fact has been stated admirably by Professor Herbert Read recently, in *Form in Poetry*, and he points out, also,[1] that 'a second characteristic of Hopkin's poetry which, while not so original, is yet a cause of strangeness, may be found in his vocabulary. No true poet hesitates to invent words when his sensibility finds no satisfaction in current phrases. Words like "shinelight" and "firedint" are probably such inventions. But most of Hopkins's innovations are in the nature of new combinations of existing words, sometimes contracted similes or metaphors, and in this respect his vocabulary has a surface similarity to that of James Joyce. Examples of such phrases are to be found in almost every poem: "the beadbonny ash," "fallowboot fellow," "windlaced," "churls grace," "foot fretted," "clammyish lash tender combs," "wildsworth." etc.'

Many of Hopkins' poems appear at first sight strange; and this is due in part to his acute and strange visual sense, a sense which pierces down to the essence of the things seen, and which, heightening the truth of it, by endowing it with attributes which at first seem alien, with colours that are sharper, clearer, more piercing than those that are seen by the common eye, succeeds in producing its inherent spirit. He does not obscure the thing seen by loading it with useless details, he produces the essence by giving one sharp visual impression, performing miracles by using comparisons which seem very remote, as when, for instance, in the lovely fragment that I am about to quote, he compares the fair hair of a youth to a sheaf of bluebells. This, to me, gives the fairness of the hair, and shows the straightness of it, and the way in which it flaps, for, of all flowers, only a sheaf of bluebells has this particular limpness. The fragment is one of an unfinished poem,[2] and how innocent and gay and rustic is the movement of it.

> The furl of fresh-leaved dogrose down
> His cheeks the forth-and-flaunting sun
> Had swarthed about with lion-brown
> Before the Spring was done.
>
> His locks like all a ravel-rope's end,
> With hempen strands in spray—
> Fallow, foam-fallow, hanks—fall'n off their
>   ranks,
> Swung down at a disarray.
>
> Or like a juicy and jostling shock
> Of bluebells sheaved in May
> Or wind-long fleeces on the flock
> A day off shearing day.
>
> Then over his turnèd temples—here—
> Was a rose, or, failing that,
> Rough-Robin or five-lipped campion clear
> For a beauty-bow to his hat,
> And the sunlight sidled, like dewdrops, like
>   dandled diamonds,
> Through the sieve of the straw of the plait.

Here we have a youth, in the midst of his walk, suddenly leaping into the air and dancing for a step or two, because of the fun of being alive on this lovely and unfading summer morning. The innocent and sweet movement of this very lovely fragment is due, partly, to the skilful interposition of an extra syllable from time to time, and an occasional rare internal rhyme; and the clearness and poignant colours of the morning are conveyed by the sounds of 'juicy,' 'bluebells,' 'sheaved,' with their varying degrees of deep and piercing colour.

This acute and piercing visual apprehension, this sharpening and heightening of the thing seen, so as to obtain its essential spirit, is found again in these lines from 'The May Magnificent' [*sic*]:

[Quotes 'May Magnificat', verses 4–6 and 10–12.]

In the sharply-seen image of the 'star-eyed strawberry-breasted' thrush—strawberry-breasted because of the freckles on her breast—in the enhanced and deepened colour of the 'bugle blue eggs,' in which the sharp U of 'bugle' melting to the softer U of 'blue' gives the reflection and the sisterhood of the deep blue heaven, the flower, and the egg, shifting and changing in the clear light, in the acutely-seen 'greybells,' we have the same piercing, truth-finding vision that produced for us the fair hair of the country youth.

But now we must turn from this exquisite and youthful happiness, this unfading spring weather, to the 'terrible' poems. Let us take, to begin with, the first verse of that great poem, 'The Wreck of the Deutschland':

> Thou mastering me
> God! giver of breath and bread;
> World's strand, sway of the sea;
> Lord of living and dead;
> Thou hast bound bones and veins in me,
>   fastened me flesh,
> And after it almost unmade, what with dread,
> Thy doing: and dost thou touch me afresh?
> Over again I feel thy finger and find thee.

In this passage we have the huge primeval swell of the sea, with its mountain-heights and its hell-depths, we have the movement before life began, conveyed by technical means.

In the slow and majestic first line, the long and strongly-swelling vowels, and the alliterative M's, produce the sensation of an immense wave gathering itself up, rising slowly, ever increasing in its huge power, till we come to the pause that follows the long vowel of 'me'. Then the wave falls, only to rush forward again.

After this majestic line comes the heaving line

> God! giver of breath and bread,

ending with the ship poised on the top of the wave. This last effect is caused by the assonances of 'breath and bread'. The sound of 'breath' is slightly longer, has slightly more of a swell beneath the surface than 'bread,' because of the 'th.' This pause on the top of the wave is followed by the gigantic straining forward of the waves in the line

> World's strand, sway of the sea,

an effect that has been produced by the strong alliterative S's, reinforced by the internal R's of 'World's strand,' followed by the internal W of 'sway.' This line, after the huge tossing up and down from the dulled A of 'strand' to the higher dissonantal A of 'sway,' ends by sweeping forward still further with the long vowel-sound of 'sea,' a sound that is more peaceful than that of 'strand' and 'sway' because of the absence of consonants.

The whole poem is inhabited by a gigantic and overwhelming power, like that of the element that inspired it. The huge force produced by the alliteration in the lines I have analysed above, and in such a line as

> Thou hast bound bones and veins in me,
> fastened me flesh,

has rarely been exceeded, even by Dryden and by Pope, those masters of the effects that can be produced by alliteration. It is true that the last line I have quoted from Hopkins is necessarily, because of its subject, more static than most of the more magnificent lines of Dryden and of Pope, yet Hopkins' line is of nearly an equally giant stature. At the end of this verse, the huge primeval power, splendour and terror which inhabit it change to the softness and tenderness of

> Over again I feel thy finger and find thee,

a line which is equalled in gentleness and sweetness by the lovely line in the ninth verse:

> Thou art lightning and love, I found it, a
> winter and warm.

How huge is the contrast between this and the black coldness and opaqueness, like that of savage waters, of the line

> And the sea flint-flake, black-backed in the
> regular blow,

The opaqueness of this is caused by the flat assonances, the thick consonants, of 'black-backed' and 'blow'.

In the same verse, we find this line:

> Wiry and white-fiery and whirlwind-swivelled
> snow.

I cannot recall any other English poet who has produced such a feeling of huge and elemental cold as Hopkins, a cold that is sometimes devouring, sometimes dulled. In the line quoted above, Hopkins produces the sensation of watching a wave receding and then plunging forward, by rhyming the first and the fourth word. A higher and more piercing dissonantal I precedes the second rhyme, and this feeling of the wave plunging forward is the result, too, of the internal R's, which always either lengthen a word or else make it flutter. In this case (as in the line

> World's strand, sway of the sea),

they lengthen it, or rather give the feeling of an immeasurable force driving forward.

This relentless and inevitable wave-stretch, this driving forward, contained in the sound of 'whirl' is followed immediately by the shrinking sound of 'wind,' the I's in 'wind' and 'swivelled' being dull with cold.

We find an equally world-huge, overwhelming coldness in this quotation from 'The Loss of the Eurydice':

> A beetling baldbright cloud through England
> Riding: there did storms not mingle? and
> Hailropes hustle and grind their
> Heavengravel? Wolfsnow, worlds of it, wind
> there?

In this, our very bones seem ground and beaten by the ropes of the harsh hail. The effect may, or may not, be partly due to the grinding harshness of the 'grind' 'heavengravel' sounds, and to the long-sustained high internal rhymes 'grind' and 'wind'. The imagery is, however, mainly responsible for the magnificence of the verse—the huge imagination, the deep consciousness that inspired the phrase 'Wolfsnow, worlds of it, wind there'....

NOTE

1 See *ante,* p. 242.
2 *Poems,* 4th edn, p. 180.

75. C. Day Lewis, *A Hope for Poetry*

Oxford, 1934, (a) pp. 6–13, (b) pp. 63–4

Cecil Day Lewis (1904–72), whose writing ranged from poetry to detective stories, was regarded in the thirties as one of the 'Auden generation,' sharing with them the 'belief that a poem is first of all an event in society and only secondarily...a verbal creation' (Julian Symons, *The Thirties,* quoted in *W.H. Auden: The Critical Heritage,* p. 13). His interest in Hopkins—and Communism (he was a party member)—is also shown in *Left Review* (see No. 96).

In the previous chapter of this book Lewis had described Hopkins as one of the founders of modern poetry.

(a)
Hopkins, Owen and Eliot are recent examples of younger sons who could not stay at home. They have little else apparently in common: whereas the Muse of Eliot would be hard put to it to say which of a dozen or so lovers was the real father, Hopkins as a poet

seems to have entered the world by a kind of partheno-genesis. The author of such lines as these—

> I caught this morning morning's minion, king—
> Dom of daylight's Dauphin, dapple-dawn-drawn Falcon, in
>   his riding.

or this—

> Or to-fro tender tram beams truckle at the eye—

is difficult to connect with anything in the past. Attempts have been made to trace his derivation back to Milton. Except for Hopkins's own statement that Milton's counterpoint rhythm, particularly as used in the choruses of *Samson Agonistes*, is apt to become identical with the 'sprung rhythm' which Hopkins himself used, I can see no warrant for such a derivation. The nearest approach to his verse texture I can find is in the Greek choruses, more especially those of Aeschylus: we may note in his work something of the same fluidity of line, the same architectural massiveness and decorated verbal accumulation.

Leaving aside verse-texture, and considering what I must call, rather vaguely, poetic merit, I find eminent in Hopkins that quality which made Shakespeare supreme. Eliot, in a recent work, has expressed it as follows: 'The re-creation of word and image which happens fitfully in the poetry of such a poet as Coleridge happens almost incessantly with Shakespeare. Again and again, in his use of a word, he will give a new meaning or extract a latent one. . . ' That 're-creation of word and image' is the last secret of poetic technique, and the extent to which Hopkins achieved it may be gauged by the excerpts printed below: the sensitive reader may discover in them, also, something of the quality and 'feel' of Shakespeare's own poetry.

> Look at the stars! look, look up at the skies!
>   O look at all the fire-folk sitting in the air!
>   The bright boroughs, the circle-citadels there!...

(Juliet might be speaking there.)

> As a dare-gale skylark scanted in a dull cage...

>   are you that liar
>   And, cast by conscience out, spendsavour salt?

But, for all this, Hopkins remains without affinities. Poets may be divided into two classes; those who assimilate a number of influences and construct an original speech from them, and those whose voice seems to come out of the blue, reminding us of nothing we have heard before. Amongst the younger present-day writers, Auden is obviously of this first class, Spender of the second. Eliot's poetry is an extreme example of the former: Lawrence's, of the latter. These categories carry no implication of poetic merit. The integration of many influences into an individual voice requires a true poet: but he is not, because of this process, to be called a greater or a lesser poet than he whose work has not undergone the process. Nor does the second category imply an absence of poetical self-consciousness: that is to say, one may have a close acquaintance with other poets, dead and living, yet remain as a poet almost untouched by them. The sophisticated critic may be the naïf poet, as witness A.E. Housman. It is possible that Housman's own definition of the class of things to which poetry belongs may be true only for the naïf poet: 'I should call it a secretion: whether a natural secretion, like turpentine in the fir, or a morbid secretion, like the pearl in the oyster': while in the sophisticated, assimilative poet more complex motive powers are at work. We do not suppose, of course, that any poet can remain entirely unaffected by the work of other poets; or that anyone can produce poetry by however skilful a blending of the best ingredients. The naïf poet, too, may sometimes write sophisticated poetry, or even turn into a sophisticated poet—it seems increasingly difficult, indeed, for him to avoid doing so. But it is possible to put the bulk of a poet's work over a number of years into one class or the other.

Though one or two of Hopkins's mature poems come into the first class ('The Blessed Virgin compared to the Air we Breathe,' for instance, which, except for a line here and there, might have been written by one of the metaphysical school), he is predominantly what I have called a 'naïf' poet. (Since writing this section, I have discovered in one of Hopkins's letters the following passage: 'The effect of studying masterpieces is to make me admire and do otherwise...') It is, therefore, all the more remarkable to find him exerting such an influence on modern verse; for poets of this type do not belong to any 'school' of poetry and are apt not to found one. We admire Blake or Housman from a distance: any closer approach to their technique would lead us into pastiche. This is, perhaps, because their technique springs more immediately and purely from their experience than is the case with the 'sophisticated' writer. Up to a point this is true of Hopkins's also: one is frequently coming across undigested fragments of his style imbedded in post-war verse. But he has had a much more real influence than this mere bequeathing of echoes: and it is due, I think, to the fact that, unlike most naïf poets, he was a technical innovator. Such poets (Blake, Housman, Emily Dickinson) are usually content to work within conventional forms: their daemon does the rest. It may seem contradictory to assert that a technical innovator can be a naïf poet, but I do not believe it is necessarily so. I should even go so far as to call Hopkins an unconscious revolutionary: in other words, his innovations are not due to a deliberate rebelling against the conventional technique of the time, as were those of Wordsworth, but spring from a kind of innocent experimenting with words, as a child of genius might invent a new style of architecture while playing with bricks.

One of Hopkins's most striking innovations is his frequent use of what he calls 'sprung rhythm'. It is not perhaps quite accurate to term it an innovation, for it approximates to the rhythm of *Piers Plowman* and the old nursery rhymes. But to all intents and purposes it is revolutionary. Wordsworth aimed at simplifying poetry, bringing it nearer to common speech: he effected this by a radical change in the use of words, not by radical changes in prosody. Hopkins was not working on any such theory of communication, but he produced in fact a result the opposite of Wordsworth: by him the language of poetry was removed almost as far as possible from ordinary language—it becomes incantation again; while his prosody swings to the other extreme, for it is based on the rhythm of common speech. We find in post-war poetry a tendency to combine these two results, to use common speech rhythms together with a mixture of simplified, superficially un-'poetical' language and highly poetical incantatory language.

Till Hopkins, almost all English verse since Langland had been written in metres divisible into feet of two or three syllables, iambic or dactylic-anapaestic in effect. It is therefore syllabically quantitative* verse. Any variations, such as the substitution of trochee for iamb, had been variations on a metre of not less than two syllables per foot, and the beat—except in a few strictly dactylic poems,

'Take her up tenderly'—had the effect of coming on the last syllable of the foot. Sprung rhythm differs from this quantitative metre in the following ways. It is based on one syllable stressed in each foot: this syllable may stand alone in its foot or it may be accompanied by a number of unstressed syllables, usually not more than four. Thus lines such as these—

Hígh there, how he húng upon the réin of a wímpling wíng.

No wónder of it: shéer plód makes plóugh down sillion...

would have the same value, five stresses, as

...When yoú shall thése unlúcky deéds reláte...

The stress, where there is more than one syllable in the foot, comes as a rule on its first syllable: but a uniformly trochaic-dactylic effect is avoided by the use of what Hopkins called 'outrides,' unstressed syllables occasionally placed before the stressed ones at the beginning of the foot. Thus in his metres the stress is the foundation, whereas in English verse as a whole, quantity—i.e. two or three syllables to a foot—is the foundation. And since stress is the basis of common speech rhythm, we may say that this sprung rhythm approximates to the rhythm of common speech.

In its favour as a poetical instrument we can put forward a greater freedom for rhythmical effects than is afforded by syllabically-quantitative metre with all its possible licences. No such lively representation of the hover and swoop of a kestrel could be achieved within the limits of the latter as we find in the first of the lines quoted above. And in the second, the heavy determination of 'sheer plod,' with its successive stresses accentuated by the three unstressed syllables before them, is again an effect which could not be procured within a conventional metre. On the other hand, the metrical foundation of sprung rhythm is so shifting and elastic that in employing it we are almost bound to lose that most desirable of rhythmical effects, the counterpoint of the line spoken according to the natural rhythm of the words working in contrast to the strict beat of the metre. As for instance we hear the metrical beat in—

...Cancél and téar to piéces thát great bónd
Which kéeps me pále! Light thíckens, ánd the crów...

counterpointed by the speech rhythm—

> Cáncel and teár to piéces that greát bónd
> Which keéps me pále! Líght thíckens and the crów...

Another objection to sprung rhythm as used by Hopkins is that it often does not conform closely enough to common speech rhythm: we find ourselves compelled to run over a number of heavy syllables, which would certainly be stressed in ordinary speech, before we come to the intended stress. The intended stress, indeed, is often difficult to find. It is comparatively seldom that a series of consecutive lines speak themselves as easily as the first verse of his great poem 'The Wreck of the Deutschland'.

> Thóu mástering me
> Gód! gíver of breáth and breád:
> Wórld's stránd, swáy of the séa
> Lórd of líving and deád;
> Thou hast boúnd bónes and veíns in me, fástened me flésh
> And áfter it álmost unmáde, whát with dreád
> Thy doing: and dóst thou toúch me afrésh?
> Óver agáin I feél thy fínger and find thée.

And even here, though the number of stresses is indicated by the setting of the lines, we are compelled once or twice to verify them from other verses.

Less questionably successful than Hopkins's use of sprung rhythm is his use of alliteration and internal assonance. He employs both constantly, yet, like all successful technical tricks, they are indistinguishable from the pattern which they help to create. These devices are seen to best advantage in 'The Leaden Echo and the Golden Echo,' a poem which is coupled in my mind with Tennyson's 'Ballad of the Revenge' as representing the most remarkable technical achievement of Victorian poetry. It begins—

> How to keep—is there any any, is there none such,
>   nowhere known some, bow or brooch or braid or brace,
>   lace, latch or catch or key to keep
> Back Beauty, keep it, beauty, beauty, beauty,...
>   from vanishing away?...

Notice how cunningly alliteration and assonance are contrived to modulate from one vowel key into another. Yet there is nothing forced, no flavour of artifice. The poem must be read aloud, and with an unprejudiced intellect, for it is a sustained sensual rhapsody; something for which our acquaintance with civilized poetry leaves us unprepared. It is the measure of Hopkins's poetical stature that, though a man of great intellectual ability, he was capable of writing this kind of rhapsody without ever degenerating into rhetoric.

> ...Only not within seeing of the sun,
> Not within the singeing of the strong sun,
> Tall sun's tingeing, or treacherous the tainting of the
> earth's air...

Alliteration, internal assonance and repetition are the chief instruments used by Hopkins in creating a poetry of rare concentration: we find them all used, though not at such high frequency, in post-war verse. The flight of his imagination is very swift: the following of it often a breathless business. What obscurity we may find when first we read him is due, not to a clouded imagination or an unsettled intellect, but to his lightning dashes from image to image, so quick that we are unable at first to perceive the points of contact. He is a true revolutionary poet, for his imagination was always breaking up and melting down the inherited forms of language, fusing them into new possibilities, hammering them into new shapes. His intense faith and his violent spiritual agonies are experiences which few of us to-day—happily or unhappily—are able to share: they caused some of his most magnificent poems: with one of these, the greatest poem to my mind that he ever wrote, we may salute him and take our leave.

[Quotes 'No worst, there is none'.]

(b)

...Hopkins is remarkable, amongst other things, for the extent of his vocabulary: no poet since Donne had drawn his material from so wide a radius, though Hopkins drew comparatively little from the specifically modern data which lay to hand. It is in his ordering of words that he is the technical forerunner of the post-war poets, the first 'modern' poet, and a most evident link between them and Donne. And, in spite of lines like—

> ...And when Peace here does house
> He comes with work to do, he does not come to coo,
> He comes to brood and sit.

it is more to the prose-style of the seventeenth-century divines, and particularly to Donne's, that Hopkins links us. The connection is obvious in such a passage as: 'In a flash, at a trumpet crash, I am all at once what Christ is, since He was what I am, and This Jack, joke, poor potsherd, patch, matchwood, immortal diamond, Is immortal diamond.' We have an idea which compels to itself a number of objects within its magnetic field, and these objects are related to each other often through an intensive alliteration and assonance. There follow a few extracts from recent verse. In A we have the mal-digested influence of Hopkins only: in B and C, verse illustrating the properly assimilated, combined influence of Donne and Hopkins, working on the lines sketched out above: in D, an example of Spender's fluid-image technique, which is affiliated to the kind of magnetically-grouped image technique noticed in Donne and Hopkins, without deriving from it.

A

Me, March, you do with your movements master and rock
With wing-whirl, whale-wallow, silent budding of cell....

(W.H. Auden.)

B

Crofter, leader of hay, working in sweat and weathers, tin-streamer, heckler, blow-room major, we are within a vein's distance of your prisoned blood....

(W.H. Auden.)

C

The quietude of a soft wind,
Will not rescind
My debts to God but gentle skinned
His finger probes, I lull myself
In quiet in diet in riot in dreams
In dopes in drams in drums in dreams
Till God retire and the door shut.
But
Now I am left in the fire-blaze
The peacefulness of the fire-blaze

283

Will not erase
My debts to God for his mind strays
Over and under and all ways
All days and always.

(Louis MacNeice.)

D

...Eye, gazelle, delicate wanderer,
Drinker of horizon's fluid line....

(Stephen Spender.)

Donne and the metaphysicals used the concentration of images and the juxtaposition of paradoxical ideas in such a way as to give the reader a series of intellectual shocks: Hopkins used an intense concentration of images in such a way as to give the reader a series of sensual shocks....

NOTE

* Quantitative is used here in the sense of a given number of syllables per foot, not in the classical sense.

76. T.S. Eliot, *After Strange Gods*

London, 1934, pp. 47–8

T.S. Eliot (1888–1963) never showed any great interest in Hopkins; certainly in temperament and technique, the two poets have little in common. Eliot's *Ash Wednesday* (1930) confirmed his recent return to Christianity, and in this essay, at the point where the following extract begins, he is demonstrating that neither Pound nor Yeats is religious in any traditional sense.

...At this point, having called attention to the difficulties experienced by Mr. Pound and Mr. Yeats through no fault of their own, you may be expecting that I shall produce Gerard Hopkins, with an air of triumph, as the orthodox and traditional poet. I wish indeed that I could; but I cannot altogether share the enthusiasm which many critics feel for this poet, or put him on a level with those whom I have just mentioned. In the first place, the fact that he was a Jesuit priest, and the author of some very beautiful devotional verse, is only partially relevant. To be converted, in any case, while it is sufficient for entertaining the hope of individual salvation, is not going to do for a man, as a writer, what his ancestry and his country for some generations have failed to do. Hopkins is a fine poet, to be sure; but he is not nearly so much a poet of our time as the accidents of his publication and the inventions of his metric have led us to suppose. His innovations certainly were good, but like the mind of their author, they operate only within a narrow range, and are easily imitated though not adaptable for many purposes; furthermore, they sometimes strike me as lacking inevitability—that is to say, they sometimes come near to being purely *verbal*, in that a whole poem will give us *more* of the same thing, an accumulation, rather than a real development of thought or feeling.

I may be wrong about Hopkins's metric and vocabulary. But I am sure that in the matter of devotional poetry a good deal more is at issue than just the purity and strength of the author's devotional passion. To be a 'devotional poet' is a limitation: a saint limits himself by writing poetry, and a poet who confines himself to even this subject matter is limiting himself too. Hopkins is not a religious poet in the more important sense in which I have elsewhere maintained Baudelaire to be a religious poet;[1] or in the sense in which I find Villon to be a religious poet; or in the sense in which I consider Mr. Joyce's work to be penetrated with Christian feeling. I do not wish to depreciate him, but to affirm limitations and distinctions. He should be compared, not with our contemporaries whose situation is different from his, but with the minor poet nearest contemporary to him, and most like him: George Meredith. The comparison is altogether to Hopkins's advantage. They are both English nature poets, they have similar technical tricks, and Hopkins is much the more agile. And where Meredith, beyond a few acute and pertly expressed observations of human nature, has only a rather cheap and shallow 'philosophy of life' to offer, Hopkins has the dignity of the Church behind him, and is consequently in closer contact with reality. But from the struggle of our time to concentrate, not to dissipate; to renew our association with traditional wisdom; to re-establish a vital connexion between the individual and the race; the struggle, in a word, against Liberalism: from all this Hopkins is a little apart, and in this Hopkins has very little aid to offer us. . . .

NOTE

1 In his essay on Baudelaire (1930) where, in a much qualified way, Eliot describes him as an 'essentially Christian poet'.

77. Joan Bennett, *Four Metaphysical Poets*

Cambridge, 1934, (a) pp. 68–71, (b) pp. 121–4

Joan Bennett (b. 1896) was appointed lecturer in English at Cambridge in 1937. She also wrote on Woolf and George Eliot. This book was later reprinted and expanded as *Five Metaphysical Poets* (1964).

(a)
. . . Herbert must start in low tones if we are to get the full impact of his climax, which consists often in a subtle change of feeling or attitude. His most characteristic gift is the power of controlling the movement of feeling in his poems. The emotional pattern is managed with exquisite tact. The attitudes he handles are subtle and delicate, over emphasis or emphasis in the wrong place, over haste or too much delay, would destroy their effect; but in such matters Herbert is a master. The opening lines of his poems are usually quiet, they place the reader at the heart of the subject just as Donne does, but, unlike Donne, Herbert maintains a demeanour of

calm and restraint, and this is so even when, like Donne, he opens
with an exclamation or question:

> Oh that I could a sinne once see![a]

> It cannot be. Where is that mightie joy
> Which just now took up all my heart?[b]

> Oh, what a thing is man! How far from power,
>   From settled peace and rest![c]

The mood is collected, it is the preparation for a discussion of the
theme. A similar difference is noticeable between the closing lines
of Herbert's poems and those of Donne or of Hopkins. Herbert
constantly achieves his effect by relaxing the tension at the end of a
poem. The struggle is over and all is peace. 'The Thanksgiving',
for instance, is a discussion with God, in which the poet tries to
offer an equivalent for all that has been given:

> If thou shalt give me wit, it shall appeare;
>   If thou hast giv'n it me, 'tis here.
> Nay, I will reade thy book and never move
> Till I have found therein thy love,
> Thy art of love, which I'le turn back on thee:
>   O my deare Saviour, Victorie!

and then the poet falters and the culminating point of the poem
suggests a lowering of the voice almost to a whisper:

> Then for thy passion—I will do for that—
> Alas, my God, I know not what.

Such a dying away in the last line is Herbert's way of suggesting
to his reader that the resources of language have been overpast,
what remains to be said can only be stated with the utmost
simplicity, as in the last line of the 'Dialogue' when he has
enumerated and attempted to compete with all the sufferings of the
Saviour:

> Ah no more! Thou break'st my heart,

or the last line of 'Miserie' in which he has described the folly and
wickedness of man and ends with

> My God, I mean myself.

The first two words of the line are not an exclamation but a vocative; it is in an entirely different key from the last line of Hopkins' 'Carrion Comfort':

> That night, that year
> Of now done darkness I wretch lay wrestling with (my God!)
> my God.

If Hopkins had written the last line of Herbert's 'Miserie' (if the fantasy may be allowed) it would have been an exclamation of agonized discovery:

> (My God!)—I mean myself,

instead of as at present a quiet, humiliated recognition of the fact. In poem no. 45 (in Robert Bridges' edition) Hopkins considers the subject of Herbert's poem 'Miserie,' the abject nature of mankind and therefore of himself: he closes his poem when the horror is at its height:

> I am gall, I am heartburn. God's most deep decree
> Bitter would have me taste: my taste was me;
> Bones built in me, flesh filled, blood brimmed the curse.
>
> Selfyeast of spirit a dull dough sours. I see
> The lost are like this, and their scourge to be
> As I am mine, their sweating selves; but worse.

Hopkins' sonnets are a crescendo of emotion, the strongest expression is reserved for the last line. Herbert, on the contrary, comes to rest on a note of quiet acceptance, some sentence that would be mere matter of fact, were it not for what has preceded. Yet the influence of Donne is unmistakably present in either case; so differently can poets of different temperament make use of a common tradition. . . .

(b)

. . . A more debatable point in our day is, whether there will be any common ground between the religious poet and a reader who has dismissed Christian beliefs. The possibility of communication between poet and reader depends upon there being something in common between them. Fortunately for poetry human needs and impulses are recurrent, though the directions in which satisfaction is sought are very varied. The state of mind in such a poem as Francis Thompson's 'The Hound of Heaven' is readily conveyed to an unbeliever, although it may have no exact parallel in his experience. The poem itself, with its abundant imagery and insistent rhythm, can communicate it:

[Quotes ll. 1–15.]

The impulse to escape from the unknown, and the longing to be at one with it, the hurry of thought to avoid contemplation, the fear of paying too great a price for what is most desired:

> (For, though I knew His love Who followèd,
> Yet was I sore adread
> Lest, having Him, I must have nought beside.)

these conflicting impulses are sufficiently common to be intelligible in the guise in which Francis Thompson's faith clothes them. The poem, like Herbert's 'Affliction', is a biography of the human spirit, its adventures may be strange, but the adventurer is familiar. This is likely to be always the case. Poets are abnormal, but this does not mean that they are different in kind from their readers, they are different in their degree of awareness, their power of co-ordinating experiences, and, chiefly of course, in the nature and degree of their command of words. For a reader of devotional poetry, as of any other kind, the most important qualification is sensibility to all the possible implications of words and their arrangement. He need not share the poet's beliefs, he may even be more responsive, because more flexible and unreserved, less tempted to foist his own experience on to the poem, if he does not: but he must be susceptible to the poet's power 'to awaken in us a wonderfully full, new and intimate sense of things and of our relation to them'.

Suppose a reader, sensitive to poetry, but repelled by or indifferent to the doctrine of the resurrection of the body, reads Gerard Manley Hopkins' poem, 'The Caged Skylark'?

[Quoted.]

The poem does not convert such a reader to the doctrine implied, in the sense in which a theological treatise might conceivably do so. And yet in some sense the thought and feeling in the poem are transferred to him. There is again something in common between poet and reader to begin with. There can be few who have not felt the body to be both prison and home, both encumbrance and delight, both an insufferable limitation and a centre of rest and refreshment. Such a background of common experience is all that is needed. The poet does the rest. Hopkins more even than most poets repays close attention to his verbal pattern. His words are like pieces in a mosaic, he composes with these fragments. This particular poem is built up in a series of contrasts, the harsh thuds of the prison motif 'Scanted in a dull cage'; 'in his bone-house, mean house dwells—'; 'This in drudgery, day-labouring out life's age'; 'Or wring their barriers in bursts of fear or rage'; contrasted with the open, liquid sound of the free-flight motif: 'Man's mounting spirit'; 'remembering his free fells'; 'Both sing some-times the sweetest, sweetest spells'; 'Why, hear him, hear him babble and drop down to his nest'; 'Meadow-down is not distressed for a rainbow footing it nor he for his bónes risen'. Finally the reader possesses, not Hopkins' belief, but his feeling of what it would be like to meet the body again in its resurrected state. A precedent knowledge of the Catholic doctrine is necessary for the poem to be understood, particularly the line which is nearest to prose statement:

> Man's spirit will be flesh-bound when found at best,
> But uncumbered:

But most poetry requires some familiarity with the tradition from which it springs. English poetry, secular or sacred, has its roots in European culture, with its inheritance of Greek, Latin, Hebrew and Christian literatures, the ideas they embody and the gods they celebrate. Given two readers of equal sensibility the more widely read has always an advantage....

NOTES

a 'Sinne'.
b 'The Temper'.
c 'Giddinesse'.

78. F.W. Bateson, *English Poetry and the English Language*

Oxford, 1934, pp. 118–20

Frederick Wilse Bateson (1901–78) was Commonwealth Fellow at Harvard, 1927–9, and editor, *Cambridge Bibliography of English Literature* (1930–40).

In the following extract he suggests that Hopkins (and Housman) tried to create a poetic idiom of their own, in reaction against the vague language of conventional Victorian poetry.

...Hopkins's abortive revolt against the Pre-Raphaelite tradition goes back to the year 1876 (the date of 'The Wreck of the Deutschland'), and that it was abortive I attribute primarily to that fact. Hopkins was too early. The language had not increased sufficiently in precision by then for the massive concrete poetry of Hopkins to be possible at all without very special precautions. The clumsy, and, as one feels now, unnecessary, concentration of his style was in fact necessary in 1876. Without the restriction it imposed the tendencies of the language would have carried him away into the vagueness and diffuseness that he was in revolt against. The danger is apparent in his earlier poems, even in the magnificent 'Heaven-Haven' (written about 1866):

> I have desired to go
> Where springs not fail,
> To fields where flies no sharp and sided hail
> And a few lilies blow.

To his contemporaries Hopkins's lines may well have seemed much the same thing as Christina Rossetti's 'Spring Quiet' (also written about 1866)

> Here the sun shineth
> Most shadily;

Here is heard an echo
Of the far sea,
Though far off it be.

The two poems are essentially at opposite poles, Christina Rossetti's representing an escape from and Hopkins's a confrontation of reality, but the condition of the language had tended to assimilate them. Mr. A.E. Housman, coming twenty years later, was able to benefit by the language's gains of precision in the interval; 'A Shropshire Lad' has exactly those qualities of directness, concision, and inevitability that Hopkins's style just misses. ...

The historical significance of Hopkins and Mr. Housman is in the sphere of diction. The tendency of Victorian poetry has been to reduce little by little the number of living words and to substitute for them the Praetorian cohorts of romantic poetic diction. Hopkins and Mr. Housman—assisted by Robert Bridges, Charles Doughty, and Thomas Hardy—rebelled against this tendency. Their efforts were tentative and sometimes mistaken—they exaggerated the value of archaisms and dialectal words and phrases; but they initiated a process that has culminated in the one indisputable achievement of post-War poetry—its catholicity of diction.

*LETTERS OF GERARD MANLEY
HOPKINS TO ROBERT BRIDGES*

and

*CORRESPONDENCE OF GERARD
MANLEY HOPKINS AND
R.W. DIXON*

edited by C.C. Abbott, London, 1935

79. C.C. Abbott, Introduction, *Letters of Hopkins to Bridges*

1935

Claude Colleer Abbott (1889–1971) was Lecturer in English at Aberdeen University 1921–32, and Professor of English at Durham from 1932. He was a poet as well as a critic, and had been publishing since 1918.

Abbott first showed his interest in Hopkins in the review of Lahey's Life in *The Nation and Athenaeum*, 28 June 1930, when he expressed a hope for the publication of the letters and the Journals. He was an admirer of Bridges's editorship, and the following extracts seem based on canons of criticism of which the latter would have approved.

Abbott also edited the *Correspondence of Hopkins and Dixon* and *Further Letters.*

... The poems [of 1918] were, generally, well received; that is, they were read with eagerness by the 'little clan' that knows 'great verse'. How small this clan was can be seen from the publisher's figures for the edition, which was not exhausted for ten years.[a] They are figures that effectively kill the legend, invented in our own day, of a public panting to read poetry arbitrarily withheld.

The taste of the 'public' in such matters is always negligible.

So much, then, for the progress of Hopkins towards publication and recognition. It is no doubt a pity that the few who might have rejoiced in him at once had to wait nearly thirty years before they knew his full measure; but such misfortunes are not unknown to literature. More striking is the fact that this work waited so long, after 1918, before its more general discovery in universities and places where poetry is studied and, on occasion, cultivated. During the last few years, however (aided by the second edition of the poems in 1930), he has been widely talked of, if not widely read; and this popularity has led to a fashion for his verses and attempts to imitate his style which as matters stand to-day may be taken as a sign of health rather than folly. He is accepted by the young as one of their contemporaries, and—a more doubtful privilege—he has even been affiliated to the Martin Tuppers of our day whose scrannel pipes have infected the field of poetry with mildew and blight.

It is easy to see why Hopkins the spare and astringent should particularly appeal to this generation, but strange to find him regarded as a poet in key with contemporary experiment and disillusion. Two things have helped towards this misconception: his originality (in which may be counted his anticipation of modern experiments in technique) and the retarded publication and realization of his work. Yet the misconception is glaring. Hopkins is an Englishman and a Victorian. How intensely he loved his country, how firmly he was rooted in her loveliness of earth, how strongly a patriot and man of his age, his poems and letters abundantly testify. He may be a strange Victorian, but he belongs to that company. No other moment could have produced him. It is a commonplace that every poet is vitally influenced by his age, either by sympathy or revolt or a combination of both. The measure of his greatness is often the measure of his apartness. This is the case with Hopkins. His modernity means not that he belongs, spiritually, to us, but that by transcending in great measure the dead conventions of his contemporaries he is free of all ages and entombed by none. The main reasons for this distinction are his searching honesty and the peculiarly personal statement that is the core of his best work. A desire to emulate these qualities would be more salutary to those who aspire to follow him than tinkerings with technique.

He has probably engaged most attention as an explorer in prosody and an experimenter in technique. Too much, and little to the purpose, has already been written about him from this point of view. He himself says what need be said in the explanatory Preface printed with his poems, and in these letters, particularly where he describes sprung rhythm to Dixon. For the system of stress which he set out to explore and methodize he had, of course, good warrant in English poetry. Stress as he conceives it is native to the genius of the language and may be taken as the logical development of his metrical studies, almost as alternative to the 'counterpoint' learned chiefly from Milton. Coleridge, among others, had felt the importance of stress to pattern, tone, and modulation, but such a work as 'Christabel' was too lightly woven and capricious to please the exacting demands of this poet who aimed 'at an unattainable perfection of language'. Where Coleridge was content to let the metre follow the tune in his mind, Hopkins demanded from himself an exact system of prosody, rules to be obeyed. Instead, therefore, of what might have been a freeing or loosening of bonds, we have a tightening and concentration, a more rigorous art. Hopkins abhorred facility, and deplored any departure from the canons he had aimed at, as may be seen from his criticism of Bridges's use of sprung rhythm. The fascination of what is difficult and yet more difficult sometimes involved him in a struggle for technical conquest to the detriment of poetry.

Despite, therefore, the fresh and characteristic loveliness of poems so various as 'Pied Beauty' and 'Spelt from Sibyl's Leaves' there are weaknesses to remark in this system of sprung rhythm as elaborated and used by Hopkins, attractive though it be. To call it a system is not altogether accurate. There may be a system implicit in the poems: he was certainly working towards one, though he never fully formulated it. Often in practice he takes complete freedom and dragoons words to fit his rhythm by a personal or capricious stress which has no more justification than a private symbolism. Beyond that comes a more important qualification: he is too greedy as poet and prosodist, and too anxious to 'load every rift...with ore'. He feels no bar to the use of stress, alliteration, assonance, internal- and end-rhyme in the same poem. This excess is probably more often a loss than a gain. He is helped towards what is often a magnificent concentration by the elimination of weak words and the determination to say nothing at second hand. At times he loses in clarity, word-music, and spontaneity. Everything he writes is written with intention, but it is often possible to question the justice of the demands he makes on word-order and grammar by omission and emphasis.[b] Occasionally his work is as much a piece of highly artificial mosaic as a mediocre passage from Pope, or one of Milton's least-inspired verse-paragraphs. He seems to have judged Old English poetry by his reading of *Piers Ploughman*.[c] Had he known the *Beowulf*, the Elegies, some of Cynewulf, and the best of the Riddles he would have seen that for one considerable body of lofty poetry stress and alliteration were sufficient, and rhyme was either an accident or intrusion. As it is, though the rhythm he evolved justifies itself triumphantly in many a short poem, it is difficult to imagine its successful use in a work of length.

His idiom, as might be expected, is very much his own. He aspired to use the language of living speech, and a few 'precious' words apart, he succeeded. His contempt for all archaisms may be seen in his remarks on Doughty's prose, or better still in his uneasy acceptance of Dixon's medievalism. His own idiom emerges as strangely and strongly personal in his best poems as Wordsworth's or Keats's; but there are in his more experimental work weaknesses and violences belonging rather to mannerism than style. What idiom he had arrived at after trial and discipline is best seen, perhaps, in the later sonnets, though these can hardly be looked on as the fulfilment of his explorations in prosody. The discipline in poetry that he had undergone, his rigorous self-honesty and habits of mind are all seen in these most poignant poems, but it is difficult to believe that their pain-swept simplicity makes them his *Samson Agonistes*. The abundant vitality of the poems following on the 'Deutschland' warrants the conviction that the crop from the mature tree should have been richer....

...The 'Deutschland' no longer seems grim and forbidding as once it did, yet, a few noble passages and images apart (how certain, for example, the mastery of rhythm in the first stanza), the reader is roused rather to astonishment at the technical strength and resource than delight in the poem as a whole. For this qualified approval the subject of the poem is principally responsible. 'All depends upon the subject,' said Arnold, 'chose a fitting action, penetrate yourself with the feelings of its situations; this done, everything else will follow'. This subject, the drowning of five exiled nuns (and forty-five other people) is unable to bear the stress of an ode so ambitious. The poet is handicapped by the academic religious subject and by his determination to make the poem safe as doctrine. The work is marred by the something of propaganda and 'presentation-piece' that pervades it, and becomes definitely smaller—excited, violent, overpitched—as the main subject[d] is approached and the poet strives to justify his choice. It is curiously built. The two parts can almost be regarded as two separate poems, and the first, loosely linked to the other, is the more important. To read this brings to mind pent-up flood waters at last released by the bursting of a dam. It is as if the turmoil in his own heart, long inarticulate, had at length forced utterance in this agonized surrender of self to the purpose and might of God. The poet in him could no longer be disregarded in confinement, and the passionate personal statement is perhaps the main factor in shaping the new rhythm that had long been haunting his ear.[e] Thence comes too that feeling of strain and stress, of lines mightily hammered out on an anvil or hewn with great strokes. Yet often the result is incommensurate with the effort. The poet pursues the spirit: he is not unobtrusively possessed by it. Hopkins never again finished anything so ambitious as the 'Wreck of the Deutschland'. The writing of it made his style, and his confidence in himself as poet, secure.

Then follow his most fruitful years as poet. To the short period 1877–9 or–80 belongs much of his more immediately attractive work, poems that seem to reflect or recall a time of rustling calm and tendrilous poetic apprehension. The torrent of the 'Deutschland', become a stream of smoother and purer flow, issues in a series of sonnets that witness to the poet's sensuous awareness. This intensity of feeling is not allowed to stand altogether alone. The senses are leashed to a purpose, praise of God.

The poems of this group are comparatively simple, and contain little that can lead to the charge of obscurity. They are written in an almost colloquial language that avoids both romantic flourish and Wordsworthian 'simplesse'. Freshness of approach, an individual music, and a temper of mind that may be called lovingkindness, characterize them. They are poems written to the glory of God by a man who is looking on the world as charged with His grandeur and revealing His bounty and presence. But always as I read them I feel that the poet is primarily seized by the beauty of earth, and that though a man of exquisitely tempered and religious mind, his senses, not his religion, are in the ascendant. Let us grant the conviction that God made this loveliness and that it bears living witness to His affection. Hopkins says little more than this on the religious side of these poems, and he says this side with no particular distinction. On the other hand, his visions of earth and her creatures make a bevy of astonishing and new felicities rarely to be matched in English poetry. These are, therefore, only secondarily religious poems. The yeast of the religious spirit has not worked through them. The fusion of earthly beauty and exemplum is often so incomplete that the second is merely the addendum of a poet captive in the first place to the beauty besieging his senses. This loveliness is here for its own sake. Thus 'Pied Beauty', that deeply moving and magical thanksgiving for things 'counter, original, spare, strange', is not a devotional poem save in the way that all poems witnessing to beauty are devotional. It is possible that these poems could not have been written unless Hopkins held the faith he did hold: even the sensuous poetry of the *Faerie Queene* might have been different without Spenser's fighting Protestantism, core of allegory, and nobility of mind. Moreover there is nothing aggressive in the religious statement, no abatement of joy in the poet's recognition of beauty. Yet the dedication of 'The Windhover' does not hinder the poem from being first of all a magnificent tribute to a natural thing perfectly done, and even in the 'May Magnificat' what matters most is not the praise of Mary, but such stanzas as

[Quotes the two penultimate verses.]

...To pass, then, to the poems of his middle mature period (roughly 1880–3: 1884 is blank) is to be conscious of a clouding over of that fresh vision in which the dappled beauty of earth proclaimed the grandeur of God. The almost lyric note gives place to a mood more charged with meditation that fathers a weightier utterance and demands for its expression a more intricate music. This tendency is already apparent in the laboured tribute to Duns Scotus, his chief among philosophers, and in his over-subtle praise (blending the parochial with the magnificent) of Purcell's divine genius; and the buffeting of his spirit by life's riddle, 'the blight man was born for', is best expressed in the tremendous and undoctrinal chords of 'Spelt from Sibyl's Leaves,' where contemplation of night's mystery conveys to his haunted mind the terror of annihilation and reverses all his former joy. This poem is perhaps the masterpiece of his more elaborate style, for the sonnet 'That Nature is a Heraclitean Fire...', where the comfort of the Resurrection jumps out of the pattern, is not 'all to one thing wrought'. With the poet's deepening experience of life's poignancy goes a fuller realization of man's pathos and importance:

> And what is Earth's eye, tongue, or heart else, where
> Else, but in dear and dogged man?

or

> To man, that needs would worship | block or barren stone,
> Our law says: Love what are | love's worthiest, were all known:
> World's loveliest—men's selves.

Such comprehension prepares the way for his last sonnets which belong to the quintessential poetry of man's spirit in travail and explore the darkest places of human suffering. These poems[f] are salt with the taste of his blood and bitter with the sweat of his anguish, the work of a man tried to the utmost limit of his strength and clinging to the last ledge where reason may find a refuge. Their authority and truthfulness cannot be questioned. Here, indeed, is a chart of despair, agony, and frustration, made by one who still believes in the justice of God. That the chart was mapped at all shows how urgent was the need for self-expression to alleviate, even though it could not resolve, his conflict[g]....

The pity of these poems is hardly to be borne: the depth of it is the measure both of his lofty devotion and his consciousness of failure. Exile, isolation, and defeat are of their essence. There is in them no rapturous one-ness with Christ that has been known to follow such self-surrender; none of the peace of God that passeth all understanding. To his fellow Jesuit and biographer 'the celebrated "terrible" sonnets are only terrible in the same way that the beauty of Jesus Christ is terrible. Only the strong pinions of an eagle can realize the cherished happiness of such suffering. It is the place where Golgotha and Thabor meet. Read in this light his poems cease to be tragic.' The critic who can read these sonnets in any light so that they 'cease to be tragic' is thinking, surely, in terms of pathological Christianity, not of poetry. Their evidence, and the evidence of the letters, is directly contrary. Four of these sonnets 'came like inspirations unbidden and against my will'. How far they must be from the spirit in which he wanted to write no one can doubt. The poet in him was too honest not to face the thought that his sacrifice had brought not peace but a sword. It is perhaps not fanciful to feel that this sacrifice of self aroused a measure of regret and a realization that his persecuted gifts should have been more fully used. Despite his determination to surrender all, the strife between poet and priest remained unsolved.

How can a poet best serve God? Milton's answer to his question in a time of great tribulation ends on a note of resignation to the divine will; but he is sure of what his service will be when opportunity offers. The sonnet 'On his Blindness' should be read again in this setting. There is a kinship of spirit between the two poets. But what was possible to the resolved will of Milton the heretic was beyond the powers of Hopkins the priest. He lacked, so it seems to me, just that serene certainty of how to serve God. It is here that the evidence of the 'spiritual' diaries would have been particularly valuable: it may happen that the more mundane records bring light. But without further witness it is difficult to believe in 'the cherished happiness of such suffering'. The emphasis for me, indeed, is on the deep regret following on the knowledge that his poetical gift had been used in part only, and that part not always to his satisfaction as priest:

> And that one talent which is death to hide
> Lodged with me useless.

It is a dilemma such as this that

> Selfyeast of spirit a dull dough sours. . . .

NOTES

a 750 copies were printed; 50 were given away; 180 sold in the first year; 240 in the second year; then an average of 30 a year for six years, rising to 90 in 1927. The last four copies were sold in 1928. The price was twelve shillings and sixpence.

b At the same time it is well to point out that he never cultivates obscurity for obscurity's sake. Any 'obscurity' that his work may hold comes from an honest concentration that expands to thought and needs no help outside itself. Whether this concentration is always poetically effective is another matter; but certainly neither laziness nor cleverness has part in it.

c *Poems*, 8,1.3, has a flavour of Old English; and *Poems*, 24,1.18, 'And ripest under rind' recalls medieval lyric ['The Starlight Night' and 'Morning, Midday, and Evening Sacrifice].

d Stanza 20.

e Is it fanciful to hear behind his rhythm something of Campbell's 'Battle of the Baltic' and Cowper's 'Loss of Royal George'?

f ... The poet's persistent use of the sonnet form is in itself evidence of the self-limitation of his powers. One feels that he chose it partly because he had some hope of concentrating on, and finishing, a poem of this length that along with discipline of form gave scope for individual pattern.

g Petty and superfluous beside it is that clever and rootless verse of our own day which apes the discovery of kindred desolation.

80. Basil de Selincourt, 'Complete Dedication', *Observer*

20 January 1935, p. 5

... It becomes clear at last that he regarded his big set pieces like 'Harry Ploughman' or 'Tom's Garland' (sonnets only, I know, but of what a size!) exactly as a musician regards his score. He does not expect you to be able to read them as reading is commonly understood. They are works for performance, and should have 'opus' numbers. You must first discover what their rhythm and tempi are, then learn how to deliver each sentence with the rhythm and tempo it requires. Moreover, to understand the rhythm of the words you must understand their meaning, though that in its turn is partly derived from the rhythm. These requirements are not novel in principle; you could not do justice to such a simple piece as Tennyson's 'Break, break, break', without having satisfied them. The novelty is the pressure put on them and the degree of technical virtuosity Hopkins asks for.

81. Fr Joseph Keating, review, *Month*

February 1935, pp. 125–36

Fr Joseph Keating, SJ (1865–1939), had been a supporter of
Hopkins in the pages of the *Month* since 1909, and it was he
who had engaged in a correspondence with Bridges for the
publication of the poems. Editor of the *Month* since 1912, he
had a strong interest in English literature and some talent for
verse of his own. As a pioneer in making Hopkins better
known, he merits the gratitude of later readers.

...The Society cannot, nor can Catholics as a body, be wholly
satisfied with the result of the labours of these various zealous
non-Catholics, and that for a fundamental reason, for which,
as it lies in the very nature of things, they are in no sense to
blame. The fact is, they do not share the Faith of their subject, they
regard it as unsound and erroneous, they are more or less hostile to
it, they resent its interference with his poetic work, and so, not
understanding or appreciating it, they cannot fully understand or
appreciate him. Dr. Bridges, his lifelong and intimate friend,
Canon Dixon his fervent admirer, Mr. Williams who has done so
much to further his fame, and now the learned Professor from
Durham, have not been able to penetrate into the soul of Father
Hopkins, have not realized or sympathized with his fundamental
'values,' and thus have failed to present an adequate picture of the
man. With the Catholic, not to say the dedicated Religious, the
claims of religion are ultimate and paramount, his life is framed
upon a supernatural basis, his citizenship of the world to come
takes precedence, in belief at least, of his citizenship in this. Father
Hopkins had freely embraced the religious state, *i.e.*, he was
pledged to celibacy and to poverty, and by his vow of obedience he
had deliberately handed over the whole disposal of his life to those
who represented God to him, and spoke, within the limits of their
authority, in His name. And so he could no longer regard his poetic
endowment, however great and manifest, as a talent to be freely

traded with. 'Surely,' cries Dixon, the most sympathetic of his critics, 'one vocation cannot destroy another,'[a] and Professor Abbott, who descries throughout in Hopkins a conflict between the 'poet' and the 'priest,' endorses the implied censure.[b] Both critics beg the whole question by assuming that a vocation to the religious state is on the same level and of the same character as a 'vocation' to be a poet, that God, by conferring exceptional talents, thereby virtually imposes an obligation to use them. That is not the Catholic view, as Hopkins pointed out at length.[c] The summons 'Follow Me' is fitly answered by 'leaving all things'; which are never, thenceforth, to be taken up again, save in the measure and for the purpose ordained by the Master. Hopkins's responsibility for the use of his poetic gift ceased when he took his vow of obedience.

This was never realized by his non-Catholic friends. Even Canon Dixon, misunderstanding the purpose of the 'third-year's probation,' hinted a desire that, at the eleventh hour so to speak, he would give the thing up.[d] And Bridges, to whom the pursuit of poetry was all his religion,[e] had even less sympathy with his friend's religious attitude. He resented it to the end, so that Father Hopkins, much as he must have desired his friend's conversion to Christianity, never apparently made more than one direct approach to the subject in his correspondence,[f] an attempt unsympathetically commented on by Professor Abbott, who for his part, approves of Bridges's rejection of such an 'intrusion into his personal faith,' and adds: 'There was always a line between them which neither could easily cross. This was inevitable. To Bridges the priesthood raised an insuperable barrier: he had, *and rightly,* a profound distrust of the Society of Jesus.'[g]

Precisely; and consequently he was ill-equipped to appreciate the spirit of so thorough a Jesuit and so holy a priest as was his bosom friend.[h] And the phrase we have ventured to italicize shows that the Professor labours under the same handicap. He speaks of Hopkins's religious ideas as 'this bleak asceticism,'[i] and contrasts unfavourably his restless urge towards a fuller perfection, and the desolation of spirit with which God appears to have tried him towards the end of his life with 'the resolved will,' 'the serene certainty,' 'the stamina and assurance' manifested by John Milton in his celebrated 'Sonnet on his Blindness.'

Here, with all respect, I think Mr. Abbott, like those other critics,[j] goes beyond his last. Even the first-year novice when he has made the 'Spiritual Exercises,' which Father Hopkins went through annually for twenty-one years, comes forth convinced that for the creature God's will is all in all, and that no sacrifice is really worth weighing in the balance against His perfect service. To picture the poet as tossed and strained by anxiety as to whether he was not absolutely right in subordinating his high natural gifts to the supernatural purposes of his priestly life, is to ascribe to him an ignorance of spiritual conditions that would shame the veriest beginner. No, he knew, far better than Milton, that 'They also serve who only stand and wait,' and that the creature's perfection lies in utter obedience to the disposition of the Creator. Accordingly, whatever experiences are reflected in those four or five 'terrible sonnets,' so full of spiritual 'desolation,' so suggestive of Gethsemane, so expressive of the 'dark night of the soul,' which those close to Christ are at times privileged to pass through, they cannot have been due to a mere human sense of failure and frustration, still less to a doubt as to whether he had chosen aright. One of the Rules (No. 16) which was expounded to Father Hopkins in the noviceship and which he heard repeated monthly during his whole religious life, runs as follows: 'Let all who have joined the Society devote themselves to the study of solid and perfect virtues and of spiritual things, and *consider these of greater importance than learning or other natural and human gifts.*' And he would have been a poor scholar, indeed, if he had not practised that doctrine from the very first. ...

NOTES

a *Correspondence of Hopkins and Dixon*, p. 90. Father Hopkins was then in his 'third year of probation' at Roehampton.

b *Letters to Bridges*, Introduction, p. xxxvi.

c *Correspondence of Hopkins and Dixon*, pp. 93 sqq.

d *Ibid.*, p. 70.

e 'Religion meant for him not assent to a particular creed, but a manner of life dependent on the discipline of his own mind and body': such is Professor Abbott's not over-clear description of his belief, *Letters to Bridges*, Introd., p. xlvi.

f Writing from Oxford, January 19, 1879, *ibid.*, p. 60.

g *Ibid.*, Introduction, p. xlv.

h Dr Bridges on his side recognized the 'barrier'. In a letter to the present writer on the eve of the publication of the *Poems*, he says: 'I cannot tell how far you will like my book, but whatever feeling or animus it may discover (lurking in it) against the medievalism which I cannot sympathize with, that no doubt will appear in anything that I write, and I do not go out of my way to express it or disguise it.' This reaction against medievalism (*i.e.*, Catholicism), was equally apparent in Bridges's relations with Digby Mackworth Dolben, another young poet whom a sudden death prevented from following Hopkins into the Church. See *The Downside Review*, January, 1935, in an article on Dolben, by Dom W. Phillipson.

i *Letters to Bridges*, Introduction, p. xxxv.

j See also in this connexion *The Poetry of G.M. Hopkins* (1933), by Miss E.E. Phare, a sympathetic and scholarly study which just fails in that one point.

82. Geoffrey Grigson and Humphry House in *New Verse*

April 1935

New Verse (1933–9), edited by Geoffrey Grigson, concentrated on printing and discussing contemporary poets, and although its circulation barely exceeded 1,000 it was probably the most important English poetry magazine of the thirties. It was enthusiastic in its support of Auden, but its editor later regretted its sometimes strident tone, as instanced here by his remarks on Bridges (see Grigson's 'Recollections of New Verse', *TLS*, 25 April 1968, pp. 409–10).

Hopkins had figured in its very first number, in January 1933, in an article by Herbert Read. The April 1935 edition was entirely devoted to him, with seven different contributors, including Grigson, House, MacNeice, Charles Madge, and Christopher Devlin. House was thanked for helping to assemble these writers.

(a) Geoffrey Grigson, Editorial

Gerard Manley Hopkins first became a public influence accessible to all poets and readers in 1918. Since then he has been elevated into a 'modernist,' praised, overpraised, underpraised for a medley of wrong and right reasons. His friends are enemies among themselves and he has suffered from them all. Most of what has been written about Hopkins is explanation and appreciation: Hopkins, writers have had to point out, is not so 'difficult' and his poems have magnificent qualities. Those conquests can be granted. It is time to begin on the real difficulties in Hopkins, in his thought and in his life as a poet and a priest. This number, in some degree, is intended as such a beginning. . . .

. . . A comment might have been expected on the relationship between Hopkins and Robert Bridges: there is comment enough in the fact that Bridges destroyed his side of the correspondence. Anyone who still believes that Bridges understood his friend will find that thoroughly and explicitly denied in his letters by Hopkins himself. Bridges is a very small poet with a very dry vein of poetry: Hopkins is even more important than himself or his own work, since both illustrate the processes, ingredients and difficulties of poetry with a definition and detail which are very infrequent in literature. The most opposite writers in this number seem to realise that, and the realisation gives it some unity. . . .

(b) Humphry House, 'A Note on Hopkins's Religious Life'

The Society of Jesus is an active and not a contemplative order; its members are missionaries and teachers; its discipline is military rather than monastic. The *Spiritual Exercises* were intended by St. Ignatius primarily as a means of testing the vocation of novices, or deepening the sense of their vocation in Jesuits of longer standing. The book was to be used normally in retreat. The late Fr. Joseph Rickaby, one of Hopkins's early friends in the Society, wrote: 'The end of the Spiritual Exercises is such amount and quality of self-denial as shall bring you to do the work given you by obedience or by Providence, wholly, steadily, intelligently, courageously, cheerfully. We make retreats either to find out our vocation or to enable us better to do the work of our vocation' (*Waters that Go Softly*, ch. vii., p. 75).

Hopkins worked through the exercises annually for his twenty-one years in the Society, and began to write a commentary on them. The Directory to the Exercises makes it clear that the chief aim of a Jesuit's continued use of them is that he may be equipped to give retreats to laymen; but this Hopkins rarely, if ever, did. His special application to the Exercises was more probably for his own purposes and seems to indicate an overtender anxiety about his vocation; and in particular it is likely that according to the suggestion of the Directory (ch. x. § 13) he meant to govern much of his life by the Ignatian methods of election, and that all his major decisions—whether to continue writing poetry, whether to make attempts to publish it, whether to learn Welsh etc.—were deliberately made by them.

'The exercises,' it has been said, 'are not a manual of perfection, but a manual of election.' They are a discipline designed for the practical guidance of missionaries and teachers. They are in no sense a school of mysticism. Hopkins was not a mystic; he was not in the narrower sense a contemplative. His vocation in the Society was a practical one, and he knew this when he joined it. The difficulty for him and for his superiors was to find the specific work he was to do. The continual changes in his appointments—Roehampton, London, Oxford, Liverpool, Stonyhurst and finally Dublin—show this uncertainty only too well. One of his contemporaries in Dublin said of him: 'Never was a squarer man in a rounder hole.' A similar lack of success is found in the many articles, essays and books which he planned to publish, but never apparently finished. He did not know what his vocational work was to be. The letters show how commonly and how bitterly he felt disappointment and failure. His practical life was lived in an almost perpetual state of crises. Yet in spite of all this he had a persistent and passionate devotion to the Society. To regret his membership of it is as useless as to regret the early death of Keats. 'There is death in that hand.'

He was not by training likely to become a mystic: nor by nature. There is nothing in the poems to show that he felt that immediate and personal *presence* of God, a consciousness of which is common to the mystics and those who can achieve the more advanced states of contemplative prayer. There is nothing of that disturbing intimacy in the love of God which is the mark of St. Theresa or St.

John of the Cross. His awareness of God is mediated in happiness by man or nature or the details of Catholic dogma; in unhappiness by the feeling of alienation, which can be overcome only by activity of his own: 'I feel thy finger and find thee.' Nothing in the letters is more moving than his confession to Bridges about 'The Deutschland':

'I may add for your greater interest and edification that what refers to myself in the poem is all strictly and literally true and did all occur; nothing is added for poetical padding.'

It is God's terror and majesty which is chiefly localised: 'Thou knowest the walls, altar and hour and night.' The physical pain of that moment is chiefly remembered. There is no familiar acceptance of God's presence: 'His mystery must be instressed, stressed. ...' Faith is sustained by an effort of intellect and will. In all this his experience, intense though it was, is the common experience of Christians; its central points are the conflict between the fear of God and the love of God, and the attempt to interpret an inscrutable will.

It is surprising that many Catholic critics have drawn an analogy between the 'terrible' sonnets and the 'dark night of the soul' of St. John of the Cross. The dark night is a defined period in a long and specialised life of contemplative prayer. The experience behind these sonnets is more elementary and universal: there is nothing of the hunger which follows on the withdrawal of unique favours. Unique favours have never been granted. Dixon's phrase 'terrible pathos' could never have been applied to the mystics; and indeed the pathos, though not non-Christian, is not specifically Christian. It is nearer in temper, as Poem 50[1] explicitly states, to Jeremiah or to Job. And also it is worse than useless to wish that the experience behind these poems had never been: it is to wish him all undone, relegated to unremitting rural gaiety.

In one vitally important way his Ignatian devotions intensified an already existing habit. Even as an undergraduate and an Anglican he was in morals over-scrupulous; and this scrupulosity must have been accentuated by the practice of the 'particular examen,' the detailed method of self-examination which St. Ignatius designed for his followers. The examen is guarded about with cautions against this very fault; and it is precarious without the evidence of the lost spiritual diary to guess how far and how often under the guidance of these cautions Hopkins was able after minute self-examination to achieve a confidence that he was forgiven. But it is known that he frequently performed long and exacting penances imposed not by his director, but by himself; and many of the poems have across them a shadow of guilt, while others (like the sonnets on Patience and Peace) show the opposing passion for the means to evade it. In this also his experience was of a conflict common to all Christians, certainly directed and heightened by the Jesuit discipline, but neither artificially fostered by it nor absent without it.

These items in his religious experience, the acute sense of sin and resulting conflict between love and fear; the feeling of alienation from a majestic and transcendent God with a correlative deep and sudden tenderness at its removal; the sense of failure to interpret the will of God in practical life with a proportionate anxiety to be able to do so—these items are not all by any means; but they are the most simple, they are those which his discipline brought into greatest prominence, and they were the direct origin of some of his greatest poems.

NOTE

1 'Thou art indeed just, Lord'.

83. C. Day Lewis, 'Records of a Great Poet', *New Republic*

22 May 1935, p. 52

It would be no exaggeration to call Gerard Manley Hopkins the strangest phenomenon of Victorian England. His mind, as revealed in these letters, in its reverence for 'character' and conservatism, was almost solid Victorian: his spirit was that of a medieval ascetic: his poetry, which was more equally the product of mind and spirit than that of any other Victorian writer, bears the indelible imprint of the exile.

That is one reason why he appeals so strongly to contemporary English poets. More so even than Eliot. For wheras Eliot's work is not so much something rootless as something uprooted, Hopkins suffered the more terrible exile of the man born out of his time. . . .

84. Bernard Kelly, *The Mind and Poetry of Gerard Manley Hopkins*

Ditchling (Sussex), 1935, (a) pp. [1]–[4], (b) pp. [14]–[19]

'Bernard Kelly was a poet, a profound philosopher, and a quiet, reserved and gentle man who died of TB shortly after or even during the War' (private information from Conrad Pepler, OP).

This unpaginated long essay was one of several sensitive pieces of writing by Kelly about Hopkins (for an earlier one, see *Blackfriars*, October 1933). According to Bottrall, *Hopkins Casebook* (London, 1975), it was privately printed 'under Jesuit auspices.' See also No. 85.

(a)
To a generation of poets very anxiously concerned for sincerity, intensity, and actuality of psychological fact came, a few years ago, the first printed volume of Father Hopkins' poetry, as a curiously ambiguous sign. Fifty years behind in time, he is probably at least fifty more ahead of the present in both spirit and achievement. His technique established a mastery, complete in its kind, in uses of language with which many of the most daring modern poets are no more than experimenting. Unhappily there is no room here to discuss his technique. But the moral character of his poetry is a synthesis of what is found in modern verse as isolated and arduous maxims: ('moral' by analogy for that in which poetry is subject to precept, to informing, disciplinary principles to which it is answerable and by which it has its perfection). Sincerity, a unity and clarity of character, forged in him by no light effort of the soul, is the mark of Hopkins the man, and is also the mark of his poetry, in which it is closely allied to that intensity and psychological actuality I have mentioned. His actuality can be seen best from a passing comparison with a great poet of an entirely different order, Francis Thompson. Where Thompson says:

I fled Him, down the arches of the years;
I fled Him, down the labyrinthine ways
  Of my own mind; and in the mist of tears
I hid from Him,...

Hopkins cries in a similar circumstance:

I wake and feel the fell of dark, not day.
What hours, O what black hoürs we have spent
This night! what sights you, heart, saw; ways you went!
And more must, in yet longer light's delay.

Arches, labyrinth, mist. These metaphors become in the sharpness
of the comparison theatrical properties for the masque of physical
flight, a masque which removes, and does not bring nearer, the
reality of spiritual flight. Hopkins walks in the deeps on which this
superstructure of imagery has been built; and his cry is exactly of
that spiritual pain which Thompson has softened, and did
habitually crowd out of his mind, by imagery. Thompson names
tears; Hopkins never had need to name them.

And intensity:* from the four lines quoted the weight of each
word may be felt, its stress falling on the mind and the emotions, to
be greater than that of common speech or of common poetry. This
intensity led him to metrical discoveries and grammatical uses
which have made him unduly difficult to many readers. He is not
likely to remain so for long, for the yardstick is relaxing its tyranny
of English metre, and the grammar of poetry is undergoing
interesting comparisons with the grammar of common speech. For
poetry takes its language from common speech directly, and not by
way of literary prose, and it perfects that language rightfully in a
way different from that of the philosopher or the litterateur. And it
is natural that poetry written to be spoken aloud, as Hopkins' was,
should avail itself of any liberties of common speech that suit its
purpose.

His sincerity will not easily be shown from a few extracts, for it
is too profound a quality to be adequately illustrated by anything
less than his whole work. By sincerity I mean rather more than
'saying what you mean' or 'meaning what you say', more too than
'saying what you feel as and how you feel it' in the modern
clinico-poetic manner. I mean, as I have said, a unity and clarity of
character, and it is the clarity here that makes the unity. What is
required for this clarity? The question involves a very great deal

that is perhaps best explained by talking about something else. One note here: the virtues of a Christian soul are not so separate that when two or more are become principles of a particular life they can easily be distinguished within that life. What is found in the concrete case is a character, formed by virtues certainly, but having in its acts a unity not easily specified in any instance as of this or that virtue separately. And this unity becomes sometimes of the whole life and of every act of it, even of the minor and indifferent. In such a character the effect of the Catholic priesthood is necessarily profound. There is very little in the latter life of Father Hopkins that has not intimate and vital reference to his priesthood, and study confirms the same of his poetry. Of the nature of his sincerity, then, it may be said that any act or utterance of his tended to imply, and by implication to express, his whole character; which is what I mean by unity. And that unity was not an accident of temperament or of physical constitution, but was achieved in him by the light, the courage and the discipline of his intelligence; which is what I mean by clarity....

(b)

...It ['The Windhover'] is the masterpiece of his metrical revision of the sonnet form. It has all the power and velocity of his mental creation. It wears the character of that joy of the senses which is the unmistakable Hopkins. Those students of poetry who find the analysis of metre dull must remember that in Hopkins each metrical discovery has the value of a formal excitement allied to his creative mind. The names he gives to his particular inventions are evidence of this. The donnish metrician does not call a handful of syllables flung against the metre of a line to give pause and echo to its movement *Outrides*; and *Paeans*, accepted from the Greek, is a loud and lovely word. A dead measure was of no use to Hopkins. His scansion is alive with values in movement. But what is more important to the less technical reader is his use of the senses by sound and image, and the life they receive in the poem by its driving intellectual force.

Returning to the beginning, patient of accidental obscurities, (accidental because we read the printed word and do not hear the poem spoken aloud as it was meant to be) we clear the ground by another reading. We find the rush of glorious words 'kingdom of daylight's dauphin' to mean 'dauphin of the kingdom of daylight', and move more securely in its rhythm as its grammar discloses itself. The juxtaposition of 'skate' and 'bow-bend' loses its absurd suggestion (our fault, our own absurdity) of an angler landing a fish on a rod bent double, and yields of its own accord the bending flight of the skater and the smooth skim of the ice. But the first lines of the sestet present a real difficulty, the difficulty of intense thought alive and aloud in words that clamour disturbingly on every joy of the senses. What is 'here', what is 'Buckle', what is 'fire', and why the emphasis of 'and', so small a word?

Firstly 'here' is not an exclamatory to attract attention, as the more vulgar 'hi' or 'oy'. It is there in the poem with work to do, and in the most important position of the line. It is a directive. To explain it will partly explain the word which follows. The poem opened with the poet in the act of seeing the windhover. Behind the masterly achievements of the bird on the wing the poet was watching unseen until he appeared at the end of the octet. 'My heart in hiding Stirred for a bird,...' and the poet, grasping the valiant beauty of the bird in his mind, exclaimed, 'the achieve of, the mastery of the thing!' 'Here', then, is in the poet's mind. He clutched at the beauty of the bird, crying aloud at its mastery. But now he commands,

> Brute beauty and valour and act, oh, air,
>   pride, plume, here Buckle!

Buckle, loud, bright, impetuous word, bidding the union closer. It was the poet first, in the act of sensation, who seized the bird. It is the bird now, present in the senses, who is commanded to lock in the embrace of the mind; the bird itself in its own power and act present in the image of it.

...*and* the fire that breaks from thee then, a billion Times told lovelier, more dangerous, O my chevalier!...

The peril and the beauty of the windhover inform, are one with, the peril and the beauty of the poet's mind, who sees and knows the bird in the dapple-dawn of daylight's kingdom. A billion times told lovelier, more dangerous, O my chevalier! The incalculable splendours of the mind meeting beauty are to be found again in Hopkins, and 'more dangerous' will be seen to be no mere epithet for valiant movement.

There it is. You may accept less from the poem, but behind it will always be the knowledge (unimaginable knowledge, almost claiming the title of mystery) of the mind in its act of knowing;

knowledge itself shining in the act of poetic creation, that shone before abstractly in the delicate precisions of Aristotle, of St Thomas, of Scotus, of the theologians he knew.

No wonder of it. . . .

The theologian which is the poet in him, here as everywhere one and the same person, explains as St Thomas might have explained, saving their differences of manner, that the intelligibility of things is in their act. It is from the act of ploughing that we know the plough. Embers blue-bleak, things dead, things bleak for lack of life, fall shining into the mind, gall themselves, expending a splendour in the act of change (act in which the world, perpetually losing its being, shines to the mind in dying) that, lost now to the thing, lives in the beholder's mind for ever. The beauty and dismay loud in the sound of those last two lines are the dismay of men in the brittle beauty of this world, that, being beauty still, lives chiefly in Christ and no one else, but in this world yields its joy only in *articulo mortis. . . .*

NOTE

* I mean the intensity of his utterance, not necessarily the utterance of intense emotions; an intensity made by the mind in the force of its creation, and visible in a condensation of grammar and of image, in the power his words and images are made to carry. A far better example is 'The Windhover'.

85. Bernard Kelly, 'Hopkins in the Nineteen Thirties', *G.K.'s Weekly*

10 October 1935, pp. 23–4

G.K.'s Weekly (1925–38), edited by G.K. Chesterton, was the *New Witness* revived (see No. 14). This article led to a correspondence about Hopkins, which included the remark 'The twentieth century, which worships oddness for its own sake, accepts him as a major prophet; his own, a saner generation, ignored him' (24 October, p. 70).

That the technical innovations of Gerard Manley Hopkins have given to many modern poets an impulse not altogether well considered or even genuinely poetic is a critical commonplace. It is easier to name at random a critic who has made the remark than it is to name one who hasn't. But it would be a pity to dismiss Hopkins as a technical experimenter whose experiments are thought by many to have been unsuccessful and whose example it is perilous to follow. In any case one of the most important maxims of his artistic conscience was 'to admire and do otherwise,' so that the blame for bad Hopkinese cannot very well rest with him. The scope of the impulse he has given is a little wider than his revision of the rules of metre, and its incidence has coincided with phases of poetic mood most likely to be sensitive to it. It certainly appears that it will be many years before our minds are cool enough to consider Hopkins objectively, dispassionately, and with the calm air of scholarly research. And there are some of us who feel quite strongly that even then we would like to die with some of the old blood still flowing in our veins. What is this impulse? Short of rhapsody, we shall have to be a little abstract. There is nothing else for it.

Firstly it will be noticed that Hopkins has an aversion to pomposity, bombast and rhetoric that at once puts him in touch with the post-war mood. People who were beginning to like T.S. Eliot found that a great many of the prejudices they might have had to Hopkins had already been (more or less painlessly) extracted. Secondly he has, in verses that from any other hand would have been merely devotional, an intensely theological excitement wedded to the poetic excitement. A rare enough thing at any time, but it came like a draught of rare and authentic wine to a generation that would far rather have stuck to its own despair than accept anything that had not the unforgettable flavour of the real. Incidentally of course his popularity must have been very largely helped by his own close acquaintance with despair. Of the shorter poems those which knock most stuffing out of the reader are bare-fist struggles against despair in the very last extremity. They are victories but not the sort of victories one wags romantic flags over. And a third point is that he does knock the stuffing out of his reader. A noble thing. A salutary thing. Those who prize their stuffing can't read him.

There are many more virtues which might be enumerated, but by far the most difficult to analyse and at the same time perhaps the most accidentally significant is the quality of his sensibility... His feeling, precisely as feeling, is exactly that which is exceedingly highly prized by the younger poets. It may be true that it would be as highly prized at any other time (I think it would, but we must decide that in fifty years or so); the point is that it is certainly highly prized now. A quality of feeling such as when he says:

> Thrush's eggs look little low heavens, and thrush
> Through the echoing timber does so rinse and wring
> The ear, it strikes like lightnings to hear him sing;

or:

> ...sheer plod makes plough down sillion
> Shine, and blue-bleak embers, ah my dear,
> Fall, gall themselves, and gash gold-vermilion.

the single line:

> I wake and feel the fell of dark, not day.

or the quatrain:

> O I admire and sorrow! The heart's eye grieves
> Discovering you, dark tramplers, tyrant years.
> A juice rides rich through bluebells, in vine leaves.
> And beauty's dearest veriest vein is tears.

has a great deal more in it than a richness of the senses and an ability to describe that richness. The extreme of a pleasurable feeling, says the philosopher (but it's quite easy to test), is painful. The joy of beauty in Hopkins is always at that point where a little more would be unbearable. There are places in which without a doubt it has become unbearable, and the whole of the poet's force is gathered in protest. And the point of this is that if you choose to take Hopkins as a poet mainly of the senses you can get sufficient kick out of him to take you over from one phase of adolescence to another. This is obviously what has happened to many of his imitators.

Hopkins is not a merely 'nature' poet, not a poet mainly of the senses as Keats too often was, not a poet of one predominant mood as I still think Eliot is, not a metaphysical poet in the sense of seventeenth century metaphysical pleasantry. Really to name him you must call him a theological poet, a poet who had to live his metaphysics and not merely amuse his friends with them. And he was a priest. The fact is not merely a marginal note. It is very deeply connected with the quality of his sensibility. His deep study of Duns Scotus, the Franciscan theologian of whom everyone has heard but whom practically no one has read, had made available to him an interpretation of natural beauty in the light of the Incarnation as a source of many of the most startling beauties of his poetry. Moreover he could not escape the Incarnation in his daily life even if he wanted to.

He said Mass every morning, just as any other priest does. And in the meantime he did not cease to be a poet. These four things pressed together, and would admit of only one ultimate solution: his sensitiveness, his active impulse to poetic creation, his theological understanding of certain divine intimacies in physical beauty, the inescapable fact of the Incarnation in his daily life. They pressed for one solution, but no amount of pressing could make that solution easy. Compromise was more than unacceptable to Hopkins. It was practically unthinkable. No amount of necessity to make a working synthesis of life would permit him to dim for a moment any of those values he held to be absolute. He could not relinquish artistic values to ease the tension of religious values. Neither could he cease from first-rate religious effort to ease the flow of poetry. If there had been about him just one trace of mental sloth, one scrap of ability to put up with the second-rate, the highly accentuated spiritual conflicts of his later poetry might never have arisen. And he might have filled as many volumes as Swinburne and done as much harm. But he could not accept the second-rate. His example has stimulated an authentic tang in many of the young poets whom so many people dislike.

Absolutely speaking there is no reason that a great fecundity of sensuous delight, provided it is part of the less selfish delight of the mind, should not be a positive help to religious discipline. It is possible. But by speaking absolutely we tend to overlook the rigour of discipline that is needed to make the senses, especially if they are peculiarly rich, minister to the incomparably greater splendours of the mind (which, if it is strong enough, includes them). The only really workable solution, which is also the only first-rate and ultimate solution, is sacrifice. Sacrifice is the most difficult thing in the world. But it is also the most fecund thing in all the fecundities that really matter. It does not produce smooth pentameters by the quart, but it does produce a sensibility pruned to the naked sanctity of the real. A sensibility which responds not so much to the urge of self expression as to the sometimes almost unendurable vitality of truth. There is still quite a lot to be learned from Hopkins.

86. Christopher Devlin, 'The Ignatian Inspiration of Gerard Hopkins', *Blackfriars*

December 1935, pp. 887–900

Christopher Devlin (1907–61) was one of the exceptional talents of the Society of Jesus. Educated at Stonyhurst, he joined the Society in 1926, taught at Jesuit schools, and studied at the Gregorian University in Rome 1935–9. A private poet himself, he found Hopkins (and hence Scotus— see his article in *New Verse*, April 1935) of special interest. He published works on Southwell and Smart, and edited Hopkin's sermons in 1958. He was a great friend of Humphry House, and originally was to have completed the biography of Hopkins which the latter started, but cancer caused his early death.

Blackfriars was founded by the English Dominicans in 1913, and although mainly religious did carry articles of literary interest.

So much has been written about the effect of Gerard Hopkins' vocation on his poetry that it may seem tedious to say anything more. Yet when the sum of things said has established a first-class misunderstanding, it is tantalising, if not requisite, to attempt a reconciliation.

Assuming, then, that Jesuits are provided with a mould *in which each after his own fashion may mould himself* (please note italics for subsequent reference), that mould being the Spiritual Exercises, and assuming further that the poet could not change his character without in some way changing his poetry, a double question arises, making room for two misunderstandings. First, as to the importance of the change—was it an inside transformation or merely an outside limitation? Secondly, as to its quality—was it for better or worse not only in Hopkins but in the general development of poetic expression?

The answer to both, which avoids alike religious enthusiasm and anti-religious dyspepsia, is that the Exercises were circumstances which channelled the poet's working just as other sets of circumstances, poverty, blindness, war, etc., have done to other poets, so that their importance though considerable is not strictly *poetic*; they make the critical occasions but are not the intimate origin of poetic thought. Their qualitative effect therefore is indifferent; not bad, because helping perhaps that chastity of mind and spare tautness of diction so much admired to-day; but hardly good because of repressions, etc. So: indifferent. If not the Jesuit training, some other thread would have assisted results poetically equivalent however widely different in other respects. This answer is balanced, and likely to prove the acceptable one. So it seems relevant to point out that it is wrong. Especially since it would certify a too extreme reaction to the original misstatement that Hopkins was a mystic in the same sense as St. John of the Cross.

I say then that the Exercises were not the occasion but the origin of Hopkins' poetic thought, and by the Exercises I mean: (1) his assimilation of them, (2) the consequent out-pouring of the Holy Spirit through this His chosen channel—'Digitus Dei est hic'....

But now, having established as I think beyond question that the Exercises formed, for better or for worse, the very stuff and not merely the accidental channel of Hopkins' poems, the next question arises: Was it for better or for worse?

The accusation that it was for worse rests on the contention that Hopkins' spiritual outlook was too subjective, too morbidly preoccupied with his own progress in perfection, his own doubts and fears about salvation, instead of with the Grandeur of God which ought to put such niggling self-scrutinies into the shade; and this criticism of Hopkins is generalized into a criticism of the disintegrating effect of the Exercises upon post-reformation spirituality. It will be best to recognize at first what there is of truth in this. There is undoubtedly in Hopkins a strain of something narrow and almost morbid. It seems to be a sort of absorption with pain, combined with scrupulosity, a struggling with God as in a sick-room with the blinds down, which is reminiscent of Kierkegaard. There is a hint of it in the opening of 'The Wreck of the Deutschland'—'Thou *mastering* me,' and it is supposed to come out most noticeably in the 'terrible sonnets' towards the end of his life as the expression of frustrated hopes and desires. Before dealing with the 'terrible sonnets' there are three things to be said:

(1) There is poem upon poem from the beginning to the end of his published works, from 'The world is charged with the grandeur of God' to 'Enough! the Resurrection, a heart's clarion!' which show that if there is a strain of scrupulosity in Hopkins it is certainly not the dominant one.

(2) To connect scrupulosity with the subjectivist trend of post-Cartesian thought by way of the 'Examination of Conscience' proposed by St. Igantius is a 'gaff' almost too crass to be taken seriously. The 'Examination of Conscience' is only a slightly more methodical form of an elementary piece of common sense designed to safeguard not only one's spiritual but even one's temporal advancement, used by Christians from the earliest times as well as by such extravert Deists as Benjamin Franklin. Since conscience is only the emotionless indication of right reason in moral questions, the examining of one's conscience has no connection with any kind of psychoanalytical introspection into one's consciousness. The especial significance of the Examination for Religious is that they have vowed themselves in marriage to Christ Our Lord, and must therefore be careful that that vow does not become undermined. But the Examination can also be usefully applied to correcting slovenly habits of mind and body.

(3) It is possible that Hopkins may have tended to dwell too much on the 'Consideration of one's Sins' which comes early in the first week of the Exercises. It is even possible that some directors in giving the Exercises may have encouraged him in this, but that is not likely nor would it have much importance, because a Jesuit priest is to a great extent his own spiritual director, and it is only towards the end of his life that any profound sadness becomes noticeable in Hopkins' poems. But the important thing to note is

that the whole scheme of the Exercises militates against sadness, self-scrutiny and subjectivism. The remorse of the first week is drowned in the mercy of God, and in its stead emerge the shining resolves of the second week. After that the eye of the soul is kept exclusively fixed upon Christ in the Gospels. The second half of the second week is devoted to the example of Our Lord in his preaching life, by the villages and roadsides and waters of Galilee. The third week is the Passion. But even the Passion is to be considered not so much as the effect of our sins but as the perfect manifestation of His love for us. Then comes the fourth week, the Risen Life, where scars are turned to radiance and we are bidden to cast off sorrow, think joyous thoughts and see how Christ in perfect joy uses all the playful devices of friendship to console his friends. The effects of these last three weeks are summed up in the words, 'Illuminare—Confortare—Transformare.' After that comes a contemplation on the Love of God of which it has been said, and the lives and writings of many saints of the Society of Jesus bear it out, that it is capable of lifting a soul to the highest possible point of prayer. Moreover it is in this spirit and in the spirit of the fourth week that those who live by the Exercises are bidden to live; and they are to return to the considerations of the first week only when it is necessary to offset by their own nothingness the goodness and sweetness of God. And it seems to me that a careful reading of Hopkins' poems shows that if he exceeded these instructions it was not to any very great extent.

Thus, though I admit there was a morbid strain in Hopkins' nature (in whose is there not?) I do not think the 'terrible pathos' of the last sonnets is best explained by it. The explanation is that Hopkins, after he had ceased for the most part to find verbal inspiration in the Exercises, did not cease but rather continued more intensely to *live* them. And their effects, increasingly now metamorphosed by his own psychological and physiological states, such as loneliness, sleeplessness, etc., are still profoundly present in his poems, not in strict but in quite remarkable chronological order.

Thus the Public Life of Our Lord (second half of the second week) comes out clearly in the poems during the years after his ordination. He does not write about Christ, in a manner he *is* Christ comforting sinners, and the bugler-boy is a boy Christ, and the farrier is Christ too, and so are all the others, as He said He would be, 'in the least of these my brethren.' But woe comes on apace.

As in the inner life of every great soul who is striving for the closest possible union with Christ there comes Gethsemane before Olivet, so there came the third week to Gerard. It came to him most overwhelmingly in Ireland. He makes no mention of the Passion; perhaps—there is evidence in the Diaries—he imagined the bodily pain too keenly to speak about it. He does not write about the Agony in the Garden, but in a manner he lives it. It was not the 'Dark Night of the Soul' but it was just desolation as St. Ignatius describes it.

Voco desolationem omne contrarium (consolationi) ut, obtenebrationem animae, turbationem in illa, motionem ad res infimas ac terrenas, inquietudinem variarum agitationum et tentationum, moventem ad diffidentiam, sine spe, sine amore; cum se reperiat anima totam pigram, tepidam, tristem, et veluti separatam a Creatore ac Domino suo.[1]

Previously in his loneliness among men he had had consolation from God, reassuring pledges of his marriage-vow, but now he has desolation. In everything the reverse side is presented. As consolation shaped his rhythm before, so now does desolation. They are still love-poems, but a hopeless, unsatisfied love that turns to bitterness in the mouth. All the signs are there. 'Darkness'd soul,' says St. Ignatius. And Hopkins says, 'Dark heaven's baffling ban'...'O what black hours we have spent.' 'Tumult in the soul': 'My cries heave, herds-long.' 'Self-disgust': 'Selfyeast of spirit a dull dough sours.' 'As it were separation from God': 'Cries like dead letters.' And the causes? St. Ignatius says, either our own tepidity, or else a mysterious visitation of God, even an attack by the Devil permitted by God to cleanse the soul for Himself.

Dark heaven's baffling ban bars or hell's spell thwarts.

God's most deep decree bitter would have me taste.

And the remedies? St. Ignatius says, to stand firmly and endure: 'Patience, hard thing!' etc.—and to recall past favours and consider how God is sure to come back soon: 'let joy size at God knows when to God knows what; whose smile...,' etc.

In these poems it cannot honestly be said that there is any absolute tragedy, any more than there was an absolute tragedy in

Gethsemane on Maundy Thursday evening. Gerard knows that it is only '*as it were* (veluti) a separation'; he knows the reason for it, however hurt and baffled at the time he is; and he knows the remedies and employs them. He knows as he knew fourteen years ago, only far more vividly now, that some day he will come to find the Risen Jesus who is now so carefully disguised:

> The keener to come at the comfort for feeling the combating keen.

And we know that it was so. The glorious paean on 'The Comfort of the Resurrection' comes after the 'terrible sonnets' and even if the joy of that is dimmed by the long wait afterwards for death, we know that his last words were: 'I am so happy, I am so happy.' I repeat that these sonnets are love-poems in a far deeper sense than his earlier ones. And it is misleading at the least to say that there is 'nothing specifically Christian about them.' I do not think that in many, if any, 'not specifically Christian' writings you will find such hints of the marriage-bond with God-made-Man as in such lines as:

> Brothers and sisters are in Christ not near.

> Mary, mother of us, where is your relief?

> To dearest him that lives, alas! away.

NOTE

1 'I call "desolation" everything that is contrary to the third rule,—as a darkening of the soul, trouble of mind, movement to base and earthly things, restlessness of various agitations and temptations, moving to distrust, loss of hope, loss of love: when the soul feels herself thoroughly apathetic, tepid, sad, and as it were separated from her Creator and Lord' (*Spiritual Exercises*, ed. Joseph Rickaby, London, 1915, p. 69).

87. F.R. Leavis, 'Doughty and Hopkins', *Scrutiny*

December 1935, pp. 316–17

This is a review of *Charles Doughty: a Study of his Prose and Verse* by Anne Treneer and *Selected Passages from 'The Dawn in Britain'*, ed. Barker Fairley. Charles Doughty (1843–1926), traveller and writer (in eccentric English), was best known for his *Travels in Arabia Deserta* (1888), which Hopkins stigmatized for its 'affectation' of style (*Letters to Bridges*, p. 284).

The minor fashion to find a parallel with Hopkins seems to have been quashed by this article.

To find Doughty in his dealings with the English language at all akin to Hopkins is to betray a complete inappreciation of Hopkins's poetry. It should not have been necessary to say this, but plainly it is. The word is being passed round that Doughty and Hopkins, Victorian rebels, will go bracketed (Blake-Burns, Dryden-Pope) down to posterity. They are both extravagantly and wilfully odd, uncouth, crabbed, and defiant of common English usage—that seems to be the argument. 'One looks forward,' says Miss Treneer, and she has the endorsement of eminent reviewers, 'to the day when young poets and critics such as Mr. Cecil Day Lewis will number the author of *Adam Cast Forth* with Wilfred Owen, Gerard Manley Hopkins and T.S. Eliot among their immediate ancestors.'

Now to appreciate Hopkins is to lose all sense of oddity; but Doughty, in the very nature of his achievement, remains insistently and essentially odd—that is why there is not the slightest danger of his having any influence at all, in verse or prose. He is a nobly massive eccentric, a great English Character. Hopkins is central and a great English poet. His apparent oddity disappears because he is working in the spirit of the living English language; all his efforts are to realize this spirit in all its vigour and at its highest intensity. He condemned archaism as manifesting a wrong attitude towards the language—the language as spoken in the poet's time. It is significant that Bridges, who would have nothing to do with his friend's 'oddity,' should have gladly acclaimed Doughty's rebellion against 'Victorian English': Doughty was merely odd and eccentric and of scholarly interest and not in the least disturbing (though he is a rich and an easy subject for academic treatises and lectures). At the best, with the aim he served, he could succeed merely in creating an impresively eccentric monument. To talk of his refreshing or renovating the language is absurd; there was not the slightest chance of his having any effect whatsoever upon it or upon subsequent literature (if there had been he would have needed denouncing as a pernicious influence).

Even to talk, with Miss Treneer, of his effecting 'a scholar's enrichment of current language' is a radical misrepresentation. Doughty pursued his word-hoarding in a spirit of rejection of current language: that comes out forcibly in his constant, extreme and wanton defiance of English idiom and word-order. He collected his words (and both Miss Treneer and Mr. Barker Fairley insist that it was individual words he was interested in) because they were strange, odd, antique and not current. What advantage did he gain by putting 'spirituous' for 'spiritual,' 'charret' for 'chariot,' 'drenched' for 'drowned,' 'girdlestead' and 'middle' for 'waist,' 'contrast' for 'resist,' 'maidenchild' for 'girl,' 'rumour' for 'noise,' 'carol' for 'dance,' or by writing: 'The truant smiling Beduins have answered again that they could no tales'? His style, in prose and verse, carries to an extreme the spirit of Victorian romanticism—except that, as Miss Treneer says, 'he did not spend his time sighing for heroic days, he tried to recreate them.' And he does marvellously succeed in making Victorian romanticism look truly heroic. But the heroism that affects the English language, English poetry and us is Hopkins's. . . .

88. W.H. Gardner, 'The Wreck of the Deutschland', *Essays and Studies*

Vol. XXI, Oxford, 1935, pp. 124–52

W.H. Gardner (1902–69) was a schoolteacher until 1946, when he took up university teaching in South Africa. He became a Catholic as a result of his study of Hopkins, and his book *Hopkins: a Study of Poetic Idiosyncrasy in Relation to Poetic Tradition* (2 vols, 1944–9) is still the most comprehensive work on the poet.

According to Dunne, this article was actually published in 1936.

I

... Alliteration, assonance, partial assonance, interior rhyme, half-rhyme, and subtle vocalic 'scales'[a] are all employed not merely as ornamental devices but as definite structural modes in the making of a complex expressional rhythm. Their employment is not regular and monotonous as it would be if determined by a prearranged and inviolable tone-pattern. Alliteration in Hopkins, for instance, is used with far greater imaginative purpose than in either Langland or Swinburne. In 'The Wreck,' alliteration and other phonal correspondences are used in conjunction with a free, creative handling of syntax as a means of giving emphasis to the rhythm—intensity, colour, and precision to the diction. The unit of variation is the 'musical phrase' rather than the line or stanza, and the result is a unique poetic design, a verbal tapestry of brilliant texture.

We may now illustrate the poet's preoccupation with expressional rhythm by quoting in full the first stanza in Part the Second:

> Sóme find me a swórd; sóme
> The flánge and the ráil; fláme
> Fáng, or flóod' goes Déath on drúm,
> And stórms búgle his fáme.
> But wé dréam we are roóted in eárth—Dúst!

Flesh fálls within síght of us, wé, though our flówer the saríe,
  Wáve with the méadow, forgét that there múst
The soúr scýthe críŋge, and the bléar sháre coríe.

The powerful, cumulative effect is produced by the judicious
placing of pauses and alliterative consonants (*fl*ange, *f*ang, *fl*ood;
*d*eath, *d*rum). Great emphasis is given to 'Some' at the end of line 1
and 'flame' in line 2 by means of the pause, or silent syllable, before
each. What a pregnant statement is 'Dust!' at the end of line 5! How
apt is the alliterative link with 'dream!'[b]

Again, in stanza 18, having told us how the brave nun rose like a
prophetess above the tumult of the wreck, the poet breaks out with

    Ah, toúched in your bówer of bóne
  Are you! túrned for an éxquisite smárt
Have you! máke words bréak from me hére all alóne
  Do you!—móther of béing in me, héart.

No rhythmic device could be more natural than the overflow in
these lines. As with a sob, each line stumbles and falters over the
threshold of the next. Each line borrows just two syllables of the
next, and the regularity of this encroachment sets up a vertical
cross-current of pure expressional rhythm without disturbing the
basic metre.

Now contrast the agitation of the above passage with the
restrained rhythm of the following:

    Jésu, héart's líght,
    Jésu, máid's són,
  Whát was the féast fóllowed the níght
    Thou hadst glóry of thís nún?—

Such hushed and reverential invocations should indeed be so
retarded. So, too, even grammar should yield to more important
considerations, and the expulsion of the relative pronoun after
'feast' (Hopkins had no use for the colourless, otiose word)
definitely improves the cadence.

A further device for varying the rhythm is the use of trisyllabic
run-on rhymes in the very next stanza (No. 31):

    Wéll, she has thée for the páin, for the
    Pátience; but píty of the rést of them.
  Héart, go bléed at a bítterer véin for the
    Cómfortless uŕconféssed of them—

These rhymes are not mere factitious ornament. The poet, wishing to dispense with the final pause, uses them as a substitute to mark the metrical divisions; so that in reading, while we are primarily conscious of the speech-rhythm, we are conscious also of the metre.

Lastly, the variety of rhythmic resources in this poem is no less apparent in the six-stress lines which terminate the stanzas. A typical or 'average' line would be that in stanza 6:

> And here the faithful waver, the faithless fable and miss.

But for the rest of these 'alexandrines', no two are metrically identical, and in rhythmic flexibility they show an extraordinary range. In a line like

> To flásh from the fláme to the fláme then, tower from the gráce
> to the gráce

we have a typical loping Swinburnian movement (with what seems also to be a share of that poet's peculiar vagueness); but this precise effect is never repeated. The poem is perhaps unique in the way it gives us a spice of one poet here and a flavour of some other poet there, yet never degenerates into pastiche. Never for a moment does it lose its own individuality.

II

...When all allowances have been made...it will be found that 'The Wreck of the Deutschland' has a completeness, an intellectual and emotional unity, a subtlety and variety of verbal orchestration which are unique not only in English but in the literature of the world. It is essentially a poem to be read aloud; but, like a sonata, it demands not a little interpretive skill. Its qualities are not to be gauged in one or two hasty, possibly peevish, readings. It is tart wine, but it mellows with keeping. The majority of sensitive readers will probably experience at first a mixture of attraction and repulsion. They will be attracted by what Father Lahey has called 'the many marvellous lines which spangle the whole poem'—an unfortunate saying, which gives an erroneous impression of mere accidental and extrinsic felicity; they will be repelled by the strangeness of its individual style. And it must be confessed that in an age like the present, when pedantry, preciosity, and super-self-conscious art forms are freely indulged by the intelligentsia in their reaction against outmoded ideals, when an artist is almost compelled to attach himself to some fashionable -ism and to address some special coterie—in such an age the stylized manner is immediately suspect. But it is the task of criticism to rescue the truly original artist from the atmosphere of charlatanism, to recognize and vindicate the work which, in spite of apparent oddity and eclecticism, is virtually a sincere reforging of universal modes and experiences:

> He swept what scope he was
> To sweep, and must obey.[1]

In the case of Hopkins it will be found that familiarity with his style dispels much of the strangeness without destroying the value of his innovation, without resultant triteness or the feeling that trickery has been unmasked. The infinite variety in 'The Wreck' is in some measure due to its difficulty. As we re-read the poem, we are continually surprised by new aspects of its poetry, but we do not exhaust its intellectual possibilities. In Dixon's words, it is 'enormously powerful'. It takes possession of the mind, fascinates, puzzles, exasperates, allures, and recaptures it once again. Some may be, indeed have been, disturbed by the fervent irrationalities of its Trinitarianism, Marianism, martyrolatry, and saint-worship; they may, at first, resent the insidious persuasiveness of its appeal; but they will probably be forced to agree with Longinus that 'it is not to persuasion but to ecstasy that passages of extraordinary genius carry the hearer'. To the ardent Catholic the poem must always stand as one of the loftiest expressions of both the central problem and the crowning glory of his creed—the problem of tragedy and the triumph of faith. To others it will perhaps rather suggest the tragedy of faith and the triumph of pure poetry. There are things in this poem which will never please the prejudiced, the occasional, the superficial, and the uninformed reader. Moreover, there will always be people of taste and judgement who, like Robert Bridges, will be unable to pronounce it uniformly successful. Yet to an ever-growing number of serious students of literature it will undoubtedly in due course take the rank it deserves beside the 'Nativity Ode,' 'Lycidas,' 'Intimations of Immortality,' and 'The Hound of Heaven.'

NOTES

a '... certain chimes', as he says, 'suggested by the Welsh poetry I had been reading (what they call *cynghanedd*).' *Correspondence of G.M.H. and R.W.D.*, p. 15.

b For a sensitive examination and analysis of the texture of the poem (especially of the magnificent opening stanza) see the chapter on G.M.H. in Edith Sitwell's *Aspects of Modern Poetry* (Duckworth), p. 59 et seq. [See No. 74.]...

1 'On a Piece of Music'.

89. Fr Geoffrey Bliss, 'In a Poet's Workshop': "The Woodlark" by G.M. Hopkins', *Month*

June 1936, pp. 528–35

For Geoffrey Bliss, see No. 19. This was the second of two articles on unfinished poems by Hopkins; the *Month* for February 1936 published Bliss's article discussing 'On a Piece of Music'.

Of the numerous 'fragments' found among Father Hopkins's papers after his death, this is one of the most delightful. It is also the nearest to being finished, and it is a puzzle to know why it was not finished. Some of the other incomplete poems appear to have said all that was to be said before the chosen form, sonnet or other, was filled up, a thing likely to happen with a poet of such concentrated expression; one, the 'Epithalamium,' begins perhaps too far away from its nominal subject, and seems to be reaching an *impasse* where it stops. But why not finish the 'Woodlark,' that 'tiny trickle of song-strain'? It is almost all there; only three and a half lines can certainly be said to be missing; the arrangement of the existing parts seems to need little consideration. And Hopkins must have loved this poem: his best poem, in his own judgement, was about a bird, the 'Windhover,' and he has two Skylark sonnets.

Before we set the poem down, which I am enabled to do here by the generous permission of the poet's Family and of the Oxford University Press, something must be said of the MS. This, by the kindness of Mr Gerald Hopkins, I have been allowed to study. Like all Hopkins's poetical manuscripts it is a thing of beauty as well as interest. It is written, as if to fit the subject, in a minute script on a small sheet of folded notepaper, three of the four pages being used. The poem is in nine separated passages, some of only two lines, with greater or lesser spaces left blank between them. Dr. Bridges printed these nine passages, inserting lines of dots between them, in the order of the MS., with scrupulous accuracy, changing, however, as he notes, the evidently erroneous 'sheaf' to 'sheath.'

In altering somewhat (below) the order of the passages as they stand in the MS. and in the editions, I rely (for justification) on the extremely draft-like character of the MS., and (for choice of order) partly on 'internal' considerations and a little on the habits of the bird-poet as watched by the woodside or read about in books. The numbers in the margin give the original order of the passages. Not regarding the various couplets and unfinished sentences as intended for stanzas I have had no hesitation in grouping them together, making but six stanzas in all; in forming the second of these I have detached the last couplet of the first passage from those that precede it. As to punctuation I have supplied full-stops at the end of passages where they were wanting, but otherwise have followed exactly the MS., as do the editions. It will be seen that for the three missing lines (I do not know what will be thought of me!) I have supplied lines of my own, enclosing them in rather unnecessary square brackets. The excuse for this impiety is a pious one: I would have the effect of a lovely piece of verse to be, at least for a moment, not interrupted by gaps in its strain.

THE WOODLARK

(1)   *Teevo cheevo cheevio chee:*
     O where, what can thát be?
     Weedio-weedio: there again!
     So tiny a trickle of sóng-strain;
     And all round not to be found

For brier, bough, furrow, or gréen ground
Before or behind or fár or at hand
Either left either right
Anywhere in the súnlight.

Well, after all! Ah but hark—
'I am the little wóodlark.
(4) The skylark is my cousin and he
Is known to men more than me.
(3) Round a ring, around a ring
And while I sail (must listen) I sing.

(2) To-day the sky is two and two
With white strokes and strains of the blue.
(7) The blue wheat-acre is underneath
And the braided ear breaks out of the sheath,
The ear in milk, lush the sash,
And crush-silk poppies aflash,
The blood-gush blade-gash
Flame-rash rudred
Bud shelling or broad-shed
Tatter-tassel-tangled and dingle-a-dangled
Dandy-hung dainty head.
(8) And down the furrow dry
Sunspurge and oxeye
And lace-leaved lovely
Foam-tuft fumitory.
(6) I am so véry, O só very glad

That I dó thínk there is not to be had
[Any where any more joy to be in.
(5) *Cheevio:*] when the cry within
Says Go on then I go on
Till the longing is less and the good gone.
But down drop, if it says Stop,
To the all-a-leaf of the tréetop.
And after that off the bough
[Hover-float to the hedge brow.]

(9) Through the velvety wind V-winged
[Where shake shadow is sun's-eye-ringed]
To the nest's nook I balance and buoy
With a sweet joy of a sweet joy,
Sweet, of a sweet, of a sweet joy
Of a sweet—a sweet—sweet—joy.'

Some brief justifications for the re-arrangement: and first as to the reversal in order of passages 2, 3, 4. The ornitho-biographic 4 is least of an interruption when it follows on the similar line 'I am the little Woodlark.' (But the couplet is more than ornithological; it gives us the humility and simple pride of this most contented little bird). Then 3 should precede 2, because 3 announces the song and 2 begins it. And 7 continues it, leading up to the canary-like burst of 'Tatter-tassel-tangled,' etc.; with 8 for the descant. No doubt the 5–6 passages could precede 7–8 as they happen to do in the draft of the poem; but the bird's joy is better asserted *after* it has been demonstrated in this outpour of song. To put 6 before 5 is the natural thought sequence: 'I am happy, therefore I sing,' not the other way round; and incidentally this order enables us to complete the passage with a single 'patch' verse. Then 9, the last-written passage, tells whither the bird is going 'off the bough' and makes, inevitably, the close.

Obviously to enjoy this poem to the full more is necessary than to be interested in the technique of poetry. You must have kept open eyes in the fields: have stared at the poppied wheat, delighting in the wind-confused petals coloured deep as blood and 'rash' as flame, or lifted the drooped buds to see where the crimson breaks through the pale-lipped wounds between the green; have pulled the half-plumped wheat-ears from their soft, lush sash* or sheath (as you surely did if you were ever a boy) and bitten on them till the milky juice of the unripe grain oozed out. Sunspurge and fumitory must be friends of yours, no less than the ox-eye daisy known to everyone; and above all you must love birds.

Those of my readers who do will not be loath if I make some attempt to identify the bird of this poem. It is not quite so simple a matter as it seems. The name woodlark is sometimes given to another bird than that to which it properly belongs. This other is the tree-pipit. Both birds are about the same size, the pipit being slightly the smaller, and are similar in colouring. Which of them did the poet meet on or a little before July 5, 1876, somewhere, presumably, in the valley of the Clwyd in North Wales? I plump, myself, for the tree-pipit; for the poem seems to me to fit him like a glove; yet this may be only because he is an acqaintance of mine, and the true woodlark is not. I had the good fortune, at Stonyhurst, many years ago, in company with an accomplished bird man, to watch the tree-pipit give his fascinating 'turn.' And since a tree may perhaps keep its pipit from one generation to another, I will add (for the benefit of Stonyhurst men) that this pipit-tree was an oak in Harry Meadow close to the Fell road. What I remember best is the 'balance and buoy' of the spiral descent from the tree-top; of the song only its charm and its joy linger in the mind. Afterwards my bird man found the nest for me in the hedge-bank with its marbled chocolate-purple eggs....

The metric of this poem is interesting, and illustrates well enough the single rule to which Hopkins (despite his famous preface!) reduced the laws of English prosody. It may be stated: 'Every verse contains a predetermined number of accented syllables.' (It has a scholion: in polysyllables the accent is fixed by the dictionary; on all monosyllables by the poet, at his own risk.) The rule had always been the only rule of English prosody to which no exceptions were admitted; the chief distinction in Hopkins (a firm traditionalist) being that he admitted exceptions to all the other rules more freely, and more skilfully, than most poets. He also admitted exceptions, cautiously, to the one rule's scholion: but in this, too, he was no absolute innovator.

In that rule the word *predetermined* is, manifestly, all-important; Hopkins ignored it twice, and twice only (in the 'Echoes' and the 'Epithalamium'), with results that are extremely interesting but extremely dangerous as a precedent. In this poem he observes it faithfully: the poem is in four-beat with a possible three-beat in one stanza (predetermination does not, of course, exclude *ordered* variety of the verse-lengths). The union of rigidity with infinite variety which the one-rule prosody provides makes a good basis, in this poem, for a music of lark-song type: monotonous yet perpetually changing. While the four accents persist the number of syllables varies from four in 'Fláme-rásh rúdréd,' to twelve in 'Tatter-tassel-tangled and dingle-a-dangled.' The MS. of this latter line is of great prosodic interest. It was first written:

Tassel-tangled and dingle-a-dangled

the dots marking the syllables to be accented. Hopkins similarly marked the four preceding and the next following lines; for his own private use, I think: it was necessary in this passage to be especially careful that the accents-number, the current-bass of the measure, was being strictly observed, just because here everything else was running free. But Hopkins wanted a rush of unaccented syllables at

the beginning of this line, to get the canary effect. So he added
'Tatter-' in front and deleted the dot under 'tassel.' If you hyphen
words together you may (though you need not) regard them as one
word and so escape the tyranny of the dictionary. Thus he could
now ignore the accents in 'tatter' and 'tassel' and have no accent till
'tangled' is reached. But if 'tangled' is the first accent there are only
three in the line: and that is the one thing forbidden! So he writes a
grave accent over the *e* in 'dangled' and puts a dot beneath it:

Tatter-tassel-tangled and dingle-a-danglèd

Dr. Bridges ignored this grave-accent mark: justifiably, I think;
you may accent the -ed in a case like this (see below) without
making it a full syllable.

The metre of passage 8 demands comment. It is a deliberate
slow-down after the excitement of passage 7, and is to be read in a
dainty, mincing manner. But I think it was intended to preserve the
four-beat of the rest of the poem. As it stands the first line is in
three-beat, but is perhaps incomplete. It was written (as the editor
printed it) with space enough for a word left between 'down' and
'the,' and possibly 'along' would have been added here, or 'all'
inserted before 'down.' You can also save the rule by accenting a
central pause, or even the initial 'And.' In the third line you can
save it by accenting both syllables of 'Lovely': rather a desperate
measure, but excused by the fact that '-ly' (like dang*led* in 7) is
rhymed to an accented word:

> And dówń the fúrrow drý
> Súnspúrge and óxeýe
> And láce-leáved lóvelý
> Foám-túft fúmitóry

The stanza thus illustrates most of the exceptions to the one rule,
or its scholion, admitted by Hopkins on occasion. They are: (a)
accent on a pause (or pause counted for accent), (b) accent on a run
of unaccented syllables (metrical pause), (c) on the secondary accent
in a polysyllable, (d) on a single unaccented syllable at the end of a
verse when this is rhymed with an accented syllable, and (e) the
equal division of an accent between two syllables. It may also be
noted here that Hopkins sometimes allows himself to *suppress* an
unimportant dictionary accent in such words as 'very,' 'ever,' etc.

It can well be asked how, with only one rule and plenty of exceptions to that, there will be any prosody left worthy the name. The answer is that there is none left in any hands save those of a subtle and conscientious craftsman. That is why the host of Hopkins imitators are so ineffective. But if the one rule is kept, with good reason for all exceptions; if these do not destroy the predetermined beat-count; *then* you have a prosody which differs from the English tradition only by going a little further in the direction in which it has always tended. They are some of our greatest poets who have adventured furthest with success in that direction: Shakespeare, Donne, Milton, Crashaw, Coleridge.

A note in conclusion on one of my own patch-lines which, since it seeks to imitate Hopkins, may need, as some of his lines are said to need, explanation. 'Shake shadow,' then, which is 'sun's-eye-ringed' is what you see under a big tree on a sunny day when there is a 'velvety wind.' The shadows of the leaves upon the ground shift and slide over one another; but in among them slide things more mysterious: circles of light now larger, now smaller, now dimmer, now brighter. I had often marvelled at these before I read in a book that they are images of the sun's disk formed by pinhole passages which his beams find through the 'rafts and rafts of leaves' overhead. (Such an image can be formed by a pin-hole opening in the shutter of a dark room.) The soft wind stirs the leaves; the openings between them change position, narrow or widen; and the sun-images move about and contract or dilate as the foci alter. That was the meaning of those magic moons. If only Hopkins had had occasion to crystallize them in his verse!

NOTE

★ I am only guessing that 'sash' (= frame) is another word for sheath. The Oxford Dictionary is no help.

90. W.H. Gardner, 'A Note on Hopkins and Duns Scotus', *Scrutiny*

June 1936, pp. 61–70

For Gardner, see No. 88. In reprinting this article, I have omitted the learned footnotes.

Some months ago Mr. Christopher Devlin, S.J., published in *New Verse*[1] an all-too-short article on the influence of Scotus on Hopkins. That essay, while throwing much light upon a difficult aspect of the poet's work, was probably, by reason of its compression and learned allusions, caviare to the general. The philosophy of the 'Subtle Doctor' does not lend itself to a popular exposition; but having acknowledged a certain indebtedness to Mr. Devlin, and a greater obligation to an enthusiastic Scotist, Mr. Francis Brand, S.J., I shall try to say a little more about the relationship between the Jesuit poet and a Scholastic who in many ways more 'swayed his spirits to peace' than the official philosopher and theologian of his Order—St. Thomas Aquinas.

We shall consider at greater length that significant 'fragment' No. 67— 'On a Piece of Music.' The poem is difficult, even obscure, unless it is interpreted in the light of Hopkins's ethical and metaphysical predilections; and as these predilections are implicit in all his mature poetry we shall be obliged to take a circuitous course through abstractions and then back to their concrete illustrations and tangible incarnations in the poetry.

'On a Piece of Music' makes an important distinction between formal beauty or 'the good' on the one hand, and moral beauty or 'the right' on the other. (We should note in passing that in another poem, 'To What Serves Mortal Beauty?' (No. 38), natural beauty tells us 'what good means'). But formal beauty is a mode of 'mortal beauty,' whereas moral beauty is immortal beauty—a supernatural state induced by man's willing co-operation with 'God's better beauty, grace'. Now the artistic faculty in man is an immediate activity of his individual nature, and it is necessary at this point to understand how, according to Scotus, the individual nature is determined.

Every finite being is composed of *ens et carentia*: the intrinsic degree of each thing is its lack of infinity in every natural activity, and the same intrinsic degree in several activities will connect all those activities and make them one individual nature by giving them the same direction. The Scotist principle of individuation embraces the celebrated and subtle *distinctio formalis a parte rei* or formal distinction between the individual nature and the specific or common nature (*e.g., humanitas*). That last formal determination, or *ultima realitas entis*, which restricts the specific form and completes it, is called by Scotus *haecceitas* ('thisness'). But '*Essentia creaturae est sua dependentia ad Deum*': underlying individuality and the common, specific nature is the universal Nature (a concept ultimately mystical rather than metaphysical), which expresses the unity of all created things.

All created substances, says Scotus, are immediately active, and not merely, as Aquinas says, '*mediantibus accidentibus.*' (For Aquinas the principle of individuation is *materia signata quantitate* or 'quantified matter,' and matter is the principle of passivity; but the Scotist *haecceitas* is an extension of the Aristotelian Form, and Form is the active principle). Individuality then is the direction given to natural activities by the *haecceitas*: it is the real relation between the creature and God.

Hopkins seized with delight on the Scotist principle of individuation, as we know from those poems in which he makes the activity of a thing a special element in that thing's being. First in 'Henry Purcell' (1879):

> It is the forged feature finds me; it is the rehearsal
> Of own, of abrupt self there so thrusts on, so throngs the ear.[a]

And the great stormfowl, to which Purcell is compared,

> but meaning motion fans fresh our wits with wonder.

Even more explicit is No. 34:

> Each mortal thing does one thing and the same:
> Deals out that being indoors each one dwells;
> Selves—goes itself; *myself* it speaks and spells,
> Crying *What I do is me: for that I came.*

338

But Hopkins is chiefly concerned with the finite being which has the richest individuality, man:

> Our law says: Love what are love's worthiest, were all known:
> World's loveliest—men's selves. Self flashes off frame and face.

Physical attributes are subordinate aspects of the total *haecceitas*, which in rational beings is the spring of all action and is therefore identified with the Will. It is the Will, and not the Intellect, which 'possesses' a loved object. Intellect is related to the specific, common nature of man; whereas Will is the expression of individuality. Another important point on which Scotus differs from Aquinas is that the former lays greater emphasis upon the freedom of the Will: in spite of God's essential co-operation in our every action, we are free to choose the objects of our love, the objects we would possess, our τέλος.[2] Thus in each man there is the individual element—*haecceitas*, Will, spring of action; and exerting a constant pressure on the Will is the fact that his intellectual and animal nature is really, though mysteriously, united to all men, and indeed to all creation.

In 1875 Hopkins was studying Scotus as a non-official part of his theology course, and we may understand now why he wrote in that year: 'Whenever I took in an inscape of the sea or sky, I thought of Scotus.' In 1879 he wrote to Bridges:

But as air, melody, is what strikes me most of all in music, and design in painting, so design, pattern, or what I am in the habit of calling *inscape* is what I above all aim at in poetry. Now it is the virtue of design, pattern or inscape to be distinctive...

His own nature had led him to attach great importance to individuality in things, to personality in men; and as an artist he had instinctively anticipated Mr. Ezra Pound's advice to 'make it new.' But distinctiveness or idiosyncrasy in itself has no metaphysical or moral value unless it is, as in the system of Scotus, a valuable link in the ontological argument. Mr. Devlin has already shown[b] that Hopkins's inspirational view of poetic creation roughly corresponds to the Scotist concept that the 'first act' of knowledge is intuitive, a particular 'glimpse' into the universal Nature, 'a confused intuition of Nature as a living whole'; and the vividness of the glimpse depends upon 'its nearness to the individual degree.' Hence to Hopkins an inscape was something more than a delightful sensory impression: it was an insight, by divine grace, into the ultimate spiritual reality. Scotus offered the poet an aesthetic sanction and the priest a moral justification for his inordinate attachment to poetry and the other arts. That is perhaps why Scotus so swayed his spirits to peace. Moreover the very multiplicity of individualities in the created universe was in itself a proof of God's infinity. This idea is expressed in the sestet of the sonnet (No. 34) already quoted, in which we see the most complete and successful union of the poet and the Scotist:

> I say móre: the just man justices;
> Keeps gráce: thát keeps all his goings graces;
> Acts in God's eye what in God's eye he is—
> Chríst—for Christ plays in ten thousand places
> Lovely in limbs, and lovely in eyes not his
> To the Father through the features of men's faces.

God the Son assumes *all* Nature; hence the individual, intrinsic degree of Christ sums up the degrees of all men. The whole sonnet is a poetic statement of the Scotist concept that individual substances, according to the metaphysical richness of their being, make up one vast hierarchy with God as their summit.

Finally, Hopkins saw in Scotism a noble tribute to the dignity of man. It was natural that a poet as sensuous as Keats should agree with the philosopher who emphasized the greater importance of the concrete over the abstractions of the mind and who stressed the close relation between activity and substance; equally natural that an anthropophile as great as Wordsworth himself should share the Scotist conviction that humanity is too noble a thing to be a mere lump of clay acted upon by outside forces: '*Oportet dignificare naturam humanam quantum possible.*' He would agree with Scotus that by the Aristotelian doctrine that free will is an imperfection and by the Thomistic that the will is a passive faculty—*valde vilificaretur natura humana*! Man must use his freedom of choice to perfect his individual nature 'where it fails,' to give the whole being its true direction Godwards:

> Doff darkness, homing nature knows the rest—

This brings us naturally back again to the main thesis of the poem 'On a Piece of Music,' No. 67—the distinction between 'the good' and 'the right.'

> How all's to one thing wrought!
> The members, how they sit!

The work of art, perfect in inscape and outscape, reminds us of the τυχῆς τέχνην στερχούσης[3] of the ashtrees described in the poet's early diary. It is an immediate spontaneous activity of the individual nature, or, to return to a more normal phraseology, a faithful expression of personality. But personality involves separation: the artist works by laws of his own fashioning; as Bacon says: 'he must do it by a kind of felicity (as a musician that maketh an excellent air in music), and not by rule.'

> Nor angel insight can
> Learn how the heart is hence:
> Since all the make of man
> Is law's indifference.

Natural beauty is good; but the moral theme has entered with the word 'heart.' That this word symbolizes man's attitude to divine law we know from a passage about the nun in the 'Deutschland':

> Ah! there was a heart right!
> There was single eye!

We cannot probe another's secret. Each man is alone with God. Man is a wayward creature, 'unteachably after evil'; waywardness or distinctiveness in genius is 'good' but not necessarily 'right.' By a volitional 'act of love' man's works must be directed Godwards:

> What makes the man and what
> The man within that makes:
> Ask whom he serves or not
> Serves and what side he takes.

It has recently been said[c] that Hopkins 'wished to achieve the "pure art, morally neutral," in which such interests as corybantic, sadistic images, etc., without being suppressed, can be controlled and philosophically employed.' This may mean that he wished to achieve an art in which moral and aesthetic motives would be present as base and acid are present in a salt; but if it means (as I think it does) an art which is innocent of, or 'unsullied' by, moral considerations, then we may cite this poem 'On a Piece of Music,' 'The Windhover,' etc., and all the letters as evidence to the contrary. There is an uncritical tendency to regard Hopkins as a thinly-disguised modernist in all his acts and attitudes. When he called himself a 'blackguard' he merely meant that he was not yet a saint. When he said that he always knew in his heart that Walt Whitman's mind was more like his own than any other man's living, he was signalizing a remarkable resemblance in personality (or individual degree), which made both poets express in nearer-to-prose rhythms particular 'glimpses' of Nature which are at times almost identical. But when he added: 'As Whitman is a very great scoundrel that is not a pleasant confession,' he is deploring the fact that all the make of a Whitman is indifferent to that regulative principle which is the Catholic Church. Hopkins admired in Whitman a natural beauty 'wild and self-instressed'.

> For good grows wild and wide,
> Has shades, is nowhere none;
> *But right must seek a side,*
> *And choose for chieftain one.*

The author of the 'Song of Myself' had certainly chosen a chieftain; but his name was not Christ: it was Whitman—or Demos. Therefore although he 'made known the music of his mind,

> Yet here he had but shewn
> His ruder-rounded rind.
>
> Not free in this because
> His powers seemed free to play:
> He swept what scope he was
> To sweep and must obey.

Hopkins is tackling the 'profound question treated by Duns Scotus'; he is trying to reconcile freedom and necessity. Robert Bridges, not realizing, apparently, the ethical significance of this poem, takes the stanza just quoted as the key to the whole:

No. 67 is the draft of what appears to be an attempt to explain how an artist has not free will in his creation. He works out his own nature instinctively as he happens to be made, and is irresponsible for the result.

Omit the last clause and this interpretation is true up to the point where the artist brings the will-guided intelligence to bear upon the inscape which he has taken in: he is not responsible for his peculiar mental pattern and rhythm, but he is responsible for their spiritual orientation. So long as the work of a Swinburne or a Whitman was 'morally neutral,' the Jesuit might have said

> Therefore this masterhood,
> This piece of perfect song,
> This fault-not-found-with good
> Is neither right nor wrong.

Unless the poet accepts responsibility for all the moral implications of his work and gives beauty 'back to God', his work can have no more immortal supernatural beauty

> than red or blue,
> No more than Re and Mi,
> Or sweet the golden glue
> That's built for by the bee.

Corroboration of the above exegesis will be found in that other remarkable fragment, No. 54, 'On the Portrait of Two Beautiful Young People', Stanza 7 is almost an epitome of the Scotist concept of the *haecceitas* as expressed in the Will:

> Man lives that list, that leaning in the will
> No wisdom can forecast by gauge or guess,
> The selfless self of self, most strange, most still
> Fast furled and all foredrawn to No or Yes.[d]

But in Stanza 5, allegiance to the right regulative principle is clearly stated as the *sine qua non* of a disciplined will:

> Where lies your landmark, seamark, or soul's star?
> There's none but truth can stead you. Christ is truth.

The very richness of Personality's regalia may prove a greater attraction to the Devil: 'favoured make and mind' and

> that most in you earnest eye
> May but call on your banes to more carouse.
> Worst will the best.

The worst moral diseases attack the finest spirits: and *corruptio optimi pessima*. Of no less a spirit than Whitman or Goethe Hopkins would have asked:

> What worm was here
> To have havoc-pocked so, see, the hung heavenward boughs?

To conclude, Hopkins's preoccupation with the *haecceitas* as the key to the common nature or *humanitas* (which, as Mr. Devlin says) 'is the source and object of all knowledge in man,' is well illustrated in the Purcell sonnet, the introductory rubric to which states:

The poet wishes well to the divine genius of Purcell and praises him that, whereas other musicians have given utterance to the moods of man's mind, he has, beyond that, uttered in notes the very make and species of man as created both in him and in all men generally.

NOTES

a *cf.* also the activity of 'Harry Ploughman' ('Harry bends–look!') and 'The Windhover'.

b *New Verse*, No. 14, April, 1935.

c By Mr. Geoffrey Grigson in *New Verse*, No. 14, April, 1935. I admit the element of truth in Mr. Grigson's own main statement. Hopkins's unconscious feeling was often in marked contrast to his controlled conscious thinking. (See Herbert Read: *Form in Modern Poetry*, p. 20.)

d There is an interesting application of this quatrain in Chap. VIII of *Practical Criticism*, to which it stands as an epigraph. Dr. Richards is saying that the final acceptance or rejection of a poem is an act of the will, a decision of the total personality: 'The personality stands balanced between the particular experience which is the realized poem and the whole fabric of its past experiences and developed habits of mind. What is being settled is whether this new experience can or cannot be taken into the fabric with advantage' (p. 303). Substitute real action for the vicarious action of a poem and that is what Hopkins meant.

1 See headnote to No. 82.

2 'Purpose', 'aim'.

3 'Chance loves art'. (See *Journals*, 2nd, edn, p. 182.)

91. W.B. Yeats, Introduction, *The Oxford Book of Modern Verse*

Oxford, 1936, pp. 39–40

Yeats, three years from death, was only moderately sympathetic towards modern poets. He included seven of Hopkins's more immediately attractive poems in this anthology, which Auden later called 'the most deplorable volume ever issued' by its publishers (quoted in Richard Ellmann, *Eminent Domain*, New York, 1967, p. 118). Ellmann points out that Yeats regarded the Introduction as a manifesto of his doubts about modern poetry.

It should be recalled that Yeats had been friendly with Bridges, and had also spoken to Hopkins in Dublin, but he could not have known that, in November 1886, Hopkins had written to Patmore criticizing the 'strained and unworkable allegory' of 'Mosada', an early poem by Yeats (*Further Letters*, p. 374).

I read Gerard Hopkins with great difficulty, I cannot keep my attention fixed for more than a few minutes; I suspect a bias born when I began to think. He is typical of his generation where most opposed to mine. His meaning is like some faint sound that strains the ear, comes out of words, passes to and fro between them, goes back into words, his manner a last development of poetical diction. My generation began that search for hard positive subject-matter, still a predominant purpose. Yet the publication of his work in 1918 made 'sprung verse' the fashion, and now his influence has replaced that of Hardy and Bridges. In sprung verse a foot may have one or many syllables without altering the metre, we count stress not syllable, it is the metre of the *Samson Agonistes* chorus and has given new vitality to much contemporary verse. It enables a poet to employ words taken over from science or the newspaper without stressing the more unmusical syllables, or to suggest hurried conversation where only one or two words in a sentence are important, to bring about a change in poetical writing like that in the modern speech of the stage where only those words which affect the situation are important. In syllabic verse, lyric, narrative, dramatic, all syllables are important. Hopkins would have disliked increase of realism; this stoppage and sudden onrush of syllables were to him a neccessary expression of his slight constant excitement. The defect or limitation of 'sprung verse', especially in five-stress lines, is that it may not be certain at a first glance where the stress falls. I have to read lines in 'The End of a War' as in *Samson Agonistes* several times before I am certain.

92. Michael Roberts, Introduction, *The Faber Book of Modern Verse*

London, 1936, pp. 2–4

Michael Roberts (1902–48), teacher and poet, edited several well-known anthologies, and his *Essays* (1937) established him, according to T.S. Eliot, as the 'most authoritative critic of contemporary poetry' (quoted Haffenden, *Auden: The Critical Heritage*, p. 84).

The Faber Book of Modern Verse was one of the best-known selections of twentieth-century verse to appear in the twenties and thirties; it contained thirteen poems by Hopkins.

...To most readers it will not be surprising that an anthology of modern poetry should begin with Hopkins: but I do not mean to suggest that his poetry made a complete break with the poetry of the past and marked the inauguration of a new age. In rhythm and in imagery, as well as in the thoughts and feelings which he intended to express, he differed from most of the English poets of his time, but there was no sharp discontinuity...[Doughty's poetry] lacks that intensity which, in the poetry of Hopkins, was the expression of an important moral conflict, related to an outer social and intellectual conflict.

...If a poet is incomprehensible to many people, but clearly intelligible to a few, as Hopkins appeared to be when his collected poems were first published, it may be because he is speaking of things not commonly experienced and is using subtleties of rhythm and imagery not used in ordinary speech, and therefore not widely understood. If it can be shown that a poet's use of language is valid for some people, we cannot dismiss his way of speaking as mere 'obscurity' and idiosyncrasy, though we may regret the necessity for such a rhetoric as we regret the necessity for scientific jargon and mathematical notation.

The significant point about Hopkins was, however, not that he invented a style different from the current poetic style, but that, working in subterranean fashion, he moulded a style which expressed the tension and disorder that he found inside himself. Good poetry is more likely to be written about subjects which are, to the writer important, than about unimportant subjects, because only on subjects of personal importance to himself does he feel the need for that accuracy of speech which itself lessens the tension which it describes. ...

93. David Daiches, 'Gerard Manley Hopkins and the Modern Poets', *New Literary Values*

Edinburgh, 1936, pp. 3–47

Daiches (b. 1912) has held a variety of university appointments in England and America. His list of publications is immense and cosmopolitan in its range, but with some leaning towards Scottish life and literature. See also No. 102.

... With Hopkins language was a servant, to be bullied and coerced into as immediate contact with the thought as was possible. The rules of grammar and of syntax were not allowed to stand in the way; if they affected the immediacy of the expression they were ignored. Thus Hopkins sacrificed an obvious intelligibility to a directness which was not even intelligible—far less direct—until the meaning had, to use Hopkins' own term, 'exploded.'[1] His obscurity is due to the fact that his meaning 'explodes' far more rarely than he anticipated. Naturally as he knew from the beginning what he wanted to say, he could not put himself in the place of the reader, who approached the meaning from the other end. A reliance on the eventual 'explosion' of the meaning, rather than on logical exposition combined with the resources of sound and suggestion, is dangerous, but if it is effective it is much more direct and powerful and immediate in its communication than the more normal way. 'Explosion' was often Shakespeare's method, especially in the later plays. What does logical analysis make of this:

> I am question'd by my fears, of what may chance,
> Or breed upon our absence, that may blow
> No sneaping winds at home, to make us say,
> This is put forth too truly,

or of this:

> The hearts
> That spaniel'd me at heels, to whom I gave
> Their wishes, do discandy, melt their sweets
> On blossoming Caesar; and this pine is barkt
> That overtopp'd them all?

The obscurity here is not so different in kind from that of Hopkins. In both there is the second kind of clearness that Hopkins talks of in a letter to Robert Bridges:

One of two kinds of clearness one shd. have—whether the meaning to be felt without effort as fast as one reads or else, if dark at first reading, when once made out to *explode*.

A passage from another of Hopkins' letters to Bridges is helpful and relevant here:

Obscurity I do and will try to avoid so far as is consistent with excellences higher than clearness at first reading.

The trouble, of course, is that Hopkins very often does not achieve that explosive clarity at second reading that he aimed at and to which he sacrificed the 'meaning to be felt without effort.' And his imitators, not perhaps grasping his principle of explosive meaning at all, fail even more frequently to achieve any kind of intelligibility. What is more distressing, they fail to realise that if you give up surface intelligibility you must submit to the much harder discipline that explosive meaning requires if it is to succeed. Each type of poetry creates its own laws, but they are none the less laws, and success is impossible if they are not respected. The poetry of Hopkins is highly disciplined—over-disciplined, some may maintain, but no one can deny that his finest poems are due to a wrestling with language which did not come easily however spontaneous the effect may be to the reader.

It was, then, his impatience with the poetic medium as generally accepted in the nineteenth century that brought Hopkins into immediate contact with the modern poets. The practice in which such impatience resulted was rationalised in his theory of 'Sprung Rhythm,' a theory highly important in its liberating effect on English metre since 1918. . . .

. . . All his life Hopkins was interested in the theory of metre, classical even more than English, and it is important to bear this in mind when comparing his work with that of his modern imitators. The difference in quality as regards metrical achievement is often explained by the fact that Hopkins had studied the subject carefully in all its aspects and came to the writing of poetry with a technical knowledge which none of the modern poets possesses. This does not, however, prevent us from realising that Hopkins' elaborate theory of sprung thythm—and he has a lot more to say than in the extract quoted—was a rationalisation of an instinctive desire to achieve more direct methods of expression in more spontaneous-sounding rhythms.

Hopkins had other peculiarities. His use of tmesis, enjambement, and coined words are three of the more important. He made frequent and often subtle use of alliteration, too, and a less frequent though equally noticeable use of peculiar rhymes, rhymes which often strike the reader as ludicrous, such as 'crew in' with 'ruin,' 'boon he on' with 'communion,' and 'Irish' with 'sire he sh(ares), 'shares' being the first word of the third line, and the line being 'rove over.' All these features sprang from the same cause—impatience with the syntactical division of language into ordered components and a desire to get behind syntax to a more cogent logic. Perhaps in less than half of his work can he be called successful in this effort, but had he lived he would probably have achieved a more uniformly successful method of attaining his aims—aims which, let it be repeated, he so largely shares with the modern poets.

When Hopkins is successful he attains a rhythmic and musical effect which is integral to the verse in a peculiar degree; it is not in any way superimposed on the meaning. The 'Echoes' song is a fine example of this, as is also the famous 'Windhover':

> I caught this morning morning's minion, king-
>   dom of day light's dauphin, dapple-dawn-drawn Falcon,
>   in his riding
> Of the rolling level underneath him steady air, and striding
> High there, how he rung upon the rein of a wimpling wing
> In his ecstasy! then off, off forth on swing,
>   As a skate's heel sweeps smooth on a bow-bend: the hurl
>   and gliding
>   Rebuffed the big wind. My heart in hiding
> Stirred for a bird,—the achieve of, the mastery of the thing!

But the dangers of this method are easily shown:

> To what serves mortal beauty—dangerous; does set dancing
> blood—the O-seal-that-so feature, flung prouder form
> Than Purcell tune lets tread to?

Here there is no white-hot welding of form and content, but only a painful stuttering. When a passion which is single struggles with a medium that consists of separate words a fusion must take place or the words scatter to the ground ineffective. At his best Hopkins does achieve this fusion. Perhaps no poet after Shakespeare shows such a sense of the infinite gap between emotion which is single and unified, and the medium of language which has to be assembled in time before the emotion can be expressed. Other poets showed no concern when faced with this fact, accepting the medium as it was and making the best of it. Only Shakespeare, with a technique that in the last resort defies analysis, was able to bridge that gap consistently. It is Hopkins' greatness that, in his own way, he also did so—occasionally. It would be idle to maintain that he did so often.

The publication of Hopkins, and the discovery by the Modern poets that he had had a problem similar to their own resulting in an attitude to the poetic medium similar to their own, led at once to imitation of every kind. The imitation, which consisted in superimposing crude Hopkinsesque fragments on to an alien style, was of no value and only did harm, but the influence was also felt in a more valuable way than that. The poets absorbed the rhythms of Hopkins and these helped to loosen up their style, to redeem it on the one hand from sloppy poetic prose and on the other from congested and unpoetic 'wit-writing.' The use a poet made of the example of Hopkins was a very good test of his understanding of Hopkins' achievement. The poet who made the example an excuse to write insensitively and obscurely was modelling his verse on Hopkins' failures.

Once we see Hopkins as a rallying point after years of experiment with the poetic medium we can attempt to consider his influence on the moderns in some detail. The work of Auden, Spender, and Day Lewis gives us examples of the influence used to loosen up the rhythm and the form of expression in a verse whose texture is much less highly wrought than that of Hopkins.

> Me, March, you do with your movements master and rock
> With ring-whirl, whale-wallow, silent budding of cell...

That is Auden. The opening of Day Lewis's 'Magnetic Mountain' is Hopkins' 'Windhover' subdued, tamed, with none of the superb movement of the original, but none the less effective:

> Now to be with you, elate, unshared,
> My kestrel joy, O hoverer in wind,
> Over the quarry furiously at rest
> Chaired on shoulders of shouting wind.

> Where's that unique one, wind and wing married,
> Aloft in contact of earth and ether;
> Feathery my comet, Oh too often
> From heav'n harried by carrion cares.

We find the rhythms of Hopkins reproduced fairly closely in a recent poem of T.H. White, 'A Dray Horse':

> Meek Hercules, passion of arched power bowed to titanic
> affection;
> Docile though vanquishing, stout-limber in vastness, plunging
> and spurning thy road;
> Taughten thy traces, triumph past me, take thy shattering
> direction

> Through misty Glasgow, dragging in a tremendous beer-wagon
> thy cobble-thundering load.

...But to return to Hopkins. For all the influence which he has had on the modern poets, there is a fundamental difference between his work and that of his imitators—even technically. In the first place, none of the moderns have the tactual and visual sense that Hopkins had; their verse is more purely intellectual. Hopkins' imagination was to a very high degree sensuous, and the difficulty of his poems is often due less to intellectual subtlety than to the welding of different kinds of sensuous experience in a struggle for complete expression. Edith Sitwell does the same sort of thing much more blatantly when she talks of the 'purring sound of fires,' the 'dark songs of birds,' the 'blue wind,' the 'creaking light,' etc. Hopkins' confusion of the senses is less obvious and based more on a preternatural sensitivity than on a desire to be effective. In his sonnet 'Duns Scotus's Oxford' we see how the senses of sight and hearing determine the vocabulary:

> Towering city and branchy between towers;
> Cuckoo-echoing, bell-swarmèd , lark-charmèd, rook-raked,
>   river-rounded;
> The dapple-eared lily below thee; that country and town did
> Once encounter in, here coped and poised powers.

None of the moderns have this sensuous awareness. Spender, for example, writes:

> My parents kept me from children who were rough
> And who threw words like stones and who wore torn clothes.
> Their thighs showed through rags. They ran in the street
> And climbed cliffs and stripped by the country streams.

There is a purely intellectual quality here that Hopkins, for all the 'cerebration' in his verse, would never have allowed. The meaning is conveyed by verbs which convey nothing to the senses. 'Their thighs *showed* through rags.' 'Who wore torn clothes.' Hopkins would never have been satisfied with the abstract verb 'showed' or the general phrase 'wore torn clothes': he would have made you see them instead of merely talking about them. Hopkins stands alone in the intensity of his perceptions, and this involved an important difference in his use of the poetic medium.

Hopkins, too, had a gift for naturalising words in foreign

contexts which the modern poets have only partly inherited. In a phrase like 'What lovely behaviour of silk-sack clouds' (from 'Hurrahing in Harvest') the word 'behaviour' is surprising and effective. This device, when it is found in modern poetry, has none of the subtlety with which Hopkins used it.

But there are more important differences than these between the poetry of Hopkins and that of contemporary poets. The main one is this. Hopkins was sure of the content, the matter, of his verse; he had no problem there—he took it for granted that the kind of subject he wished to write about was a fit subject for poetry and he wrote only when the inspiration came. All his conscious attention was devoted to form. His experiments and innovations were all due to a striving after new means of expression, not after new matter to express. The new matter he may have had, but it came without striving, and his desire to justify his themes theologically had no relevance to his poetic activity. As a poet he was concerned with originating a new technique, and it was to this that all his conscious experimentation was directed. But his modern imitators are even more preoccupied with content than with form. Indeed it may be questioned whether they are fundamentally concerned about form at all. When we see how unscrupulous a poet like Auden can be in using trivial and unworthy forms in order to ensure that a certain point will be 'got across' to a certain audience, when we see him and others taking advantage of every meretricious trick available in order to achieve a purpose which is not poetic at all, we begin to wonder how far the poets of to-day are concerned to write *good* as distinct from temporarily *effective* poetry. Many of them have adopted sprung rhythm ready-made without any understanding of its organic nature or appreciation of its οἰκείη ἡδονή, its peculiar pleasure. In technique their only concern seems to be towards a looseness *ad infinitum,* counterbalanced, when they remember, with a stiffening of intricacy by some such method as the Wilfred Owen type of assonance. And all the while they grow more and more concerned about their subject, what they are to write about. This was not Hopkins' attitude, and it puts a big gulf between his poetry and that of his modern imitators.

So while Hopkins and the modern poets have similar attitudes to the poetic medium, they differ in their more fundamental attitudes to poetry. To Hopkins, an attitude to the medium was identified with a complete theory of poetry—at least the other elements in the theory were obvious and taken as a matter of course. If you had some thing to put into poetry and came seriously to your subject, that was all that mattered. 'A kind of touchstone of the highest or most living art,' he wrote Bridges in 1886, 'is seriousness; not gravity but the being in earnest with your subject—reality.' He was not worried about what the poet ought to say—as long as he meant what he did say. The matter for poetry was not itself poetry: the way the matter was used was what made poetry. He wrote to Bridges of the Irish that 'they always mistake the matter of poetry for poetry.' The modern poets have not yet decided on what the matter of poetry is, though they seem to have reached some agreement on what it is not. The reasons for this state of affairs in modern poetry cannot be discussed in such a sketch as this; it would require a closer study of contemporary literature and society than is possible here. Here the fact can only be noted, and stressed as an important point of difference between Hopkins and his followers.

A less fundamental but equally interesting point of difference is that Hopkins did not allow his preoccupation with technique to interfere with his lyrical faculty—he retained the ability to *sing*, which the modern poets have lost through over much self-consciousness. The self-consciousness of the modern poet is twofold: he has too much knowledge of the psychology of poetic creation, of his own mental processes, to be comfortable in creation, and, secondly, undue social sensitiveness makes him worried and apologetic in his artistic activity. Hopkins suffered from neither of these ills, and that was his good fortune rather than his merit: had he lived to-day he could hardly have avoided the influence of modern psychology or the effects of an altered social atmosphere. But as things were he retained a remarkably fresh lyrical vein.

> Look at the stars! look, look up at the skies!
> O look at all the fire-folk sitting in the air!

There is nothing like this in contemporary poetry—nothing, either, like the more meditative mood of 'God's Grandeur' and 'The Sea and the Skylark', which show a restrained lyrical quality rare in any poet. This lyrical faculty of Hopkins is akin to that startling directness of approach which produces some of his most effective lines:

> The Eurydice—it concerned thee, O Lord,

or

> And you were a liar, O blue March day.

The verse of the contemporary poets is technically much simpler and more elementary than that of Hopkins. Auden and Spender, for example, though they show considerable Hopkins influence, generally use loose iambic feet with simple counterpoint and equivalence which gives something of the effect of sprung rhythm without being so technically accomplished or so highly wrought. This is the third major difference between Hopkins and his imitators. ...

NOTE

1 *Letters to Bridges*, p. 90. See *post*, p. 392 and note.

94. C.K. Ogden, 'Sprung Rhythm', *Psyche*

1936, pp. 5–50

Charles Kay Ogden (1889–1957) wrote *The Meaning of Meaning* (1923) with I.A. Richards, and became editor of *Psyche*, 'An annual of general and linguistic psychology' in 1922.

The editorial reprinted here is a witty commentary on the views of many earlier critics of Hopkins.

...An understanding of stress is quite as essential for the interpretation of English literature as for talking naturally and intelligently. We hear much nowadays about the need for better methods of interpretation, and the more we insist that the meaning of a word is dependent on context the more necessary it becomes to realize that stress may be more important than any other contextual factor.

Take a simple question like—What is a man? Before we begin to consider the implications of multiple definition, we should, in accordance with Basic methods, at least try the simple key of stress—which gives us the four possibilities:

> *What* is a man? Were it not for his too too solid flesh many a murderer would have got away with it.
> What *is* a man? The ultimate reality veiled by any existential proposition may lead us to a discussion of symbolic machinery in its emotive aspects.
> What is *a* man? The problem of individuality was first concretely raised by *amoeba*.
> What is a *man*? The lawyers are still undecided whether Eve was a person.

Only a liberal use of italics would make the rhythm clear. Context may or may not be conclusive, but if we know the rhythm the ambiguity is removed. In prose, rhythm is conjectural, in verse it may be obvious; and in stress-verse, provided we can interpret the poet's metrical intention, at least one source of ambiguity is removed. Hence the importance of stress in the study of poetry, and hence the importance of prosody in studying the work of a poet like Hopkins.

In the twenty years which have elapsed since the *Poems* were introduced to a small public by the late Robert Bridges, then Poet Laureate, in 1918, most of the leading critics have expressed themselves for or against what they have regarded as his essential contribution. Though it is sometimes urged that the MSS. which his friend and editor preserved and copied with such exemplary devotion and scrupulous scholarship might with advantage have been given to the world at an earlier date, there is every reason to doubt whether a more judicious moment could have been chosen.[a] Everything goes to confirm the verdict of Professor Abbott, that 'no poet has ever been treated by a contemporary with greater reverence. The volume of 1918 is a masterpiece of editing.' Bridges himself was subsequently too engrossed by his *Testament of Beauty* to continue his editorial supervision but the manuscripts were left in such order that anyone concerned with the puzzles which his

Notes left unsolved has all the material at his disposal.

These puzzles are of two kinds. The first concern the sort of emotional cross-word divination in which literary critics delight. 'Solving riddles,' as Mr. Aldous Huxley has remarked, 'is an occupation that appeals to almost all of us. All poetry consists of riddles, to which the answers are occasionally, as in Dante's case, scientific or metaphysic(al).' Poetry may thus be valued because it is obscure, ambiguous, or over-determined, and though there are many who seek satisfaction 'in the sonnets of Mallarmé and the more eccentric verses of Gerard Hopkins' as an alternative to the low-brow acrostic, there are others to whom even this degree of arm-chair concentration is anathema. The emendation of classical texts is nevertheless a hobby which has not been confined entirely to pedants, for only when the text is established can appreciation be more than speculative.

In the case of Hopkins, the text cannot be established till we know how the poet intended it to be read—which brings us to the second sort of puzzle and a second sort of appreciation. And here the modern expositor tends to part company with the classicist whose emendations are frequently concerned with prosody. The fiftieth anniversary (June 8, 1939) of Hopkins' death will find prosody, in spite of the labours of Saintsbury and his emulators, much where he left it. But where did he leave it? Few will pause for an answer, but the subtler critics of today, such as Dr. Richards and Mr. Empson, would, of course, be the first to admit that the inquiry may bear directly on questions of literary interpretation. It is therefore in the interests of interpretation no less than as an illustration of the stress technique that the following glosses are here tentatively offered for the delectation of the pausing few.

At no point shall we be concerned with the sort of exegesis which is exercised by Hopkins' beliefs, or with the so-called 'terrible sonnets' which are associated with discussions of poignant pathos, the suffering of desolation, and the devastations of doubt. But amongst the unpublished scraps which commentators have so far overlooked is one dated January 1, 1888, from St. Stanislaus' College, Tullamore:

I was a Christian from birth or baptism, later I was converted to the Catholic faith, and am enlisted 20 years in the Society of Jesus. I am now 44. I do not waver in my allegiance. I never have since my conversion to the Church. The question is how I advance the side I serve on.[1]

357

Was he advancing the side in Ireland? It did not seem obvious; bodily energy and cheerful spirits had been denied him. And his poems—for which in 1883 (September 3–10) he prayed that 'they might not do me harm through the enmity or imprudence of any man or my own'? Here certainly there was room for conflict and doubt. 'You ask,' he wrote to Canon Dixon in 1878, 'do I write verse myself. What I had written I burnt before I became a Jesuit and resolved to write no more, as not belonging to my profession, unless it were by the wish of my superiors; so for seven years I wrote nothing but two or three presentation pieces, which occasion called for. But when in the winter of '75 the Deutschland was wrecked in the mouth of the Thames...I was affected by the account and happening to say so to my rector he said that he wished someone would write a poem on the subject. On this hint I set to work and, though my hand was out at first, produced one. I had long had haunting my ear the echo of a new rhythm which now I realized on paper.'[b]

'The Wreck of the Deutschland,' to which attention was drawn in this connection in our last issue, is primarily a challenge to prosodists; and prosodists, it would seem, have deliberately eschewed it. Even Bridges, who is generally regarded as an innovator, and whose metrical skill was remarkable, seems always to have shied. He started (1878) by telling the author that he would not for any money read it again,[c] and ended (1918) by explaining that 'both subject and treatment were distasteful to him,' and recommending the reader to circumvent 'the great dragon folded in the gate'[2] by attacking stanza 16 first.

Why not start at the beginning? It is surprising that Bridges nowhere informs the reader that the metrical scheme of the poem follows the alignment of the MS, that Part II has, therefore, one more stress in the first line than Part I, and that the number of stresses in lines 2–8 of every verse, in both parts, is 3-4-3-5-5-4-6. Before he came to edit the poem, he may not have realized that the metre was regular throughout. If, in spite of copying it with such care (in B), he still failed to make certain lines fit into the scheme apparently intended, he may have remained doubtful. It is true that Hopkins wrote: 'Your parody reassures me about your understanding the metre;'[d] but he required reassurance, and by 'the metre' he may merely have meant sprung rhythm. And if Bridges regarded such a note as unnecessary because the pattern is obvious, why did he print the first stanza in 'The Spirit of Man'[e] with even alignment? So printed, the pattern vanishes, and even with the correct alignment there is no guarantee that those who claim to base themselves on Hopkins will read it as he intended.

Take, for example, the recent attempt of Mr. C. Day Lewis,[f] who claims that though the intended stress is often difficult to find 'it is seldom that a series of consecutive lines speak themselves as easily as the first verse.' This he prints as follows:

> Thóu mástering me
> Gód! gíve of breáth and bréad:
> Wórld's stránd, swáy of the séa
> Lórd of líving and déad;
> Thou hast boúnd bónes and veins in me, fástened me flésh
> And áfter it álmost unmáde, whát with dréad
> Thy doíng: and dóst thou toúch me afrésh?
> Óver agáin I féel thy fínger and fínd thée.

In an erratum slip, the missing stress on *over* in line 8 is added, but the alignment (with lines 5 and 6) remains wrong, 'though the number of stresses is indicated by the setting of the lines.' And, in addition to four changes of punctuation (in lines 2, 3, 5, and 6), there are three demonstrable errors of stress:

1. In the first line, since *me* must be stressed for the rhyme with *sea* and *thee, Thou*, which comes, by anacrusis, in the half foot before *mastering*, cannot be given a stress mark in the two-stress line.

2. After telling us that we are compelled to verify the number of stresses in any line from other verses, Mr. Lewis gives four stresses to the second line. But every second line in every one of the 35 stanzas has three stresses, and *God* (balancing *Thou* in the first line) is clearly in the half foot before the first stress.

3. In line 6, the stress should be on the first syllable of *unmade*, whether for rhythm or to mark the contrast with *fastened* (= made fast).

On such principles it is not surprising that Mr. Lewis often finds himself 'compelled to run over a number of heavy syllables, which would certainly be stressed in ordinary speech,' before coming to the intended stress; or that Mr. Yeats reads Hopkins 'with great difficulty.'[g] Indeed it seems certain that most of those who have expressed admiration for the 'Deutschland' have read it as if the metre were irregular, disregarding the carefully studied stresses (on an even beat)[h] and pausing for breath or emotion where they felt inclined.

This is confirmed by the curious fact that anyone who has bought the *Poems* since 1930 would have been led to assume that the alignment was *not* intended as a guide to the metrical pattern. In the first edition, published in 1918 and long out of print, the first lines of Part II were correctly aligned as three-stress; i.e. they were not indented as are the two-stress lines. But in the second edition the printers seem to have scented an irregularity, and to have eliminated it without anyone who read the poem during the next seven years being aware of the fact. Deprived of this essential guidance, the conscientious student might well reject the evidence of alignment elsewhere and assume regularity only where he could not escape it. It is to be hoped that the correct alignment will be restored at an early date, though unfortunately the error remains in the new (1937) edition by which Hopkins is for the first time made accessible to a wider public.

It is significant that Mr. W.H. Gardner, who devotes nearly thirty pages to an exposition of the metre and doctrine of this poem,[i] ventures to stress only one complete Stanza (the first of Part II), in which there seems to be no good reason for the awkward

Sóme find me a swórd; sóme

rather than 'Some fínd me'.

He also marks sixteen other lines, preferring, in Stanza 31, 'Stártle the poor sheep báck! is the' to the paeonic 'Startle the poor shéep back! is the.' There is an argument for either; but in No. 31,

Wéll, she has thée for the páin, for the

the stress on *well* is definitely wrong. *Well* is the half foot before the stress on *she* to chime with *thee* and contrast with *the rest*.

It is curious that Mr. Gardner, who follows the misprinted alignment of Part II, though he correctly marks the four first lines quoted as three-stress, should also align the fourth line wrongly on four occasions through *not* following the printed text. Thus on page 137, stanza 4 appears as follows:

I am soft sift
In an hour-glass—at the wall
Fast, but mined with a motion, a drift,
And it crowds and it combs to the fall;

from which the reader would infer that Hopkins, or the printed version, indents the fourth line in this manner. This impression is heightened by the comment: 'The rhythmic felicity of this quatrain is noticeable even in the manner of the indenting.' But, in fact, the indenting is uniform with that of every other Stanza in Part I. This, then, can hardly be a printer's error;[j] the other deviations being in Stanzas 18, 30, and 31 (pages 130–1). Elsewhere, except in the equation of lines 3 and 4 of Stanza 10 on page 143, the printed alignment is carefully followed.

Miss E.E. Phare, who finds something in the 'Deutschland' which 'strikes one as artificial in the bad sense,' and contrasts its 'lack of balance, shallowness, and febrility' with the 'poised, deep, calm' of 'The Windhover' (written only eighteen months later, though she speaks of a poetic progress summed up in the passage from 'Fancy to Imagination') aligns no less than eighteen lines wrongly in the six stanzas which she quotes.[k] And of four lines from Part II, she indents two, in accordance with the error in the later editions, while two are correctly aligned as in the first printing. In this poem, she adds, (p. 86), 'Hopkins is not sure enough of himself, not certain enough that the traits which he is expressing are those of his own individuality and not foreign to him, not to impress the reader with a sense that the poet is deviating into oddity.' But 'odd in the sense of being the product of a mind which deflects from the normal in a way not to be desired, Hopkins' poetry considered as a whole is not.' This may seem to beg a knotty question for those who cannot accept religion as (p. 150) a normal 'way of keeping all the facts in mind without losing sanity.'

Hopkins indeed seems fated to maltreatment at the hands of printers and critics, and even Miss Sitwell,[l] who indents the first line of each of the two verses she quotes from Part I, prints all other lines (including one first line from Part II) with even alignment. It is significant that Miss Sitwell, who nowhere refers to the metrical problem, criticizes Mr. Empson for missing out half a syllable in the line

Your well fenced-out real estate of mind[m]

so that 'there is a gap between "out" and "real"; though the poet, who presumably treats *real* as a dissyllable, in the same way that Hopkins made two syllables out of *heir*,[n] must have deliberately juxtaposed the two main stresses as in Hopkins' sprung rhythm. And why *half* a syllable?

The ineptitudes of prosodists have clearly made it impossible for most contemporary writers on verse to regard Hopkins' specific contribution to the subject as more than an aberration of genius. 'Hopkins originality,' we are told[o] 'was radical and surprising: there was, as he owns, some excuse for the dismay of his first readers. He could not himself, as the Author's Preface shows, be reconciled to his originality without subterfuge;' i.e., apparently, he introduced the red herring of prosody.

There are exceptions, of course. Of the *Note-Books* the *Times Literary Supplement* says: 'The Journal in point of poetic eloquence and fantasy is the chief thing in this volume. Next come the incomplete notes on "the various shapes of speech called verse".'[p] Indeed one might have expected a literary critic to turn first to anything which promised to throw light on the rhythmic principles which have baffled two generations. Yet of these same notes, running to more than 10,000 words, Mr. Desmond MacCarthy, in reviewing the new material three weeks later, says: 'The lecture notes on Rhetoric and metres I have not read.' For him the book contained 'too much that was remote from my constant interests or contingent upon inquiries I had no immediate inclination to pursue—the problems of metre and scansion for example.'[q] Poetic justice is doubtless responsible for the curious coincidence that in dealing with metrical minutiae, Hopkins refers to the need for taking care that syllables shall be really assonant: 'some of MacCarthy's are not, as *entangled* and *many*.'[r]

To the majority even his simplest rhythms are too original to be tolerated. Mr. Sturge Moore goes so far as to rewrite the poem of which Hopkins said 'I never did anything more musical,' in such a way as to discard 'his most ludicrous redundancies.'[s] Particularly disquieting is the suggestion that some readers may require guidance. 'The very fact that nearly all these rhythms need stressing in the text and explanation in the notes reveals their artificiality; the vision only too often is forced into them and not expressed by them.'[t] The moral being that one should not write for specialists. Indeed, any attention to prosody is a waste of time if it leads to novelty. 'The metrical effects which Mr. Hopkins studies with such assiduity do not seem to us worth the pains bestowed on them. . . . Lyrics which do not sing themselves would in our opinion be better in prose.'ᵘ

The only point on which all the critics seem to agree is the novelty of the rhythm, *exceptis excipiendis*,ᵛ whatever the metre may be. It is 'something for which our acquaintance with civilized poetry leaves us unprepared.'ʷ This is partly the fault of the Latinists who have looked at Medieval Latin Verse through syllabic eyes and have failed to see in St. Peter Damiani's *Quis est hic?* the authentic prototype of 'The Deutschland,'ˣ and of the Hebraists who have insisted that the rhythms they were studying had no parallel in English. When simple stress-verse or sprung rhythm is found in Latin the critics have accepted the view of the experts that its rhythm is merely execrable; and when the student of Hebrew metre records the fact that 'the accentuation, the rhythmical beat dominates everything' so that it is immaterial 'whether one, two, or three syllables intervene between the consecutive beats,' he adds 'in English poetry the line has a fixed number of feet and each foot has a fixed number of syllables.'ʸ Apart from such problems as the scansion of Browning's 'Grammarian's Funeral,' the science of prosody will suffer more than partial eclipse if it continues to be pursued by candle-light. In 1879 Hopkins could write

> Some candle clear burns somewhere I come by.

But its to-fro tender trambeams have for the most part given place to neon signs. The poet himself has been among the signs of the times for more than forty years;ᶻ and that *The Times* has been consistently aware of so signal a luminary is obvious from its recent verdict—'It would hardly be an exaggeration to say that Hopkins was the most original of the poets of the second half of the nineteenth century.'ᵃᵃ

In this connection, and with the fifth printing of the Second Edition before us, it is instructive to note that in May 1919, *The Dial*, then the organ of modernist opinion in America, after remarking that 'the chief interest in these posthumous poems lies in their metrical eccentricities,' and referring to the 'unwise condensation' which makes the writing obscure, concludes that it shows 'a strong talent, but will claim few readers.'³

There are those who, while admitting that stress-verse may have its merits, regard Hopkins as a sort of Holman Hunt, labouring vainly, in a Pre-Raphaelite literary atmosphere, to create effects.

With Bridges, they find his Mariolatry distasteful; and like *The Spectator* they prefer their sprung rhythm neat—in prose. But the most formidable indictment has come from a writer who goes so far as to say that Hopkins' theories of metre are 'as demonstrably wrong as those of any speculator who has ever led a multitude into the wilderness to perish,' and that 'the root of his error lay in an ignorance of the subject so profound that he was not aware that there was anything to know.'bb

Here is indeed a Kuczynski[4] among the Malthusiasts, for the influence of Hopkins 'has been as pernicious as it has been potent, and unless the rising generation has enough poetic learning to see where it is taking them, and enough poetic vigour to throw it off, I am afraid the next and last *Oxford Book of Verse* will bear as its sub-title, "Or, the End of an Old Song."'

What Hopkins failed to realize was:

> 1. A line only scans when, 'without any straining of the words or melody, it can be sung to an easy and popular tune.'
> 2. The least impeded way of speaking English 'is so to arrange the sounds that we are not called upon to make two successive discharges of vocal energy, or to inhibit that energy over too long a sequence of unstressed syllables.'
> 3. The Choruses of *Samson Agonistes* 'taken line by line are counterpointed or not according to the judgment of the poet'—and not 'throughout,' as the Preface states.
> 4. That his principles would cause 'not a development but a catastrophe, a gash at the root of our poetry, to which I can recall no exact parallel in literary history,' and that 'The Deutschland' would make every poet but one unable to write 'verse which shall be verse as well as modern'—that poet being the author of the *Canons of Giant Art*.[5]

To this it may be replied seriatim:

> 1. That the public ear may sometimes require a little training before a given tune becomes popular, as all attempts to adapt Donne's Satires for Community Singing have shown.
> 2. When Matthew Arnold wrote
>
> > Dówn, dówn, dówn
> > Dówn to the dépths of the séa
>
> he asked the smoothest Victorians to make four successive discharges of vocal energy, such as Hopkins' sprung feet demand; and that in

normal English prose we frequently insert a sequence of more than twice as many syllables as Hopkins normally used between two beats, at the same tempo as those in 'The Deutschland.'

3. That by 'throughout' Hopkins did not mean *every line* as is shown by his amplified statement (*Correspondence of Hopkins and Dixon*, p. 15): 'the choruses are in my judgment counterpointed throughout; that is, each line (or nearly so) has two different coexisting scansions.'

4. That if those who profess themselves admirers of Hopkins have had no more conception of his rhythmic principles than the evidence would suggest, these principles can hardly be made responsible for 'the cacophonies which naturally result when the metrically deaf write verse;' and that Miss Sitwell, the only other critic who has advocated the immediate canonization of the author of *Giant Art*, is convinced that the technician already in occupation of the adjoining niche is—the author of 'The Deutschland'. ...

★   ★   ★   ★

... We have dwelt at some length on certain problematic lines in the ninety poems which exemplify the metrical system under discussion. These poems were not prepared for publication and the notes which elucidate their intricacies were written over a period of more than fifteen years in the course of an informal correspondence with poets whose queries and comments have only occasionally been preserved. The result is very far from confirming the judgment of *The Observer* that Hopkins 'made an unnecessary mystery of his effort to put speech rhythms into verse.'[cc]

What does emerge is that the effects for which Hopkins was striving, especially in poems like 'The Deutschland,'[dd] are frequently hard to obtain in an ordinary room where carpetings, furnishings, and dimensions tend to inhibit the sort of interpretation he required. He frequently refers to the fact that his poems are not to be read but (though he does not use the word) chanted. ...

NOTES

a This point was well made by Miss Louise Imogen Guiney in *The Month* shortly after the first reviews appeared. In her own review (March, 1919), by a curious slip, Tom Navvy was turned by the printers into an Irishman—'Tom Mavoy.' [See No. 16.]

b *Correspondence of Hopkins and Dixon*, p. 14.

c *Letters to Bridges*, p. 46.

d *Letters to Bridges*, p. 44.

e 1916 (Fourteenth impression, 1934), No. 53.

f *A Hope for Poetry*, 1934, p. 11. [See *ante*, p. 281.]

g *Oxford Book of English Verse*, 1936; Introduction, p. xxxix.—'I cannot keep my attention fixed for more than a few minutes; I suspect a bias born when I began to think.' [See *ante*, p. 345.]

h See *Psyche*, Vol. XV (1935), pp. 8–13, for a general account of Sprung Rhythm in relation to 'The Deutschland.'

i *Essays and Studies*, by Members of the English Association, Vol. XXI, 1936, pp. 124–152. [See No. 88.]

j Such as is clearly responsible for the omission of a stress mark on *towers* in the last line of Stanza 3; or slips like *settlers* for *settler* in the third line of Stanza 12, *snows* for *snow* in the first line of Stanza 13, and the Americanism, *go bleed* for *go and bleed* in the third line of Stanza 31.

k E.E. Phare (Mrs. Duncan-Jones), *The Poetry of Gerard Manley Hopkins*, 1933, pp. 17 and 109–113. [See No. 67.]

l *Aspects of Modern Poetry*, 1934, pp. 59–64. [See No. 74.]

m The line is so printed in *Poems* (1935), p. 23. Miss Sitwell hyphens *well-fenced*.

n 'The Bugler's First Communion,' Stanza 8, line 4; cf. *Letters to Bridges*, p. 43.

o *New Bearings in English Poetry* (1932) by F.R. Leavis, p. 167. 'His prosodic account in terms of Logaoedic Rhythm, Counterpoint Rhythm, Sprung Rhythm, Rocking Feet and Outriders will help no one to read his verse—unless by giving the sense of being helped.' *Ibid.*, p. 167. [See No. 63.]

p January 23, 1937.

q *Sunday Times*, February 14, 1937.

r *Note-Books*, p. 243. [2nd edn, p. 284. Denis MacCarthy was a nineteenth-century translator of Calderón.]

s *Criterion*, July, 1930. The result must be read to be believed; and as Dr. Leavis well remarks, *Op. cit.*, p. 173 'all the action and substance of the verse' has been discarded.

t *Oxford Magazine*, May 23, 1919. [See *ante*, p. 112.]

u *Spectator*, May 10, 1919. [See *ante*, p. 111.]

v All of which are invariably quoted, with or without acknowledgment, from Hopkins' Preface.

w C. Day Lewis, *Op. cit.*, p. 12.

x See the Note on *Quis est hic?* printed as a Supplement to *The Song of Songs*, translated into Basic English by Ma Than É (1937).

y W.O.E. Oesterley, *A Fresh Approach to the Psalms*, pp. 127–8. It is perhaps equally surprising that there has been no discussion of 'sprung

rhythm' in relation to what is known as the 'pointing' of the Psalms.
Incidentally, we know that Hebrew was part of Hopkins' normal
curriculum (*Letters to Bridges*, p. 31).

z Eleven of his poems were printed in A.H. Miles' *Poets and Poetry of the
XIXth Century*, 1893.

aa *Times Literary Supplement*, December 25, 1936. Cf. *The Glasgow
Herald*, January 1, 1931, 'Hopkins is now, perhaps, the most potent
influence on the finest spirits of the younger generation.'

bb G.M. Young, 'Forty Years of Verse,' *The London Mercury*, December
1936.

cc February 15, 1931. [See *ante*, p. 210.]

dd 'Take breath and read it with the ears, as I always wish to be read and
my verse becomes all right.'—*Letters to Bridges*, p. 79.

1 *Sermons of Hopkins*, ed. Devlin, 1959, p. 261.

2 See *ante*, p. 83.

3 See *ante*, p. 116.

4 Robert Kuczynski, a population scientist, writing at the beginning of
the twentieth century.

5 A collection of poems (1933), written in sprung rhythm, by
Sacheverell Sitwell.

THE NOTE-BOOKS AND PAPERS
OF GERARD MANLEY HOPKINS

edited by Humphry House, London, 1937

95. G. W. Stonier, review, *New Statesman and Nation*

23 January 1937, pp. 124–6

...One can say with certainty that no poem dated earlier than 1876 ('The Wreck of the Deutschland') is fully characteristic of Hopkins. His conversion to the Catholic Church in 1866 had marked a change of current, a coming-of-age, in his spiritual life, and ten years later—after a long pause for discovery—his poetry revealed the impact. In the journal for these years, which contains both verse and prose, we see his false start as a poet reaching its climax in 'Heaven-Haven' (1866),

> I have desired to go
>   Where springs not fail,
> To fields where flies no sharp and sided hail
>   And a few lilies blow...

and side by side with this, in prose jottings, the germs of his real development. The point about 'Heaven-Haven' and all his poems of that kind is not so much that they are bad—some indeed are exquisite—as that they are *wrong*. Wrong from Hopkins's point of view (he disliked the 'enervating qualities' in Keats), and in the light of a whole literature which has opposed personal truthfulness to decorative grace in art.

...Apart from the fact that his early poems are sustained by little emotion except (as with Swinburne) the emotion of writing poetry, he does not succeed till much later in fusing spiritual with visual and rhythmic intensity. The terrific force of 'Spelt from Sibyl's Leaves', and other poems of his last period, is held by exact imagery.

96. C. Day Lewis, 'Gerard Manley Hopkins, Poet and Jesuit', *Left Review*

April 1937, pp. 172–5

Left Review (1934–8) was edited by Edgell Rickword, a Communist Party member and distinguished literary critic, and stressed the role of literature and the arts in the political struggle. For Lewis, see No. 75. His article was an example of the contemporary fashion for involving Hopkins, as well as living poets, in the social and political arguments of the day.

In this volume [*The Note-Books and Papers of Gerard Manley Hopkins*] are contained extracts from the early diaries of Gerard Manley Hopkins written during his first two years as an undergraduate, a Platonic dialogue 'On the Origin of beauty', the Journal which he kept for a number of years after entering the Jesuit novitiate, and a selection from his sermons, drawings, and shorter essays. It is emphatically a book for the specialist, the scholar or the poet, rather than for the general reader. At the same time, there are certain implications which I believe it is important to realise.

First, in the matter of poetic development. If we consider the work of any major poet as a whole, we are bound to be struck by the continuity of its development, both in technique and content. The best example of this is Shakespeare, in whose later plays we find a deepening of thought and emotional experience, together with a greater freedom, elasticity, adaptability in the verse structure: but—and this is the important thing—the later work is in no way a fresh start, an isolated phenomenon; it is based on and has grown out of the earlier. It is also true that poetic development proceeds, as far as the finished product is concerned, in leaps. Though his experience is all the time at work, behind the scenes, on the poet's imagination and technique, the changes which it brings about take place with relative suddenness: we can lay our finger on the play of Shakespeare, for instance, or the poems of Hopkins or Yeats, where this revolutionary development has taken place and the poet's work has advanced to a new stage.

This is only one more corroboration of a dialectical law. It is also a point which cannot be too much stressed and amplified by Marxist literary criticism. In so far as it is possible to distinguish between 'major' and 'minor' poets, we may fairly say that the work of the former embodies this dialectical development, while the work of the latter remains relatively static.

Most of the poems Hopkins wrote in his first period were destroyed. But there are enough of them in this book to provide comparison with those which were produced in his second period, beginning with 'The Wreck of the Deutschland' in 1876. The difference, at first sight, is quite extraordinary. There are flashes of vision and phrase in these earlier poems which show the original poet; but for the most part they are derivative (there is a strong Shakespearean influence) and ill-organised, and often exhibit that archaic diction which Hopkins came later to criticise with severity. Yet, if we look closer, we will find here the seeds of his mature work; the lines on page 39 beginning, 'Boughs being pruned, birds preenèd, show more fair,' is one of the more obvious instances.

Mr. Charles Williams, in his introduction to Hopkins' *Poems*, wrote: 'It is arguable that this is not the greatest kind of poetry; but it is also arguable that the greatest kind of poetry might easily arise out of this.'[1] I would prefer to put it in a somewhat different form. If Hopkins had lived and continued to write, would he have emerged into another—'greater,' if you like—stage of development than that which produced his finest work, the 'terrible' sonnets? I am a little inclined to doubt it. Mr. House, the indefatigable editor of the volume under review, comments that Hopkins' mind 'worked at its best in a delimited intellectual and moral tradition.' That is certainly one way of describing the effect of Jesuit orders upon the poet's mind. It is, of course, easy enough to say that Hopkins's poetic potentiality was partly frustrated by his religious vocation; but that also would be an over-simplification. The truth is that on the one hand his orders severely limited the time and energy he could give to the writing of verse, made him look upon it as a hobby, or at least a highly personal and private acitivity; while, on the other hand, they provided him with an external discipline and—in the widest sense—a 'subject,' neither of which should necessarily have been anything but beneficial.

In this sense, Hopkins was working under conditions by no

means dissimilar to those of the Communist poet to-day. There was nothing in the nature of those conditions to prevent the poetic activity being at once autonomous and subservient to a tradition and purpose wider than its own. But, as it happened, their effect on Hopkins was to make him look upon his verse as 'a highly personal and private activity'; and not only this, the 'terrible' sonnets, his finest work, are negative in the sense that they represent the 'dark night of the soul,' the periodic doubts of his religion and the sense of separation from God at which he hints from time to time in the Journal.

> I am gall, I am heartburn. God's most deep decree
> Bitter would have me taste: my taste was me. . . .

> That night, that year
> Of now done darkness I wretch lay wrestling with (my God!) my
> God. . . .

> Comforter, where, where is your comforting? . . .

> Wert thou my enemy, O thou my friend,
> How wouldst thou worse, I wonder, than thou dost
> Defeat, thwart me? Oh, the sots and thralls of lust
> Do in spare hours more thrive than I that spend,
> Sir, life upon thy cause. . . .

If it is true, as I believe, that his poetry was never thoroughly integrated with his religious life and belief, was raised to its greatest heights by despairing doubt—the very negation of religion—then it is difficult to see how Hopkins, having committed himself to Catholicism, could have come through to a further stage of poetic development. Even supposing he had achieved this integration between his religion and his poetry, the very nature of his orders and—as far as one can tell—of his personality was calculated to prevent that deepening of human sympathy and wider exploration of reality on which a further poetic advance might have been based. One has only to read the sermons printed in this volume to see what a blight the trivial and ludicrous minutiae of Catholic doctrine had cast upon the poet's intelligence. In his youth, retiring, sensitive, neurotic (at school he abstained from all drink for three weeks, as an experiment, we are told), Hopkins in later life was still more deeply cut off from society. We cannot fail to notice, in the

Journal as well as in the Letters, how fundamentally uninterested in people he was. The Journal, admittedly, is intended first and foremost to be a nature-diary; but we look in vain for those extraordinary minute and original powers of observation which he exercises on trees, waves and cloudscapes to be applied to human lineaments. This is not to say that Hopkins was incapable of friendship; we know very well that his affections were strong; but between him and common humanity and the ideas and events of his time, there was a barrier which we feel he had neither the power nor the will to leap.

Yet, if we consider the two extracts which follow, we see what Hopkins might have been had he not gone into the voluntary self-abdication of Jesuit orders.

> Maidens shall weep at merry morn,
> And hedges break and lose the kine,
> And field-flowers make the fields forlorn,
> And noonday have a shallow shine,
> And barley turn to weed and wild,
> And seven ears crown the lodgèd corn,
> And mother have no milk for child,
>   And father be overworn.
> And John shall lie, where winds are dead,
> And hate the ill-visaged cursing tars,
> And James shall hate his faded red,
> Grown wicked in the wicked wars.
> No rains shall fresh the flats of sea,
> Nor close the clayfields' sharded sores,
> And every heart think loathingly
>   Its dearest changed to bores.

(Early Diaries, 1865)[2]

However, I am afraid some great revolution is not far off. Horrible to say, in a manner I am a Communist. Their ideal bating some things is nobler than that professed by any secular statesman I know of. ... Besides it is just—I do not mean the means of getting to it are. But it is a dreadful thing for the greatest and most necessary part of a very rich nation to live a hard life without dignity, knowledge, comforts, delight, or hopes, in the midst of plenty—which plenty they make. They profess that they do not care what they wreck and burn, the old civilisation and order must be destroyed. This is a dreadful lookout, but what has the old civilisation done for them? As it at present stands in England it is itself in great measure founded on wrecking....

(Letter to Robert Bridges, 1871)[3]

There is no need for me to draw the moral, or to point out the more subtle connections between that beautiful early poem and the passage of social criticism (one of the few he ever wrote) in the letter to Bridges. Hopkins' passionate intelligence enabled him to arrive independently at conclusions which, in spite of Marx and Lenin, are still ignored by many people to-day....

NOTES

1 See *ante*, p. 173.
2 See *Poems*, 4th edn, p. 160.
3 *Letters to Bridges*, p. 27.

97. W.H. Gardner, 'The Religious Problem in G.M. Hopkins', *Scrutiny*

June 1937, pp. 32–42,

The chief problem presented by the poetry of Hopkins derives from the repressed conflict between two sets of values—those of the poet and those of the priest; between the psychic individuality, or what I shall for convenience call the *personality* on the one hand, and the *character*, as determined by a strict regulative principle (the Jesuit discipline) on the other. Hence the central problem to be discussed may be stated as follows: How far and in what manner was the personality of Hopkins the poet stultified, or assisted, by the character of Father Hopkins, S.J.?

It is by now common knowledge that Hopkins, on becoming a Jesuit, burnt most of his early poems and resolved to write no more except by the wish of his superiors. Fortunately that sanction was not withheld; but the creative Hopkins was at all times, from 1868 till his death in 1889, profoundly influenced or even dominated by the devotional text-book of the Society of Jesus—the *Spiritual Exercises* of St. Ignatius. The basis of this 'manual of election' is Self-abnegation, or rather (for the principle is really positive), the complete dedication of the Self to God and salvation, to a life of poverty, chastity and obedience. Right 'election' in all crises of the soul entailed the renunciation of all attachments and pleasures which were not contributory to God's service and the soul's weal: 'Take, O lord, and receive my liberty, my memory, my understanding, and all my will.' Hopkins acquiesced; yet how idiosyncratic his gesture of renunciation could be we hear in

> O feel-of-primrose hands, O feet
> That want the yield of plushy sward...

and in

> What life half lifts the latch of,
> What hell stalks towards the snatch of
> Your offering, with dispatch, of!

By a rigorous method of daily self-scrutiny called 'the particular examen,' the priest searched his conscience for the impure motive, the intrusive Self; it is therefore not surprising that a man so devout as Hopkins should carry the same moral scrupulosity into his poetry. We proceed to observe how the regulative principle affects the imagination, the highest conscious function of the personality.

Hopkins is continually examining the claims of what Keats called 'the principle of Beauty in all things.' To Keats, Beauty was single and good—it was Truth: to Hopkins it was two-fold—'mortal beauty' and immortal (or supernatural) beauty, and its influence or 'instress' was equivocal; for Hopkins saw that beauty could be both an insidious lure to the lower levels of being and a constant admonition to the higher. It all depended upon the state of the receptive mind, the character. On the analogy of the sensitive soul's response to the transient beauty of this world, the Christian, by a definite motion of the will towards 'the highest spiritual poverty,' aspires to the immortal beauty of the super-natural world, union with God in the Beatific Vision. The necessary check put upon sensibility by the disciplined will is first stated in 'The Habit of

Perfection.' The enjoyment of beauty is a sacrament, and the implied obligation is an act of sacrifice:

> Give beauty back...back to God.[a]

In a later poem, 'To what serves Mortal Beauty?' Hopkins faces the danger of over-indulgence, and asks:

> What do then? how meet beauty?

and the answer is an attempt to bridge the gap between the transient and the permanent, to reconcile the poet with his impulse of acceptance and the priest with his doctrine of 'detachment':

> Merely meet it; own
> Home-at-heart, heaven's sweet gift; then leave, let that alone.
> Yea, wish that though, wish all, God's better beauty, grace.

Recognition of this fundamental belief helps us to understand those poems in which direct sensuous enjoyment of natural beauty leads up to a doctrinal, dogmatic, or quasi-mystical consummation—the spiritual exegesis of nature's parable: I mean the early nature sonnets, 'God's Grandeur,' The Starlight Night,' 'Spring,' etc. On the other hand, failure to grasp or to sympathize with the poet's metaphysic leads to misconceptions like the following:

The sensuous insistency with which, in these sonnets, earth and air are claimed for Christ is to my sense taut and artificial, suggesting a profound emotional dislocation, with the ensuing desolation of 'Carrion Comfort' as its inevitable counterpart.[b]

The last part is merely a euphemistic way of saying that Hopkins was a victim of self-deception, that the poet dragged in the name of Christ simply to mollify the conscience of the priest. To anyone who has no use for Christian Theism the Christ-symbol will almost certainly appear 'taut and artificial'; yet that is no reason for saying that the frequency of this symbol betokens a 'profound emotional dislocation' in a sincere believer like Hopkins. (Unless the *Letters* and *Notebooks* are grossly disingenuous, it is difficult to maintain now that Hopkins seriously questioned his faith.) To a fellow-Theist, the Christ-symbol indicates rather a profound and spontaneous unification of the intellect and the senses, that mystical fusion of the Many and the One which is at the root of all great conversions to the religious attitude and mode of life. As we know from his remarks on Keats and Whitman, Hopkins was not satisfied with a poetry which rested in the senses and the emotions alone; he desired intellectual satisfaction as well—what another Jesuit describes as 'the unity and order and ultimate satisfaction of the intellect' which for him 'the grandeur of theism'[c] could alone provide. Theism dressed not only his 'days' but his thoughts about man and the universe 'to a dexterous and starlight order'; and the nature sonnets are evidence not of 'emotional dislocation' but of his discovery of a philosophy about which he could say, with confidence and joy, 'On this principle hang the heavens and the earth.'

To Hopkins nature was (in Milman's phrase) 'a sublime theophany.' In his own words:

'God's utterance of Himself in Himself is God the Word, outside Himself is this world. This world then is word, expression, news, of God.

Then follows a statement which is vital to a complete understanding of Hopkins's mind and poetry: 'Therefore its end, its purpose, its purport, its meaning, is God, and its life or work to name and praise Him.'[d] When he writes

> I walk, I lift up, I lift up heart, eyes
> Down all that glory in the heavens to glean our Saviour.

we hear not a suggestion of emotional dislocation but rather of peace and certainty—that ecstasy which Dr. Richards once said Hopkins failed to reach. To most people, it is true, Christ stands for an ideal (or Utopian) code of morals, and they would see no connection between a code of morals and a mystical vision of external nature: to them such an arbitary connection might well be a token of self-deception, a symptom of neurosis. But the phenomenon cannot be explained away so easily; for even in the earlier Wordsworth we find something like it. Speaking of the 'tranquil restoration' of remembered, assimilated beauty, he says:

> feelings too
> Of unremembered pleasure: such perhaps
> As have no slight or trivial influence
> On that best portion of a good man's life,
> His little, nameless, unremembered acts
> Of kindness and of love.[e]

From this it is but a step to Hopkins's comment on a bluebell: 'By its beauty I know the beauty of Our Lord.'[f]

No one will deny that a profound emotional dislocation informs the later sonnets of despair; but before dealing with this question we will examine a poem which, although variously interpreted by agnostics and Roman Catholics, evinces in its final effect a perfect fusion of the poetic personality and the religious character: I mean 'The Windhover.' The fact that Hopkins dedicated the sonnet 'To Christ our Lord' suggests, first, that he saw in the kestrel, as in the bluebell and all things of beauty, a symbol of Christ; and secondly, that he found a deep relief and self-justification in the writing of the poem. The resolution of spiritual conflicts, and the reconciliation of opposite or discordant tendencies in the active personality and the consciously controlled character is a process similar to that which Coleridge defines as the highest poetic imagination—'the balance or reconciliation of opposite or discordant qualities.'

In 'The Windhover' the reconciliation is between the rival claims of this life and of the next;[g] between the value and the danger of mortal beauty; between the desire for freedom of expression—the natural function 'wild and self-instressed,' and 'the will to suffer, to subject oneself to the ascetic rule, to dedicate all one's powers to Christ's employment.' The resolution of the conflict depends upon recognition of the fact that 'mastery' and 'achieve' in those mental and physical acts which excite the admiration of onlookers (activities of personality) may be sub-limited—assimilated by the character and revealed with equal or greater merit in the supreme act of sacrifice, which is derived from, due to, and rewarded by, Christ.

> 'Brute beauty and valour and act, oh, air, pride, plume here
> Buckle!...'[h]

The wild beauty and instinctive self-discipline of the kestrel are symbols of the controlled beauty given 'back to God' and the military self-discipline of the Ignatian ideal. The likeness between the bird and the partially repressed personality of the poet is obvious, and is emphasized rather than obscured by the subtle ambiguities in the poem: 'chevalier,' for instance, can with equal force refer to the kestrel, the poet's 'heart in hiding,' and Christ. The equally obvious difference is that Hopkins, as a Scotist, believed his own self-discipline to be ultimately a function of the will, which was free to choose or to reject the Ignatian character. That it was the poet's intention to point this likeness-with-a-difference is proved by the phrase 'O my chevalier.' This is addressed ostensibly to the bird, but also, by the clear implication of what follows, to himself. Hopkins the poet was, when free to act, a curvetting and caracoling knight-errant; but the mental transition from 'chevalier' to 'chivalry', and thence to 'soldier of Christ' (the Jesuit priest) makes the next symbol of humble useful toil—the plough—both natural and moving. Because of the sacrifice, the fire that breaks from the plodding priest and inhibited poet is all the 'lovelier' in the eyes of Christ and all the more 'dangerous' to the powers of evil:

> No wonder of it: sheer plod makes plough down sillion
> Shine...

But the price must be paid. How unlike the swoop of a hawk is the following symbol of the jaded drudge, the slow decline into age or infirmity, the gradual cooling off of youthful zeal—'blue-bleak embers.' Yet the consolation is there:

> and blue-bleak embers, ah my dear,
> Fall, gall themselves, and gash gold vermilion.

—words which suggest, as Mr. Empson[i] says, both the martyr's blood and the crown of gold. They also foreshadow the 'terrible pathos' and unique poetry of his later sonnets.

No doubt 'The Windhover' expresses a great deal more of the poet's unconscious than he was himself aware. It is a poem essentially of the tragic order. To the Catholic reader, the sense of loss is diminished by the compensatory sense of moral gain, of the Self over-mastered. But the final impression for any reader must be one of catharsis, 'that sense of relief, of repose in the midst of stress, of balance and composure, given by Tragedy; for there is no other way in which such impulses, once awakened, can be set at rest without suppression.'[j]

The appeasement and resignation expressed in 'The Windhover' were not absolutely decisive. Yet up to 1885, when 'Carrion Comfort' was 'written in blood,' Hopkins's works cannot as a whole be called unhappy. Many of these poems—'Henry Purcell,' 'Brothers', 'The Blessed Virgin,' etc., are as much the consummation of pure joy as any in the language. In 'Spelt from Sibyl's

Leaves,' however, we hear harsh repercussions of the particular examen:

> Let life, waned, ah let life wind
> Off her once skeined stained veined variety upon all on two spools...
> ...black, white: right, wrong;

There, no doubt, is the dislocation which Dr. Richards and Mr. de Selincourt have deplored—that the rich variety of such a poet's intellect, imagination and potential experience should be levelled down to this stern 'dichotomy of right and wrong.' Yet if we discount that moral aspect and consider only the poetry, can it truthfully be said that his cry 'O our tale, our oracle' is justified?—that the poet's dapple is really at an end?—that his valuable personality is quite steeped, pashed and dismembered in the larger unit of the Jesuit discipline? The answer is in the poem itself: diction, rhythm, imagery, organization of experience—all are new, individual.

An interesting pendant to 'The Windhover' is the sonnet 'In honour of St. Alphonsus Rodriguez' (1888). Despite its objective theme, it is, one feels, strongly subjective, and goes to prove that Hopkins's loyalty to the regulative principle had moulted no essential feather up to the year before his death. Like 'The Windhover,' the poem deals with the 'unseen war within the heroic breast' of the humble plodding servant of Christ: and the note of triumph is unmistakable:

> Yet God that hews mountain and continent...
> *Could crowd career with conquest* while there went
> Those years and years by of world without event
> That in Majorca Alfonso watched the door.[k]

As with King Lear, this projection of the self into another was a kind of relief. The hurtle of the poet's own 'fiercest fray' we hear in the sonnets Nos. 40, 41 and 45.[1] Yet commentators on the so-called tragedy of Hopkins's whole life (Dr. Richards, for example) are so anxious to give full weight to these utterances that they ignore the psychological significance of first-rate poems of quite a different outlook. 'Harry Ploughman' (1887) and the incomplete 'Epithalamion' (1888) are both joyous products of the unimpeded personality. (There is no need to discover a pathological symptom in the violent physical action of the former or in the missing nuptial exegesis of the latter). Moreover to anyone who can entertain even only the smallest wistful hope of Immortality, 'That Nature is a Heraclitean Fire' must surely present as perfect a collaboration of priest and poet as 'The Windhover.'[1]

How far the ill-health and depression so frequently mentioned in the 'Letters' were due to thwarted physical impulses would be a dangerous matter for speculation by one who is not a trained neuropathologist. It is certain however that many of the later sonnets are concerned with the poet's struggle to live in accordance with the Ignatian rule. 'One step,' says a commentator on the *Exercises*, 'is patience and meekness under affronts.' Touching the former virtue Hopkins laments:

> Patience hard thing! the hard thing but to pray
> But bid for Patience is!

And that his 'elected silence,' whether as patriot, priest, poet or plain man could at times prove almost unbearably irksome we learn from No. 44.[2] In this he may be uttering a repressed desire to write an ode to England, a political pamphlet, or perhaps merely to speak his mind freely to those about him. But to some ears the sestet vibrates with a deeper, more tragic note, which hints at something more personal and essential than a sporadic patriotism or what Dr. Richards somewhat curiously calls 'self-consciousness':

> Only what word
> Wisest my heart breeds dark heaven's baffling ban
> Bars or hell's spell thwarts. This to hoard unheard
> Heard unheeded leaves me a lonely began.

No doubt Hopkins suffered greatly; yet he had been prepared for periods of dejection and disillusion by the *Spiritual Exercises*, in which moods of desolation are minutely described and dogmatically accounted for. In the words of Father Keating, S.J.:

Whatever experiences are reflected in the four or five 'terrible sonnets,' so full of spiritual 'desolation,' so expressive of 'the dark night of the soul,' that those close to Christ are at times privileged to pass through, they cannot have been due to a mere sense of failure and frustration, still less to doubt as to whether he had chosen aright.[m]

We may cite in corroboration Hopkins's own words: 'I have never wavered in my vocation, but I have not lived up to it.'[n] And as for suffering, he had explicitly stated, 1869, that suffering, nobly endured, was a mark of special grace:

What suffering she had!...But sufferings falling on such a person as your sister was are to be looked on as the marks of God's particular love, and this is true the more exceptional they are.°

Yet those who maintain that much of his trouble was due to unsatisfied creative impulses have no mean evidence to go on. There is first the significant passage in a letter, where he regrets his inability to carry out his literary projects—'it kills me to be time's eunuch and never to beget'; and frustration could hardly be more articulate than in No. 50, from its cry

> Why do sinner's ways prosper? and why must
> Disappointment all I endeavour end?

to the poignant repetition of

> ...birds build—but not I build: no, but strain,
> Time's eunuch, and not breed one work that wakes.

The mortification expressed here and in No. 44 is intensified in the acute anhedonia and spiritual dyspepsia of No. 45:

> I am gall, I am heartburn. God's most deep decree
> Bitter would have me taste. My taste was me...
> Selfyeast of spirit a dull dough sours...

The active personality has not been perfectly assimilated by the passive religious character. 'Selfyeast of spirit' suggests the individual vital principle, the psychic individuality, rather than the immortal soul of the Christian, which strives to annihilate the Self either in works of charity or in a perfect union with its Creator. The souring of the personality and the consequent loss of inspiration is a foretaste of perdition:

> I see
> The lost are like this, and their scourge to be
> As I am mine, their sweating selves; but worse.

—the mere husks of men, without vision or hope. Contrast this with the Scotist ecstasy of No. 34—'Selves, goes itself; *myself* it speaks and spells.'ᴾ 'What I do is me' seems to have become 'What I cannot do is what I want to be'. The last two words of the poem, placed in emphatic isolation, must not be misread: they safeguard the priest's sincerity, for with a sudden twist the poet diverts our attention from himself to what without some saving grace he would become. As in 'Carrion Comfort,' having groaned 'I can no more' he immediately cries 'I can.' Yet when he remonstrates with God, or attributes the bitter taste of himself to 'God's most deep decree' ('baffling ban'), he seems to confess that the mortification he endures is very much more than the voluntary mortification of the patient ascetic. The complaint we hear seems to come from a personality which is prevented by ill-health, overwork, or inhibition from reaching its full stature.

I think it probable that Father Keating has underestimated the agonies of failure and frustration which creative genius, without any religious complications, can undergo, and has ignored the neuroses which may be caused when powerful instincts and impulses are repressed or imperfectly satisfied. But this qualification does not, to my mind, altogether invalidate his belief in the supernatural origin and purpose of Hopkin's desolations. Such experiences have been regarded by many serious thinkers as a phenomenon worthy of consideration in any complete study of man. Admit the possibility and it follows that God's purpose with the spirit, as with the body, might well work itself out in ways which are clearly explainable in the light of psychology and physiology.

To sum up, whether the cry of anguish in the later sonnets was due to mutilation or to probation, the gain to poetry, on the whole, seems to me to outweigh the loss. Had Hopkins been physically stronger, less devout, less sensitive, less neurotic, we should have had more poems but not the ones we now treasure. His output was restricted but at the same time intensified—allotropized from graphite to diamond (Dixon's 'terrible crystal') in the stringency of his 'bleak asceticism.' Being one of those described by William James as needing 'some austerity, wintry negativity, roughness and danger to be mixed in to produce the sense of an existence with character, texture and power,'q his moral fastidiousness, in union with his ritualistic sensualism, had valuable repercussions in the rigours and splendours of his poetic style. On the other hand, the religious life probably fostered that unsophisticated, intuitive approach to nature, life and language which, as Vico says, is an essential condition of the true 'original' poet. So far from 'whirling dizzily in a spiritual vacuum,'r the personality of Hopkins found in its delimited experience a medium of considerable resistance through which it could at times beat up to heights unattempted before in English poetry.

NOTES

a The Golden Echo.

b Basil de Selincourt: *The Observer*, Jan. 20th, 1935. [See No. 80.]

c M.C.D'Arcy, S.J., *Mirage and Truth*, p. 89.

d Quoted by G.F. Lahey, S.J. *Life of G.M.H.*, p. 124.

e Lines Written Above Tintern Abbey.

f *Notebooks and Papers, Etc.* (Oxford), p. 134. [2nd edn, p. 199.]

g 'I am a eunuch—but it is for the kingdom of heaven's sake' (*Letters to Bridges*, p. 270).

h Despite Mr. Empson's ingenious suggestions, the primary meaning of this word is that of Shakespeare's 'buckle thy distempered cause within the belt of rule.'

i *Seven Types of Ambiguity.* [See *ante* p. 170.]

j I.A. Richards: *Principles of Literary Criticism*, Chap. xxxii, p. 246.

k The italics are mine.

l *cf.* 'Hopkins's best poem for me is 48 (the "Heraclitean Fire"); this has the fusion required by a "metaphysical" mind which had to work in harmony on two planes at once.' (Louis MacNeice: *New Verse*, April, 1935).

m *The Month*, July, 1935.

n Letter to Dixon: *Correspondence*, p. 88.

o *Letters to Robert Bridges*, p. 25. The same idea is expressed in 'The Wreck of the Deutschland (1875), Stanza 22.

p *cf.* also: 'Nothing else in nature comes near this unspeakable stress of pitch, distinctiveness, selving, this selfbeing of my own.' (*Notebooks and Papers of G.M.H.*, p. 309). [Now printed in the *Sermons*, ed. Devlin, p. 123.]

q *Varieties of Religious Experience*, p. 298.

r Mr. Middleton Murry: *Aspects of Literature*. [See *ante* p. 127.]

1 64, 65 and 67 in the 4th edn.

2 'To seem the stranger'.

98. Charles Trueblood, 'The Esthetics of Gerard Hopkins', *Poetry*

August 1937, pp. 274–80

...The supposed obscurity of Hopkins' poetry is chargeable, perhaps in major share, not to the poetry but to a generation of readers to whom the reading of poetry is very nearly a lost art. Those who attempt to read Hopkins merely with the eye, as we do, deserve the chagrin they will undoubtedly experience. Hardly since Milton has there been a body of verse which more demands to be uttered, to be variously tried in the organs and imagery of breathing and speech, to be listened to and heard, until its intricate spreading patterns of response develop themselves and possess the reader....

99. Cornelius Weygandt, *The Time of Yeats*

New York, 1937, pp. 386–8

Weygandt (1871–1957) taught in the English Department of the University of Philadelphia from 1897, and was professor 1907–42. Katherine Brégy in her reminiscences in the *Catholic World*, February 1939, wrote that she studied under the 'devout all-round scholar, Dr. Cornelius Weygandt'. He was the author of several works on English literature.

...It had been better for the fame of Gerard Manley Hopkins... had his admirers taken their cue from what Robert Bridges

wrote of him. ... It had been better, too, if the considerable
number of verse-writers who seized upon Hopkins's new methods
as the way out from what they considered an exhausted mode of
poetry had not had such utter faith in him as guide. 'Sprung
rhythm' and breathless elliptical expression, exclamation and
coined adjectives are well enough in their way, but they are a small
part of poetry. Hopkins bulks bigger today as an influence over
younger poets than as a poet, but his value as an originator of new
effects has been overemphasised, as well as the intrinsic worth of
his poetry.

There are in Hopkins a good few poems of arresting onset, but
there is no single one of great and sustained power from first line to
last. ...

100. John Pick, 'The Growth of a Poet: Gerard Manley Hopkins, S.J.', *Month*

February 1940, pp. 106 ff

John Pick (1911–?80) was Professor of English at Boston
College 1939–41, and later a Professor at Marquette.

This was the second of two articles (which appeared in
successive numbers) relating Hopkins's poetry to his Jesuit
life and background. Only the opening is reprinted here;
Pick's work on Hopkins appeared in book form in 1942 as
Gerard Manley Hopkins, Priest and Poet, which is still in print.

The poems composed by Hopkins in 1877 and 1878 show how the
world expresses and praises God. But his growing concern is now
with man. Does man perceive the world as 'word, expression,
news, of God' and as a constant call to perfection? Does he use
created things to pursue his end, which is also God? Does he fulfil
his own purpose as outlined in the opening of the Spiritual

Exercises? The contrast between the waywardness of man and the beauty of created things which offer an avenue to God, gives to many of Hopkins's poems their vitality and beauty.

The poems of these two years are full of joyous wonder at the beauty of the world, of a joy enhanced and made exuberant because the poet sees creation as 'word, expression, news, of God,' and because he himself is using beauty to praise his Maker. No longer do we find the versifying of unrealized abstractions as in his Oxford poems. Nor are the poems surfeited with the lushness and luxuriance of his 'Vision of the Mermaids.'

The senses become instruments and means with which to praise God. There is an integration of sense, intellect, and emotion in a single act in which the whole man seeks God. He had attained that integrity of mind which correlates all perceptions and thoughts, the spiritual and material, in one single God-ward attitude....

101. Terence Heywood, 'Gerard Manley Hopkins: His Literary Ancestry', *English*

Spring 1940, pp. 16–24

English is the magazine of the English Association and has been published since 1907. In this article, Heywood claims to refute C. Day Lewis's contention (in *A Hope for Poetry*, see No. 75) that Hopkins has no literary ancestry.

...Now masculinity and ruggedness were, as we know, a special cult of the metaphysicals. It is probable that Hopkins would not have considered Dryden 'the most masculine of our poets' had he known Donne whose 'words' masculine persuasive force' so impressed his disciples, and of whom Carew wrote in his Elegy 'Thou hast...drawn a line/Of masculine expression' and 'to the awe of thy imperious wit/Our stubborn language bends, made only fit,/With her tough-thick-ribb'd hoops to gird about/Thy

Giant phansie'. To me it seems certain, though I know some still doubt it, that Donne and many of his followers were striving for a natural speech-rhythm in English poetry. That the harshness of some of their verse was intentional is at any rate unquestionable. Hopkins's words about sprung rhythm in earlier poets, 'if they could have done it they would', seem peculiarly applicable here. The metaphysicals could not: the most they could do was on occasion to reduce prosody to a mere counting of syllables: a decasyllable, for example, was literally a decasyllable and no more. As Donne says, 'And this unpolisht rugged verse I chose/ As fittest for discourse and nearest prose.'

But of course the tykishness[1] no more occurred free in Hopkins than it did in the metaphysicals, nearly all the ingredients of whose style he possesses, above all 'the peculiar blend of passion and thought, feeling and ratiocination' which Grierson calls their greatest achievement. There is the same condensation and resultant explosiveness, the surprise technique (though differently applied), and in most of the later sonnets the same subtle argumentativeness. In imagery, however, there is a difference: Hopkins's figures are neither learned, nor, usually, far-fetched—they are drawn mostly from nature (the nature he knew at first hand) and from everyday life; or concern suffering and destruction (anvils, blow-pipes, blood, gashing, grinding, torturing, drowning, &c.)—images that some would call sadistic, and of a type especially common in late Elizabethan drama and again in Beddoes. The range of the metaphysicals was far greater (not that Donne or Herbert eschewed homely striking figures any more than Shakespeare). The chief resemblance is in the intensity, accuracy, and vividness, being likewise the outcome of a highly unified sensibility.

And what of the conceit, the metaphysicals' central method of revealing the latent unity in the universe? There are a fair number of conceits in Hopkins: the whole of 'The Blessed Virgin' and 'The May Magnificat,' many stanzas of 'The Deutschland' (4, 8, 21, 22, 23, 31), parts of 'The Bugler's First Communion' and such a line as 'I all my being have hacked in half with her neck'. The conceits seem more numerous (though rather external) in his Juvenilia: 'My prayers must meet a brazen heaven/And fail or scatter all away', 'My eyes hold yet the rinds and bright/Remainder of a miracle'; the 'Margaret Clitheroe' fragment abounds in them and contains even this: 'Fawning fawning crocodiles/Days and days came round about/With tears to put her candle out'. As Pope remarks, 'Some to conceit alone their task confine', but Hopkins was not one of those. It seems that he could dispense with the conceit altogether, and yet, owing to his direct sensuous apprehension of thought, be (as in 'The Windhover') far more metaphysical than certain modern poets who repeatedly use the conceit in the baroque fashion as an end in itself. This may be because the unification is often achieved directly through Christ: it becomes the great conceit of religion, the paradox of the universe. Applying George Williamson's distinction between the conceit and the ordinary image—that the former shows more brainwork, makes use of material of little innate poetic value, and achieves greater imaginative distance—we could say perhaps that most of Hopkins's figures resemble the conceit in the first and third respect but not often in the second. This can be seen not only in compressed images like 'wolfsnow', 'selfyeast', 'flockbells', epithets like 'wading light' and 'lashtender combs', but in the working out of his recurrent winch, cage, and bird images, and in the whole procedure of poems like 'The Windhover', 'Carrion Comfort', 'Hurrahing in Harvest,' 'Sibyl's Leaves', 'That Nature is a Heraclitean Fire', The Candle Indoors'—all of which 'fan fresh our wits with wonder'.

What particular metaphysicals does Hopkins most resemble? I think it was F.R. Leavis who first coupled him with Donne. He is most like Donne in the intensely personal record of his religious experience, in his ability to convey moods of extraordinary complexity (notably in 'The Windhover'), and in his mastery of rhetoric. He has often a similar dramatic manner: an abrupt opening like 'No, I'll not, carrion comfort, despair'; questions and imperatives hardly less fierce; rhetorical repetitions; and a fine control of tempo (most obviously in 'The Echoes', and Beuno's Speech). The parallel is perhaps closest between the terrible sonnets and Donne's 'Holy Sonnets', especially 'Batter my heart' and 'At the round earth's imagined corners' with their remarkable periods of monosyllabic piledriving; while Donne with his extremely slow movement gave to the sonnet the extra length that Hopkins felt it required. The main difference is that Hopkins is sensuous rather than sensual, and is without obscenity or pedantry (his algolagnia, however, could be considered a substitute?)

Although he had dipped in Marvell ('a rich and nervous poet' he calls him) and Vaughan, George Herbert is the only metaphysical he studied and was influenced by. Herbert, we are told, was actually 'his strongest tie to the English Church'. It is easy to imagine how congenial the poet who called his *Temple* 'a picture of many spiritual conflicts that have past betwixt God and my soul' must have been to him about the time of his conversion. And it is from this period that we have the group of devotional poems in Herbert's manner. At the time he could hardly have had a better master: Herbert, in his rather stripped, very accurate, and highly finished poems, had what one of his editors calls 'a deliberate plan to push thought into the foreground and fix attention on harsh, intricate and veritable experience'. Technically, the Herbert who could write 'Church-bells beyond the stars heard, the soul's blood', 'Thou and alone thou knowst', may well have assisted in leading him towards a sprung rhythm: at any rate there are many lines in his undergraduate poems like 'Handle the fig, suck the full-sapp'd vine-shoot', 'Beat, heave and the strong mountain tire', which suggest it; in the second draft of 'St. Dorothea' the stresses are actually marked ('Í am só light and faír'). The later Hopkins, as we might expect, has moved beyond Herbert; there is a difference in the devotional attitude (a greater reliance on the reason and will); there is greater complexity and profoundity; more passion, intellect, colour; and a far greater intensity in the pressure and fusion of his images. Herbert, however, appears to have had a lasting influence, spiritual as well as technical.

At a first glance there would appear to be a striking resemblance between Hopkins's coruscations and the brilliantly flaming odes of Crashaw (also a convert to Romanism). But not on closer inspection. Crashaw's rockets are pyrotechnic, rarely more than 'happy fireworks'; while Hopkins's are signals or life-rockets. A flashing iridescence is common to both, but that is about all.

There is one other metaphysical worth considering, a little-read eccentric whom Hopkins had almost certainly never heard of. It may seem outrageous to mention him in the same breath as Edward Benlowes, a wilfully odd writer whose style includes all the worst faults of the age and a good many more peculiar to himself. But Benlowes, though extremely uneven, is a poet of many good passages; and in parts of his long divine poem, 'Theophila' (1652), he comes nearer to anticipating Hopkins than almost anyone: 'Wrack'd is with bitter-sweet extremes my mind,/Shell'd, sheath'd, cag'd, coffin'd in her treacherous friend',

'Vast cares, long dumb, thus vent. Flow tears, soul's wine,/Juice of an heart opprest', 'Top and top-gallant hoise; we will outroar/The billowing storms, though shipwrackt more/Healths are, than temptings't sirens did enchant of yore', 'How from the rock, rod-struck in ire,/Did cataracts gush out? How did the seas retire?' He has great devotional intensity; what he calls 'a fulgurance of mind'; a powerful urgency of rhythm; and a highly elliptical style, phrases being telescoped, and transitional phrases and relatives omitted: 'Wh' on sky, seas, earth, rocks doth rays disperse,/Stars, rainbows, pearls, fruits, diamonds pierce;/The world's eye, source of light, soul of the universe.' His imagery is glaringly and overwhelmingly dynamic; he loves storms, shipwrecks, forcible verbs like 'shoot', 'sluice', 'sprout', 'unbowel', military images—in fact, 'with zeal's fireworks storms heaven's roof'. Compound words are very frequent ('woolly-curdled clouds', 'shot-bruis'd mud-walls', 'bough-cradles', 'hope-blades'); there are double possessives ('sin's asp's womb'); even Hopkinsian phrases like 'Deprav'd of vice, depriv'd of grace'....

And so we find that Hopkins, like most revolutionaries, instead of breaking with tradition altogether, only went back to earlier traditions; l arned from a greater variety of poets and languages than any English poet before him, some of which poets he in certain ways resembled, and others not; and that there are also resemblances between him and certain poets who never actually influenced him, or whom he had never heard of. The mature Hopkins had so thoroughly assimilated his influences that they never emerged as echoes. 'The authentic cadence was discovered late', but it *was* discovered.

NOTE

1 'Rawness... the unrefined in the refined and educated' (*Further Letters*, p. 392, and see *ibid.*, p. 390).

102. David Daiches, *Poetry and the Modern World*

Chicago, 1940, pp. 30–4

... Though certain defects in Hopkins's poetry may derive from unresolved conflicts in the poet's personality, it is equally true that the virtues derive from a very similar source, namely, the complexity and many-sidedness of his feeling. Both his obscurity and his brilliance arise out of this complexity, as the following example—the opening stanza of his poem on Henry Purcell—will show:

> Have fair fallen, O fair, fair have fallen, so dear
> To me, so arch-especial a spirit as heaves in Henry Purcell,
> An age is now since passed, since parted; with the reversal
> Of the outward sentence low lays him, listed to a heresy, here.

The urgence of the adjective in the first line, the rapid movement of the verse which seems to want to keep the reader's reaction in suspense until it has completed the thought, the order of the words, the cadence of the phrases ('low lays him, listed to a heresy, here'), are all the marks of a poet whose attitude to his subject is compounded of many different and even conflicting visions, all of which he must communicate at once if the truth is to be told. This will be made clear if we compare Hopkins's stanza with one from Tennyson:

> Now sleeps the crimson petal, now the white;
> Nor waves the cypress in the palace walk;
> Nor winks the gold fin in the porphyry font:
> The fire-fly wakens: waken thou with me.

Here diction, rhythm, and cadence contribute to a single and simple mood; there is no breathless haste to get the qualifying statements in before the reader can pause, no problem of fusion: there is but one level of statement, to which all undertones are carefully and placidly subordinated. Hopkins's verse, however, is not made up of dominant meaning to which undertones contribute;

his meanings are all equal tones, which must be fused, not subordinated. An analysis of that difficult but fascinating poem 'Tom's Garland' will show Hopkins wrestling with the same problem. All the devices which for the casual reader produce only obscurity are really intended to prevent the reader from understanding anything until he can understand everything. For the complete statement alone—elaborated, qualified, compressed, unified—is the truth. As he said in a letter to Bridges: 'One of two kinds of obscurity one should have—either the meaning to be felt without effort as fast as one reads or else, if dark at first reading, when once made out to *explode*'.[1] This term 'explode' is significant: it conveys the sense of everything happening at once, which is so important for Hopkins. What Hopkins seems to be saying in this sentence is that one should write either as Tennyson does, from a single point of view, with one mood, one meaning, one simple truth to tell, in which case that mood is set right away and the lines merely continue it without modifying or complicating it; or else in the many-visioned way that he employs himself, where the truth is kept in suspense until all is told, for to understand a line before completing the stanza would be to learn a half-truth or a falsehood.

...Hopkins was a poet with unusual problems of personal adjustment who was driven to seek a kind of integrity in his poetry that demanded a new technique and also a denial of the poet's public function. For what audience did he write? He probably could not have answered that question himself. Though he told Bridges that he wrote not for the public but for him,★ we are obviously meant to take this in a symbolic rather than a literal sense. There is no doubt that Hopkins did wish for some kind of readers, 'fit audience though few', yet he is never explicit on the subject. He certainly had no desire to appeal to the great public who read and enjoyed Tennyson, though not for reasons of snobbery. This uncertainty about his audience he shares with many of the poets of our own generation, who, faced with the splitting-up of the poetry-reading public, cannot make up their minds for whom to write. This was a much wider problem in the world after 1919 than it was in Hopkins's time, for in the former period the widespread disintegration of older values and beliefs had taken the solid ground from underneath the poets and they were doubtful alike of their function and of their readers. . . . . Different as he was in so many important ways from the young English poets of the late 1920's and early 1930's, Hopkins shared many of their problems. His problems derived largely from personal factors, while theirs was the result of the general state of culture and even of civilization as a whole. Yet both he and they were faced with the problem of communicating on several levels at once, of determining anew not only who was to be their audience, but what was the nature and function of their art, of building something to replace the Tennysonian tradition. That the metaphysical poets of the 17th century were also faced with this manifold problem, for yet different reasons, is in part the explanation of why John Donne and Gerard Manley Hopkins lie behind so much modern poetry. . . .

NOTES

* *Letters to Bridges*, p. 46.

1 For Daiches' commentary on this passage four years before, see *ante*, p. 348 (Hopkins said 'clearness' not 'obscurity').

103. Lord David Cecil, Introduction, *The Oxford Book of Christian Verse*

Oxford, 1940, pp. xxx–xxxi

Lord David Cecil (1902–86) was fellow of New College Oxford 1939–69, and author of books on Cowper, Scott, and others. In the Introduction to the *Oxford Book of Christian Verse* he favourably compared the religious verse of the second half of the nineteenth century with that of the seventeenth. From Christina Rossetti he moved on to Hopkins.

. . . Hopkins is also a virtuoso. His effects are not so certain as hers. A natural juggler with words, intoxicated by the fertility of his own invention, he sometimes strained the resources of language beyond their strength; in his efforts to extend the bounds of expression he becomes obscure. But at its best, his verbal invention has a Shakespearian boldness and felicity. And he conveys with extraordinary fire and immediacy the more full-blooded religious emotions; the ecstasy of the rapt worshipper, the black night of the soul cut off from its vision of God. Like Christina Rossetti he had nothing very unusual to say. He voices the typical feelings of a Roman Catholic devotee as she voices those of a high Anglican. But this gives his poems a general appeal of which their eccentricities of expression might otherwise deprive them. ...

Bibliography

The Poems of Gerard Manley Hopkins, ed. Robert Bridges, London, 1918.

The Poems of Gerard Manley Hopkins, 2nd edition, with Introduction by Charles Williams, London, 1930.

The Poems of Gerard Manley Hopkins, ed. W.H. Gardner and N.H. Mackenzie, 4th edition, London, 1967 (reprinted with corrections 1970).

The Note-Books and Papers of Gerard Manley Hopkins, ed. Humphry House, London, 1937.

The Journals and Papers of Gerard Manley Hopkins, ed. Humphry House and Graham Storey, London, 1959.

The Letters of Gerard Manley Hopkins to Robert Bridges, ed. C.C. Abbott. London, 1935.

The Correspondence of Gerard Manley Hopkins and R.W. Dixon, ed. C.C. Abbott, London, 1935.

Further Letters of Gerard Manley Hopkins, ed. C.C. Abbott, 2nd edition, London, 1956. (1st edn, 1938.)

The Sermons and Devotional Writings of Gerard Manley Hopkins, ed. Christopher Devlin, London, 1959.

Gerard Manley Hopkins: Selected Prose, ed. Gerald Roberts, Oxford, 1980.

Tom Dunne, *Gerard Manley Hopkins: A Comprehensive Bibliography*, Oxford, 1976.

W.H. Gardner, *Gerard Manley Hopkins: A Study of Poetic Idiosyncrasy in Relation to Poetic Tradition*, 2 vols, London, 1944 and 1949 (reprinted).

Alfred Thomas, *Hopkins the Jesuit*, London, 1969.

Bernard Bergonzi, *Gerard Manley Hopkins*, London, 1977.

G.H. Hartman (ed.), *Hopkins: A Collection of Critical Essays* (Twentieth Century Views), Englewood Cliffs, NJ, 1966.

Select Index